Education for an Information Age

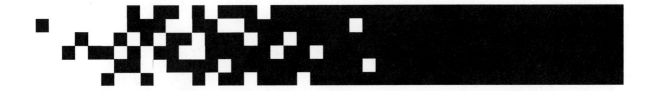

Education for an Information Age

Teaching in the Computerized Classroom

■ **Bernard J. Poole**
University of Pittsburgh at Johnstown

WCB **Brown &
Benchmark**
P U B L I S H E R S

Madison, Wisconsin • Dubuque, Iowa

Book Team

Managing Editor *Sue Pulvermacher-Alt*
Developmental Editor *Suzanne M. Guinn*
Production Editor *Michelle M. Campbell*
Photo Editor *Rose Deluhery*
Art Processor *Jodi Banowetz*
Visuals/Design Developmental Consultant *Marilyn A. Phelps*
Visuals/Design Freelance Specialist *Mary L. Christianson*
Marketing Manager *Liz Haefele*
Advertising Coordinator *Colleen Howes*
Production Manager *Beth Kundert*

WCB Brown & Benchmark

A Division of Wm. C. Brown Communications, Inc.

Executive Vice President/General Manager *Thomas E. Doran*
Vice President/Editor in Chief *Edgar J. Laube*
Vice President/Marketing and Sales Systems *Eric Ziegler*
Director of Production *Vickie Putman Caughron*
Director of Custom and Electronic Publishing *Chris Rogers*

Wm. C. Brown Communications, Inc.

President and Chief Executive Officer *G. Franklin Lewis*
Senior Vice President, Operations *James H. Higby*
Corporate Senior Vice President and Chief Financial Officer *Robert Chesterman*
Corporate Senior Vice President and President of Manufacturing *Roger Meyer*

The credits section for this book begins on page 445 and is considered an extension of the copyright page.

Cover and interior designs by Lansdon Design.

Cover illustration by Telemation, Inc.

Line art generated by Bernard J. Poole unless noted otherwise.

Copyedited by Toni Good

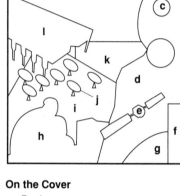

On the Cover

a. Book
b. Silicon disk
c. Globe
d. John Vincent Atanasoff—inventor of electronic digital computer
e. Satellite
f. Desktop computer tools
g. Earth
h. Students and teacher at computer
i. Course plan
j. Satellite dish
k. Desktop computer on-screen display
l. Computer chip

To my wife, Marilyn

Brief Contents

Contents

Chapter 7

Software Systems for Microcomputers 169

Part III **Computers in the Classroom 193**

Chapter 8

Educational Computing Environments 195

Chapter 9

Computer-Managed Instruction (CMI) 229

Part IV **No Problems, Only Solutions 357**

About the Author

Bernard John Poole has broad experience in education. He understands the needs of teachers who may not be naturally inclined to get excited about the latest technology. He has 25 years of experience teaching at all scholastic levels in Europe, the Middle East, Africa, and North America. For 15 of his 27 years in the classroom, he has taught in nontechnical subject areas in elementary and secondary, private and public schools. His undergraduate degrees are in English, history, French, and data processing; he has postgraduate degrees in education and in information science. His teaching responsibilities have also included work with special-needs children.

About This Text

Purpose of the text. This text has been written for preservice and in-service teachers who want to learn about computers and their use in the classroom. In-service teachers need help making the transition to computer-based teaching and learning, and preservice teachers need to be prepared for a profession in which the computer will become an increasingly indispensable tool. *Education for an Information Age* addresses all aspects of this need from the basic level of computer literacy to the more cutting-edge issues related to the integration of computer-based technology into the curriculum.

The approach has, therefore, been to make the text as accessible as possible to K–12 teachers, many of whom work under conditions that are far from ideal as far as technology-based education is concerned. The text presents the potential powerful effects of learning in the technology-rich classroom while acknowledging unequivocally that teachers can create and sustain such a learning environment only if they have strong moral and financial support from the community of parents, school boards, and administrators, at all levels.

Because of the breathtaking rate of progress in the computer field, it is impossible to publish a textbook that is as current as monthly publications such as journals and magazines. *Education for an Information Age* makes no pretense of trying to compete with these publications. The focus here is on concepts rather than keystrokes. For this reason, there is no extensive coverage of specific hardware or software systems. Such systems are profiled only where such treatment is useful to amplify conceptual material.

Professionals in the field of education are no different from professionals in any other job. They must commit to an ongoing upgrading of skills and knowledge in order to remain current in their field. Thus, there is an appendix that lists recommended reading for teachers who use technology in the classroom. There is also an appendix that lists some of the sources of funding for technology projects.

Organization of the text. The book has been organized into four distinct parts in order to facilitate flexible use in the context of a course for preservice or in-service teachers. Each part can be studied independently and in any sequence. The impact of the text is not necessarily cumulative. In the next section, Content of the Text, the rationale for the organization of the book as published is given, but it is appreciated that no two courses are identical and different emphases will always require alternative approaches to the subject matter. Users of the text should feel free to select parts and chapters in a sequence that suits their needs.

Content of the text. Part I of *Education for an Information Age* presents an overview of computer use in schools and society at large.

Chapter 1 presents the outcomes of research based on studies of computer use in schools. Teachers should be familiar with this research as a prerequisite to, and justification of, their efforts to incorporate the computer into the curriculum.

Chapter 2 examines the history of computer use in schools, and **chapter 3** examines their impact on society in general. Students are children of the Information Age. They are in tune with the reality of instant access to data; they are conscious of how tiny the world has become; they are intuitively aware of the global impact of even their most insignificant actions. Teachers need to develop the same awareness in themselves, if only so that they can get some sense of their students' frame of reference.

In **chapters 4** and **5,** we will examine ethical and legal issues arising out of computer use in the classroom and in society in general. It is, perhaps, unusual to include chapters on these matters so early in a text on computer literacy. The majority of such texts relegate this material to the latter half of the book, which often results in its being presented, if at all, as a hurried afterthought at the end of a semester. But teachers have a special responsibility to contribute to the preparation of children for life in today's world. A text for teachers should, therefore, recognize this responsibility, and give it the priority it deserves.

Part II introduces computer hardware and software.

Chapter 6 examines the basic hardware components of desktop computers, along with those specialized devices of which multimedia systems are comprised.

Chapter 7 will review the different kinds of software necessary to drive the computer at what are called the **systems** and **applications** levels of general computer use. Computing machinery is useless without the software that controls its operations. The more one understands about the software systems (called operating systems) that control the operations of the computer, the more comfortable one will feel at the machine.

PART III examines how best to incorporate the computer into the curriculum.

In **chapter 8**, we will look at the different ways in which computers are set up in typical school environments. We will also discuss some innovative ideas for organizing computing resources, whether in the classroom or in the purpose-built laboratory setting.

Chapters 9 and 10 examine the wide spectrum of software for computer-managed instruction (CMI) and computer-assisted instruction (CAI). These chapters will inform the teacher's experience, explaining the different types of educational software and providing sets of criteria for making sound judgments about the quality of that software.

Chapter 11 examines computers and communications (C&C) as it applies to classroom management and learning. The demands of the corporate world have brought communications technology—the technology that links computer systems over local and wide area networks—to the point where it has powerful applications in the classroom—and in the community served by the school—for collaborative, intercultural, and distance learning. This is important reading for the teacher who will work in the classrooms of tomorrow.

Chapter 12 looks at specialized technologies that are giving a new meaning to the term *multimedia* and that are slowly finding their way into the schools. Teachers will more than likely be called on to make decisions about the use of multimedia hardware and software in their classrooms. They will, therefore, benefit from as broad an experience as possible with the technologies involved. Ideally, readers will have access to some or all of the different types of educational software and hardware discussed in **chapters 8 through 12.**

Part IV answers the question: "How can I get this technology for my classroom when my school district can barely afford to maintain the equipment already in place?"

Chapter 13 examines the process of applications development along with the various ways, from traditional programming to modern authoring systems, in which teachers and students can get involved. This chapter will be of interest to those preservice or inservice teachers who want to try their hand at creating their own software, or who are interested in what would be involved in getting their students to do the same.

Chapter 14 deals with the subject of grant writing. Needless to say, for the most part, teachers can reasonably expect that their school districts will provide the hardware and software they need. However, money—always in short supply—is generally allocated according to priorities that reflect the educational philosophy—or lack thereof—of those in control of the budget. So, teachers and administrators may have to take matters into their own hands.

In the last chapter of part IV, **chapter 15,** you will have the opportunity to sit back and reflect on what you have learned through the book. You will review teaching philosophy as it applies to computer-based learning. Methodologies will be examined and a case made for an ongoing commitment to the needs of individual students in the computerized classroom. This debate will best be appreciated if you have had the opportunity to experience, either firsthand or in discussion, all aspects of computer-based learning—hence, the positioning of this chapter at the end of the text. This is not to imply that it is less important than the other chapters. Indeed, it is the most important chapter of all. A convincing rationale both informs and stimulates motivation.

About the Pedagogy

The following learning aids have been designed into *Education for an Information Age:*

- The main body of each chapter begins with a summary of anticipated learning outcomes and closes with a review of material covered.

- Chapters conclude with case studies based on the experience of teachers using computer-based learning in the K–12 classroom. Each case study is accompanied by a set of topics for discussion.

- At the end of every chapter is a set of suggestions for projects related to the subject matter of each chapter.

- Also at the end of every chapter is a references section, which can act as a resource for recommended reading beyond the text.

- Chapters are clearly divided into "mind-size" sections and subsections to aid reading and understanding. Where applicable, listed items are indented and "bulleted" for easier assimilation.

- Illustrations are used throughout the text to increase interest, promote understanding, and provide rest for the reader's eyes as they progress through the material covered.

- In general, the writing style is immediate, friendly, and engaging. The reader often is addressed in the first or second person ("we" and "you") in order to foster commitment and sustain interest.

- There is a glossary of terms which may be unfamiliar to the reader.

- There is also an extensive index to aid the reader who wants to browse selected sections of the text.

- Supplementary materials include an optional set of Microsoft *Works* tutorials, a test item file, test items on disk, an instructor's manual, including transparency masters and a set of lecture outlines for instructor and/or student use.

Acknowledgments

My thanks to the many teachers, past and present, whose skill and dedication have fueled my own enthusiasm for this rewarding profession. In particular, I owe a huge debt of gratitude to the Brothers of the Christian Schools, whose exemplary commitment to teaching inspires me to this day.

I am grateful to Patty Riddle, assistant director of the University of Pittsburgh at Johnstown (UPJ) Regional Computer Resource Center (RCRC), who recognized the contribution I could make and who was instrumental in getting me involved with the Pennsylvania Information Technology Education for the Commonwealth (ITEC) program. That involvement led directly to the creation of this textbook. Rob Eckenrod, Director of the UPJ RCRC, has been a valuable resource. Dr. David Dunlop at UPJ and Dr. Ken Mechling at Clarion University, Pennsylvania, also deserve special mention in this context because of their efforts formulating and supporting the ITEC program, both at UPJ and statewide, since its inception in 1984.

I must thank the following reviewers of various drafts of the manuscript:

Norman Sterchele
Saginaw Valley State University

John Achrazoglou
The University of Iowa

Charles Mlynarczyk
S.U.N.Y. College at Potsdam

Albert P. Nous
University of Pittsburgh

J. Steven Soulier
Utah State University

Debra A. Mathinos
Bucknell University

Neal Strudler
University of Nevada-Las Vegas

Marilyn Shelton
California State University-Fresno

Their encouragement motivated me to stay the course, and their criticism has led, I hope, to significant improvements in this final draft.

A special note of thanks must go to Toni Good, copy editor, whose close criticism, corrections, and suggestions have also significantly improved the quality of the manuscript.

Next, I am grateful to my sister-in-law, Susan, who spent many hours reviewing the text, assembling artwork, and helping with the development of supplementary materials.

Finally, I thank my wife, Marilyn, who ranks among the most dedicated and best teachers I have known and whose example and companionship have sustained me on the journey that has led to the completion of this book.

Introduction

Thus education forms the common mind;
Just as the twig is bent, the tree's inclined.

Alexander Pope (1688–1744)

I have hope that society may be reformed,
when I see how much education may be reformed.

Gottfried Wilhelm von Leibnitz (1646–1716)

The audience for *Education for an Information Age* is the pre-service/in-service K–12 teacher. The primary goal of the text is to help you incorporate the computer into the curriculum. A secondary goal is to support your endeavors toward being the most effective educator you can be.

To this latter extent the book cannot be taken in isolation. The ideas and skills presented form part of the continuum of learning and experience related to your profession that began when you were yourself on the receiving end as a K–12 student, continues during your college studies as an education major, and ultimately bears fruit in your role as a teacher in the classroom. The computer, along with the expanding range of associated technology, is just one of many tools and techniques that can improve the learning environment that you provide for your students.

I.1.1 The Need for Change

There has been a great deal of hype about the computer as a tool for teaching. Perhaps it is in the nature of the profession, but teachers are more skeptical than most about the advent of yet another fad, yet another experimental methodology, yet another pedagogical imposter destined to come and go like so many others.

Change, in and of itself, is not usually welcomed with open arms. As Machiavelli observed:

> It must be remembered that there is nothing more difficult to plan, more doubtful of success, nor more dangerous to manage, than the creation of a new system. For the initiator has the enmity of all who would profit by the preservation of the old institutions and merely lukewarm defenders in those who would gain by the new ones.[1]

People in general are resistant to change even when it is for the better. A certain inertia is built into time-tested ways of doing things. "If it ain't broke, don't fix it," as they say, and the fact is that time-tested methodologies—chalk and talk, competition, rote learning, regimentation—have been successful until relatively recently in achieving the goal of turning out at least an educated elite from our schools.

With the collapse of agriculture, and then of industry, as the primary provider of people's bread and butter, today's increasingly service-oriented, information-based societies are waking up to the fact that an educated elite will put food on only a small number of plates on a nation's table. Today we have to ensure that *everyone* has a realistic opportunity to develop the intellectual skills required to prosper in an information age.

To this end education needs help. We continue to be *A Nation At Risk* (National Committee on Excellence in Education, 1984). A growing number of young people graduating from our schools are ill-prepared to find gainful employment in tomorrow's workplace, where the majority of jobs require higher-order intellectual skills—strong communication skills, information gathering and analysis skills, interpersonal skills, learning skills, and creative skills.

---

[1] Niccolo di Bernardo Machiavelli, 1469–1527.

This is not to deny the progress that American education has made over the years. In fact there is cause for great optimism as pointed out in the report *Workplace Competencies: The Need to Improve Literacy and Employment Readiness* (Information Services Office, 1990). A century ago one was considered literate if one could sign one's name. Today almost all young adults can do that. Fifty years ago the criterion for literacy was the ability to read at a fourth-grade level. Today 95% of young adults meet this criterion. Twenty-five years ago one was deemed literate by the War on Poverty standards if one could read at the eighth-grade level. Today 80% of young adults read at that level. These are indeed grounds for optimism.

But young-adult preparedness for a productive and prosperous life requires more than merely the ability to read at an eighth-grade level. To quote from the above-mentioned *Workplace Competencies* report:

> The requirements [for America's work force] are likely upward, at least in many important sectors of the economy and in particular employers' needs. The present technological environment has enlarged some workers' responsibilities. The lines between workers and supervisors and managers blur as "work teams" or "quality circles" are used to raise creativity and productivity. The team members put their heads together and solve problems. The members can do each other's jobs. They must be flexible. And they have to deal with print, often in more complex forms than before. In short, the requirements are rising in some areas that are highly visible to employers and to observers of the economy in general, and it is against these growing demands and expectations that the adequacy of preparation for the entering work force must be viewed.

I.1.2 Teachers Can Make a Difference

The challenge is enormous, but we must hold on to the conviction that each one of us, in making our contribution, can make a difference. There indeed *is* the source of joy in teaching—the act, day by day, of "putting a spark" in young minds. As Anatole France observed, "If there is some good inflammable stuff, it will catch fire."

In the pages that follow, you will have the opportunity to learn about computing in general and about computer-based education in particular. The computer is obviously not the whole solution to the challenge of broadening and deepening the base of educational opportunity, but it may be part of the solution. This text examines all aspects of computer-based technology as one among the set of tools in a teacher's methodological toolbox.

The reader should bear in mind that it is beyond the scope of this book to profile in more than cursory fashion specific courseware or other applications for teaching and learning. Here we are concerned with concepts, rather than keystrokes. Keystrokes are essentially ephemeral; concepts endure. The ideal accompaniment to the study of the material here would, however, be hands-on experience with, and review of, a wide range of applications for education. It is hoped that the reader will have this opportunity.

▪ I.2 Objectives of the Text

1. **To encourage the use of computers in the classroom by removing the mystery that surrounds the technology**

   Many teachers resist using computers in their classrooms because they are intimidated by the technology. For this reason, another objective of *Education for an*

Information Age is to take away the mystery that often surrounds these machines by emphasizing their use as tools. You will read about the hardware and software of electronic computers at a level that will help you understand what makes them tick. You will learn about the differences among the machines that are most popular in schools today. You will also be introduced to several of the most important communications and audiovisual innovations, such as networks, scanners, overhead display panels, interactive video, and multimedia systems, that have come to depend on computer technology.

2. **To apply the principles of educational theory to the use of computers in the classroom**

    Another objective of this text is to help the teacher at all levels of education, but especially K–12, to discern quality educational software among the plethora of packages available today. In pursuit of this objective, you will review educational theory (at various points throughout the text, pulling everything together in chapter 15) and apply it to the use of computers in education. Over thousands of years, philosophers and educationists have promulgated various theories of learning, from mental discipline to constructivism, which you have no doubt studied in your education courses at college, and applied, or will apply, in your professional life. As a result of reviewing learning theory, you will be more informed in your selection of computer-based materials for classroom use, ensuring that they meet the objectives that you have set for the learning experience to which you plan to introduce your students.

3. **To provide opportunities for hands-on computer experience**

    The most effective way to overcome fear is to face it. A set of tutorials for Microsoft *Works*™ (Poole, 1994) are an optional accompaniment to this text. They introduce the teacher to the fundamental features of the software along with exercises and practical recommendations for using *Works* in the classroom.

    Ideally, you will also have at hand a wide selection of software designed for use in the learning process. Reviewing the myriad examples of computer-based learning systems that are available today can be a valuable experience. By the time you have completed your journey through this text, you will have strengthened your commitment to keeping abreast of developments in educational computing. You will also have laid a solid foundation for the classroom of the future in which you will recognize and pursue opportunities to integrate the computer into the curriculum.

    Every hour you spend physically and mentally interacting with the computer will increase your familiarity with the technology and your competence in its use. Indeed, you will come to marvel at its applicability to the learning process. Most important, you will empathize with your students' enthusiasm for computer-based systems and become caught up in it yourself.

4. **To help teachers understand the effect that computing and communications are having on the society in which their students are raised**

    Our times are variously referred to as The Computer Age, The Information Age, and The Age of Technology. There is no doubt that the last twenty to thirty years have brought about a dramatic change in the very infrastructure of developed societies. Technological innovation has permeated so many areas of our lives—in the home, in medical care, in travel, in communications, in government, in finance, in industry, in recreational activities—and, of course, in schools.

Children growing up in these societies will have a different frame of reference from those of previous generations. As Marshall McLuhan pointed out: "The medium is the message." The very technological transformation that is taking place will have an impact on the culture that adopts it, and those most likely to experience the acculturation at its deepest level will be the children of the culture. As teachers, we must at least keep an open mind on the ever-changing world of our students' experience, and if we can integrate the changes into our own experience, so much the better.

This is not to say that teachers should shift gears into the era of classroom computerization just for the sake of it, just because it is there. There must be a rationale, a conviction born of research and experience, that makes the adjustment part of their general predisposition to provide the best possible educational opportunity for the children in their care.

I.3 Computers in the Classroom

The International Society for Technology in Education (ISTE), the largest nonprofit professional organization supporting computer-using educators in the world, has drawn up a set of fundamental skills and concepts as Foundation Standards for teacher preparation programs. Table I.1 lists these skills and concepts and shows where they are dealt with in this text and the accompanying tutorials. Four aspects to computers in the classroom should be considered when deciding to what extent one will adopt their use.

I.3.1 Computers Can Be Used to Support Learning

We will examine various specific types of computer-based educational systems—drill and practice, tutorials, simulation, collaborative learning, distance learning, integrated learning systems, and multimedia—that take different approaches to helping children assimilate knowledge.

I.3.2 Computers Can Be Used to Support Children's Socialization

Children's socialization can come about not simply by exposing them to computer programs that help them learn about themselves and their world, but also by creating cooperative learning. The computer is a tool to share. For example, it is fascinating to see how easily a group of children will work together on a writing project in which all the materials are captured electronically. Each individual brings his or her own special abilities to the project and unhesitatingly calls on others to help with skills that they lack but which they recognize in others.

I.3.3 The Computer Is an Effective Tool to Support Classroom Instruction and Administration

The individual teacher gains a great deal of extra efficiency out of computerized record-keeping. Preparation of syllabi, schedules, and printed classroom materials of all kinds can be more efficiently and professionally produced using the computer, especially if, as is more and more likely the case, the printer is a high-quality laser printer. It is anachronistic today to use the typewriter, or even a dedicated word processor, for this kind of work.

Table I.1	ISTE Set of Fundamental Skills and Concepts for Today's Teachers (ISTE, 1992)

Skill or concept	Where covered
1. Demonstrate ability to operate a computer system in order to successfully utilize software.	Part II MS-*Works* tutorials
2. Evaluate and use computers and related technologies to support the instructional process.	Part III
3. Apply current instructional principles, research, and appropriate assessment practices to the use of computers and related technologies.	Part I Part IV
4. Explore, evaluate, and use computer/technology-based materials, including applications, educational software, and associated documentation.	Part III
5. Demonstrate knowledge of uses of computers for problem-solving, data collection, information management, communications, presentations, and decision making.	Throughout this text MS-*Works* tutorials
6. Design and develop student learning activities that integrate computing and technology for a variety of student grouping strategies and for diverse student populations.	Throughout this text MS-*Works* tutorials
7. Evaluate, select, and integrate computer/technology-based instruction in the curriculum of one's subject area(s) and/or grade levels.	Part III
8. Demonstrate knowledge of uses of multimedia, hypermedia, and telecommunications to support instruction.	Throughout this text, especially chapters 11 and 12
9. Demonstrate skill in using productivity tools for professional and personal use, including word processing, database, spreadsheet, and print/graphic utilities.	Chapter 10 MS-*Works* tutorials
10. Demonstrate knowledge of equity, ethical, legal, and human issues of computing and technology use as they relate to society and model appropriate behaviors.	Throughout this text, especially chapters 4 and 5
11. Identify resources for staying current in applications of computing and related technologies in education.	Throughout this text, especially chapter 14 and appendix B
12. Use computer-based technologies to access information to enhance personal and professional productivity.	Throughout this text, especially chapter 11
13. Apply computers and related technologies to facilitate emerging roles of the learner and the educator.	Throughout this text MS-*Works* tutorials

Networking—the linking of computers over communications lines—is opening up a world of opportunity for students, teachers, and administrators alike. Many schools are establishing on-line interactive hookups for students to communicate within the school as well as between schools, whether locally, nationally, or internationally. More and more states have established networks to facilitate communication between school administrations and a central state-administrative office. Nationwide, schools can now take advantage of federally funded communications highways, which are encouraging data sharing as never before, with the potential for significant information gain by individuals.

Figure I.1
Children at work in
the computer lab
Photo courtesy Susan
Giorgio Bond

Figure I.2
Students
collaborating on a
project
Photo courtesy Hilary
Englebert

Figure I.3
The computer is the
teacher's productivity
tool.
Photo courtesy Susan
Giorgio Bond

I.3.4 Software That Is Well-Designed to Support Learning Enables a Teacher to Duplicate Excellence

A growing number of examples of educational software are recognized as pedagogically sound. Many teachers are now using productivity software—word processors, database management systems, spreadsheets, communications software, drawing tools—to manage the whole process of teaching and learning. Well-designed and integrated systems such as these support successful learning environments for children, thus duplicating excellence when they are made available to all.

Taking this idea one step further, in chapter 13 we will discuss authoring systems. These products help take the creation of learning systems out of the hands of technologists and put it into the hands of the teachers themselves. Innovative teachers are thus able to share their expertise—to duplicate excellence—by developing lessons that incorporate the ever-increasing stock of computer-based teaching aids and by making these lessons available to colleagues.

At one time or another all teachers have those magic moments when they touch the hearts and minds of their students and, thus, as the saying goes, "touch the future." But even the best teachers in the world find it difficult to be their best all the time. We all have professional ups and downs and as long as we have to rely solely on our own devices to manage the educational process, we inevitably subject our students to a roller-coaster educational experience. Thoughtful integration of appropriate computer-based learning, however, can take some of this pressure off teachers, enabling them to offer, on their own account as well as with the help of the computer, consistently excellent learning experiences both in their classrooms and in their students' homes.

Most, if not all, teachers choose the profession because they are excited by the challenge of education. Most teachers are sustained in the profession by the joy that comes

Figure I.4
Multimedia in the classroom
Photo courtesy Optical Data Corporation

from seeing the light of newfound knowledge gleaming in a child's eyes. If this book helps you to discover the value of computers in an educational setting, it will have succeeded in its objectives—you will be a better teacher in some small but significant way.

None of this will happen overnight, so you will need a good dose of patience and perseverance during the initial stages of your journey toward becoming a computer-literate teacher. But you will find that the rewards of successful integration of computers into the curriculum and into your classroom administration will be incalculable. You are going to be glad you set out on this adventure.

It is not unusual during these early days of computerized education to find just one computer in a classroom. Sometimes it sits there gathering dust. The children would love to get their hands on it, but the teacher perhaps does not know where to begin supervising its use in a pedagogically powerful way and understandably fears that uncontrolled use will probably result in its being destroyed!

If you are one of those many teachers who recognize the need to start using computers but have hesitated till now to take the plunge, know that every step you take will lessen any fear you may feel and will increase your potential as a teacher in this Information Age. If this book helps you take this step, all the effort that has gone into its creation will have been worthwhile.

■ References

Information Services Office. *Workplace Competencies: The Need to Improve Literacy and Employment Readiness.* Publication of the Information Services Office of Educational Research and Improvement, U.S. Department of Education, 1990, p. 1.

ISTE. *Curriculum Guidelines for Accreditation of Educational Computing and Technology Programs.* Eugene, OR: The International Society for Technology in Education, 1992, pp. 7–8.

National Committee on Excellence in Education. *A Nation At Risk.* Publication of the National Committee on Excellence in Education. Cambridge, MA: USA Research, 1984.

Poole, Bernard J. *Essential Microsoft Works: Tutorials for Teachers.* Madison, WI: Brown & Benchmark, 1994.

Computers in Schools and Society

A Review of the Research

The greatest wrong, the greatest treason,
Is to do the right thing for the wrong reason.
T. S. Eliot (1888–1965)
Murder in the Cathedral

◤ Learning Outcomes

This chapter will review a cross-section of the research into the effectiveness of computer-based teaching and learning. The objective is to provide a rationale for acquiring and applying the skills that will be presented in the remainder of the text. The outcomes of the research support what most teachers who have incorporated the computer into the learning process have already concluded: that it can add value to that process when it is integrated thoughtfully.

The material covered in this chapter, coupled with the evidence that you gather from your own experience using the computer in the classroom, will also provide solid justification for the requests that you make to local, state, or federal agencies for grants and other support of technology-assisted learning. To quote Bailey (1992): "Your response to the question: 'What does research say about the impact of technology on education?' has a direct bearing on how school board members, parents, teachers, and students view and support technology."

Later, in chapter 14, you will learn about writing grants—the skills involved in creating proposals that request support of all kinds for your educational endeavors. You will be most successful at writing grants if you can convince the providers of financial support—parents, administrators, board members, state and federal agencies—that they are investing in an endeavor that has proved successful and that they are likely to get a worthwhile return on their investment. Hence, you need to be able to reference the research regarding the successful incorporation of computer technology into the curriculum.

This chapter will examine the following aspects of this research:

- Sources for research findings
- Computers, the three R's, science, and social studies
    - Reading
    - Writing
    - Arithmetic and problem-solving
    - Science
    - Social studies
- The challenge of change

This is by no means an exhaustive set of those instructional areas that have been researched in any depth. But it is likely to be of interest to those preparing for, or already engaged in, teaching at the precollege level because it addresses broadly based topics that relate to key areas of responsibility within the K–12 educational process.

◤ 1.1 Introduction

The goal of *Education for an Information Age* is to help teachers incorporate computer-controlled technology into the educational curriculum. The significant investment of time and effort, not to mention money, in pursuit of this goal is a relatively recent phenomenon in schools. Computers first started to appear in K–12 classrooms in the late 1970s—less than 20 years ago. Since then, federal, state, and local governments, corporations, and even teachers and students themselves have spent hundreds of millions of dollars to provide schools with computer-related equipment. Hundreds of thousands of teachers worldwide have been trained in the use of the technology. It is possible that more has been invested in the effort to incorporate the computer into the K–12 curriculum than in any other educational innovation in the history of formal schooling—and we've only just begun!

Such an investment presupposes a consensus that the myriad applications of this technology currently flooding into the educational marketplace are an improvement on tried and true teaching methodologies. Is this the case? Dickson (1984) quotes Joseph Weizenbaum, Professor of Computer Science at the Massachusetts Institute of Technology, who cautions: "Everyone agrees that in principle computers are powerful, but too often teachers . . . find they are following a common scenario: First you get the hardware, then you get the software, then you train the teachers, and only then do you start trying to work out what you are going to do with it all."

"The mark of fertility in a science," according to Jean Piaget (1926), "is its capacity for practical application." Can the science of computing be practically applied in schools? What evidence is there that computer-based teaching tools make a difference in the learning process? Is this merely another pedagogical fad destined to come and go like so many others? How well have these systems been designed? Do they reflect the wisdom of educational philosophies born of centuries of cumulative educational experience?

Has the research been done to answer these important questions? The answer is: Yes—to some extent at least; though more needs to be done. The many studies that *have* been done indicate that definite aspects of the learning process can be significantly augmented by computer-based educational technologies. Indeed, as Kinnaman (1990) and Tierney (1992) remind us, much of the research that has been done might have been more impressive if it had *not* been conducted in traditional learning settings, but rather in settings designed to gain maximum benefit from integration of computers. As Selfe (1992) points out, computer-based teaching and learning presents a whole new set of pedagogical and logistical realities that will need to be thought through before technology can be integrated into the curriculum in the best possible way.

■■ 1.2 Sources for Research Findings

In what ways, then, is computer use in schools effective? Many resources are available to help answer this question. For example, Apple Computer, Inc. (1990) has made available in electronic form an extensive review of the research that has been done to assess the impact of computers on K–12 education. The project was managed by Dr. Lyn Allen of Apple Computer, Inc. and edited by Dr. Dan Gibbs. Although sponsored by a company that is not disinterested in the outcomes of the study, the review nonetheless does a good job of directly or indirectly summarizing the findings of several hundred published studies. The results outlined later in this chapter are to a large extent corroborated by similar reviews carried out by more manifestly disinterested parties (OTA, 1988; Kinnaman, 1990).

The research reviewed in the Apple project is prefaced by the observation that "the answers [to whether or not computer-based instructional materials are effective] are only as good as the questions" (Rockman, 1988). The three "big" questions Rockman poses are:

1. When should technology be used?
2. Under what conditions can it be used effectively?
3. How can the instructional effectiveness of computer-based materials be increased?

Roblyer et al. (1988) are more specific when they ask:

1. Can computer applications help improve student performance in basic skills and other areas?
2. For what specific skill areas, grade levels, and content areas are computers most effective?
3. Which students seem to profit most from using computers?
4. Which computer applications are most effective for which skills/content areas?
5. Can computer applications affect students' attitudes toward school, learning, and the ability to learn?
6. Will improved attitudes lead to better performance and lower dropout rates?

The remainder of this chapter will present the results of the research. Later, chapters 8 through 12 will examine computer-based learning systems in some detail. For now it will be useful to see how computers have actually been used in recent years to improve the quality of teaching and learning in elementary and secondary schools.

1.3 Computers, the Three R's, Science, and Social Studies

Reading, writing, and arithmetic, since the early 19th century at least, have been hailed as the basic ingredients of education for literacy[1] at the elementary level. This is still largely the case in primary schools worldwide. The vast majority of children are born equipped with the intellectual prerequisites for literacy—the ability to read, write, and handle enough math to cope with the demands of the modern world.

What evidence exists that computer technology can augment our efforts to help children learn to read, write, and do math? For the most part, the sections that follow will use studies that review the research literature, this being the most convenient resource in view of the plethora of data generated by the ever-increasing number of publications dealing with computer use in education. Capper (1988) carried out such a review for the Congress of the United States Office of Technology Assessment (OTA). Capper's work, with that of others contracted by OTA, supplied the data for the OTA (1988) publication titled: *POWER ON! New Tools for Teaching and Learning*. The Apple Computer, Inc. project (1990) already cited also provides useful reference data. We will further draw on publications

---

[1]*Literacy* here used in the sense of "possession of education" (Random House, 1991). It should be remembered that in these waning years of the 20th century, there are still countries where the universal right to even an elementary education is a novel and barely implemented phenomenon.

such as Electronic Learning's Special Editions: *Hands-on Math and Science* (1992a), *School Reform: Why You Need Technology to Get There* (1992b), and *Turned on to Reading and Writing* (1992c).

As you read the conclusions that follow, bear in mind that the learning outcomes complement each other. For example, when computer-using students "displayed more subject/verb agreement" in their writing than other students who did not use the computer, this may well be because the computer-using students "reread and revised their compositions more frequently than a control group using pen and paper." Also bear in mind that, in general, students thought of technology education as "fun" because it was "hands on" and relevant to their world (Thode, 1988).

But the computer is only a tool in the hands of both student and teacher. The effectiveness of that tool depends entirely on the skills that the student and teacher bring to the learning process. Students are no more passive soakers-up of knowledge than teachers are robotized imparters of knowledge. As constructivists from Dewey on have emphasized, children learn best when they are actively engaged in, and in control of, their own education (Harris, 1991). Constructivism also emphasizes the dual role of teacher and student in maintaining a "zone of proximal development" (Vygotsky, 1962), which is defined by Harris (1991) as "the area between what a learner can do independently (mastery level) and what can be accomplished with the assistance of a competent adult or peer (instructional level)." The outcomes of the computer-based systems for teaching and learning described in the following are likewise not automatic; they are the result of a collaboration between the teacher, the student, and the designers of the technology.

1.3.1 Reading

One of the most celebrated computer-based systems for teaching early reading and writing is that developed by Dr. John Henry Martin in cooperation with IBM. This system, called *Writing to Read*™, has been in use since 1982 and has been thoroughly evaluated both by the Educational Testing Service (ETS), commissioned by IBM, and by other independent researchers.

We are interested in how effective the *Writing to Read* program has been in improving on more traditional methodologies for helping children of kindergarten and first-grade age to learn to read and write. If rapid progress and joy in learning are a measure of a program's effectiveness, then *Writing to Read* has been very successful. The program is in operation in schools across the United States, and one cannot help but be impressed by the philosophy and pedagogy that has guided its development. In fact, one is reminded of the methodologies employed in the Montessori schools where children "explode" into writing after learning the letters and the sounds associated with those letters (Standing, 1962); however, Montessori's children do not need computers to discover reading by themselves once they are ready to make the leap from writing the letters associated with the sounds that make up language. So do the computers in the *Writing to Read* program make any significant difference?

Studies such as Murphy (1984) note that the program has been more effective in teaching writing than reading, putting *Writing to Read* students significantly ahead of non-*Writing to Read* students in terms of writing skills. But, the results also showed that eventually the non-*Writing to Read* students caught up with their *Writing to Read*

Figure 1.1
Children using the
Writing to Read
program
Photo courtesy IBM
Corporation

counterparts. The program gave participants a jump start on basic literacy skills, but neither the advantage gained over non-*Writing to Read* students nor the rate of progress were sustained after the program was completed. Indeed, a year later, the *Writing to Read* students' writing skills had declined slightly while the non-*Writing to Read* students continued to improve.

Olson (1987) provides a further caveat. Teachers involved with *Writing to Read* classes tended to have their students spend more time reading and writing than had been the practice in previous years. So any conclusions about the effectiveness of the program as compared with other well-researched alternatives remain tentative.

A major question about *Writing to Read* relates to cost-effectiveness. Slavin (1990) indicates that first-year costs per lab range anywhere from IBM's listed cost of about $20,000 per lab to the $65,000 paid for each of the labs installed in 43 elementary schools in Baltimore. The reason for the discrepancy is that IBM's list price does not cover all expenses involved with the system. By contrast, research has shown that reading programs sponsored by the U.S. Department of Education (Alphaphonics, MECCA, TALK, MARC, and INSTRUCT) that cost just a few hundred dollars per class have been at least as effective as *Writing to Read*.

Larter (1987) corroborates the conclusions of the research into the *Writing to Read* program when she notes that using computers did not significantly improve students' reading in either the first, third, or sixth grades. Some researchers have found that students of all ages have difficulty reading and writing on-line. One reason may be that computer-based reading and writing requires that users learn to

Figure 1.2
A young student
using the *Discis Book
Library*
Photo courtesy Susan
Giorgio Bond

cope with on-line texts, screens, and file directories instead of the printed page and tables of contents—what Selfe (1992) calls a "multilayered literacy."

Certainly, good old-fashioned books take some beating when it comes to reading in general. Ergonomically speaking,[2] there is a lot to be said for reading a book curled up in an armchair in front of a warm fire or lying out in the sun on a lawn, a deck, or a beach. Scrolling through the text on a notebook computer does not have the same carefree, relaxed feel to it; it is almost as if the machinery might get in the way of one's enjoyment and interfere with one's concentration. The goal of any learning environment, however, is to foster learning and the data confirm that the *Writing to Read* program achieves this goal. If money is no object, and the learning is enjoyable, too, then so much the better.

The jury is thus still out on the effectiveness of using computers to help children learn to read. Roblyer (1988), in his review of the research from 1980 to 1987, found that the use of computer applications for reading resulted in "educationally significant effects," and that "tutorials[3] seem more effective than other kinds of tools in reading." As for so many aspects of using computers in teaching and learning, success may depend on a shift in paradigms. New products, such as the *CCC Instructional System*™, or the *Discis Book Library*™, that use **CD-ROM**[4] technology to bring a book to life with text, full color illustrations, *and sound,* need to be studied.

---

[2]*Ergonomics*—also called Human Factors Engineering—is the study of the interfacing (interaction) between people and machines.

[3]Software that interactively walks the student through a reading exercise.

[4]Compact Disk–Read Only Memory: Laserdisc-based computer systems that enable users to work more easily with full-color graphics and sound along with text. The technology will be discussed in more depth in chapters 2 and 8.

Figure 1.3
Students at work on word-processed projects
Photo courtesy Susan Giorgio Bond

According to Computer Curriculum Corporation, its *CCC Instructional System*™ helped Credle Elementary School in North Carolina raise average student reading scores by 57% in two years. Granted, the average reading ability of the students was low to start with, but the progress was sufficiently significant for the U.S. Department of Education to recognize the school as a 1989-90 National School of Excellence. Teachers who use CD-ROM are enthusiastic about a technology that "has made reading exciting," as one kindergarten teacher at York Central School in Retsoff, New York, put it, "The children feel empowered, and we're definitely seeing an improvement in reading skills" (Electronic Learning, 1992).

Of course, anecdotal evidence is easy to come by and therefore should be taken with a grain of salt. But when positive anecdotal evidence abounds, it reinforces the outcomes of more rigorous research.

1.3.2 Writing

Unlike reading, there is a good deal of positive research feedback regarding student use of computers for writing assignments. The conclusions listed below are consistent whether the research focused on learning disabled students or regular students.

■ Students using the computer and word processor for writing assignments generally felt more positive about the writing instruction they received and about their own writing skills (Kurth, 1987a,b; Roblyer, 1988; Klenow, 1991);

Figure 1.4
MECC's *My Own Stories* uses pictures and songs to help children bring their stories to life
Photo courtesy of MECC

improved the quality and fluency of their writing (Burnett, 1984; Bigley, 1986; Cirello, 1986; Muldrow, 1986; Larter, 1987; Klenow, 1991);

were more self-motivated with regard to the subject matter of their writing (Rosegrant, 1985);

were motivated to achieve literacy because of the computer's visual, auditory, and physical support (Rosegrant, 1985);

improved in literacy because they were encouraged to read what they had written (Rosegrant, 1985);

found software useful for tutoring, writing theory, getting ideas, organizing thoughts, composing, providing feedback, and communicating with others (Frase, 1987);

wanted to write more (Roblyer, 1988).

■ With regard to revising their work, students using the computer and word processor for writing assignments

were more self-motivated to revise drafts and spent more time on the process (Hague, 1986; Hawisher, 1986; Muldrow, 1986; Pearson, 1986; Souviney, 1986; Dalton, 1987; Katz, 1987; Kurth, 1987a; Eastman, 1988, 1989; Klenow, 1991);

produced higher quality revisions than revisions completed using pen and paper (Daiute, 1986; Muldrow, 1986; Kurth, 1987a; Kurth, 1987b; Eastman, 1989);

when using the computer's readability measure competed to see who would write at the highest grade level and increased grade level from first draft to revised draft which encouraged them to revise their drafts (Hague, 1986);

adapted more easily to composing on a computer when emphasis was put on revising as opposed to advance planning[5] (Lansing, 1984);

reread and revised their compositions more frequently and more readily than a control group using pen and paper (Rust, 1986; Butler-Nalin, 1987; Kurth, 1987a; Eastman, 1988, 1989);

made revisions that involved an increase in the length of the composition (Bigley, 1986; Cirello, 1986; Daiute, 1986; Rust, 1986; Kurth, 1987b; Eastman, 1989).

- With regard to the mechanics of writing, students using the computer and word processor for writing assignments

more readily developed conceptual abilities since they did not have to physically create the symbols with which they expressed those concepts (Daiute, 1985b; Rosegrant, 1985; Souviney, 1986);

composed more fluently than they would have with pencils and pens because of the automatic recopying and printout features of computers (Daiute, 1985b; Rust, 1986; Souviney, 1986; Eastman, 1989; Klenow, 1991);

found that triple-spaced copy made editing easier (Rust, 1986);

felt that keyboarding did not interfere with writing[6] (Muldrow, 1986; Cheever, 1987);

prepared computer drafts that contained fewer words than pen and paper drafts when composing time was limited to 15 minutes, and longer drafts than with pen and paper when more time was allowed (Daiute, 1986);

were more concerned with the aesthetic quality of their text—layout, appearance, and so forth (Daiute, 1985b);

preferred the word processor over pen and paper for writing (Burnett, 1984; Larter, 1987; Klenow, 1991);

produced significantly enhanced science-related documents through the use of the word processor (O'Brien, 1986).

- With regard to the reduction of errors in writing, students using the computer and word processor for writing assignments

showed the most dramatic gains in reducing grammar, punctuation and capitalization errors, and in displaying more subject/verb agreement when they initially demonstrated the lowest ability (Muldrow, 1986; Cheever, 1987; Dalton, 1987);

overlooked fewer errors than when using pen and paper (Daiute, 1986; Klenow, 1991);

made fewer grammar, punctuation and capitalization errors (Cheever, 1987);

displayed more subject/verb agreement than those who did not use the computer (Cheever, 1987).

---

[5]Students who planned their written work in advance would not need the help of interactive revision as much as those who did not plan their work ahead of time.

[6]This conflicts with Selfe's (1992) caveat about "multi-layered literacy" discussed earlier in the chapter.

Figure 1.5
Students
collaborating on a
writing assignment
Photo courtesy Susan
Giorgio Bond

■ With regard to effects not directly related to writing, students using the computer and word processor for writing assignments

> may more easily have made the difficult transition from speech to writing (Daiute, 1985b);

> may more easily have developed self-awareness because of the interactive capacities of a computer (Daiute, 1985b);

> may have found the computer to be a catalyst in the development of writing skills as adolescents (Curtiss, 1984; Cirello, 1986; Pearson, 1986).

Computer-assisted collaborative learning, including writing

Teachers in all subject areas are discovering that computer-based learning lends itself to collaboration between groups of students. This is especially true when students are encouraged to work together on writing assignments. Such students

> worked best in small groups of two, three or four students (Daiute, 1985a; Ayoubi, 1985);

> were more often girls than boys, suggesting that collaborative work is more successful with girls (Johnson, 1985);

> shared more ideas with classmates than those using traditional methods of composition (Daiute, 1985a; Heap, 1986; Kurth, 1987a; Klenow, 1991);

> appeared to help each other learn appropriate writing techniques (Daiute, 1985a; Daiute, 1985b; Eastman, 1988, 1989; Klenow, 1991);

were encouraged to collaborate because it was simpler to add to and arrange common text (Heap, 1986; Muldrow, 1986);

produced a higher level of achievement in terms of mastery and application of factual information as compared with individualistic learning (Johnson, 1985);

had very little interaction with the teacher (Johnson, 1985).

Using prompting programs to help students compose

As Daiute (1985c) observed, in some schools students have been given the opportunity to use the computer and word processor in conjunction with a prompting program such as *Writing Process Workshop* (from Educational Activities), or *Success with Writing* (from Scholastic). These programs are designed to stimulate interaction between the students and their writing.

Students using the computer and word processor in conjunction with a prompting program:

made more interactive revisions than when using only the word processor especially if they were beginning writers of all ages (Daiute, 1985c; Daiute, 1986);

increased their level of reading and rereading their written work (Daiute, 1985c).

Caveats re: computer use for writing

The following research findings remind us that no methodology, no tool, is suited to all situations, and that sometimes the methodology or tool can create or reveal new, unanticipated problems.

Children of seven years of age or younger may lack the cognitive skills necessary to socialize and collaborate effectively, in writing or otherwise; the writer's age, level of cognitive development, and composing style is critical to how the computer tool is used (Daiute, 1985a; Daiute, 1985b);

Students working collaboratively will not find collaboration effective for all writing tasks, and should work independently on some writing tasks in order to assure maturation of the writing process (Daiute, 1985a);

The computer is less useful if the hardware or software design is complicated; all computers should ideally be of the same brand and model so as to facilitate group instruction and interaction (Daiute, 1985b; Frase, 1987; Eastman, 1988);

Computer writing needs to be integrated with the use of other traditional writing and drawing tools (Daiute, 1985b);

Some students found using the keyboard and working with text on line inhibited their writing ability (Curtiss, 1984; Dalton, 1987; Eastman, 1988, 1989; Selfe, 1992);

Some students neglected planning when using the word processor (Dalton, 1987)[7];

There need to be an adequate number of computers for students to work simultaneously and individually (Eastman, 1988);

---

[7]Perhaps because revisions were so much easier to make—which is a problem, since planning is always important.

Figure 1.6
Students using
MECC's *Number
Munchers*
Photo courtesy Susan
Giorgio Bond

Pedagogical styles will need to change to accommodate the use of computers (Daiute, 1985b; Eastman, 1988, 1989; Tierney, 1992);

Sixth-grade students using the word processor did not produce better-quality writing than those using pencil and paper (Larter, 1987);

A few researchers found the computer made practically no difference as regard many aspects of the writing process (Lansing, 1984; Kurth, 1987a; Strickland, 1987; Roblyer, 1988);

Viewing written work on a computer screen does not appear to help the writing process—hard copy may be the preferred medium for review of written work (Lansing, 1984).

1.3.3 Arithmetic and Problem-Solving

Let us now review the research conclusions regarding the effectiveness of computer use in teaching and learning math and problem-solving.

Students who used the computer for these learning activities

showed math achievement gains that were significantly greater than the control groups who did not use the computer (Foley, 1984; Roblyer, 1988; Fletcher, 1990);

spent 50% of all computer time learning programming skills (problem-solving) at the high-school level (Becker, 1987);

were more likely to be helped in basic math and language skills if they were lower-ability students; higher-ability students benefited in terms of higher cognitive skills such as problem-solving and programming (Ayoubi, 1985; Samson, 1986; Becker, 1987; Thode, 1988);

improved problem-solving skills when using Logo as a platform for programming (Spence, 1987; Roblyer, 1988);

learned concepts such as fractions and binary operations of fractions, graphing, and algebraic precedence conventions significantly more effectively when provided with computer-based experiences in addition to teacher-directed activities, as opposed to students who received only teacher-directed activities (Marty, 1985; Al-Ghamdi, 1987; Ball, 1988);

scored significantly higher on measures of their ability to transfer skills learned with the aid of the computer to other areas of mathematics (Al-Ghamdi, 1987; OTA, 1988).

Caveats re: computer use for learning math and problem-solving

Joseph Weizenbaum, professor at the Massachusetts Institute of Technology, points out that there is "no more evidence that [problem-solving in the form of computer programming] is better for the mind than Latin is, as sometimes claimed" (Spence, 1987). Other researchers found that students using computers for math and problem-solving:

were not affected as to their attitudes towards math or computers (Foley, 1984; Marty, 1985);

were not affected with regard to class attendance (Foley, 1984);

were as likely to find math and computer programming equally difficult (OTA, 1988).

1.3.4 Science

In the science classroom, students interacting with computers running simulations of experiments enjoyed a more effective learning experience than students watching a demonstration accompanied by teacher–student interaction. Simulated or real experimentation seems to provide the benefit of *involvement*—a characteristic of quality learning so ardently advocated by Thomas Edison. "The most important method of education," Edison once remarked, "always has consisted of that in which the pupils were urged to actual performance."

Here is some of the feedback from research into computer-integrated science education. Students who used the computer in the science classroom:

achieved more from computer-based laboratory activities and/or computer simulations than students who studied in a conventional learning environment (White, 1984; Shaw, 1985; Roblyer, 1988);

were more likely to benefit than when using computers for learning in other content areas (Roblyer, 1988);

Figure 1.7
Students in a
microcomputer-
based laboratory
Photo courtesy IBM
Corporation

learned more effectively to generate graphs, to identify trends in graphs, and to understand the meaning of information presented in graphs developed during experiments than students developing graphs by hand (Linn, 1987);

were more easily able to transfer understanding from one type of physical activity to another when generating graphs during experiments in microcomputer-based laboratories (Linn, 1987; OTA, 1988);

were able to use the computer as an oscilloscope, temperature probe, pressure sensor, light sensor, and so on, by connecting sensors and probes to it, thus extending the use of the computer as a laboratory instrument for science studies at a fraction of the cost of the actual instruments (McCarthy, 1992);

gained skills likely to be valuable throughout their lives when learning how to collect, analyze, and interpret data (Rash, 1990);

produced science-related documents that were significantly enhanced through the use of word processing (O'Brien, 1986).

Caveat re: computer use for teaching and learning science

Not all researchers came to the same conclusions. Ayoubi (1985) and Choi (1987) found that students who were given the opportunity for computer-based learning of science gained no advantage in computer-simulated experiments over students who conducted the same experiments hands-on, when the students were of average ability. It was also noted that students were involved mostly in drill and practice when using software related to the physical sciences (Hegelson, 1988).

Figure 1.8
(*a*) Students facing the challenges of the Oregon Trail; (*b*) *The Oregon Trail*™ and *The Amazon Trail*™ (*a*) Photo courtesy Susan Giorgio Bond; (*b*) Photo courtesy MECC

a

1.3.5 Social Studies

The following are some outcomes of research into the effectiveness of computer use for social studies.

Social studies benefit from the increasingly varied access to computerized databases of appropriate information (Hunter, 1987). **Database management systems (DBMS)** simplify access to large volumes of data covering most subjects in the social studies curriculum. The databases are both local and remote, the latter being accessed via communications media such as the telephone system.

Cohen (1987) drew conclusions similar to those of Hunter. Students were given access to electronic information via on-line databases. As expected, access to information was quicker, and students developed research skills as well as skills related to computer use and telecommunications.

Studies across the curriculum benefit from using the computer to create, store, retrieve, and randomly display data. Students are more easily motivated when using the computer for these activities (Ferguson, 1989). Massialas (1987) found teachers K–8 enthusiastic about the use of computers for social studies, even though the integration of computers into the curriculum proved complex. The introduction of computers may result in the beginning of curriculum change. It is interesting that Massialas also found that computer use led to an increase in social skills.

Figure 1.8
Continued

b

Figure 1.9
Students using Compton's CD-ROM *Encyclopedia* for a history project
Photo courtesy Susan Giorgio Bond

Teachers from fourth through twelfth grade found that interactive videodiscs provided a multimedia environment that simplified the sequencing and presentation of relevant, high-quality visual information as a supplement to traditional social studies lessons (White, 1990). White noted that videodisc technology was most effective when used in conjunction with a microcomputer running software such as *HyperCard.*

Audio-telecommunications systems such as voice mail promote the bridging of oceans and cultures, increasing students' global awareness and international understanding (Galvin, 1989). Voice mail cuts across time zones because it allows students to take up a conversation at any time they choose. Conversations can also be duplicated and shared with other users. Diem (1989) reports on video-conferencing technology used to teach students the nature and importance of global interdependence. Chapter 11 will expand on these technologies when discussing the effectiveness of computers and communications (C&C) in the learning process.

The computer is a useful tool (word processing, database management, simulations, tutorials) for learning traditional social-studies concepts (Lengel, 1987; OTA, 1988). Budin (1987) identified the following as directions to pursue in the use of computers in teaching social studies:

1. Develop more software that involves students in decision making in regard to social studies issues, and expect more input from them;
2. Use software that makes more use of graphics to convey subject matter;
3. Use technology such as telecommunications to increase students' global understanding;
4. Use the computer to stimulate more social interaction on the part of the students.

Students are learning to be more effective in finding meaning in data because of the ease with which large amounts of data can be displayed graphically using microcomputers (Hinze, 1989).

Caveats re: computer use in social studies

Teachers were concerned about the lack of software, and found a lack of correlation between some of the available software and instructional goals. Teachers also considered themselves inadequately prepared to use computers in the social studies classroom (Massialas, 1987).

According to White (1987), incorporation of the computer into social studies education was most effective when teachers were well trained and were prepared to spend extended time to make the computer-based programs work. Success was also associated with cooperation from institutions outside the school who served as partners.

Schug (1988) found that far more teachers had received training than were presently using computers, even though most teachers expected to be using them more. This suggests that either the training was inadequate, or that access to computers was too restrictive to warrant incorporating them into the curriculum, or that the available social-studies applications were considered unsatisfactory.

1.4 The Challenge of Change

If computers are such a boon to education, why is it that so few teachers have developed curricula that incorporate their use? Here are some obvious reasons.

- **Until the mid-1980s desktop computers were unable to run sophisticated learning programs because they were not powerful enough.** Early software was therefore very limited in what it could do. If the program used graphics, it ran too slowly, and the images were primative. If it lacked graphics, its interest value was diminished significantly.

- **Still today, well into the 1990s, computers are too expensive to justify their purchase in sufficient numbers to make a significant impact in a school.** Few teachers have computers on their desks, which means that most teachers, whether they like it or not, have to do without them most, if not all, of the time. The same is true of students. As observed in Borrell (1992), quoting Herb Lin of the National Academy of Sciences: "Even if there were one computer per classroom, that's less than two minutes per student for a one-hour class." A survey conducted by the Software Publishers Association (1992) found that in spite of a $2.7 billion investment in computers and software in the 1991–92 academic year, of which $1.9 billion had been spent for instructional purposes, "most students and teachers get very little computing time." Bulkeley (1988) noted that even schools that were among the first to purchase computers are now faced with the expense of replacing those old machines before they can even think about adding more computers.

- **Educational systems in general are slow to change.** Elmer-Dewitt (1991) points out that at most age levels in most schools, the time frame around which lessons are planned is about 40 minutes. But when students work together on a project that uses the computer for research, data analysis, and presentation, this time frame is too short. To some extent, computer technology will begin to be used most effectively when schools allow for a schedule in which the day is divided up along more flexible lines, with a mix of time frames depending on the topic and medium of instruction.

- Cuban (1986) and Bulkeley (1988) add the following reasons for the uneven and limited penetration of technology into teachers' instructional repertoires:

    1. Teachers have inadequate opportunities for training and poor access to technology; strategies for implementation are thus often flawed. In 1988, 32 percent of the computer-education coordinators in elementary schools admitted they were uncomfortable with computers, according to an Educational Testing Service survey (Bulkeley, 1988).

    2. A surprisingly large number of colleges of education still do little to prepare student teachers for a technology-based teaching paradigm.

    3. Using computers to teach classes is much more difficult than expected and demands considerable preparation even for well-trained teachers.

    4. Classroom demands of various kinds—class size, heavy teaching schedule, other teacher responsibilities unrelated to teaching, and so forth—take away from a teacher's commitment to computer-based teaching and learning. As one teacher put it: "I've been too busy teaching to integrate the computers" (Bulkeley, 1988).

A useful exercise would be to come up with other reasons for the slow pace of change in terms of introducing computer-based technology into the classroom. These might reflect your own experiences in the classroom, as either a student or a teacher. This discussion is offered as one of the exercises in the Do Something About It section at the end of this chapter.

That the transition to computer-integrated curricula is slow should not surprise us; nor should it deter us from continuing to move forward. In Electronic Learning (1992b), Bruder references the April 1992 report of the Council of Chief State School Officers with its call for access to technology "for all students" along with a proposal for "a series of sweeping measures to integrate technology on a broad scale in schools." Since effective leadership is so crucial to success, let us hope that the council's report will lead to real action on the part of its members and those they represent.

▦ Looking Back

This chapter has presented feedback from the collective experience of many educators and educational researchers with regard to the effective use of computer-based tools in schools. More work needs to be done. Current conclusions remain tentative though predominantly positive, suggesting that experimentation should continue with a view to helping teachers make wise decisions about ways and means of incorporating the computer into the curriculum. Experience also bears out the obvious caveat that any application of computer-based technology should be carefully evaluated as to its effectiveness. We will return to this theme in part III when we examine the technologies and methodologies involved in computer-based learning and teaching.

Lewis Perelman, Director of Project Learning 2001 at the Hudson Institute, fires something of a broadside at people who continue to question the potential contribution of computer-based technology in schools. "Two decades of research," Perelman (1990) writes, "show that computer-based instruction produces at least 30% more learning in 40% less time at 30% less cost compared to traditional classroom teaching. Other research demonstrated 125 technologies and methods that proved to at least double the productivity of teaching—yielding at least twice as much learning for each unit of labor, cost, or time."

The leviathan that is education is stirring. When people look back on this period in the history of education, they will conclude that the invention of the computer was a critical catalyst for fundamental change in the way people learn, just as it is proving to be a catalyst for change in the way people live. Today we are on the threshold of this change, which means that these are difficult times. No one likes to let go of successful but outmoded methodologies. Teachers in training do not have much experience on which to base innovation since, for the most part, they were taught in traditional ways. But the pioneers are out there in the schools, and some of them are profiled in the case studies that accompany each chapter. Others are profiled in the many publications related to teaching in general, and to teaching with technology in particular. Appendix B reviews a selection of this recommended reading.

■ Looking Forward

Ideas are one thing, innovation another. Computer-integrated curricula yield significant benefits for students. This is recognized time and again in the hundreds of articles on this theme published every month in magazines and journals devoted to educational issues. Attend any of the dozens of conferences on educational computing that take place every year around the world and you will meet, unfortunately still very much in the minority, those who are taking the technology into their classrooms and, as we shall see in chapters 8 through 12, making it work for them and for their students.

But innovation requires hard work, planning, and discipline. It does not just happen. Multitudes of teachers have attended seminars, workshops, conferences, even semester-long courses, where they have had the opportunity to learn how to use computer technology as a tool for teaching. A large proportion of these teachers have come away with a new found enthusiasm for the new methodologies involved. Too often, however, they have returned to their schools only to have that enthusiasm and excitement wane as reality brought home to them the extent to which they would have to change the way they have routinely run their classrooms.

The translation of ideas, and enthusiasm about those ideas, into practical implementation is often difficult. We should therefore not be surprised if change is slow in schools. Peters (1984) references the work of Theodore Levitt (1981) on the subject of ideas (creativity) and innovation in the business world. Levitt describes how difficult it is to effect change through innovation and makes a distinction between creativity and innovation. "Creativity," he says, "is thinking up new things. Innovation is *doing* new things." Many people come up with good ideas that will improve the way things are done in schools; too few people are prepared to *do* what is necessary to implement their ideas.

Ideas take on life when they are realized through action. As Levitt points out: "Ideas are useless unless used." So we should resolve to be innovative as well as creative. Better yet, we should resolve to help others be innovative by our example, by our encouragement, and by our willingness to give our time and energy to promote the integration of technology across the curriculum at all levels of teaching and learning in our schools.

■ Do Something About It: Exercises and Projects

1. Break up into groups. Each group is responsible for finding software for each of the subject areas that have been the topic of discussion in this chapter. Evaluate the software's effectiveness as a learning instrument.

2. Work in teams, having each team discuss one of the subject areas focused on in this chapter and draw up a list of other benefits you think would accrue from computer-based learning in that subject area other than those presented in the chapter.

3. Draw up a list of subject areas other than those discussed in this chapter which you believe would especially benefit from well-designed computer-based learning.

4. Identify one other subject area other than those discussed in this chapter (fine art, music, and so forth) and evaluate the impact that the computer might have in helping children develop skills related to those subject areas. Write up your conclusions.

Just because a person can't speak, it doesn't mean he has nothing to say

Jeff Lavin, Springfield High School, Burlington, Vermont

I first met Hudson two years ago, passing him in the hallway of the high school where I teach. He was barely able to see or walk, totally unable to speak, drooling, and moving spasmodically. I felt sorry for him.

I had heard the arguments about mainstreaming severely handicapped students many times before. One camp holds that it's a waste of money to try to educate children like Hudson because they cannot learn. The other side argues that we can't know for sure what goes on inside another person's head, and, in any case, all kids should be given an opportunity. Who is right?

Many people in the school avoided getting too close to Hudson. Perhaps they were embarrassed by his strange behavior and the weird noises he made. Whatever the reason, there he was: at 16, a severely disabled boy condemned to silence, isolated and shunned in a supposedly progressive educational institution. What should be done with him?

Then the incredible happened. A new method called facilitated communication, in which a nonverbal person can communicate by pointing to letters on a keyboard, was tried with Hudson.

It worked. Using the keyboard, Hudson showed that he knew the street on which he lived, the name of the president of the United States, his favorite television show, and so on. It became clear that Hudson had taught himself how to read without any formal training.

This came as a complete shock. The possibility that he was literate had not even been considered. Without warning, Hudson's thoughts burst into the open. His parents and teachers learned for the first time of Hudson's hopes, fears, and feelings.

In September, Hudson entered my U.S. history class. I wondered if a kid whose optimum challenge a couple of years earlier had been sorting mail in the school office could possibly learn history like other kids. A few weeks into class, I asked Valerie and Gary, Hudson's teachers, to let me "converse" with Hudson so I could better understand his deficits. We went to the computer lab and sat down together. I had no idea what to expect.

I watched as Hudson pointed his finger to the letters on the computer keyboard. The process was slow. It was physically difficult for him to hit the letter he wanted. Finally his first message appeared: "WHY ARE YOU HERE?" he had typed. I gulped.

"Since I am your history teacher, I thought I could help you more in my class if I knew you better," I replied. I braced for the response.

(continued)

Jeff Lavin, author of the case study

Hudson Lamb working with his teachers, Valerie Gasco-Wiggin and Gary Pool.
Photo courtesy Jeff Lavin

Case Study 1 (continued)

"GOOD IDEA," he shot back.

"Hudson," I said, "what would you like to say to me to help make history class easier for you?" His involuntary movements increased a bit as his finger headed for the keyboard.

"I WANT YOU TO BELIEVE I CAN DO THIS," he responded.

I was astounded. I decided then and there that I would not only believe that Hudson could "do this," but that I would not assume there was any limitation on what he could learn in social studies.

Soon Hudson started to talk in his own way: He began to lead the class on tests, scoring one 100 after another.

Many of his classmates did not believe it possible. "It must be the aide guiding his finger to the keyboard," they thought. "How could a kid like that be so smart?" (Read: "smarter than me.")

Then, for an academic tournament on the topic of U.S. history since 1950, Hudson was assigned to a team, just like the other students.

Now, Hudson was noticeable in a different way. During the competition, question after question went around the room without response until the answer was found on Hudson's keyboard.

"Name the first recipient of an artificial heart." "BARNARD CLARK," rolled off the end of his finger. "What was the name of the North Vietnamese offensive in 1968 that became the turning point of the Vietnam War?" "THE TET OFFENSIVE," said the boy who couldn't talk.

Hudson spoke and his classmates listened to the kid who made funny noises and drooled. His teammates began to congratulate him and slap his back each time he answered a question correctly. Now he was valuable, at least to the students on his team.

Hudson's competitors—the students who now were the victims of his smarts—were more skeptical than ever. One of them came up to me after class. He said, "I can't believe there's really a person in there, let alone one who is capable of coming up with those answers over and over again."

"There's a person in there all right," I responded. "One who has hopes and dreams just like the rest of us. He happens to be trapped in a body that doesn't work, but his brain works just fine. You know those right

answers he keeps coming up with? That's his way of hoping we will hear him despite his silence. That's his way of asking us to accept him as fully human."

The final week of school arrived and I finally finished this article. I realized I could not publish it without giving Hudson the chance to read it and comment, and, if he wished, veto its publication.

One morning I asked Gary and Valerie to show it to him. Later that day Valerie returned with Hudson's response. It appears here just as he wrote it, even before he had a chance to edit out the typos:

"I LIKE WHAAT HEE WROTE. IT IS TRUE. GO FFOR IT, PUBLISH IT. PEOPLE WILL FINNALLY BBELIEVE ME. OOK TOO SHARE WITH ALL. NO CHANGES IN ARTICLE FOR ME. IT IS NICE TO HEAR GOOD UTHINGHS ABOUT ME THAT ARE SO TRUE. YOU DO BELIEVE! NOW OTHER PEOPLE WILL TOO. I AM SMART. I CAN LEZARN. IT IS JUST SLOWERE FOR,ME YTO SPEAK ONE LETTEER AT A TIME, I MAY BE SLPOW TYPING BUT THAT DOESNT MEAN IM STUPID!!! END LETTER.

I fought back tears as I read Hudson's words.

Valerie had taught me a line earlier in the year, familiar to everyone who works with facilitated communication: "Just because a person can't speak, it doesn't mean he has nothing to say." I knew Hudson was living proof. But I will always remember these words as well:

"It's a very ancient saying, but a true and honest thought, that if you become a teacher, by your pupils you'll be taught."

Thanks, Hud. You're a great teacher. I've heard your voice loud and clear.

Talk About It

Topics for discussion based on the case study

1. Can you recall being in a situation where you have judged someone on the basis of appearances, only to discover later that you were quite wrong? How do you feel about that?

2. What other circumstances commonly lead to people being incorrectly or prejudicially labeled? How can we as teachers help children develop appropriate

(continued)

Case Study 1 (concluded)

attitudes toward others which will reduce the likelihood of a repeat of Hudson's predicament?

3. Discuss strategies that you can use as a teacher to help sensitize children to the need to treat all people fairly and as they themselves would like to be treated.

4. Mainstreaming, the integration of mentally and physically handicapped children into regular classrooms, is the subject of heated debate as to whether it is in the best interests of all concerned. Where do you stand on this? Are you prepared to manage a class in which there may be handicapped children whose needs will be significantly different from the other children?

■ References

Apple Computer, Inc. *The Impact of Computers on K–12 Education: A Resource for Decision-Makers.* Computer Software, 1990.

Bailey, Gerald, Dan Lumley. "Prove It!" *Electronic Learning,* vol. 11, no. 4, January 1992, p. 10.

Becker, Henry Jay. "Using Computers for Instruction: The Results and Implications of a National Survey May Surprise You." *Byte,* vol. 12, no. 2, February 1987, pp. 149–62.

Borrell, Jerry. "America's Shame: How We've Abandoned Our Children's Future." *MacWorld,* September 1992, pp. 25–30.

Bulkeley, William M. "Computers Failing as Teaching Aids." *Wall Street Journal,* June 6, 1988.

Capper, Joanne. *Computers and Learning: Do They Work? A Review of Research.* Washington, DC: Center for Research into Practice, 1988.

Cuban, L. *Teachers and Machines: The Classroom Use of Technology since 1920.* New York: Teachers College Press, 1986.

Dickson, David. "Better Education Software Seen Tied to More International Cooperation." *Chronicle of Higher Education,* July 25, 1984, p. 30.

Electronic Learning. *Hands-on Math and Science.* Special edition, September 1992(a).

Electronic Learning. *School Reform: Why You Need Technology to Get There.* Special edition, May/June 1992(b).

Electronic Learning. *Turned on to Reading and Writing.* Special edition, May/June 1992(c).

Elmer-Dewitt, Philip. The Revolution That Fizzled. *Time,* May 20, 1991, pp. 48-49.

Ferguson, Jim. "Computing Across the Curriculum." *Social Studies,* March/April 1989, pp. 69–72.

Harris, Karen R., Michael Pressley. "The Nature of Cognitive Strategy Instruction: Interactive Strategy Construction." *Exceptional Children,* March/April 1991, pp. 392–404.

Hunter, Beverly. "Knowledge-Creative Learning with Databases." *Social Education,* January 1987, pp. 38–43.

Kinnaman, Daniel E. "What's the Research Telling Us?" *Classroom Computer Learning,* vol. 10, no. 6, March 1990, pp. 31–39.

Klenow, Carol, Janet Van Dam, Rebecca Rankin. *Teaching and Learning with Technology: Executive Summary of the Evaluation Report.* Oakland Schools, MI: Division of Information Resources, 1991.

Levitt, Theodore. "Ideas Are Useless Unless Used." *Inc.,* February 1981, p. 96. Referenced in Peters.

McCarthy, Robert. "Hands-On Math and Science." *Electronic Learning,* Special Edition, September 1992.

Murphy, Richard T., Lola Rhea Appel. *Evaluation of the Writing to Read Instructional System 1982–84.* Princeton, NJ: Educational Testing Service, 1984.

Olson, Richard, Barbara Wise. "Computer Speech in Reading Instruction." In *Computers and Reading: Issues for Theory and Practice,* David Reinking, ed. New York: Teachers College Press, 1987. Referenced in Capper.

OTA. *POWER ON! New Tools for Teaching and Learning.* Congress of the United States Office of Technology Assessment, OTA-SET-379, Washington, DC: U.S. Government Printing Office, September 1988.

Perelman, Lewis J. "Luddite Schools Wage a Wasteful War." *Wall Street Journal,* September 10, 1990.

Peters, Thomas J., Robert H. Waterman, Jr. *In Search of EXCELLENCE: Lessons from America's Best-Run Companies.* New York: Warner Communications, 1984.

Piaget, Jean. *The Language and Thought of the Child.* New York: Harcourt, Brace, 1926.

Roblyer, M. D. "The Effectiveness of Microcomputers in Education: A Review of the Research from 1980–1987." *Technological Horizons in Education,* vol. 16, no. 2, September 1988, pp. 85–89.

Selfe, Cynthia. "The Humanization of Computers: Forget Technology, Remember Literacy." In *Dialogs: Reading and Writing in the Disciplines,* Jeffrey Carroll, ed. New York: Macmillan, 1992.

Shaw, Edward, James Okey. "Effects of Microcomputer Simulations on Achievement and Attitudes of Middle School Students." *National Research in Science Teaching,* April 1985.

Slavin, Robert E. "IBM's Writing to Read: Is It Right for Reading?" *Phi Delta Kappan,* November 1990, pp. 214–16.

Software Publisher's Association. Referenced in *Chronicle of Higher Education,* October 7, 1992, p. A17.

Spence, Cathie Slater. "New Ideas For Computers in Schools." *Christian Science Monitor,* October 10, 1987, pp. 21–22.

Standing, E. M. *Maria Montessori: Her Life and Work.* Fresno, CA: The New American Library of World Literature, 1962.

Tierney, Robert J. "Shortchanging Technology." *Electronic Learning,* vol. 11, no. 8, May/June 1992, p. 10.

Vygotsky, L. S. *Thought and Language.* Cambridge: Massachusetts Institute of Technology Press, 1962. Referenced in Harris.

White, Barbara. "Designing Computer Games to Help Physics Students Understand Newton's Laws of Motion." *Cognition and Instruction,* vol. 1, no. 1, 1984, pp. 69–108. In OTA.

The following are secondary references cited in Apple Computer, Inc. *The Impact of Computers on K–12 Education: A Resource for Decision-Makers,* Computer Software, 1990.

Al-Ghamdi, Yousif Abdullah Sanad. "The Effectiveness of Using Microcomputers in Learning Algebraic Precedence Conventions." Doctoral dissertation, Florida State University, 1987.

Ayoubi, Zalpha Rachad. "The Effect of Microcomputer Assisted Instruction on Achievement in High School Chemistry." Doctoral dissertation, University of Michigan, 1985.

Ball, Stanley. "Computers, Concrete Materials and Teaching Fractions." *School Science and Mathematics,* vol. 88, no. 6, October 1988, pp. 470–75.

Bigley, Ann C. "An Investigation of Microcomputer Use in Three High School Writing Programs." Doctoral dissertation, Columbia University Teachers College, 1986.

Budin, Howard, Robert Taylor, Diane Kendall. "Computers and Social Studies: Trends and Directions." *The Social Studies,* January/February 1987, pp. 7–11.

Burnett, Jeanie H. "Word Processing as a Writing Tool of an Elementary School Student (A Single Case Study with Nine Replications). Doctoral dissertation, University of Maryland, 1984.

Butler-Nalin, Kay. "How Composing Aloud and Computer Composing Influence Composing Processes. *ERIC Files ED 292115,* 1987, 36 pp.

Cheever, Maureen Susan. "The Effects of Using a Word Processor on the Acquisition of Composition Skills by the Elementary Student. Doctoral dissertation, Northwestern University, 1987.

Choi, Byung-Soon, Eugene Gennaro. "The Effectiveness of Using Computer Simulated Experiments on Junior High Students' Understanding of the Volume Displacement Concept." *Journal of Research in Science Teaching,* vol. 24, no. 6, 1987, pp. 539–52.

Cirello, Vincent J. "The Effect of Word Processing in the Writing Abilities of Tenth Grade Remedial Writing Students." Doctoral dissertation, New York University, 1986.

Cohen, Mollie. "Doing Research Electronically in Social Studies Classrooms." *The Social Studies,* January/February 1987, pp. 26–29.

Curtiss, Damian H. "The Experience of Composition and Word Processing: An Ethnographic, Phenomenological Study of High School Seniors." Doctoral dissertation, Boston University, 1984.

Daiute, Colette. "Issues in Using Computers to Socialize the Writing Process. In *Educational Communication and Technology Journal,* vol. 33, no. 1, 1985, pp. 41–50. (a)

Daiute, Colette. "Writing and Computers." *Writing and Computers.* Menlo Park, CA: Addison-Wesley, 1985. (b)

Daiute, Colette, John Kruidenier. "A Self-questioning Strategy to Increase Young Writers' Revising Processes." *Applied Psycholinguistics,* vol. 6, no. 3, 1985, pp. 307–18. (c)

Daiute, Colette. "Physical and Cognitive Factors in Revising: Insights from Studies With Computers." *Research in the Teaching of English,* vol. 20, no. 2, 1986, pp. 141–59.

Dalton, David W., Michael J. Hannafin. "The Effects of Word Processing on Written Composition." *Journal of Educational Research,* vol. 80, no. 6, 1987, pp. 338–42.

Diem, Richard A. "Technology and Global Education." *Social Studies,* January/February, 1989, pp. 25–27.

Eastman, Susan, et al. "Computers and Writing: 1987–88 Report." Report to Indiana Consortium for Computers and Higher Technology Education, September 1988.

Fletcher, J., P. Hawley, P. Piele. *Seventh International Conference on Technology and Education,* vol. 1, March 1990, pp. 46–48.

Foley, Margaret U. "Personal Computers in High School General Mathematics: Effects on Achievement, Attitude, and Attendance." Doctoral dissertation, University of Maryland, 1984.

Frase, Lawrence T. "Creating Intelligent Environments for Computer Use in Writing." *Contemporary Educational Psychology,* vol. 12, 1987, pp. 212–21.

Galvin, Jene M. "Using Audio-Teleconferencing to Teach Global Awareness." *Social Studies,* November/December 1989, pp. 246–49.

Hague, Sally. "Using the Computer's Readability Measure to Teach Students to Revise Their Writing." *Journal of Reading,* October 1986.

Hawisher, Gail E. "Studies in Word Processing." *Computers and Composition,* vol. 4, no. 1, 1986, pp. 6–31.

Heap, James L. "Collaborative Practices During Computer Writing in a First Grade Classroom." Paper presented at the American Educational Research Association Annual Meeting, San Francisco, April 1986.

Hegelson, Stanley. "Microcomputers in the Science Classroom." *ERIC Clearinghouse for Science, Mathematics, and Environmental Education,* no. 3, 1988.

Hinze, Kenneth E. "PC Datagraphics and Mapping." *Social Science Computer Review,* vol. 7, no. 1, Spring 1989, pp. 72–75.

Johnson, Roger T., David W. Johnson, Mary Beth Stanne. "Effects of Cooperative, Competitive, and Individualistic Goal Structures on Computer-Assisted Instruction." *Journal of Educational Psychology,* vol. 77, no. 6, 1985, pp. 668–77.

Katz, Catherine, Frederick B. Hoffman. "Teaching Writing through Word Processing: A Case Study." *Computers in the Schools,* vol. 4, no. 2, 1987, pp. 99–115.

Kurth, Ruth J. "Using Word Processing to Enhance Revision Strategies during Student Writing Activities." *Educational Technology,* vol. 27, no. 1, 1987, pp. 13–19. (a)

Kurth, Ruth J. "Word Processing and Composition Revision Strategies." Paper presented at the annual meeting of the Educational Research Association, Washington, D.C., April 1987. (b)

Lansing, Margaret L. "Student Writers and Word Processors: A Case Study." *ERIC Files ED249491, Report no. CS-208-577,* 1984.

Larter, Sylvia. "Writing with Microcomputers in the Elementary Grades: Process, Roles, Attitudes, and Products." *ERIC Files ED284261,* 1987.

Lengel, James G. "Thinking Skills, Social Studies, and Computers." *Social Studies,* January/February 1987, pp. 13–16.

Linn, Marcia C., John W. Layman, Rafi Machmias. "Cognitive Consequences of Microcomputer-Based Laboratories: Graphing Skills Development." *Contemporary Educational Psychology,* vol. 12, 1987, pp. 244–53.

Marty, James F. "Selected Effects of a Computer Game on Achievement, Attitude, and Graphing Ability in Secondary Algebra." Doctoral dissertation, Oregon State University, 1985.

Massialas, Byron G., George Papagiannis. "Toward a Critical Review of Computers in Education: Implications for Social Studies." *Social Studies,* January/February, 1987, pp. 47–53.

Muldrow, Elizabeth. "On Writing and Word Processors in a Ninth Grade Classroom." *English Journal,* vol. 75, 1986, pp. 84–86.

O'Brien, George, Edward Pizzini. "Righting Research Writing with a Word Processor." *Science Teacher,* March 1986, pp. 26–28.

Pearson, Howard, Andrew Wilkinson. "The Use of the Word Processor in Assisting Childrens' Writing Development." In *Educational Review,* vol. 28, no. 2, 1986.

Rash, Polly, Helenmarie Hofman. "GOES Weather Satellite Model Program." *The Seventh International Conference on Technology and Education,* vol. 1, March 1990, pp. 16–18.

Roblyer, M. D., W. H. Castine, F. J. King. "Assessing the Impact of Computer-Based Education: A Review of Research." *Computers in the Schools,* vol. 5, no. 2, Fall 1988.

Rockman, Saul. "The Answers Are Only as Good as the Questions." *Apple Education News,* Fall 1988, p. 10.

Rosegrant, Teresa. "Using the Microcomputer as a Tool for Learning to Read and Write." *Journal of Learning Disabilities,* vol. 18, no. 2, 1985, pp. 113–15.

Rust, Kathy. "Word Processing: The Missing Key for Writing." *The Reading Teacher,* February 1986, pp. 611–12.

Schug, Mark C. "What Do Social Studies Teachers Say about Using Computers?" *Social Studies,* May/June 1988, pp. 112–15.

Souviney, Randall, Barbara Miller-Souviney. "Integrating Computers and the Writing Process." Report #11. Interactive Technology Laboratory, University of California, San Diego, March 1986.

Strickland, James. "Computers, Invention, and the Power to Change Student Writing." *Computers and Composition,* vol. 4, no. 2, 1987, pp. 7–26.

Thode, Terry. "Technology Education in the Elementary School." *The Technology Teacher,* September/October 1988, pp. 12–15.

White, Charles E. "Interactive Multimedia for Social Studies: A Review of *In the Holy Land* and *The '88 Vote.*" In *Social Education,* February 1990, pp. 68–70.

White, Charles S. "Teachers Using Technology." *Social Education,* January 1987, pp. 44–47.

The History of Computers in Schools

A people without history is like wind on the buffalo grass.

Sioux proverb

If I have seen further than other men, it is because I have stood on the shoulders of giants.

Sir Isaac Newton (1643–1727)

All the child is ever to be and become lies in the child, and can be attained only through development from within outward. The purpose of teaching and instruction is to bring ever more out of a man rather than to put more and more into man.

Friedrich W. Froebel (1782–1852)

History provides perspective. The mystery surrounding a familiar technology is diminished when one learns that it took hundreds, if not thousands, of years to reach its current state of the art. It is beyond the scope of this book to traverse in more than a superficial way the thousands of years that led to the development of the modern computer. In this chapter you will have the opportunity to learn more about the two-decade history of the desktop computer, since this is the machine that you are most likely to use in your teaching career, both inside and outside the classroom.

We will look especially at the families of Apple computers (Apple II™ and Apple Macintosh™) and at the IBM PC™ and PS/2™ and compatible machines. These are the systems that predominate in K–12 schools in the United States. The Commodore Amiga™ is another machine that we should profile since you may have the opportunity to use it as well.

After reading this chapter, you will be more knowledgeable about the following aspects of the history of computers in schools:

- Early uses of computers in school
    - Sowing the seed
- The microcomputer in schools
    - The Apple II family of personal computers
    - The IBM PC family of personal computers
    - The Commodore family of personal computers
    - The compatible computers on the IBM PC's bandwagon
    - Apple's counterpunch—the Macintosh family
    - The Apple IIGS
    - The Apple Macintosh LC
- Educational computing in the 1990s and beyond
    - Future horizons in personal computing

▟ 2.1 Early Uses of Computers in Schools

Table 2.1 represents a time line detailing the broad history of computing from the earliest years of recorded human existence until 1971, when Intel Corporation invented the first microprocessor.[1] Nicknamed "the computer on a chip," this invention resulted directly in the invention of the microcomputer, which led eventually to today's proliferation of computers in K–12 schools. The photo on page 39 is of Steve Wozniak (left) and Steve Jobs (right) holding the logic board of their first Apple computers. These microcomputer pioneers were from the outset conscious of the potential for computer use in education.

2.1.1 Sowing the Seed

The idea of using computers in education took shape long before the advent of microcomputers in the latter half of the 1970s. In fact, before the modern electronic digital

---

[1]Blissmer (1993) is a source for some of the data for this time line.

Table 2.1	**A History of Computers Time Line**

Pre-mechanical computing, earliest times–4000 BCE (Before Common Era)

Counting on fingers
Making hash marks on cave walls and animal bones

Mechanical computing, 4000 BCE–1880s CE (Common Era)

4000 BCE	**The Abacus** (probably invented by people living in the Middle East)
1617 CE	**Napier's Bones**(logarithmic tables invented by *John Napier*)
1621	**The Slide Rule** (invented by *William Oughtred*)
1642	**The Pascaline** (a mechanical counting device invented by *Blaise Pascal*)
1673	**The Stepped Reckoner** (a more advanced counting device invented by *Wilhelm Gottfried von Liebnitz*)
1802	**The Jacquard Loom** (built by *Joseph Marie Jacquard* and considered the prototype for later computing devices that were controlled by punched cards)
1812	**The Difference Engine** (sophisticated, mechanical computing device invented by *Charles Babbage* while he was an undergrad. This machine earned Babbage the title "*Father of Computers.*" His friend *Lady Ada, Countess of Lovelace,* wrote programs to control Babbage's machine, which earns her the title of "*First computer programmer.*"
1854	**Boolean Logic** (invented by *George Boole* and used in the design of modern computer circuitry and for control instructions in computer programs)

Electro-mechanical era, 1890–1944

1890	**The Census Counting Machine** (invented by *Herman Hollerith*)
1936	**The Turing Machine** (a theoretical logic machine which *Alan Turing* used to prove the "universal" problem-solving potential of the modern electronic computer)
1944	**The Harvard Mark I** (a massive electro-mechanical computer built by *Howard Aiken* with funding from IBM)

Electronic era (1939–   )

1939	**The Atanasoff-Berry Computer** (the ABC—the first electronic digital computer, invented by *John Vincent Atanasoff* and *Clifford Berry* at Iowa State University)
1946	**The Electronic Numerical Integrator and Computer** (the ENIAC—the first fully operational electronic digital computer built by *J. Presper Eckert* and *John Mauchly*)
1951	**The Univac I** (the first commercially available electronic computer—also built by *Eckert and Mauchly*)
1959	**The Transac 2000** (the first transistorized computer developed by a team led by *Saul Rosen* at Philco Corporation)
1964	**IBM System/360** (one of the first computers to use integrated circuits)
1971	**The microprocessor** (the "Computer on a chip" invented at *Intel Corporation,* still the #1 supplier of microprocessors to the computer industry)
1976	**Apple Computer, Inc.** (founded by *Steve Wozniak* and *Steve Jobs*)
1981	**The IBM PC** (first IBM desktop computer)

Figure 2.1
A microprocessor
Photo courtesy Intel
Corporation

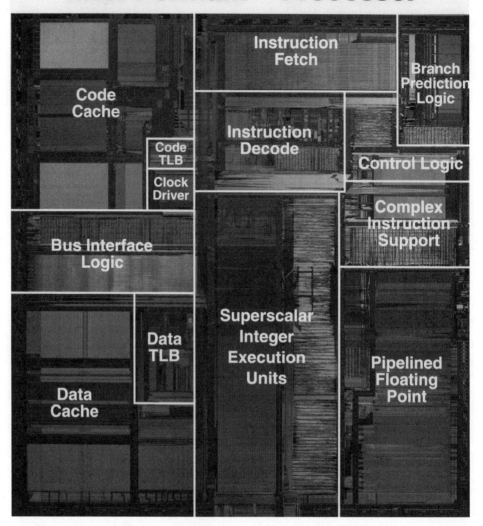

Intel Pentium™ Processor

computer was even invented, it had been shown conclusively (Turing, 1937) that such a machine could be built and that, in theory at least, it could be programmed to handle almost any problem demanded of it. The original "necessity" that became the "mother of the invention" in 1939 was the determination of one Dr. John Vincent Atanasoff (pronounced with the stress on the third syllable—Ata-NA-soff) to build a machine which would take the drudgery out of the routine calculations involved in graduate-level physics research at Iowa State University. Clifford Berry, who was a graduate student studying under Dr. Atanasoff in the Department of Physics at Iowa State University, helped Atanasoff realize in practical electronic form the theoretical machine described by Alan Turing nearly three years before.

Figure 2.2
John Vincent
Atanasoff (*left*),
inventor of the
electronic digital
computer
Photo courtesy Iowa State
University, Office of
University Relations

Figure 2.3
Clifford Berry (*right*)
Photo courtesy Iowa State
University, Office of
University Relations

The computing machine that they built was called the **Atanasoff-Berry Computer (the ABC).** We need not concern ourselves here with the process whereby Atanasoff achieved the conceptual breakthrough that led to the ABC's design, nor with the details of its construction. Atanasoff wrote up the full specifications for the machine and, in accord with academic custom, asked his university to take care of securing the patent with the U.S. Patent Office. Unfortunately, the patent was never filed on Atanasoff's behalf.

The ABC was nonetheless the prototype for every electronic digital computer that followed, including, by the way, another famous early computer called the **ENIAC (Electronic Numerical Integrator and Calculator).** The ENIAC was commissioned by the U.S. Department of Defense and completed in 1946. Its builders, John Mauchly and J. Presper Eckert, had had the opportunity to see the ABC and had discussed its design with Atanasoff as early as 1941. Indeed, Atanasoff had loaned his written specifications to Mauchly when Mauchly visited him in Ames, Iowa, in 1941. Yet for some inexplicable reason, Mauchly and Eckert applied for, and were granted, the patent for the electronic digital computer without due acknowledgement of Atanasoff's contribution.

Fortunately, in 1972 this injustice was rectified when, after a protracted six-year legal battle between two giants of the computer industry—Honeywell representing Atanasoff, and Sperry Rand representing Mauchly and Eckert—Atanasoff was judged to be the inventor of the electronic digital computer (Mollenhoff, 1988).

By the 1950s, researchers were very much aware of the computer's potential as an artificially intelligent machine with applications at all levels of education. In the late 1950s and early 1960s, Dr. Seymour Papert, now head of the Learning and Epistemology research group at the Massachusetts Institute of Technology, studied in Geneva, Switzerland, with the renowned educationist Jean Piaget. Papert went on to lead the

Figure 2.4
Atanasoff-Berry
Computer (the ABC)
Photo courtesy Iowa State
University, Office of
University Relations

development of the Logo programming language, a powerful computer-based, problem-solving environment for students of all ages from kindergarten on up. The subject of Logo programming in the context of Computer-Assisted Instruction (CAI) will be discussed in chapter 10.

In the 1960s and 1970s, high school teachers of mathematics were taking advantage of local corporate-computing facilities to give their students the opportunity to learn computer-programming skills. There was no doubt that computer technology would have a place in education at all levels once it became affordable and easy to use. The miniaturization enabled by the microprocessor was the key to the computer's affordability and to its introduction in schools K–12.

The microcomputer industry in America is governed largely by two companies, each of which has its own distinctive family of microcomputer systems. The giant in the industry is, of course, International Business Machines Corporation (IBM) with its PC and PS/2 desktop computer systems. But the company that controlled the lion's share of the PC market before IBM's debut in 1981 was, in fact, Apple Computer, Inc. with its long-standing flagship product, the Apple II.

2.2 The Microcomputer in Schools

2.2.1 The Apple II Family of Personal Computers

Apple Computer, Inc. was founded by two college undergraduates, Steve Jobs and Steve Wozniak. In 1976 Wozniak built the first Apple microcomputer designed around a microprocessor developed by Motorola Corporation. The machine greatly impressed his engineering friends. Jobs and Wozniak recognized that they had a potential moneymaker

Figure 2.5
The Apple IIe
computer system
Photo courtesy Apple
Computer, Inc.

on their hands and, as Shurkin (1985) recounts, Jobs sold his Volkswagen bus and Wozniak sold his two HP calculators to raise some cash. On the strength of an order for 50 Apples, they set up their business in Jobs's garage in Cupertino, California.

In 1977 a second generation of Apples was born and within a year or two the Apple II was carving a comfortable niche for itself in homes, computer hobbyists' workshops, and at all levels in educational environments. Then, in 1978, Daniel Bricklin and Robert Franston, students in the Graduate School of Business at Harvard University, wrote a program that gave every business in the United States a reason to buy the Apple II+, especially the smaller businesses that had been wondering how they could afford to buy into the advantages that computing could bring. This program, called *VisiCalc,* was the first electronic spreadsheet.

VisiCalc revolutionized accounting practices by providing a tool that was designed specifically to handle numeric data, as such it took much of the drudgery out of financial record-keeping. *VisiCalc* was written for the Apple II family of computers, and with its advent into the marketplace, Apple Computer, Inc. experienced a demand for its machine that skyrocketed the company into superstar status. The Apple II+ was quickly followed by the Apple IIe, the Apple III, and the Apple IIc. Apple struggled to keep up with the demand.

As funding allowed, many schools made piecemeal purchases of Apple IIs during the 1980s. For this reason, if there is an Apple laboratory in your school, you should not be surprised to find that it consists of a mixed bag of computers, which are more or less compatible, but not identically set up. Some may have more speed and more features than others.

Apple Computer, Inc. has, to date at least, dominated the educational computing market largely because the company focused on that market from the outset. Steve Wozniak in particular was conscious of the potential value of the computer in the classroom. Apple also made many grants of computer equipment to schools in order to

Figure 2.6
The IBM PC
Photo courtesy IBM
Corporation

encourage them to get started. Above all, Apple had a three-year head start on IBM in the K–12 educational arena. The Apple II was introduced in 1978; the IBM PC was not made available until 1981. In the meantime several companies, notably Atari, Commodore, and Radio Shack, joined Apple as pioneers in educational computing.

2.2.2 The IBM PC Family of Personal Computers

Apple's dominance of the personal computer market was short-lived. Within months of the introduction of the IBM PC in 1981, Apple Computer, Inc. suffered a serious loss of market share. Within 18 months IBM had vaulted to the top of the microcomputer market. This was largely because of IBM's superior business credibility. At that time Apple Computer, Inc. had been around for just five years and was directed by two entrepreneurs, Jobs and Wozniak, who were barely into their twenties. On the other hand, IBM, since its founding in 1924, had established an enviable and, for the time being at least, unbeatable reputation as a company that could be relied on to be in the microcomputer race long after many smaller, less prestigious computer manufacturers had come and gone.

The business world in particular preferred to invest data-processing dollars in IBM. Thus, only one year after entering the microcomputer market, IBM had garnered well over 50% of the sales of personal computers to corporate America. The original PC was soon followed by the PC Jr (otherwise known as the "Peanut"), the PC XT (Extra Technology), the PC AT (Advanced Technology), and the PC RT (Reduced Instruction Set Technology). Another computer family was born.

All the IBM and IBM-compatible desktop computers were, and still are, built around microprocessors supplied by Intel Corporation. Unfortunately, the software created for the Apple II (with microprocessors supplied, you may recall, by Motorola Corporation) could not run on the IBM PC and vice versa, with the result that there has been a wasteful scramble to produce more-or-less duplicate software for both families of computers.

a

b

Figure 2.7
Commodore
Business Machines'
(*a*) Amiga 4000 and
the (*b*) Amiga
CD32™ CD-ROM
drive
Photos courtesy
Commodore Business
Machines

2.2.3 Focus on the Commodore Amiga

Commodore Business Machines, headquartered in West Chester, Pennsylvania, was one of the first personal computer manufacturers. The Pet, Commodore's first commercial machine, is still used in a few schools, as is the Commodore 64. Both machines enjoyed initial success by virtue of the fact that they were considerably more advanced than the competition at a price that made them much better value for money. Because of this it is probably not an exaggeration to say that Commodore has helped establish computer use in schools as much as any other company.

Figure 2.8
Radio Shack TRS-80
Photo courtesy Radio
Shack

Today the Commodore flagship product is the Amiga 4000, a superb machine with outstanding graphics and multimedia capabilities. The Amiga 4000 is also capable of running software developed for the Apple Macintosh as well as IBM and compatible computers. Commodore machines have established less of a foothold in the U.S. educational market even though the Commodore Amiga has always had a significant technological edge on any comparably priced machines developed by Apple or IBM. The company has, in fact, survived thus far because of its popularity in Europe.

2.2.4 The Compatible Computers on the IBM PC Bandwagon

In a pluralistic world there is room for a wide variety of players. Other companies did not stand idly by while Apple, IBM, and Commodore slugged it out in the early 1980s. NCR, DEC, Wang, Radio Shack, Osborne, and Compaq, to name but a few of the dozens of microcomputer manufacturers that have come and gone since the invention of the microprocessor in 1971, have all at one time or another enjoyed their moment in the sun. Each came out with state-of-the-art machines that caught the buying public's eye because they were, on the grounds of price and performance, highly competitive, especially with both IBM and Apple.

Some school systems, especially at the high school level, have decided to rely on IBM PC or compatible systems for all their educational computing needs. Many others have set up separate laboratories of both IBM and Apple computers, the former to provide a learning environment for older students whose needs are primarily vocational (business courses, for example), and the latter for students K–12 with more general educational needs.

IBM has tried, thus far unsuccessfully, to dislodge Apple as the leading supplier of computers to schools. In the early 1980s, the IBM PC Jr (the "Peanut") was targeted at the home and educational markets, but it was poorly designed and was dropped within a

Figure 2.9
The IBM PS/2 Model
25
Photo courtesy IBM
Corporation

year of introduction. The many thousands of Peanuts that had already been built were packaged along with innovative software developed by Dr. John Henry Martin (the *Writing To Read* program discussed in chapter 1 and later in chapter 10) and sold for use in kindergarten, first-, and second-grade classes.

More recently, in 1988, IBM introduced the PS/2 along with a new operating system, OS/2™, which has a graphics-based interface much like the Apple Macintosh. In 1992 IBM set up a separate company called EduQuest™, which has been "dedicated to helping to improve K–12 education through the use of technology" (EduQuest, 1993).

2.2.5 Focus on the Apple Macintosh

Meanwhile, in 1983 Apple Computer, Inc. introduced a revolutionary new computer system targeted for the business market. Its name was Lisa™, and its distinguishing feature was a user interface that was particularly easy to learn and use—its Graphical User Interface (GUI). Most users do not want to have to learn a difficult series of commands in order to use a computer. They want to be able to complete their work without having to spend more time than necessary figuring out how to use the machine.

Apple's Lisa, the immediate precursor to the Macintosh, was an "easy" system to use because just about everything you needed to know about the system was displayed on the screen.[2] The computer was designed using what is often called a desktop metaphor—the

---

[2] Much to Apple's surprise, however, ease of use did not immediately prove to be a highly marketable quality in a computer product. In fact, a senior majoring in computer science at a university that shall go unnamed was overheard saying, shortly after the Lisa's release, that he did not like the machine because "it's *too* easy to use!"

Figure 2.10
The Apple Macintosh
Plus computer
system

interaction with the system simulated the environment of an office.[3] The Lisa also came with a handheld input device called a mouse to control much of the user's interaction with the system. Finally, the Lisa was the first true WYSIWYG personal computer: **W**hat **Y**ou **S**ee **I**s **W**hat **Y**ou **G**et. In other words, the way the data appear on the screen is the way they will look on the printed page.

As it happened, Apple's Lisa failed to make an impact in the business world largely because, at $10,000, it was at that time considered too expensive for most companies to risk buying on the off chance that it would be as good as it looked. The corporate world still did not trust Apple; however, less than a year after the release of the Lisa, Apple introduced another system called the Macintosh, popularly known as the Mac. The Mac was to all intents and purposes the same as the Lisa at less than half the price.

The Mac, which was not compatible with the Apple II and therefore not immediately popular in schools, might not have survived the competition from the IBM PC had it not been for a stroke of marketing genius and a little luck. Apple produced a reasonably priced laser printer for the Mac. Another company, Aldus Corporation, came out with a powerful software package called *PageMaker*™, which put professional page-layout tools into the hands of Mac users. The combination of a sophisticated page-layout program, a **WYSIWYG** display on the screen, and a laser printer added up to desktop publishing which, like *VisiCalc* for the Apple II, gave corporations a bottom-line reason to invest in the Mac technology.

---

[3]We will return to the philosophy behind the design of the *Lisa's* operating system in chapter 7.

Figure 2.11
The Apple IIGS
computer system
Photo courtesy Apple
Computer, Inc.

The Mac has thus made a considerable impact in the personal computer marketplace and has restored Apple's credibility and market share in the corporate computing world. It is also well on the way to supplanting the Apple II in schools. The Apple II will survive for some time, however, because there are several million of these machines in schools— quite an investment. Moreover, as already noted, a large proportion of the software written for educational purposes has been designed for this family of machines. It is the software that sells the hardware, after all. So the Apple IIs already in use in schools will not be relegated to the scrap heap yet. Do not be surprised if you find yourself designing classes around this technology even into the next century.

The Mac, however, will be the Apple computer of choice for the time being. As we shall see, it is a far superior machine to the Apple II and in its Mac LC™ version it has the added advantage that it can behave as if it were an Apple II, thus allowing it to run all that educational courseware.

2.2.6 The Apple IIGS

The Apple IIGS was introduced in 1986 as a replacement for the Apple IIe. It turned out to be the last of the Apple II line. Fully compatible with the Apple IIe, it is able to run almost all of the thousands of pieces of educational software developed for that machine. Moreover, its user interface is much like that of the Mac, and the newer educational programs (often now called courseware) use the mouse and pull down menus which have always characterized interaction with the Mac.[4]

---

[4]Although we may never know for sure, it is possible that the Apple IIGS was part of a strategic plan drawn up by Apple Computer, Inc. to wean schools away from the Apple II line. After the introduction of the Macintosh, a far superior machine, Apple was frustrated that it had to continue manufacturing the Apple II because of demand from schools. The Apple IIGS was close enough to a Macintosh for schools to look on the two systems in the same light. But it was still not until Apple introduced the Macintosh LC, with its Apple II compatibility, that schools made the transition. Finally, Apple Computer, Inc. was able to put the Apple II assembly lines to rest.

Figure 2.12
Teacher working on
the Apple Macintosh
LC computer system
Photo courtesy Susan
Giorgio Bond

2.2.7 The Apple Macintosh LC

Apple made the Mac a viable alternative to the Apple II in schools when the company introduced the Macintosh LC in 1991. Since 1991 the LC family has expanded to include a multimedia PC (MPC) called the Macintosh LC 520 which has a built-in CD-ROM drive. Other companies such as Tandy and IBM's EduQuest are also delivering MPC systems to serve a market which is coming to expect easy access to high quality video, still images, and sound along with text.

There are several reasons why a school or school district would today decide to migrate to the Mac from the Apple II as the hardware platform for their educational computing needs.

- The Macintosh family of computers is now well established and is likely to be supported by Apple for some time to come.
- The Mac LC is targeted for use in schools. LC stands for *low cost,* indicating Apple's long-standing commitment to helping financially strapped schools take advantage of the computer as a tool for teaching and learning. The Mac LC has an optional, high-resolution color monitor and enough power and extendibility to accommodate just about any current educational need whether as a networked or standalone machine.
- More and more educational software is being developed specifically for the Mac to add to the existing base of Mac and Apple II software.
- Software designed specifically for the Mac can take advantage of the Mac's superior graphics capabilities and speed as compared to the Apple II. This increases the potential for high quality educational systems supporting inquiry-based learning.

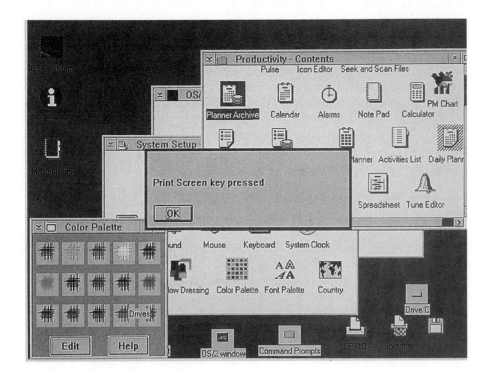

Figure 2.13
IBM's *OS/2* graphical
user interface
Photo courtesy IBM
Corporation

These systems will be increasingly capable of realistically simulating reality and of providing rapid access to selected volumes of data (text, images, and sound) in local or remote databases.

■ The way the user interacts with the Mac computer, called the user interface, is standardized across applications. This means that the user will learn new software relatively easily once interaction with the basic machine has been mastered. The pull-down menus, icons, desktop, windows, mouse, buttons, and so forth behave the same way no matter which Mac-designed software you are using. Fortunately this is now becoming the case for most other computer systems.

Graphical user interfaces (GUIs) will be discussed in more detail in chapter 7, but for now suffice to say that systems that use a GUI, such as Apple's Macintosh operating system or Microsoft's *Windows/Windows NT* or IBM's *OS/2,* are simpler to learn and use.

■ 2.3 Educational Computing in the 1990s and Beyond

The price of computing continues to fall even as the power and usefulness of computing machines continues to rise. There is not a school district in the United States that is not looking at its budget in terms of allocating some proportion to either initiating or more likely expanding its educational computing inventory.

In 1983, $10,000 bought a desktop computer, the Apple Lisa, which had one megabyte of internal storage (a megabyte is 1 million bytes or characters, equivalent to about 500 pages of text); a 10-megabyte, hard disk drive for secondary storage; and a processing speed in the hundreds of thousands of instructions per second. Today, one quarter of that amount of money will buy a "work station" that will have up to 32 megabytes of internal storage, well over 100 megabytes of hard disk secondary storage, and processing speeds in the range of 14 to 17 million instructions per second (abbreviated to MIPS). These measures of memory and speed will be discussed in chapter 6.

Since the introduction of the powerful PS/2 line of computers in 1988, IBM continues to make a strong bid for the educational computing market. In 1990 the company introduced the PS/1, a scaled-down version of the PS/2 priced to capture the home market in particular. In 1993 EduQuest, the company formed to represent IBM in schools, introduced a series of MPC machines which have built-in networking capability along with CD-ROM drives.

Although there is a growing library of educational software for the IBM and compatible systems, it does not yet compare with the variety and quality of that available for the Apple machines. It is likely that Apple will continue to enjoy the lion's share of the educational hardware market into the foreseeable future. Many new companies, however, are responding to the increasing demand for more and more sophisticated and pedagogically sound, educational software applications.

Many states have established programs to support the integration of computer technology into the K–12 curriculum. In Pennsylvania, for example, the Information Technology Education for the Commonwealth (ITEC) program has, since 1984, had centers statewide called Regional Computer Resource Centers (RCRCs), which provide graduate, credit-bearing introductory, and advanced courses for in-service teachers on the subject of incorporating the computer into the curriculum. The RCRCs have extensive libraries of educational software as well as state of the art computing laboratories. These centers are also used by undergraduates majoring in education at the institutions where the Centers have been established.

More and more colleges are making the financial and philosophical commitment to helping pre-service and in-service teachers prepare for a classroom in which computing technology will be a tool integrated into the teaching and learning process.

2.3.1 Future Horizons in Personal Computing

When, if ever, will the rapid rate of growth in the personal computer arena end? No time soon. It is reasonably safe to say that by the year 2000, one can expect to have on one's desktop a computer the size of the IBM PC or the Apple Macintosh which will have the power and performance of a present-day supercomputer. The machine will be able to process billions of instructions per second. Internal memory will be measured in the hundreds of megabytes (millions of bytes), and secondary memory will be described in gigabytes (billions of bytes). These machines will probably still cost less than $2,000, even though $2,000, by then, will be worth considerably less than it is today.

The big question is whether the software can keep up with the advances in hardware capabilities. One thing is for sure: The creators of educational software systems will not be limited in their ingenuity by the performance of the machines; rather, they will be limited by the inherently complex nature of the programming involved.

Today the distinction between the machines developed by different companies is beginning to blur. Not only has Apple's Mac computer made huge inroads into the business environment, but IBM and Apple have also set up a joint company—Taligent—that is developing a new operating system for Apple and IBM machines (code named "Pink") to

a

Figure 2.14
(*a*) IBM multimedia
PC; (*b*) Apple's
Macintosh LC520
multimedia PC.
(*a*) Photo courtesy IBM
Corporation; (*b*) Photo
courtesy Apple Computer,
Inc.

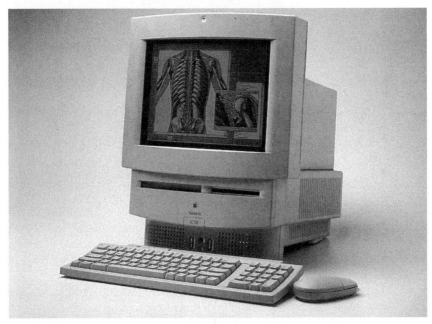

b

A day in the life of a computer coordinator
Denise Ryan, Tanque Verde Unified School District, Tucson, Arizona

Denise Ryan is a teacher in the Tanque Verde School District in Tucson, Arizona. Her work involves her in three different, yet related, areas of responsibility. She teaches mathematics at various levels; she teaches computer electives at the junior high; and she is the computer coordinator for the three schools that make up the Tanque Verde School District. The purpose of this profile is to show how Denise uses computers in each setting.

Computers in the Math Class
By trade Denise is a teacher of mathematics, and still has three classes of various levels of math every day. The computer is used in these classes as one of several tools to present a topic. Basically it serves as a manipulative, along with other more traditional techniques, for translating mathematical theory into some practical, tangible form. Some days it might mean a trip to the computer lab to work on drill and practice programs. On other days students practice problem-solving strategies while competing against the computer, or each other, in math simulations.

The Computer as a Tool for Writing across the Curriculum
A math class may not immediately strike one as an obvious forum for developing writing skills; however, as a firm believer in the importance of communication skills in an age of information, Denise is incorporating more

writing into her mathematics classes. All of her students have been taught *AppleWorks* word processing, which comes in handy for writing assignments.

For example, she will give her students an assignment to write stories about the number "23." Some of these stories invariably turn out to be extremely creative! When the class hits the geometry section of the **(continued)**

Denise Ryan, author of the case study

make them compatible with each other. Time alone will tell where this development will lead in terms of computer use in schools. At least it promises a future where software development companies may no longer need to expend enormously expensive effort creating duplicate systems for incompatible hardware platforms.

So, by the year 2000 it is reasonably safe to say that computer manufacturers will have standardized hardware and system software design to the point where the current mishmash of incompatible machines will have become an anachronism, a bad dream best forgotten. Computer systems will be universally easy to use compared to what must be put up with in many computing environments today. They will be powerful, inescapable, and woven intricately into the fabric of our lives.

Multimedia technology, such as computer-based interactive videodisc, capable of storing all kinds of data, from text and still images to stereo-quality sound and high-definition video, will cause school districts to reaffirm, and teachers to rediscover, their commitment to audiovisual aids in the learning process. As such it will take its place as a powerful new tool in the pedagogical process.

Case Study 2 (continued)

curriculum, the students work in cooperative learning groups to write a play, for which a typical theme might be a love story between a point and a line. The day after a test, the class visits the computer lab and the students write a few paragraphs, telling Denise how well they think they performed on the test, which problems they felt were exceptionally difficult, and where they think they need more work. They often have to write a short piece explaining how to perform a certain skill without using numbers. For example, the students must compose a letter to a lower-grade-level classmate detailing the process used for borrowing when subtracting fractions.

The computer is also a valuable tool in higher-level mathematics classes. Here Denise uses an LCD projection panel in tandem with the overhead projector to display the graphical results of plotting linear and quadratic equations onto the overhead screen. Having the computer do the tedious graphing allows her to lead discussions on how changing certain coefficients can affect the graph.

After ten years experience using the computer in the classroom, Denise has found that it has not lost its novelty in math classes. Sometimes just doing word problems on a spreadsheet can provide that extra motivation to get some students through the chapters. Remember those problems in which you had to figure out when Train A (going 150 mph) would meet Train B (going 125 mph)? Using a spreadsheet, the students can insert different estimates to determine a reasonable answer to the problem and then check their work through an algebraic equation. Math is used to set up the spreadsheet and again to verify the findings.

A Tool for Teaching Computer Electives

Denise Ryan's second job is to teach two computer electives at the junior high. One of the classes is applications oriented, focusing primarily on all aspects of *AppleWorks*. The children learn to use the word **(continued)**

The computer basically serves as another manipulative

processor, database, and spreadsheet with the objective of helping them become comfortable using the technology for productivity purposes.

These students are taught the basics of the various components of *AppleWorks,* then they practice their skills in a variety of assignments. Some of the tasks assigned to them have been to design a database of students at Emily Gray Junior High, enter the survey information, and then compare the results to those obtained when they interviewed students via modem from another junior high across town.

Telecommunications is thus used to exchange information with various junior high and middle schools in the valley. The students experience "logging on" and various "telecomputing prompts." In a world where the global village is becoming more and more a reality, telecommunications is a tool for preparing these students for the future.

Junior-high students use their word-processing skills to write stories for kindergarten students.

Denise's junior high students use their word-processing skills to write stories for kindergarten students. These stories are based on drawings the five-year-olds have created in art class. The culmination of this project is a trip to the elementary school to read the literary masterpieces to the original artists.

A final project is to simulate the management of a store in a mall. Students use all aspects of *AppleWorks* to hire employees, do payroll, set up mailing lists for sales, and write letters to the Internal Revenue Service. Graphing programs such as *Print Shop* and *GraphWorks* are used to print sales flyers and chart employee salaries. This, of course, is not an original idea, but the students really get into this project; the results are fun and allow the children to express and develop their creativity.

In the first of her two computer electives classes, Denise also touches on artificial intelligence, software evaluation, and telecommunications. While students study various programs that are purported to promote artificial intelligence (such as *Dr. Know, AI, Eliza, Animals,* etc.), they constantly revise their own personal definition of this topic.

These junior high students learn to evaluate software with the goal of making them intelligent consumers. They are given packages to preview without any directions. With each package they are to write a software review, following the guidelines they use for book reports in their language arts classes. They also keep a list of priorities they would look for in purchasing a specific piece of software—priorities such as price, machine compatibility, age level, and so forth.

Computer Graphics a Lure to Computer Programming

Denise also teaches a BASIC programming class. Here the computer itself is the object of instruction as students learn to take control of the machine. The content is very structured, introducing the students step by step to the **(continued)** skills involved in programming a computer. She explains: "I try to include a graphics exercise with each new BASIC programming language statement learned. Middle and junior high school students like to display their programming expertise, and graphics is a great model to accomplish this end." Denise notes that this is because graphics programming gives children the chance to use their creativity in the design of an object along with the design of a program. The display of their work is a way of publishing their accomplishments. A bulletin board of graphic designs holds much more student interest than a list of BASIC code.

At the beginning of the year the graphic might incorporate details of their summer vacation. During the second semester, returning to the theme of Writing Across the Curriculum, the students are asked to portray some facet of a book that they have read—a character, a scene, or a theme—for the annual "Love of Reading Week."

School District Computer Coordinator

Denise's last job is that of computer coordinator for the three schools in the Tanque Verde School District. "The computer," she says, "is my means for keeping everyone happy, for keeping on top of current technological issues, and for my peace of mind. I am on this machine every night to complete a wide range of tasks. It is my tool for software and hardware inventory; it is my method of communication via memo or newsletter; it is my artist's drawing board for creating announcements and cards for special events; and it is my calculator to make sure I am never over budget."

The Computer as Administrative Assistant

"The computer assists me in all aspects of my job. All my lesson plans, class objectives, and even a database for seating charts are on my computer. I do not have to reinvent the wheel' every year or semester. I can easily adapt my class requirements to the group of students I am currently teaching and make my classes the best they can be for that particular environment.

"For all these reasons," Denise goes on to say, "I am a great believer in making backups. Losing this information would be like losing my monthly calendar. My colleagues would then know how disorganized I can really be!" It sounds as if Denise, along with the rest of us, has at some time or another been afflicted with Murphy's machinations.

Denise has received many compliments from parents on how much easier her assignment sheets and handouts are to read because they are done on a computer, rather than by hand. She can keep her students informed of their current grades weekly because of a computerized grade book. Parent contact is much more accurate and usually much more positive. She believes every teacher should have easy access to a word processing package and grading program for their personal use. This would reduce the amount of time spent on the paperwork that is required of teachers, and allow them more time to spend with the students.

Talk About It

Topics for discussion based on the Case Study.

1. What are the advantages/disadvantages of having a district technology coordinator versus a computer "coach" at each school site?

2. What are the benefits of having a district curriculum for computer education as opposed to individual teachers developing their own technology integration? What are the disadvantages?

3. What technology skills do you think are mandatory for securing any teaching position?

4. How will technology change what or how current curricula are taught?

5. What aspect of math (or any other specific subject area) would be better taught using technology? How? Why?

6. Is technology for everyone?

7. Cite examples of how technology can benefit teachers.

■ Looking Back

Many people believe the computer to be a modern invention with no link to the pre-electronic past. But much credit is due the individuals and groups responsible for advancing the state of the art of computing in schools. Teachers, in particular, have made important contributions to the use of computers in educational settings.

It is a fascinating story, well worth more in-depth study. Several good sources are available on the broader history of computers, the most readable of which is Shurkin (1985). A blow-by-blow account of the legal battle that established John Vincent Atanasoff as the inventor of the electronic digital computer is excellently described in Mollenhoff (1988).

The goal of education is to stimulate children to learn by making the process enjoyable. As Montessori observed, and as any teacher knows, children work hard and single-mindedly when they are interested in what they are doing. History, which is storytelling after all, is a great source of interesting lesson material. It also gives context to knowledge, making it more understandable, more meaningful, and therefore more memorable. For this reason teachers should deepen their knowledge of the origins of the subject matter that they teach—whether it be math, English, or history itself.

■ Looking Forward

So much for the history of the computer in schools, which is still in its infancy. It is now time to turn our attention to the impact this machine has had, is having, and will have on society in general, and on education in particular. To do this we will shift our focus from the computer as an entity in itself to the computer as a factor in social change.

Chapter 3 will examine a selection of social impacts of advances in computing science. How has the computer enabled the extension of our capabilities both as individuals and as social groups? How has the computer enabled us to effect significant change in our social institutions, including education? The accelerated pace of this change (Toffler, 1971) means that we cannot afford to wait on the sidelines. Nonparticipation will do a disservice not only to ourselves, but more important, to the children with whose future we are entrusted.

■ Do Something About It: Exercises and Projects

1. Take one unit's lesson plan per semester and incorporate some aspect of technology into it.

2. Compile an annotated bibliography on articles from a variety of computer journals for teachers,—for example, *The Computing Teacher, Teaching with Computers.*

3. Brainstorm writing exercises for each class/subject you teach. Use word processing to develop these ideas.

4. Have your students develop a class almanac based on questions they have developed. Use word processing and graphing software to express the survey results.

5. Begin a list of software to match a specific curriculum topic.

6. Prepare software reports, using a book report format, for three different software titles.

7. Use graphing or desktop publishing software to help the front office staff develop a project such as notices for the school carnival, annual book fair, basketball schedule, and so on.

8. Adopt a teacher. Become the "technology buddy" for another teacher—sharing computer problems, your expertise in specific terms, newfound software titles.

■ References

Blissmer, Robert H. *Introducing Computers, Concepts, Systems and Applications.* New York: John Wiley, 1993.

EduQuest. *EduQuest Committed to Full Circle of K–12 Education.* Press release, summer 1993.

Mollenhoff, Clark R. *Atanasoff: Forgotten Father of the Computer.* Ames: Iowa State United Press, 1988.

Shurkin, Joel. *Engines of the Mind.* New York: Washington Square Press, 1985.

Toffler, Alvin. *Future Shock.* New York: Bantam Books, 1971.

Turing, Alan Mathison. "On Computable Numbers, with an Application to the Entscheidungsproblem." Proceedings of the London Mathematical Society (2), 42, 1937.

Educational Computing and Society

The most fundamental element in education is change. This is implicit in its very definition. All learning requires change. Education as a "process" must 'proceed' or move ahead. Stagnation is therefore directly and fundamentally opposed to education. It is the basic evil for education.

Philip H. Phenix (1915–   )

It is useless to bemoan the departure of the good old days of children's modesty, reverence, and implicit obedience, if we expect merely by bemoaning and by exhortation to bring them back. It is radical conditions which have changed, and only an equally radical change in education suffices.

John Dewey (1859–1952)

61

Our examination of the sociological impact of computers begins with a broad sweep across the canvas of our world. We will consider the computer as a tool that supports research, enables discovery, stimulates invention, fosters environmental and organizational control, and facilitates communication between individuals and groups, which in turn fosters understanding, cooperation, and accord. Then the focus will narrow somewhat to concentrate on the increasingly central importance of computer-integrated education to the survival of the individual in a modern, computer-controlled, information-based society.

In this chapter, therefore, you will learn about the following aspects of the computer's impact on society in general and on education in particular:

- The social impact of advances in computer science
  - Extending the capacity of the mind
  - Extending the capability of the body
  - Extending the boundaries of the feasibly finite
  - The world of work
  - The global village
  - "High tech, high touch"
- The computer revolution
  - "Revolution" is a relative term
  - The revolution has not yet run its course
  - Information overload
- Education and the information society
  - Information and wealth
  - Computers, control, and systems of education

.ᴵ 3.1 The Social Impact of Advances in Computer Science

What an awesome responsibility teachers have! For good or ill, they touch the future of each and every young mind they encounter in our schools. Their task is much more than that of imparting a body of knowledge in a particular subject area, important as that task may be. The task, *in loco parentis*[1] and in cooperation with parents, is to prepare students to take advantage of as complete a spectrum of societal opportunity as is consonant with their motivation and ability.

Public education was prohibited or rigidly controlled by many regimes in the past because of its liberating impact on people. Today the battle for the right to education, and thus to freedom, has been won more or less worldwide. Educators are responsible for ensuring that the environment they provide gives students of all ages, but especially children K–12, the opportunity to lay the foundation on which to maximize their potential as free human beings.

---

[1]Latin for "in the place of the parents."

In order to appropriately shape educational environments, educators must consider the kind of world children will experience. The objective of this section is therefore to paint a picture of what living in an increasingly computerized society might mean so that educators can plan their teaching with a better perspective on the future.

This chapter argues that *revolution* is not too strong a term to describe the impact of the computer and looks briefly at some of the ways in which this machine has undeniably changed our world in general, and our schools in particular. We should begin with a caveat.

Not all computerization is for the better. Weizenbaum (1976) reminds us of the words of John Dewey, who wrote: "Every thinker puts some portion of an apparently stable world in peril and no one can predict what will emerge in its place." The invention of the computer has indeed changed the world, though not necessarily for the better. According to Weizenbaum, the very existence of a machine, the computer, that makes it possible to manage more data than ever before has resulted in our *collecting* more data than ever before. This possibility came along at a time when our bureaucracies were in danger of being overwhelmed by the fast-rising flood of facts. Today, like pack rats, we discard nothing. Memory is no longer defined by whatever facts one can remember; it is defined by whatever facts one can *find.*

While this is a boon to researchers, it also affects the way we solve problems. As Weizenbaum points out, "the computer did arrive 'just in time.' But in time for what? In time to save—and save very nearly intact, indeed to entrench and stabilize—social and political structures that otherwise might have been radically renovated or allowed to totter under the demands that were sure to be made on them." Weizenbaum is speaking about the United States, but what he says may apply equally well to nations everywhere: the computer "buttressed" and "immunized" social and political structures "against enormous pressures for change."

Weizenbaum goes on to question the use of the term *computer revolution,* arguing, as in the above quotation, that computers have done more to *prevent* change than bring it about. For the most part, however, increased control, as Beniger (1986) makes clear, is a key ingredient of advances in any field of endeavor. Artists and artisans from all walks of life—including teaching—have recognized the potential of the computer to extend people's capabilities in the realms of creativity and problem-solving. The computer thus seems destined to have a beneficial impact on our world, as this chapter shows.

3.1.1 Extending the Capability of the Mind

Is the computer like the human brain?

Alan Turing was an English philosopher and mathematician who published a paper in 1937 which anticipated the invention of the modern electronic-computing machine. Turing described a theoretical, logical machine (Turing, 1937), now known as the Turing machine, capable of processing any *computable* function. Kurt Gödel (1931) had already shown that there was a class of problems in mathematics that were simply unprovable. But what Turing established for the record was that, given time, we could build a machine that could come up with the solution to any computable problem we set our minds to! He called his theoretical machine "The **Universal Machine.**" In practice the "universality" of the machine will always be severely restricted by the essentially limited (finite) nature of the universe in general, and of the computing machines in particular. In other words, no matter how long intelligent life survives, we will never build a machine that will have unlimited (infinite) capabilities.

A mind-boggling corollary of Turing's thesis (more correctly referred to as the Church–Turing thesis) is that there is theoretically *infinite* potential for technological advance. In other words, no matter how awestruck we might be by the myriad inventions that have been developed to date, the human brain—augmented by increasingly powerful, computerized systems—has barely begun to realize its problem-solving potential.

Turing might be called the Father of Artificial Intelligence because of his early recognition of the electronic computer's extraordinary potential as a "thinking machine." He liked to compare the computer to the human brain. As Hodges (1982) notes, Turing had always been interested in physiology, and showed a thoroughly modern understanding of neurophysiology when, in 1930, he observed: "We have a will which is able to determine the actions of the atoms probably in a small portion of the brain. . . . The rest of the body acts so as to amplify this." The brain proposes, the body disposes. By analogy the computer, like the brain, processes data, which results in the emission of electronic signals that spread tentaclelike along electronic, nervelike pathways to control a potentially infinite series of other machines, other activities.

Much of the electronic computer's functionality is thus modeled after the human brain. It will therefore be useful to consider briefly some facets of our understanding of this awesome product of the evolutionary process.

The capabilities of the human brain

How the human brain works is still far from fully understood; however, one does not have to be a neurologist to recognize that one's brain, arguably the repository of "mind" (Churchland, 1986), has many diverse intellectual capabilities. It is a logical processor, which largely accounts for our ability to develop math-based skills; it is a language processor; it handles and controls motor activity; it is a memory bank; it is an image processor; it is a generator of new ideas, new insights, new ways of looking at things; it is a source of commonsense reasoning—not necessarily logical, more perhaps intuitive, as in "I have a hunch"; it is the seat of emotions of all kinds. In short, it is an extraordinarily complex machine which we have scarcely begun to understand.

The limitations of the human brain

Wonderful as the human brain is, it leaves much to be desired in certain respects. Let us examine two of these limitations with the goal of understanding how the computer can help us overcome them.

Memory   As Miller (1956) observed, our short-term memory is capable of keeping track of about seven items at any one time. Some of us are proverbially absentminded, and just about everyone forgets things. Most of us are less than meticulous when keeping calendars and records of appointments. Although the human brain is unquestionably unmatched in its ability to *make associations* between the data that it stores, encounters, or processes, it is easily surpassed by the computer when it comes to the simple process of storing and speedily accessing limitless volumes of data. The computer, especially when networked with other computers, is a natural extension of the memory capacity of the human brain, thus significantly enhancing our intellectual capabilities. So much for the human memory. What about our mathematical ability?

Mathematical ability   Most people recognize the value of being able to do math. But curiously enough, we are not born with an innate ability to add numbers together, or to carry out the various other mathematical functions. We have to learn how. Arithmetic is one of the key skills we teach in our schools. Very few people, in fact, are naturally gifted in math.

Yet math is recognized as a fundamental skill—one of the three R's—because it is one of the bases for our ability to control our lives. Fortunately, though it is important for us to understand how certain mathematical conclusions were arrived at so that we can use the results intelligently, we ourselves do not need to *do* the calculations that led to those conclusions. This is where the computer comes in handy. The unaided human brain cannot come close to matching the speed with which a $10 calculator, let alone a full-blown computer, can carry out computations.

The limitations of computers

Humans have certain intellectual skills that will be beyond the competence of the most powerful computers for at least the foreseeable future. Some philosophers, such as Dreyfus (1979), argue that certain human intellectual capabilities will *always* elude machine computation. Others, Churchland (1986) included, argue cogently that there is no logical reason why computers should not be able eventually to match the full capability of the human brain. Still others (Fjermedal, 1986), albeit on the far fringes of science, are convinced that within the next hundred years or so we will be able to "download" the mind–brain into a robot, thus presumably making at least our mental selves both immortal and endlessly clonable! Only time will tell which of these philosophical viewpoints will be borne out.

Some examples of the computer's mind-extending capability

Moving from the abstract to the concrete, let us now consider some actual implementations of computer technology, to get a flavor of the ways in which it has already extended the capability of our minds.

Computers as organizers   It is commonplace today to use computer systems to electronically store data of all kinds so that they are easily accessible for informational purposes. There is software to help one plan one's time: interactive calendars, memo pads, diaries, project planners, schedulers. There is software to help one organize one's thoughts: word processors, outliners, lesson planners. There also is software to help one capture, manipulate, and access the data one needs to make decisions: database management systems, spreadsheets, electronic grade books.

Nothing is particularly exciting here, unless you consider that because of computerized management systems, one person is able to control and accomplish so much more than ever before. More and more administrative environments, educational or otherwise (especially "otherwise" since schools are typically slow to follow in the footsteps of business organizations), are using this mind-enhancing software as a matter of course.

Computers as controllers   Modern automobiles have dozens of computer-controlled functions that save us from having to *think* about how the vehicle is behaving. Computers can tell us how many miles are left in the gas tank, based on the variables that affect a vehicle's mileage. Other computers control the brakes to ensure that, no matter how much we might panic in a crisis situation, those brakes will not lock and cause us to lose control of the vehicle.

Controlling energy consumption in the home is a significant intellectual activity requiring not only an understanding of the factors that increase or decrease cost, but also an almost neurotic attention to the detailed application of criteria for reducing energy consumption, such as turning off lights when they are not needed, maintaining optimal water temperature depending on time of day and usage, opening appropriate vents, or turning on fans instead of the air-conditioning unit when such action would be equally effective, but more economical (and environmentally responsible). Computerized climate control relieves us of this energy-saving burden.

Computers are being used in the classroom to coordinate access to data and the integration of audiovisual materials into the teaching and learning process. Multimedia systems, for example, can help teachers manage and control the learning experience.

"Smart" cars, "smart" homes, "smart" devices in general that go far beyond this level of sophistication are becoming more common and will eventually be the norm.

Expert systems   Expert systems are another interesting extension of the capabilities of the human mind. These systems are designed to model the thought processes of a human expert, storing in the computer all the accumulated knowledge of years of experience so that it can be tapped when required, by less-experienced individuals. According to Vitek (1990), close to 200 expert systems are "in various stages of research, development and use—in agriculture, chemistry, computers, electronics, engineering, geology, information management, law, manufacturing, mathematics, medicine, meteorology, physics, and space technology."

A good example is the expert system based on the knowledge of Al Cimino at Campbell's Soups. A few years ago Al was coming up for retirement. The company was aware that he knew more about how to make soup than any other employee. So they hired knowledge engineers, as they call the people who build expert systems, to spend time with Al, siphoning from his mind every last drop of expertise he had stored there. The knowledge engineers took Al's ideas, rules, guidelines, and advice about making soup and poured everything into their expert system shell.[2] Today Al is retired, but his presence lives on in the company, thanks to the computer. Youngsters new to the job can tap Al's expertise by calling up the expert system whenever they need to know the best way to handle a situation.

More and more companies are creating systems such as this for all kinds of applications in which the precious commodity of individual or collective expertise can be shared by all. At the University of Pittsburgh, for example, Professor Jack Myers has been working on an expert system called *Caduceus,* which is considered to have the expertise equivalent to a good general practitioner (GP) of medicine. "The program's database consists

---

[2]"Shell" is more computerese, and refers to the outline of a system inside which can be built the various modules that make up the completed system.

of information on more than 500 diseases, with about 75% of all possible diagnoses" (Shurkin, 1985). Potentially, a patient could interact with the system, responding to prompts about symptoms, and *Caduceus* would come up with a diagnosis that might act as a corroborative or cautionary second opinion, helping the GP to prescribe appropriate treatment or recommend further tests.

Artificial intelligence promises other applications that, for the time being at least, might appear esoteric. Consider, for example, a system that comes to you, an elementary or secondary school teacher, with the data you need without you even asking for it. How about a system that is on-line to an ever-expanding database that would include an encyclopedic array of data of all kinds? Included would be relevant historical records for each of the students in your charge, especially those in your homeroom, those for whom you might feel a special responsibility, a special parental (*in loco parentis*) care.

Imagine that intelligence is programmed into the system, which instructs it to rummage around looking for connections between bits of data that you would never have the time to find. When you turn it on, it informs you that Johnny Doe's grade in a test he took with another teacher the day before was much improved over previous scores and that a word of congratulation might reinforce Johnny's resolve to do well. Or the system might come up with details of a seminar on American Indian culture coming up in a week which might provide useful background for the segment on the same subject that you covered with your class two weeks ago.

Garbage In, Garbage Out (GIGO)

One issue that should be borne in mind with regard to computers is that they are just "dumb machines." Any intelligence they appear to demonstrate is nothing more than rote processing of instructions fed into them by humans. It stands to reason that computers will be only as accurate as the people who program them. So we should always be at least a little skeptical about the results of computer operations. In other words, we should double-check computer output. This is an important aspect of computer literacy.

Unfortunately, most people are careless in this regard. How many of us, for example, check whether the amount we are charged for our groceries at the computerized supermarket checkout tallies with the amount we should be paying according to the prices marked on the shelves? It is easy for a store owner to change the prices in the computer database, and then forget (or neglect) to update the prices marked on the shelves. Likewise, an education information system that offered data about our students or made suggestions that might help us improve our teaching would be only as good, accurate, or useful as the data in the database, which would have to be current and consistent at all times.

3.1.2 Extending the Capability of the Body

Computer literacy is all about knowing how, when, and what computer technology can serve one's needs, optimize one's existence, and expand one's opportunities. This applies as much to the body as to the mind. Even animals use tools to help them accomplish different physical tasks. Computers are no different from other machines in this respect, except insofar as they can be programmed as electronic controllers of those other machines. This gives them a dimension of flexibility and versatility that goes beyond most other machines. The following are a few examples of computer-based systems that extend our physical capabilities.

Remote-controlled devices

Scientists are able to pick up rocks on the surface of distant planets by wearing gloves that are connected by radio signals to the "hands" of robots that have been sent to those planets to do their exploring for them. The robot has a camera to transmit pictures of the object to be collected, and the scientist just moves her fingers as if she were there on the planet alongside the robot. The robot responds precisely and delicately, controlled from hundreds of thousands, maybe millions, of miles away.

Other remotely operated vehicles (ROVs) are used to study the ocean depths, or to investigate unexploded bombs, or to check out areas that may have been contaminated as a result of toxic emissions. In general, ROVs allow us to go where it would be either very difficult or very dangerous for us to go in person.

Help for the handicapped

Human-factors engineering involves the study of the human considerations that come to play in the design of machines. The August 1990 volume of *Human Factors Journal* contains a special section devoted to "Assisting People With Functional Impairments." One paper in this special issue (Vanderheiden, 1990) titled "Thirty-Something Million: Should They Be Exceptions?" points out that "there are over 30 million people in the United States with disabilities or functional limitations . . . and this number is increasing." According to Koenig (1992), this number had indeed increased to closer to 43 million people.

Vanderheiden and Koenig agree that the sheer size of this segment of the population coupled with the mandates of the Americans with Disabilities Act, should provide impetus to the introduction of mass-market, computerized products with features that address the needs of the disabled or functionally impaired. The nascent industry for computerized devices to assist this segment of the population has already produced inventions that give one reason to hope that the term *handicapped* will eventually all but disappear from our vocabulary.

Consider what has already been achieved.

Consider the quadriplegic, paralyzed from the neck down, who has a voice-controlled robot programmed to be his companion, preparing his meals, feeding him, fetching and carrying for him, and so forth (NOVA, 1985).

Consider the paraplegic, paralyzed from the waist down, and now able to walk because of computer-controlled functional electrical stimulation of the leg muscles (NOVA, 1985).

Consider the blind person able to see faint images for the first time in his life because of a computer-based system that literally plugs into the visual cortex at the back of his brain and transmits pictures captured by a video camera, bypassing the eyes altogether.

Consider Hudson Lamb (Lavin, 1993), whose brain was injured at birth. Until the age of 16 he was considered educationally beyond reach, even though he was in fact highly intelligent. Then he was introduced to "facilitated communication"—where someone sits with him and holds up his arm while he types at a computer keyboard. To everyone's astonishment, it was discovered that without much help from anyone, Hudson had learned a great deal, including how to read. He immediately went to the top of his

Figure 3.1
Hudson Lamb
communicating with
the help of his
teacher, Gary Pool
Photo courtesy Jeff Lavin

class in tests and in the process made a mockery of most people's stereotypes of those whose physical disabilities are related to motor control and speech. As Hudson put it so eloquently: "Just because a person can't speak doesn't mean he has nothing to say."

"The blind see, the lame walk." The more aware we become of the many extraordinary applications that are being designed around the computer by inventors and researchers all over the world, the more we can appreciate the relevance of the term *computer revolution* as a description of the transformation that is taking place in every nook and cranny of our world.

You can probably come up with other examples where the computer has allowed us to perform some physical function that would previously have been simply beyond our capability. There is not a single area of life that has not, or will not eventually, feel the computer's impact. Another interesting discussion could be generated by focusing on ways in which computers can enrich the educational experience for handicapped children. The Do Something About It section at the end of the chapter offers exercises that center on such a discussion.

Augmenting normal human capabilities

Powell (1992) describes the Artificial Intelligence (AI) system developed by Dr. Geoffrey Hinton at the University of Toronto to monitor women for early detection of cancer.

This image recognition system is able to examine a pap smear, which typically contains about 500,000 cells, and identify the 128 cells that are most likely candidates for closer examination in case they are cancerous. "A human operator," Hinton explains, "makes the final decision about whether these are really cancerous cells. Not only is this system faster, but it makes fewer mistakes because a person inevitably overlooks a few cells when facing such a huge number. . . . [The system] can afford to look at all the cells. As a result, the error rate in diagnosis has decreased by a factor of 10."

This example underscores the true power of the computer as a tool in intelligent—that is, human—hands. The same applies to computer use in schools: It will be most effective when it supports, rather than replaces, the skilled and experienced teacher.

Enriching human experience

As we discussed in chapter 1, research has shown that children's writing skills are enhanced considerably when they use the computer, because they are liberated from the constraint of having to form letters by hand. Children at ages four, five, and six are already learning to touch type, their fingers flying over the keys as fast as their minds can conjure up ideas.

Once voice-recognition systems are generally available, they will liberate children from much of the typing at the keyboard. They will tell stories or describe situations orally, and the computer will capture the data, echoing it back to the child as text on the computer screen. This will encourage the child to *read* the text in order to verify that it has been successfully recognized by the computer. More important, because the computer captures everything in a form that is infinitely malleable, the child will also be encouraged to *revise* the text, a key ingredient of good writing. So the physically liberating computer will enable the child to extend mental capabilities, too.

Teachers thus have a golden opportunity today to improve the educational experience for their students by creating an environment in which children can take advantage of computer-based technology to extend mental and physical capabilities.

3.1.3 Extending the Boundaries of the Feasibly Finite

The *feasibly finite* describes whatever is doable in the context of current human capabilities. For example, thanks to the level of command and control enabled by computers, we have been able to achieve the feat of landing people on the moon. We are able routinely to put people into orbit using the NASA shuttle orbiters, and it is only a matter of time before the U.S. has a space station that will serve as a platform to leap off in further exploration of our universe.

All this has been feasibly finite since the end of the 1960s. It also is now feasibly finite for our students to enter into dialogue in real time with other students in other countries and other cultures thanks to computers and communications (C&C) networks.

The technology is available for video conferencing, where the participants can both hear *and see* each other. This technology is expensive; it is therefore currently feasibly finite only in corporate environments. But it is just a matter of time before schools will be able to enjoy this technology, with all the educational opportunities that it implies. For

example, imagine the day when children in, say, Cape Coral, Florida, will be able to join a video conference with children in Sydney, Australia; Birmingham, England; Ilorin, Nigeria; and Riyadh, Saudi Arabia.

You will recall Weizenbaum's (1976) caveat that computers have caused us to avoid facing up to some aspects of social and economic change by enabling us, "just in time," to continue with management policies that were in grave need of revision and reform. There is much wisdom in Weizenbaum's words and we should nurture a healthy skepticism that should cause us to question unbridled change. Computerized systems of mass destruction, for example, are also extending the boundaries of the feasibly finite, but they are hardly laudable advances. It is, however, plain that the computer is helping us find solutions to previously intractable problems by enabling us to identify those problems in time to deal with them before they overwhelm us.

Look at weather forecasting. Take Hurricane Andrew, which devastated communities south of Miami in 1992. A feasibly finite, advance warning made possible by computer-coordinated monitoring and satellite transmission meant that hundreds of thousands of people were given time to move to safety before the storm.

The list could go on and on. The computer, in conjunction with other enabling technology, is helping us increase the domain of the feasibly finite at an ever-accelerating pace. This change, as Weizenbaum and others have observed, is not always beneficial, our task as a global society is to forge ahead, learn from experience, and take those two steps forward and one step back that have characterized all of human progress. The steps, forward or back, will be taken more purposefully if, as teachers, we have faith in people's fundamental good will, hope for a better future, and love for the children with whose education we are entrusted.

3.1.4 The World of Work

Government and corporations were the first to use computers in a big way to manage their operations. First it was control of data—employee records, payroll, accounting, and so forth. Next it was control of strategic decision-making—"Where do we go from here?"—based on what-if analyses of accounting, sales, and marketing data. Then computer-controlled automation began to transform the workplace with robotized systems of all kinds. Word processors enabled one secretary to do the work of three. Expert systems captured the knowledge of experts so that the expertise could be preserved and duplicated for others to apply.

Today there are corporations where all functions of the business—planning, design, manufacturing, accounts, inventory, marketing, sales, personnel, customer relations—are computer-coordinated. **Computer-integrated manufacturing (CIM)** is the term coined to describe this new approach. It means that ideas conceived at the planning stage are electronically mapped to design. Designs are transformed by computers into prototypes before being approved for manufacturing. Robots ("steel-collar workers," as they are sometimes called) make the parts and assemble them into the final product. Computers track sales and monitor market conditions so that no more than the required number of products is produced, thus keeping inventory to a minimum. For the manufacturing process itself, required parts are available in the right quantity "just in time" (JIT). Shipping is tracked by the same system, along with invoicing and other electronic paperwork.

The efficiency and productivity that result from *effective* CIM[3] inevitably lead to greater profitability. Unfortunately there is a downside to CIM. Approximately 20 percent of layoffs in all sectors of the workforce is attributable to automation. Fewer people are needed at all levels of corporate life, especially people who have failed to update intellectual skills that as yet cannot be equaled or replaced by computers. In some cases whole communities have been destroyed.

The people hardest hit are those with the least ability to adapt and move on. This is where education comes in. Later, chapter 14 will review the competencies required for today's workplace and examine how schools can best prepare students for these new workplace realities. But how must society as a whole adapt to the new realities brought on by the integration of computer-based technology into working environments? Should government intervene to ensure that a nation's wealth is enjoyed fairly by all citizens? If so, how can this be done? Will people work less for a living wage? In the early years of this century it was not unusual for a blue-collar worker to put in 80 hours a week—without overtime pay. Today, 40 hours a week is considered full-time work. In some European countries overtime begins after 30 hours of work a week. What will be a normal working week 50 or 100 years from now?

Computer-based systems are at the heart of fundamental change in the workplace. Are our social structures flexible enough to accommodate this change without significant social upheaval?

Implications for education

What implications does this change in the workplace have for education? It is fair to say that the societies best equipped to survive in the future will be those that guarantee the right of open access to lifelong educational opportunity for all members of the population. Computers will be an increasingly important component of that educational opportunity. Computers will never replace teachers since children need adult help, guidance, supervision, caring, and love. Indeed, society will need *more* teachers in the future as awareness of the importance of education leads to improved teacher–pupil ratios.[4]

3.1.5 The Global Village

Computers and communications (C&C) have accelerated the advent of the realities of Marshall McLuhan's Global Village (McLuhan, 1989). These realities are characterized by the following:

- Near instantaneous access to the remotest corners of the earth.
- The responsibility of all nations for the plight of each nation because of increasing economic and political interdependence.
- The slow but sure—and largely unnoticed—homogenizing of cultures and national identities because of global multicultural exposure. For example, Moyers (1988)

---

[3]Remember that computers are only ever as effective as the people using them.

[4]Currently about 1:17 on average according to the *Digest of Education Statistics* (1992), which belies the fact that many classrooms still have a ratio of teacher to students that is closer to 1:30.

observed that American English is becoming the *lingua franca* of the world because of U.S. economic dominance in the global marketplace.

- A global labor market providing global opportunities for those personally and educationally qualified to take advantage of them.
- The erosion of barriers between people and nations.

Chapter 11 will examine C&C as it relates to education. In a world reduced electronically to villagelike proportions, our schools have a responsibility to provide students with every opportunity to learn about, communicate with, and experience, peoples from cultures other than their own. The goal is to remove the prejudices that go with ignorance.

Education, which begins the moment a child is born,[5] is our only hope in this regard. As Fersh (1982) pointed out: "To change and add to our perspectives is not as difficult as it may first seem. The ways in which we view the world, other peoples, and ourselves are, after all, the results of education, formal and informal. Humans are not born with conceptions; we learn them. And we can unlearn them as well."

The global village is actually a relatively narrow concept now that we have developed the technology to escape earth's bounds. The boundaries of the feasibly finite now extend out into the universe. As the Russian scientist Tsviolkovsky remarked, "Earth is the cradle of humanity. But humanity cannot live in a cradle forever."

3.1.6 "High Tech, High Touch"

This phrase "high tech, high touch" was coined by Naisbitt (1982). Contrary to the skeptical view that technology alienates people, Naisbitt noticed that high tech, either directly or indirectly, is more likely to put people more closely in touch with each other. Telecommunications, for example, bring the world to our door. Computerized scanning devices have enabled doctors to detect life-threatening conditions earlier than ever, often soon enough to arrest further deterioration. Automobiles are sprinkled with microprocessors that increase safety and efficiency, thus giving us more control in diverse driving conditions.

Recall the story of Al Cimino, retired blue-collar worker at Campbell's Soups. Not only did the high-tech expert system described earlier put the company in touch with Al's expertise even after he had retired, but it also had an unexpected "high tech, high touch" side effect as far as Al was concerned. When he saw the extent to which Campbell's Soups depended on his knowledge and experience, he became aware, sadly for the first time in his life, of his own importance and self-worth.

In schools, computers are making possible the elusive dream of individualized education, even as they facilitate collaborative learning and intercultural communication. As Melmed (1988) observed: "The application of science and technology, which has had such a powerful effect in other social and economic sectors, can be the basis of a new instructional model with much improved learner productivity."

Computers also appear to produce some surprising and moving "high tech, high touch" outcomes. Dr. Rena Upitis at the Hennigan school in Boston, Massachusetts, relates the story of "one little girl—classified as non-verbal because she had never spoken

---

[5]Some would argue that it begins while the child is still in the mother's womb.

in school—[who] spoke for the first time at the computer, asking her teacher to come and see her work" (Spence, 1987). In another example, an autistic child was able to be mainstreamed because of the computer's capability of voice synthesis. As the child said: "In time I will utter the truth of my plight. I will remember the people who helped me. I cannot do this without help."[6] The child recognized that without the computer he would probably have been trapped forever inside his disability.

■ 3.2 The Computer Revolution

Revolution is a strong word. It means "great upheaval," or "complete change in outlook, social habits, or circumstances," to quote one dictionary (Macdonald, 1974). To quote another, "revolution is a complete or radical change of any kind" (Random House, 1991).

3.2.1 "Revolution" Is a Relative Term

A time frame for revolution does not enter into the preceding definitions. Time, after all, is relative to one's perception of events. It must also be relative to the nature of the society that has been affected by the "complete change," and relative to the type of change taking place. So-called developed countries such as the United States, while capable of broad-based implementation of technological change, will be less dramatically affected by that change than, say, a wealthy *under*developed country such as many of the oil-rich states in the Middle and Far East. In these latter countries citizens have, in the space of 20 to 30 years, leapt from being preindustrial, even preagricultural societies, to postindustrial, information-based societies. For these societies the term *computer revolution* is very meaningful indeed.

On the other hand, many peoples, constituting perhaps 70% of the world population, have barely felt the impact of the technological revolution brought on by computerization. Their way of life still relies on either hunting and gathering or agriculture and their pace of life is dictated by the rhythms of nature. Alvin Toffler (1971) calls them "people of the past."

From the perspective of the industrialized and computerized societies with their frenetic pace of life and problems with environmental degradation, depersonalization, and overcrowding, it is understandable that one might entertain a wistful longing for a return to the halcyon days of a preindustrial era. Ironically, however, "the people of the past" are the first to recognize that ultimately their survival depends on catching up with the rest of the world.

As John Naisbitt (1982) observed, and as discussed earlier in this chapter, electronic technology is bringing us closer together. It is also enabling us to haul in the reins on uncontrolled growth, ill-managed development, and the conflicting consequences of individual and collective desire to improve our lot. Beniger (1986) corroborates Naisbitt's observation, acknowledging the computer's place as a key tool in political, economic, and social control.

---

[6]From a TV documentary on autism.

3.2.2 The Revolution Has Not Yet Run Its Course

The change that has been made possible by computer-based technology since John Vincent Atanasoff invented the ABC in 1939 has thus already transformed those societies that have been able to afford to take advantage of it. Yet the impact of the computer on society has barely begun. Hardly a year goes by without some new development in computing capability making what was previously state of the art outmoded by comparison. Companies buy the new technology resigned to the fact that a five-year life cycle is as much as they can hope for before the quickly antiquated machines must be updated. Schools, too, face a similar dilemma: Should they buy new equipment now, to give today's students the opportunity to share in the benefits of computer-based learning, or should they wait a year or two to take advantage of the inevitable increased capability of newer machines?

Alvin Toffler (1971) wrote of the "acceleration in the rate of change." He observed that more inventions had come about during the 50 years before publication of his book than during the rest of human history. He acknowledged the central role of the computer in fueling the change. The computer is a skill-enhancing tool that directly supports the realization of technological, sociological, scientific, as well as artistic dreams. Moreover, this general-purpose, programmable computer is more than a tool at the service of inventors. It is a component in their inventions, woven into the very structure of revolutionary designs.

Earlier this chapter examined some ways in which the computer has changed our world. The following examples will further underscore the revolutionary nature of these changes.

The most dramatic example is, of course, exploration of space. Humankind could never have journeyed into space without the aid of machines that could process vital data fast enough to control the Sputniks, Apollos, Soyuz, or Shuttles of our age.

In 1961, when President John F. Kennedy laid down the challenge to American scientists to put a man on the moon by the end of that decade, he did so with full knowledge that the capability was in place. Computers coordinated the planning of the various projects initiated to develop the technology that would take the astronauts to the moon. Computers carried out the calculations required to control the flights from start to finish. Computers monitored and controlled the in-flight environment and the various systems that were critical to success. Computers processed and analyzed the enormous stream of data that was generated by the various missions.

Such dependence on computers has its disadvantages, of course, in that we may be becoming too dependent on technology. Leveson (1992) reported a problem that occurred during a NASA Space Shuttle mission to rescue the IntelSat satellite. Authorized changes made to the rendezvous software did not work quite as expected and, though no ultimate harm was done, alarm bells sounded in the launch director's mind. To use Hale's own words, referenced in Leveson (1992), "We are concerned about the safety of all the other software on the orbiter—*if the computers don't work, nothing on the orbiter works.*" [Emphasis added.]

Computers have revolutionized medical technology. They are embedded in heart pacemakers, programmed to monitor and adjust the ailing heartbeat so that it can pulse at a rate compatible with the demands made of it. They are embedded in all kinds of medical imaging systems (X-ray, magnetic-resonance, fiberoptic, ultrasound) to give medical experts the kind of data they need to make informed decisions regarding suitable treatment. No longer does a brain surgeon attack tumors by probing around inside the skull. Imaging systems locate the tumor, and computer-guided probes administer appropriate treatment under the surgeon's skilled control.

Computers have revolutionized research, the very seedbed of change. As Penzias (1989) points out, doing science today literally depends on the computer as a tool to generate, store, analyze, visualize, organize, document, communicate, and publicize the results of painstaking investigation of hypotheses across all academic disciplines.

Computers may one day revolutionize government. Mowshowitz (1976), echoing the ideas of others, foresees the scenario where "every home [is] equipped with a communications terminal connected to a nationwide computer network, and . . . the network's (presumably rich) information resources [are] accessible to all users." He goes on to surmise that in such a state, "the ordinary citizen would have the means for making intelligent decisions and communicating opinions to others." Such a scenario, as McLuhan (1989) pointed out, would enable the implementation of local, state, and national referenda at a moment's notice. Putting power like this into the hands of the people would, of course, increase the demand for a responsible, informed electorate. Is our education system adapting to address this demand? We will have to wait and see.

One could go on and on. Indeed, we are becoming so inured to spectacular technology that it is becoming humdrum. This is especially so for the children in our schools for whom the world of the Jetsons must seem not simply feasible, but imminent. Revolution, indeed!

3.2.3 Information Overload

But revolutions create chaos as readily as they bring change. A significant concomitant of the computer revolution has been an information explosion which threatens to overwhelm the decision maker at every turn. While too little data, like too little knowledge, is a dangerous thing, so too is too much data, otherwise known as information overload.

This problem is not new. Francis Bacon (1561-1626), the English essayist, philosopher, and statesman, was perhaps one of the last people to have had the temerity to say: "I have taken all knowledge to be my province." A century later, Voltaire (1694-1778), the French writer and philosopher, was forced to admit that "the multitude of books is making us ignorant." Information overload was definitely a problem in the 18th century, and it is getting worse rather than better even *with* the data-processing capabilities of the computer. This is because the computer can only process data—the raw material of information; you need the human brain to process information, a topic discussed more fully in chapter 15.

Take, for example, the proposed space station that has been commissioned by the U.S. federal government and which is scheduled to be operational by the year 2005. It is estimated that the data that will be generated *each day* by that orbiting space station will be equivalent to the contents of the Library of Congress.

Clearly we will need to develop systems to capture, store, organize, sieve, and manipulate this data so that it can be useful to us. The North American Space Administration (NASA) has already awarded a grant to the Consortium for International Earth Science Information (CIESIN) to coordinate the development of a new system that will make it easy for researchers to access worldwide-distributed data collected from the various satellites monitoring the biosphere (Lisker, 1993). It is estimated that these satellites alone will be sending a trillion bytes of data each day back to Earth by the end of this decade—that is the equivalent of about 600,000 five-hundred-page books! The computer revolution, in giving birth to this unprecedented explosion of information, leaves us no choice but to commit to pushing the frontiers of computer hardware and software technology just to cope with the data spawned by the advances we have already made.

Fortunately, well before the year 2005 data storage technology will be available that will be capable of coping with the kind of volume of data generated by the space station. Researchers in Japan have developed a method for storing data on disks which involves aligning the molecules in the very structure of the materials used in making the disk. At this submicron level[7] we will be able to store the equivalent of one million 300-page books on a single 3½″-diameter disk.

By the time the space station comes on line, such density of data storage will undoubtedly seem insignificant. Meanwhile, expert systems will have to be designed and built which will be able to sift through the data stream coming in from space, using artificial intelligence to draw scientists' attention to just those patches of data that will require further analysis by natural—that is, human—intelligence.

Technology will thus be driven by its own success, like a dog chasing its own tail. Computer hardware and software engineers will be increasingly challenged to develop the highly complex systems of control that will allow us to maintain political, economic, and social equilibrium in the technologically turbulent times ahead.

Like most of those who have made outstanding contributions to society, John Vincent Atanasoff could never in his wildest dreams have anticipated that the machine he invented in the late 1930s would be effecting such radical social change on into the 21st century.

3.3 Education and the Information Society

3.3.1 Information and Wealth

In a preindustrial society, the source of wealth was land. Then, in the 18th century the Industrial Revolution caused a shift to capital as a primary constituent of wealth. Today, data is the raw material of financial empires. Information, in the form of organized and assimilated data, not only provides companies with a leading edge over the competition by enabling them to efficiently conduct their affairs, but also is itself a commodity, a direct source of wealth. An increasingly large percentage of the workforce in an increasingly large percentage of companies earns a living from transmitting, receiving, and processing information.

Since 1890 the numbers of those employed in agriculture in the United States has fallen from 95% of the population to no more than 3% today. Since 1950 the number of those employed in manufacturing (blue-collar labor) has fallen from 62%

---

[7]The optically assisted human eye, using microscopes, can see objects magnified about a thousand times. Beyond that level, the submicron level, computerized electron microscopes are necessary, and with their aid we are able to see objects magnified in excess of one million times.

to less than 25%. By 1995, it is projected that close to 80% of the workforce will be processing data in information-intensive or service-oriented jobs (U.S. Bureau of Labor Statistics, 1986). As John Sculley, President and CEO of Apple Computer Corporation, observed in his autobiography (1988): "Thinking skills are replacing manual skills in the new age." Education, of course, will have a vital role to play in preparing tomorrow's citizens for a world thus transformed.

3.3.2 Computers, Control, and Systems of Education

Here are some key questions that must be addressed in order to understand and anticipate the role of computers in educational settings that reflect the realities of an information society:

- To what extent can computers be used to control the process whereby an individual acquires the set of information expected of students in schools K through college?
- What role will teachers play in "schools" where much of the learning is computer-based?
- Are schools as physical plants likely to disappear as students have home-based access to learning systems?

Let us address each question:

To what extent can computers be used to control the process whereby an individual acquires the set of information expected of students in schools K through college?

First, there is no such thing as total control, since this would imply a perfection that is a contradiction in terms in an imperfect world. But, a good measure of control is a desirable objective in all organizations, educational environments included.

Government, business and industry—administration in general—will attest to the fact that economies and efficiencies are invariably predicated on control. Quality, too, is predicated on control, and is more likely to be achieved when everyone involved in producing an end product becomes actively involved in the pursuit of excellence. Progress, of course, is concomitant with the pursuit of quality and therefore predicated on control. All this applies as much in education as in the more esoteric worlds of music, theater, and sports where the purpose of practice—"which makes perfect"—is to increase levels of control in the pursuit of excellence.

However, balance is necessary to arrive at the best outcomes. Too much control can stifle creativity by inhibiting the kind of freedom of expression that leads to ideas and to the implementation of those ideas in terms of innovation (Levitt, 1981). As Peters and Waterman (1984) observed when describing the "simultaneous loose–tight properties, the last of [their] 'eight basics' of excellent management practice": "Organizations that live by the loose–tight principle are on the one hand rigidly controlled, yet at the same time allow (indeed, insist on) autonomy, entrepreneurship, and innovation from the rank and file."

Applying all this to the classroom, control is fundamental to our success with students. When we are teaching we are searching for excellence in terms of quality in both our own and our students' performance. Along the lines of the loose–tight principle, we "allow (indeed, insist on)" the independent pursuit of knowledge ("autonomy"), creativity ("entrepreneurship"), and discovery ("innovation") from our students ("the rank and file"). Obviously, we expect progress on the part of our students, and we also like to think that, as teachers, we too make progress (get better at our job) with experience. Inevitably, because the education budget constrains the very lessons that we plan as well as the methodologies that we use, we have to practice economies and keep a watchful eye on efficiency so as to make the best of the scarce resources that are put at our disposal. These objectives of economically and efficiently achieving the level of quality in the end product where each of our students has made the progress that is consonant with his or her age, interests and ability are more likely to be achieved when we exercise an appropriate measure of control over all aspects of our professional life in and out of the classroom. This is where the computer comes in.

Economy, efficiency, quality, progress—these are the yardsticks (objectives) by which it is possible to measure the extent to which computers can be used to control the process whereby an individual advances educationally in schools K–college. If the computer, wisely integrated into the curriculum and used as a productivity tool by the teacher, economically and efficiently fosters program quality and student progress, then there is no limit to the extent to which it can be used to control and enhance the educational process.

Of course, you can be an excellent teacher without having anything to do with computers. The profession managed very nicely without them for centuries. But the profession also managed for centuries without books (and still does in some parts of the world). Yet no one would argue against books as valuable tools for learning.

Chapters 8–12 present ideas on which to base planning for computer-integrated curricula. Studying them should form a starting point, a foundation perhaps, for your own very special, unique approach to using the computer as a tool for teaching and learning. You have a responsibility to take advantage of a tool that, as shown in chapter 1, has been demonstrated to have many powerful applications in schools, applications of value to both you and your students.

What role will teachers play in "schools" where much of the learning is computer-based?

The myriad computer-based learning applications developed for education K–12 can help you as a teacher by releasing you from the primary burden of responsibility for knowledge transfer. Learning, after all, is ultimately the responsibility of the individual student. You, the teacher, through the thoughtful incorporation of computer-based technology into your curriculum, can become the facilitator of knowledge acquisition—a knowledge broker, if you like. Your role is to create and sustain an environment in which children can seek, find, and assimilate data, thus becoming informed through the acquisition of knowledge.

The teachers of the future will need intellectual skills of a different kind. Teachers will still need to know math, history, geography, chemistry, and so on, but this kind of knowledge will be less important than knowing how to manage a learning environment: how to select and set up appropriate individualized learning experiences for children based on their age, propensities, capabilities, and interests; how to motivate children; how to recognize and work with the subtlest of learning disabilities; how to create positive and productive interaction between the child, the school, and the home.

Further discussion of the qualities and skills of the teacher of the future is a suggested activity in the Do Something About It section at the end of the chapter. A report based on four National Science Foundation workshops that took place in 1987 noted that "America is in rapid social and economic transition. Changing circumstances are undermining the effectiveness of traditional classroom instruction. A different educational model may be required, rather than reform of the present system" (Melmed, 1988).

Aspects of that "different educational model" are discussed throughout this book. However, the way schools operate cannot change overnight. All the technology in the world will not transform education if the people in control of education do not themselves understand and initiate appropriate change. Older, more experienced teachers welcome change as much as their younger counterparts, but for the most part they look to younger teachers to be the agents of change. Assuming a continuation of the long-term trend toward improved teacher–pupil ratios continues, there will be a steady infusion of young teachers into the schools. These young teachers will lead education into the 21st century. The following account of one teacher's experience working with children in a technology-rich classroom offers a glimpse of what that 21st century educational environment might resemble.

Researchers (Van Dam, 1991) monitoring a classroom where computer-based technology was integrated intensively into the curriculum, noticed that the teacher seemed to have very little to do. The children were working alone or in groups—some with and some without computers. There was a quiet hum of activity; everyone was involved in the learning process. The teacher was attentive to everything that was going on, moving easily from one group to another, sometimes in response to a verbal or nonverbal call for help, other times to more precisely feel the pulse of the learning process as it occurred.

One of the researchers asked one of the nine-year-olds, "What does the teacher do?"

The youngster replied, "Oh, he's very important."

The researcher was not satisfied with the response. What did the youngster mean? So the question was put again: "Yes, but what does the teacher *do?*"

"He's there in case we need him," said the boy, after a moment's pause.

"He's very important. . . . He's there in case we need him." What a beautiful description of the role of the teacher in the student-directed learning environment.

The teacher does not direct the entire learning experience. Rather, the teacher sets up and maintains an environment that fosters learning for the student participants.

The teacher does not pass on all the knowledge. Rather, the teacher ensures optimal conditions for knowledge acquisition.

The teacher is not an officer in a regimented educational system. Rather, the teacher is a "knowledge broker," acting as an intermediary between students and the data they seek to fulfill their individual information needs.

Children need teachers more than ever in a world where information overload creates confusion in immature minds. But they need teachers less and less as imparters of knowledge, and more and more as imparters of wisdom.

"He's very important. . . . He's there in case we need him." Attendees at educational computing conferences know that there is an increasing number of classrooms worldwide where this concept of the teacher as facilitator of learning is a reality.

Are schools as physical plants likely to disappear as students have home-based access to learning systems?

Maybe—but not any time soon. Schools will surely be on-line. This is nothing new. At the adult level the British Broadcasting Corporation's Open University, which has been in operation for more than 30 years, has provided educational programming for undergraduate degree studies leading to a highly regarded academic diploma. Elementary and secondary schools all over the world are introducing innovative programs where youngsters cross local, state, national, even international boundaries for educational interaction. Using programs such as DIALOG's *CLASSMATE* students are already tapping into a wide range of on-line information retrieval systems.

It is foreseeable that the home of the not-too-distant future will contain not an entertainment center, but an **information center.** The TV, videophone, sound system, and computer will be coordinated into an integrated unit. Students in small teams of perhaps half a dozen per teacher will go to school electronically. The large screen will be divided up into an appropriate number of subscreens (windows) so that everyone can see everyone else. The systems will be easy to use, the technology designed so that it is largely transparent[8] to the users.

But there will still be the need for schools as physical locations for students to learn practical skills related to social, cultural, athletic, vocational, communicational, and managerial excellence. The schools of the future will be far from dull. It is not the fault of the teachers that too many students dislike school today. The fault lies in the way schools are organized. Bruder (1992) states the case plainly:

Today, there's not a person involved or interested in education who hasn't heard the call to reform American schools. Math education is stuck somewhere in the 15th century. Science education made it all the way to the 19th century and then hit a roadblock. Our language arts curriculum is designed for a school population that walks in the door knowing how to speak English. And how do we keep kids in high school when they've already emotionally and mentally dropped out by the fourth grade?

Bruder goes on to profile schools, which, "armed with new ideas and tools," are meeting the challenge of reform head on.

---

[8]*Transparent* here means unnoticed, as if the user sees right through the intricacy of the technology to the point of being unaware of it.

■ Looking Back

Computers have been incorporated into every product under the sun. They have been woven into the fabric of our systems of transportation, administration, information, communications, manufacturing, finance, and government, to name but a few. They have begun to transform the way we live, the way we work, and the way we play. Inevitably they will be woven into the fabric of our education systems, too, and they will transform the way we teach and learn.

Computers have demonstrated their usefulness in their own right as stand-alone, desktop, personal machines. But they become doubly useful when linked to other computers on local and global communications systems. Whether as stand-alone or networked machines, computers have demonstrated their value in the learning process and it is only a matter of time before the full effects of the computer revolution are felt in our schools.

■ Looking Forward

Any technology that has had a significant impact on society has been accompanied by controversy reflecting ethics and law. The computer is no exception. The incredible spread of computer technology throughout the world and into the neighboring universe has spawned gross invasion of privacy, inequities and theft of various kinds, vandalism, trespass, and intrigue. No one has been immune from the negative side of what, on the surface, should be an innocuous technology.

Chapters 4 and 5 will examine some of these problems related to advances in technology. They represent the darker side of the seemingly unstoppable infiltration of society by computer-controlled instruments, an infiltration that raises ethical and legal considerations of which we and our students should be aware.

■ Do Something About It: Exercises and Projects

1. The chapter talks about the qualities and skills required by the teacher of the future. How do they differ from what teachers are expected to know and be good at now? Are colleges preparing teachers for the kind of future discussed in this chapter? Brainstorm with a group of colleagues or co-students to come up with as complete a scenario as possible for the teacher education program of the future.

2. Discuss each of the impacts on society of advances in computing presented in this chapter. Do you agree with the chapter's conclusions? What examples from your

own life corroborate the ideas presented? What other aspects of society are being affected by advances in computer-based technologies, and what are these effects?

3. Come up with examples where the computer has allowed us to perform some physical function that would previously have been simply beyond our capability. There is not a single area of life that has not been, or will not eventually be, affected in this way.

4. How can computers enrich the educational experience for handicapped children?

■ References

Beniger, James R. *The Control Revolution: Technological and Economic Origins of the Information Society.* Cambridge, MA: Harvard University Press, 1986.

Bruder, Isabelle, Herbert Buchsbaum, Maggie Hill, Louise C. Orlando. *School Reform: Why You Need Technology to Get There. Electronic Learning,* vol. 11, no. 8, May/June 1992, pp. 22–28.

Churchland, Patricia S. *Neurophilosophy: Toward a Unified Science of The Mind/Brain.* Cambridge, MA: MIT Press, 1986.

Dreyfus, Hubert. *What Computers Can't Do: The Limits of Artificial Intelligence,* 2nd ed. New York: Harper and Row, 1979. Referenced in Turkle, Sherry. *The Second Self: Computers and the Human Spirit.* New York: Simon and Schuster, 1984.

Fersh, Seymour. "Becoming Self-Educating and Culture-Creating by Being Educated Transculturally." *Reflections,* Winter 1982, pp. 17–24.

Fjermedal, Grant. *The Tomorrow Makers: A Brave New World of Living-Brain Machines.* New York: Macmillan, 1986.

Gödel, K. "Über Formal Unentscheidbare Sätze der Principia Mathematica und Verwandter Systeme, I." *Monatsheftefür Mathematik und Physik,* 38 (1931), pp. 173–98. Referenced in Hofstadter, D. R. *Gödel., Escher, Bach: An Eternal Golden Braid.* New York: Vintage Books, 1980.

Hodges, Andrew. *Alan Turing: The Enigma.* New York: Simon & Schuster, 1983.

Koenig, Dennis. "Look On the Disabilities Act As an Opportunity Rather Than a Burden." *InfoWorld,* November 23, 1992.

Lavin, Jeff. "The Brilliant Boy Inside." *USA Weekend,* July 30–August 1, 1993, pp. 6–7.

(References continue on page 87)

ACCESS Pennsylvania: A statewide network
by Lisa M. Dallape Matson, Head Reference Librarian, University of Pittsburgh at Johnstown
"Who learns by finding out has sevenfold the skill of he who learns by being told."
Auther Guiterman, 1871–1943 American Poet

Introduction

During the past 20 years technology has vastly altered the way in which information is generated, stored, accessed and used. In contemporary education, learning through independent inquiry requires a vision of one's self as an end-user searcher. This entails not only having the skills needed to use traditional printed sources but also an understanding of on-line databases and search strategies.

The development of optical disc technology in the 1980s provided the impetus for the idea of designing and implementing a statewide database in Pennsylvania which would allow high school students to access on-line not only the holdings of their own school's library collection, but also the collections held in other high school libraries, as well as public, academic, and special libraries.

Achieving this ideal was not easy. Obstacles were apparent: lack of administrative commitment, lack of funding, inability to do retrospective conversion to MARC (machine readable record catalog) format for high school collections, lack of technical support, and lack of librarians trained in on-line searching. However, *ACCESS Pennsylvania,* the State Library of Pennsylvania's Division of School Library Media Services (SLMS) program, is one nationally recognized, statewide program that has overcome all these obstacles.

Its agenda is twofold. First, it integrates on-line, end-user searching into school library media curricula. Second, it brings school, public, academic, and special libraries into a CD-ROM based, resource-sharing network.

Since its inception in 1984, *ACCESS Pennsylvania*'s success at linking dissimilar institutions and creating a cooperative database in a cost-effective manner makes it a prototype and a case study worth closer attention.

The Project

When introduced to *ACCESS Pennsylvania* in 1984, some librarians already had on-line searching skills on which to draw, thanks to *LIN-TEL* (**Lin**king **I**nformation

Lisa Dallape Matson, author of the case study

Needs—**T**echnology, **E**ducation, and **L**ibraries). This on-line database-searching system was set up in 1982, and thus preceded *ACCESS Pennsylvania* by two years.

LIN-TEL is funded by the Pennsylvania State Department of Education and the State Library of Pennsylvania. Its primary mission is to train librarians to conduct on-line searching on the commercial database vendor, Bibliographic Retrieval Services (BRS). Librarians are then expected to introduce on-line searching skills into the school library media curriculum. *LIN-TEL* users obtain a list of citations from one of two hundred databases available through the BRS database and then utilize the electronic mail component to request materials not held locally.

LIN-TEL gave librarians the opportunity to hone their on-line database-searching skills before the introduction of *ACCESS Pennsylvania.* In addition, the computer hardware used to support *LIN-TEL* can also be **(continued)**

used to support *ACCESS Pennsylvania,* allowing libraries to participate in both projects simultaneously.

ACCESS Pennsylvania's objectives expand those stated for *LIN-TEL* by creating a searchable catalog database. Under the direction of Dr. Doris Epler and Mr. John Emerick, SLMS has primary responsibility for coordinating efforts and creating the networks needed to make *ACCESS Pennsylvania* work.

Schools may submit applications to join the project in one of three ways:

■ create a consortium that includes at least one public or nonpublic high school library together with a public and/or academic library which already has MARC tapes;

■ join an already existing consortium; or

■ develop a consortium of at least two public school districts.

SLMS pays for retrospective conversion of records from public and nonpublic high schools, combined junior/senior high schools, or junior/senior collections from a K–12 library.

Brodart Automation of Williamsport, Pennsylvania, was contracted to create a database that combined the collections of the *ACCESS Pennsylvania* libraries that had an easy, fast search methodology on author, title, subject, and keyword as well as holding-library location. Brodart was also responsible for the retrospective conversion of libraries' paper shelf lists to MARC records. Finally, Brodart merged existing and new MARC records into a master database on compact disc.

Costs

SLMS pays union catalog costs. Schools pay fifty dollars per year for updated discs. Capital investment by schools includes paying for on-line catalog hardware, circulation hardware, circulation software and supplies.

The Schuylkill Intermediate Unit 29 provides consulting and end-user support. Many feel that *ACCESS Pennsylvania* could not be as successful as it is without such support. Schools participating in the union catalog have access to 17 million records, 3 million of which represent unique titles from just under a thousand libraries. Since the average high school in

The library is a multifaceted information source.

Pennsylvania owns a collection of 12,000 resources, the effects of this resource sharing is considerable.

Impact on Education

ACCESS Pennsylvania reflects Pennsylvania's goal of providing information and knowledge through libraries. The impact on public education is transforming. As Cynthia Hudson, library media specialist at Conemaugh Valley Jr.–Sr. High School in Johnstown, Pennsylvania, put it: "Students don't think of the library as just a place for books, but also a place for computers."

Hudson notes that the database makes it necessary to teach students to think of themselves as information consumers; they are taught to analyze their information needs, evaluate the sources available, and consider the scope of the presentation they plan to make. Moreover, students are taught to compare the value of information in various formats. These needs convinced Hudson and others at SLMS that an educator's guide integrating the *ACCESS Pennsylvania* database into the public school curriculum was not only important but also unquestionably necessary to build students' information literacy and critical thinking skills.

Therefore, the *ACCESS Pennsylvania Curriculum Guide* was published in 1991 by a committee of practicing **(continued)**

Students are information consumers.

school library media specialists and the SLMS staff. The *Guide,* a resource for those participating in the project, is designed to delineate for students the purpose and function of the *ACCESS Pennsylvania* database in addition to providing the instruction students need to become information literate. It also encourages the integration of the *ACCESS Pennsylvania* database into the total school curriculum.

The *Guide* contains 16 lesson plans with learning objectives, a list of activities needed to complete each lesson, and a list of necessary resources. The lessons introduce students to a variety of skills including:

- comparing the database to the card catalog;
- identifying hardware necessary to use the database;
- correct search strategies;
- boolean logic;
- locating holding libraries;
- generating working bibliographies for course work;
- completing interlibrary loan requests;
- downloading from the database.

Image of Libraries

ACCESS Pennsylvania has had a positive impact on the relationship librarians have with their communities, their administrators, their teaching colleagues, and their students. Librarians participating in the project have expressed satisfaction at being able to thus extend the usefulness and effectiveness of their libraries to the community.

There have been four other positive outcomes. First, managing the information needs of the citizens of Pennsylvania has given librarians an increased standing in the eyes of the community. Second, administrators have noted the 200–300% increase in their own library's circulation. Interlibrary loan statistics make it possible to justify monies for enhancing local collections. Also, librarians are being granted release time for training in interlibrary loan and on-line searching.

Third, teachers and librarians are working in a spirit of reciprocity, teaching students the value of the library in all of their courses. Teachers are also depending more on their libraries for information for professional development.

Finally, improving the management of the school library by automating the routine circulation functions has liberated librarians to spend more time using their professional skills with those who matter most, the patrons.

ACCESS Pennsylvania provides librarians and teachers a vehicle to cultivate critical thinking skills and nurture curiosity by empowering students to learn on their own. As such, it supports liberal education at its best.

Special thanks to Dr. Doris Epler and Mr. John Emerick, School Libraries and Media Services Program, Pennsylvania Department of Education.

(continued)

Levitt, Theodore. "Ideas Are Useless Unless Used." *Inc. Magazine,* February 1981, p. 96. Referenced in Peters and Waterman, 1984.

Lisker, Peter. *Environmental Concerns Spur Electronic Index System. Network World,* August 9, 1993, pp. 42–44.

Macdonald, A. M., ed. *Chambers 20th Century Dictionary.* Edinburgh, Scotland: W & R Chambers, 1974.

McLuhan, Marshall, Bruce R. Powers. *The Global Village: Transformations in World Life and Media in the 21st Century.* New York: Oxford University Press, 1989.

Melmed, Arthur S., Robert A. Burnham. "New Information Technology Directions for American Education: Improving Science and Mathematics Education." *T.H.E. Journal,* vol. 16, no. 1, August 1988, pp. 64–68.

Miller, George A. "The Magical Number 7±2: Some Limits On Our Capacity For Processing Information." *The Psychological Review,* vol. 63, no. 2, 1956, pp. 81–97.

Mowshowitz, Abbe. *Conquest of the Will: Information Processing in Human Affairs.* Reading, MA: Addison-Wesley, 1976.

Moyers, Bill. *The History of English.* Series broadcast on PBS TV, 1988.

Naisbitt, John. *Megatrends: Ten New Directions Transforming Our Lives.* New York: Warner Books, 1982.

NOVA. *Those Miraculous Machines.* Boston, MA: WGBH Educational Foundation, 1985.

Penzias, Arno. *Ideas and Information.* New York: Touchstone, 1989.

Peters, Thomas J., Robert H. Waterman, Jr. *In Search of Excellence: Lessons from America's Best-Run Companies.* New York: Warner Communications, 1984.

Powell, Douglas. "AI, Expert Systems Researchers Honored in Canada." *Computing Research News,* November 1992.

Random House. *Webster's College Dictionary.* New York: Random House, 1991.

Sculley, John, Byrne, John A. *Odyssey—Pepsi to Apple, A Journal of a Marketing Impressario.* New York: Harper & Row, 1988. Reviewed by H. Eric Branscomb in *Thought and Action: The NEA Higher Education Journal,* vol. 5, no. 2, Fall 1989, pp. 117–19.

Shurkin, Joel, *Engines of the Mind.* New York: Washington Square Press, 1985.

Spence, Cathie Slater. "New Ideas For Computers in Schools." *The Christian Science Monitor,* October 10, 1987, pp. 21–22.

Toffler, Alvin. *Future Shock.* New York: Bantam Books, 1971.

Turing, Alan M. "On Computable Numbers, with an Application to the Entscheidungsproblem." *Proceedings of the London Mathematical Society* (2), 42, 1937.

U.S. Bureau of Labor Statistics, 1986. Referenced in Blissmer, R. H., *Introducing Computers, Concepts, Systems, and Applications.* New York: John Wiley, 1990.

Van Dam, Janet, Carol Klenow. "Teaching and Learning with Technology." Report to the National Educational Computing Conference, June 1991.

Vanderheiden, Gregg C. "Thirty-Something Million: Should They Be Exceptions?" *Human Factors, Journal of the Human Factors Society,* vol. 32, no. 4, August 1990, pp. 383–96.

Vitek, Jan. "Computerized 'Experts.' " *World Press Review,* October 1990.

Weizenbaum, Joseph. *Computer Power and Human Reason: From Judgement to Calculation.* San Francisco: W. H. Freeman, 1976.

What's the effect on the graph?

$f(x) = x^2 + 3$

$g(x) = x - 3$

$f(g(x)) = (x-3)^2 + 3$

Ethics and Computers: Invasion of Privacy and Computing Inequities

Science cannot stop while ethics catches up.
Elvin Stackman

The system of private property is the most important guaranty of freedom, not only for those who own property, but scarcely less for those who do not.
Friedrich August von Hayek (1899–   )

Your education begins when what is called your education is over.
Oliver Wendell Holmes (1809–1894)

Many societies today are faced with serious problems regarding the upbringing of their children. This is especially true in the so-called developed world, where half of all marriages fail and where, even when the marriages last, both parents often feel constrained to work to make enough money to have a decent standard of living.[1] With the best will in the world, parents in such families have difficulty giving their children the close comfort and companionship they have every right to expect from the dependable and attentive presence of a nurturing adult. Many children are latchkey kids, coming home to an empty house and left to fend for themselves for several hours until a parent returns. Other children come home to a house where the parents have little energy left to respond to their need for attention.

Too often, the children *are* finding at home all the wrong kinds of role models, pacifying them hour after hour over largely unsupervised, dubiously educational, TV channels. As Postman (1986) observed, "We are now a culture whose information, ideas, and epistemology are given form by television, not by the printed word." Shanker (1992) further reminds us that "studies and statistics—and our own observations—tell us that American families are increasingly fragile and unstable, and we fear that, as a result, many children are being seriously damaged." In a culture where the immediate family appears to have less and less control over their well-being, children need all the help they can get.

In some countries, such as in the kibbutzim (collective farms) in Israel, children are put in the almost total care of specially appointed nurses and educators from a very early age. Today, this type of responsibility is more important than ever. Societies are having to rely more than ever on professionally managed institutions such as schools to act *in loco parentis*. Acting *in loco parentis*—not *instead of* but *in the place of,* as in *standing in for,* parents—is nothing new for teachers because children have always spent a large proportion of their waking day in school.

Teachers are significant role models for children—they are often looked up to, respected, admired, even loved. One rewarding aspect of being a teacher is the thrill that comes from "touching a child's future." This is true even for the most hard-bitten teachers who might sometimes come across as mean and morose, yet make a difference in their students' lives because they are professionals in a profession governed by standards and expectations that are set by the community. In their role as caregivers, teachers inevitably have an impact on the ethical code that governs a child's behavior, a code that becomes clarified as the child grows to adulthood. A code of ethics is formed as much by culture as by any innate sense of right and wrong. Put another way, a system of ethics is not only instinctive; it is also *learned.*

Many teachers feel uncomfortable discussing matters of an ethical nature with their students. Here, we examine a rationale for why teachers should discuss with their students the ethical and legal issues surrounding computer use in society. The remainder of the chapter, along with chapter 5, will explore some of those issues in more depth.

---

[1] Both spouses work full time in roughly 70% of all marriages as of October 1992.

Topics covered in this chapter include:

- Why should teachers discuss ethical and legal issues?
  - Teachers have a role in preparing students for the computerized society
  - Education should empower students
  - Issues of computer-related liability may affect our students' lives
- The invasion of privacy and the illusion of truth
  - Big Brother
  - Privacy invasion: is it all for a good cause?
  - Data is a source of wealth in an information society
  - Is it possible to control invasion of one's privacy?
  - Privacy, faulty files, and the right of public access
  - Disinformation and doublethink
- Computers and Inequities
  - Haves and have-nots: rich versus poor
  - Haves and have-nots: girls versus boys
  - Haves and have-nots: whites versus minorities
  - Haves and have-nots: the lack of equal access to information
  - The problems of the haves and have-nots are founded on more than just financial inequities

4.1 Why Should Teachers Discuss Ethical and Legal Issues?

4.1.1 Teachers Have a Role in Preparing Students for the Computerized Society

Although this chapter discusses the negative side effects of computing, it should be understood at the outset that computers have had, are having, and will continue to have an overwhelmingly beneficial effect on our world. There is one simple reason for this: the vast majority of people want it to be so. Abuse of the power of computing technology is practiced by the few.

It is our responsibility to make students aware of how they may become at the very least victims of this abuse. They may even themselves be perpetrators. Edmund Burke, the 19th-century Irish philosopher-statesman, wrote: "All that is necessary for the triumph of evil is that good men do nothing." As teachers, we could confine ourselves to teaching the narrow field of knowledge which may have been, or is, the focus of our college studies and which we are expected to teach in the school district that hired, or will hire, us. But we cannot turn a blind eye to the needs of maturing students in the face of the "evils" that they must cope with from day to day in the increasingly computerized society.

We will examine two of these "evils"—the routine invasion of privacy and the inequities that arise from unequal access to computer technology.

Everyone has a code of ethics of some kind. One purpose of the socialization that goes on in homes and schools is to attempt to bring individuals to the point where they can appreciate and try to stand by the common set of rules and behaviors that bind the society to which they belong. Idiosyncrasy will still prevail; individuals and subgroups will always adhere to rules and behaviors that are particular to them. But even those idiosyncratic individuals and subgroups cannot live together unless they familiarize themselves with the ethical common ground.

Hence, the Constitution of the United States, originally patterned after English law, which, since 1789,[2] has evolved toward the ideal of protecting equally the rights of every individual in an ethnically, socially, economically, and religiously diverse population. Children count on their parents and their teachers to help them prepare for full participation in the life of their country according to the fundamental principles of human rights as laid down in the Constitution. A testament to the quality of this Constitution is the fact that it has become the model for many other nations in modern history striving toward democracy.

But this same Constitution may be interpreted as presenting a barrier to the open discussion of ethics-related issues. The separation of church and state is called for by the First Amendment of the Constitution of the United States, which, among other things, mandates freedom of religion and freedom from the establishment of religion. This is perhaps one of the reasons why many teachers, at least in the United States, are loath to discuss with their students issues related to ethics. Unfortunately, religion easily becomes inextricably intertwined with ethics, even though ethics is, strictly speaking, above and independent of religion. Ethical people are not necessarily religious in the formal sense of the word *religious,* just as religious people are not necessarily ethical.

There are other reasons why many teachers shy away from discussing ethics-related issues. One is the problem of objectivity. It may be difficult for a teacher to keep his or her own prejudices out of a debate in which the goal should be to arrive at a commonly accepted interpretation of a moral issue. Another is the problem of competence. A teacher may not feel competent to lead a discussion of ethics-related issues. One final reason teachers may feel loath to discuss these issues is that they may be embarrassed to do so. Many people simply feel uncomfortable discussing matters of right and wrong, aware as they are of their own vulnerability on the same issues.

Whatever the reason, avoiding the topic of ethics with students is unfortunate because it denies them the opportunity to openly discuss problems that need to be aired. Invasion of privacy, inequity, trespass, and theft are examples of such problem areas. The purpose here and in the next chapter is to show: (1) how computer technology has blurred the perception of what is right and wrong with regard to these illegal practices, thus making us more likely to fall into the trap of unethical conduct; (2) how easily we can become unwitting victims of the unethical practices of others who take advantage of computer-based systems to commit crime.

For the most part, people who become elementary and secondary school teachers are talented individuals who are motivated primarily by the desire to serve. In their role as educators they have an ideal opportunity to have a positive influence not only on the individual students that come under their care, but, through them, on the society to which they belong. Schools are responsible for inculcating not just the three Rs, but the five Rs: reading, writing, arithmetic, right, and wrong!

---

[2]The year of the French Revolution, which rallied around the tricolor—the three-colored flag symbolizing the battle cry of "Liberté, Egalité, Fraternité!"—"Freedom, Equality, Brotherhood!"

4.1.2 Education Should Empower Students

The collected folklore of a society can sow seeds of confusion even when it represents the wisdom of the past. For example, we recognize that "knowledge itself is power," as the 16th-century philosopher-statesman Francis Bacon pointed out. If I know how to read or how to wisely invest money, I can compete more effectively in a society where, for the time being, so much of what I need to know is conveyed in written form and where money tends to be the means of exchange for the goods and services that I need and want. At the same time, we are told that ignorance is bliss. For example, all of us at one time or another have denied ourselves or others some new experience, some new knowledge out of fear of the consequences of the heightened perceptions the experience or knowledge would bring. Such a rationale is at work when people argue that it is dangerous to discuss certain issues with children because it will "give them ideas." They may be right; certainly it is a debate that will never be fully resolved.

Both aphorisms—knowledge is power and ignorance is bliss—though seemingly contradictory, are in fact complementary. They are equally relevant depending on the circumstances, hence the need to discuss all sides of every case. When it comes to the interweaving of computer-based technology into the fabric of our world, teachers have a duty to make students fully aware of the advantages to be gained from the appropriate and skillful use of computers as well as of the dangers inherent in a society where computers are used increasingly to control our lives.

Ignorance is definitely not bliss when it puts us at a disadvantage. It is said that a little knowledge is a dangerous thing, but learning has to start somewhere and the job of teachers is to guide children in their quest for the knowledge that will empower them to become fully contributing and honorable members of their local, national, and global communities.

4.1.3 Issues of Computer-Related Liability May Affect Our Students' Lives

In recent years, computer-related liability issues have spawned a dramatic increase in litigation. Poorly designed systems have been blamed for various ills such as gross infringements of people's rights, crippling business losses, major public inconvenience, serious individual injury, and victimization of one kind or another. Students should be given the opportunity to become aware of how they may become victims of the abuse inflicted on society by individuals and groups who either design and market systems that represent a threat to our mental or physical well-being or who use computer-based technology for illegal purposes.

4.2 The Invasion of Privacy and the Illusion of Truth

George Orwell (1949), in his famous novel *1984,* warns us of the dangers inherent in the abuse of power. Among these are the concept of **Big Brother**—a force that is surreptitiously or otherwise watching our every move and monitoring our every thought. Then, there is the concept of *doublethink,* which we will define later. Computers, especially when they are linked together over the wide area networks (which will be covered in chapter 11), make these concepts all too easily a reality even in so-called free and democratic states.

Figure 4.1
George Orwell's *1984*

Computer technology makes it easier than ever for Big Brother to monitor the comings and goings of an increasingly large proportion of the populace. The integration of computers and communications (C&C—discussed further in chapter 11) enables nearly instant mass media and makes it easier than ever for professional doublethinkers—"spinners" of the truth—to distort any reality, using "conscious deception while retaining the firmness of purpose that goes with complete honesty" (Orwell, 1949). The verbiage generated during any political campaign bears witness to the relevance of Orwell's words.

4.2.1 Privacy and Big Brother

"Privacy," observes Rothfeder (1992), "is an issue charged with emotion. Nothing makes Americans angrier than the suspicion that somebody is looking over their shoulders or peering into their private affairs. And people often describe privacy deprivation with the same words used by rape victims: We say we feel violated, vulnerable and ineffectual." However, Johnson (1985a) reminds us that "much to the surprise of many Americans there is no explicit constitutional guarantee to privacy," as will be discussed later in the context of the various privacy-related acts passed by the United States government in the last 30 years.

All over the world, the institutions established by government for the maintenance of law and order, along with most major and many minor corporations and private investigative agencies, use technology to an ever-increasing extent to spy on people. It is surprising that most of the spying is legal, either sanctioned by law or at least not proscribed by it—which does not necessarily make it right. On the other hand, some of the spying is illegal, but because we do not know it is going on, we do not become concerned. Is ignorance bliss, in this case? Do students need to be sensitized to the reality of privacy invasion? Is there any harm in it, anyway, especially if one is behaving oneself? And, in any case, is there anything we can do about it?

We have all read about the private detective who boasts to need only a person's first and last name, and maybe an address if the person happens to be named John Smith, to come up with a detailed record of that individual, right down to the Social Security number, complete medical and credit history, credit card and bank account numbers, life-style as indicated by credit-card spending records, telephone number and the names and numbers of anyone the individual has called on the phone—all at the touch of a few keys on a computer keyboard. If all this data were made available to someone with malicious intent, one can see how easily a targeted person's life could be destroyed.

People should be aware of the extent to which their lives are now the subject of public record. In a computerized society, it is easy to capture, store, and manipulate almost limitless amounts of data. Modern Data Base Management Systems (DBMS) take much of the drudgery out of amassing data. Local, state, and especially federal governments allocate significant sums of taxpayer money to establish and maintain records on the citizenry. The National Crime Information Center (NCIC), "the single most complex communication system operated by the federal government" (Burnham, 1983), is a huge and mushrooming database of stolen property and criminal activity in the United States with links to databases in other cooperating countries. Separate databases of records pertaining to people living in the United States are maintained by other branches of government, such as the CIA, the Census Bureau, and the Internal Revenue Service.

Fortunately, this process of amassing data is not totally uncontrolled. Turn (1985) reminds us of the outrage caused by the 1965 recommendation by the Committee on the Preservation and Use of Economic Data to establish a federally managed National Data Bank which would be "a centralized database of all personal information collected by federal agencies for statistical purposes." The idea drew strong protest from all sides. Already, less than 20 years after the delivery of the first working electronic computer, society was becoming wary of the uses to which the computer could be put. During the 1980s, there was another move to coordinate all these databases so that records could be cross-referenced, but the proposal was again the focus of strong protest because it was felt that this could lead to abuse by putting too much power into the hands of those who controlled access to the data.

Other attempts to create monolithic databases containing material about private citizens for sale to those who could afford it have been quashed thanks to the efforts of active minorities working in the public's interest. Lotus Development Corporation planned such a database in the late 1980s. The company decided to scrap the idea in response to a huge upswelling of popular protest organized over electronic mail by a few watchdogs who recognized the danger of privacy invasion inherent in the proposed system.

The United States is not alone in its attempts to protect the privacy rights of its citizens. For example, a Swedish data security law passed in 1973 was used in 1986 to shut down a University of Stockholm research database "which had been secretly gathering data on all aspects of the lives of its subjects for more than 20 years" (ComputerWorld, 1986).

4.2.2 Privacy Invasion: Is It All for a Good Cause?

Those who invade our privacy in the name of doing good will argue either that they are providing a service that improves the quality of our lives, or that they are protecting us from the bad guys. Those who claim to be providers of services when they perpetrate invasion of privacy argue that the benefits of easy access to public data outweigh the disadvantages.

People who claim to be protecting us from the bad guys are usually the forces of law and order. They argue that they must be able to ferret out whatever they need to know about anyone and everyone so that they can isolate the bad guys and keep an eye on them.

Recent years have seen advances in communications technology—especially all-digital transmission media (microwave and fiber optics)—that have made it more difficult to carry out wiretaps and conduct covert surveillance. The FBI has therefore felt it necessary to lobby for a new law that would force communications companies to make it possible for the FBI to return to the predigital status quo when the agency was easily able to "remotely intercept suspect communications" (Network World, 1992).

But who decides what is "suspect"? Is there nothing that is off limits to investigators? Is a member of an organization such as the National Organization of Women suspect? How about a paying member of the American Civil Liberties Union? Does it depend on who is in power at the time? Is one suspect if one writes a piece in a local paper expressing reservations about the behavior of some government bigwig?

Providers of services—insurance companies or corporate marketing departments, for example—also need to be controlled. As Rothfeder (1992) points out, "It's an information free-for-all, and even people with little computer expertise can get [most any data they want]." The problem is that, in many instances, we are content to have our privacy invaded. Hospitals need to keep a record of our medical history so they can more efficiently take care of us when we need treatment. Banks need to keep a record of our accounts so they can help us manage our hard-earned money. Credit companies need records of our credit history so they can help us get loans and shop with the convenience of a plastic card. Telephone companies need to be able to trace a number to a name and address because the data can be critical for emergency services.[3]

Insurance companies need to check up on people who abuse the system with fraudulent claims. Corporate marketing departments need to gather data about the marketplace in order to limit the number of people they target for sales pitches of one kind or another. But where do these companies get their information, and what do they do with it?

4.2.3 Data Are a Source of Wealth in the Information Age

Today, there are companies whose entire business consists of collecting and selling lists—lists that contain data about everything and anything. These companies often invade privacy. Sometimes they break the law by acquiring lists from illicit sources. Typically, for example, an employee in a company's computer department might steal a copy of corporate data to sell to the highest bidder. A company that sells lists will use a powerful computer and a technique called profiling to quickly dredge lists of people who fit a certain set of characteristics as specified by a customer. No attempt is made to check out what the customer wants to do with the list.

---

[3]Witness the case where a man suffered a serious heart attack while home alone with his three-year-old daughter. She had been taught to dial 911, but she gave the wrong address. The computer quickly traced the call and she—and the system—saved her father's life.

4.2.4 Is It Possible to Control Invasion of One's Privacy?

This is an interesting debate for teachers to raise with their students, and is therefore included as one of the Do Something About It exercises at the end of this chapter. To some extent, the answer is "yes." You are entitled to make it as difficult as possible for all but the most determined electronic invaders to get at you by supplying as little data as you can get away with whenever you are called on to give out personal information.

If privacy is important to you, an unlisted telephone number is a smart move, though, unfortunately, there is usually a premium on your telephone bill for the privilege.

Think of all the times you are asked to fill out forms—at gas stations, stores, hotels, restaurants, travel agencies, banks, hospitals, schools, and so on. You do not have to provide all the information requested, nor, for that matter, are you obliged to supply correct information. "N/A" (not applicable) or "none of your business" should be your response to all but the most obviously essential questions—unless, of course, you believe that the quality of your life depends on your receiving an armful of junk mail every day.

Read the fine print. You are entitled to reword a document before you sign it if you think the conditions are compromising to privacy, health, or financial well-being. Burnham (1983) points out that "more and more nongovernment agencies are allowed access to [some governmental] databases for purposes of checking out people's credentials." Insurance companies, banks, private investigative agencies and the like are taking advantage of the right of public access, perhaps at your unwitting expense, to protect their own interests and that of their clients. You may unwittingly give up your right to privacy, for example, when you sign an application form which, in the small print, gives a company access to your records.

You may need to work with an attorney to get the wording changes right—which can get expensive—and you may risk being turned down for whatever you are applying for, but at least you would be exercising judgment in regard to matters that may otherwise come back to haunt you.

Ultimately, you can best control invasion of your privacy by being sensitive to the fact that it does go on more than you think. That awareness alone should give you a healthy skepticism whenever you are in the situation where you are asked to divulge personal data. Teachers should help students to become sensitive to this negative side to the otherwise predominantly positive social change brought on by computer technology.

The problem of confidentiality

It would be nice to think that all the personal data we share with doctors, bankers, attorneys, schools, and federal institutions goes no further than the initial data depository. This was largely true in the days when data were recorded on paper and stored in manually managed systems of files and file cabinets. Indeed, before electronic filing became the norm, institutions collected a fraction of the data they collect today simply because the data were too expensive to maintain. This meant that the data were also easier to control and less likely to find their way into other hands.

As Norton (1989) makes painfully clear, however, computerized electronic filing makes data easily available to anyone. "The demands for information," according to Norton, "have grown so much that the orderly flow has become a nearly unchecked torrent. In a single month, the Stanford University Hospital medical records department receives

1,500 requests for medical records information—from insurers, physicians, attorneys, federal and local law officers with subpoenas, and other sources." Thus, confidentiality has largely gone out the door along with filing cabinets and their keys.

4.2.5 Privacy, Faulty Files, and the Right of Public Access

An invasion of privacy is one thing when the data gleaned are correct. It is quite another when data gathered about us are incorrect. Burnham (1983) has noted that one of four people with criminal records in the state of California who bothered to check their records discovered flaws. Only one in ten of this group bothered to exercise the right to force corrections to the records. Quinn (1991) cites one example where 647 out of 1,500 mortgage applications were delayed while mistakes in peoples' credit files were investigated. Errors in data records lead to situations ranging from the mildly amusing to the annoying to the decidedly dangerous.

Neumann (1992) reports the experiences of individuals involved in all three kinds of situations. First, the mildly amusing: Here is an incident that involved a database that contained incorrect data about Archbishop George Cram of Toronto. "Archbishop Cram," quotes Neumann, "enjoys a banana once in a while, but he's not the kind of primate that ape researchers had in mind. The University of Wisconsin's Regional Primate Research Center sent Cram, primate (senior archbishop) of the Anglican Church of Canada, a questionnaire while preparing an international directory of primatology. The envelope was addressed to: George Cram, Primates World Relief and Development Fund."

Next, Neumann reports on an example of a decidedly annoying outcome of incorrect correspondence between the data in different records in a database: "[A medical health insurance] computer system in New York had difficulties distinguishing between hospital patients with the same sex and birthdate when they are treated by the same doctor on the same date. Thus, parents of twins, triplets, etc., have had horrible problems getting reimbursement for hospital expenses."

Finally, here is an incident that underscores the dangerous outcomes of incorrect data in computer records; this one occurred in England. "The National Audit Office," according to the article, "issued a report blaming 'unreliable computer data' for failing to identify high risk groups of women being screened for cervical and breast cancer, which reduces the chances of successful scanning, and so contributes to the deaths of 15,000 women in England each year."

Similar incidents have, of course, occurred in the United States. The only difference in the United States as compared to other countries has been the size of the settlements that have resulted from the inevitable litigation.

What you don't know may hurt you a great deal

Students should be told that they have a right to know what data are stored about them. The United States government as long ago as 1966 passed the Freedom of Information Act, which, in tandem with the 1974 Privacy Act, ensured controlled public access to any database maintained by the federal government. To be more specific, the Freedom of Information Act opened up governmental databases to public scrutiny, and the Privacy Act limited access by making it dependent on the permission of the individual whose records were to be made available.

Meanwhile, the Fair Credit Reporting Act was passed in 1971 to protect peoples' rights of access to data gathered by the financial credit reporting industry. The Family Educational Right and Privacy Act of 1974 guaranteed public access to student reports in the files of federally-funded educational institutions. The Right To Financial Privacy Act of 1978 prohibited federal government access to banking records without either the permission of individuals who are the subject of the search or a search warrant. Other similar legislation has been passed, and more will follow as situations arise in which individual freedoms are violated in more and more creative, and no doubt computerized, ways. Ethics continues to plod along in pursuit of science.

Some of these laws have been duplicated in many U.S. states today. Unfortunately, the ritual involved in actually getting to examine one's record in any particular database discourages most people from trying, even though, as already pointed out, the odds are that there are errors in the record.

What should you and your students do to protect your right to privacy?

Here are some dos and don'ts with regard to protecting your own and your students' right to privacy.

1. **Don't give away your right to privacy.**

   Read the small print when you sign forms of any kind and look for these words: "I agree to allow XYZ company the right to check my credentials however they choose."

2. **Don't feel obliged to answer questions, especially when someone asks you over the phone.**

   This seems obvious, but because people are normally polite, they are often loath to come across as aggressive by challenging another person's questioning. Salespeople in particular count on this natural deference in most customers in order to lead them to commit to a sale. There are cases where computer hackers have broken into computer systems simply by calling up the company and duping one of the employees to give up his or her log-in name and password over the phone (Dateline, 1992).

3. **Do check your credit report periodically.**

   By law (the Fair Credit Reporting Act), you may obtain a credit report at no charge if you have been denied credit by anyone, provided you apply to your local credit bureau within 30 days of being denied. You may also get a free report once per year from a credit-reporting company called TRW. Send a written request. Remember: what you don't know can hurt you. Table 4.1 lists the information required in order for TRW to send consumers their credit report (Ruis, 1992).

4. **Do check the records that are kept on you in local, state, or federal government databases if you have reason to believe there may be errors in your files.**

   If you have no reason for concern, then it is probably fair to assume that your records are correct. There is no point to becoming paranoid. But if, let us say, you are an activist in your union or support any of the politically extreme causes, watch out! Someone may be watching you and collecting data that may come back to haunt you.

Table 4.1	Data Required for Obtaining Credit History from a Credit Information Service

- Full name including middle initial and generation such as Jr., Sr., II, III, etc.
- Current address with zip code.
- Previous addresses with zip code for the past five years (if the consumer has moved).
- Social Security number.
- Year of birth.
- Spouse's first name, if married.
- Verification of current address such as a photocopy of a driver's license or telephone or utility bill. (This is needed to protect the security of a consumers' personal information.)

Send your request to:

TRW Consumer Assistance
P.O. Box 2350
Chatsworth, CA 91313–2350

(Telephone requests will *not* be accepted)

Courtesy Nancy Ruis, Johnstown Credit Bureau, Inc.

Remember, knowledge is power and, as Mowshowitz (1976) points out, "Power has a built-in tendency to preserve itself. . . ." Control of information may very well provide a basis for 'adjusting' the world to suit a particular government agency.

4.2.6 Disinformation and Doublethink

Disinformation can be defined as the deliberate manipulation of truth. The classic disinformation approach is to tell the truth, and nothing but the truth, but *not the whole truth.* **Doublethink,** mentioned earlier, is related to, though not quite the same as, disinformation. George Orwell (1949) describes it thus: "*Doublethink* means the power of holding two contradictory beliefs in one's mind simultaneously, and accepting both of them." The Party[4] intellectual knows in which direction his memories must be altered; he therefore knows that he is playing tricks with reality; but by the exercise of *Doublethink* he also satisfies himself that reality is not violated. "The process," continues Orwell, "has to be conscious, or it would not be carried out with sufficient precision, but it also has to be unconscious, or it would bring with it a feeling of falsity and hence guilt." Doublethink thus "uses conscious deception while retaining the firmness of purpose that goes with complete honesty."

Here is an actual example of disinformation that has a ring of doublethink. A United States bank, which shall go unnamed, mass-mailed applications for a new credit card to thousands of preapproved customers. Spelled out in the sales literature was a complete statement of all the details, beneficial or otherwise, to be kept in mind by potential users of the card. What was curious was that all the numbers that were deemed either attractive or neutral to a customer, such as credit limit or number of days of free credit before interest would be applied on monies owed, were printed in numeric form (say, $5,000,

---

[4]For the "Party," read your friendly banker, insurance company, politician, or any individual or group that has a vested interest in concealing the whole truth.

25 days), which made them stand out among regular text on the printed page. Numbers that the bank wanted to conceal, such as the annual fee or the annual interest rate, were spelled out as text (for example, twenty-one point five percent, thirty dollars).

Check the effect of this for yourself. Quickly scan the foregoing paragraph. Where are the numbers? Are the numerically depicted numbers easier to find than the ones that are depicted textually? The answer is obviously yes. Did the bank in question act unethically in thus disinforming potential customers? You be the judge. Of course, if you are the employee of the bank who came up with this neat idea and who no doubt applied doublethink to assuage any guilt that might have accompanied such deviousness, you will be praised for your cleverness. After all, is the employee not the servant of the company and therefore morally bound to foster the company's profitability? Doublethink, indeed.

There is the story of the chief accountant who for many years got away with embezzlement from his company while faithfully recording in the books every single one of his illegal transactions. At the annual board meeting, he presented each board member with a foot-thick volume of the firm's accounts. Who was going to examine it with more than a cursory glance before signing off on it?

It is clear what this kind of deception has to do with ethics. But what does it have to do with computers? The answer is that computers have made this kind of deception easier to perpetrate even as they have made data more accessible than ever. It is now routine to use the computer to search large volumes of text. Scientific, legal, or other research that once took hours, days, even weeks can now be accomplished in a few seconds. On-line catalogs in libraries have taken much of the drudgery out of research. Finding the material that pertains to an area of study is now a snap. But this simple facility—textual search—is also used to disinform the public.

For example, candidates for political office will conduct searches of the personal files and speeches of their opponents in order to come up with data that they can manipulate in the hopes of alienating voters. Fax machines, e-mail, and other means of rapid and mass dissemination of data are the tools of the disinformation trade. That their opponents have privacy rights and may have since changed a particular position or philosophy is neither here nor there. And if their opponents declare that they have changed viewpoint, they are derided for flip-flopping on the issues. It is almost as if the very enunciation of convictions and commitments leaves one open to misinterpretation through disinformation. Perhaps this is why some politicians studiously avoid having actual opinions on anything at all!

Another way in which computers foster disinformation is by making it easy to produce eye-catching graphics in support of dubious arguments. In general, as Tufte (1990) points out, the less information a graphic contains the less it is to be trusted as a conveyor of information. *Chartjunk* is a term coined by Tufte to describe "creative concepts, where everything counts, but nothing matters." Notice how the contemporary press is peppered with charts. The charts are accurate, but they do not tell the whole truth. How can they? The truth is not that simple. But a few strokes at a computer keyboard will generate a slew of fancy-looking charts from a tiny set of data. The rationale is that the charts sell ideas—and help sell newspapers. Unfortunately, truth often gets muddled along the way.

A final note of warning on the privacy issue comes from Rothfeder (1992):

'Society could pay in the end for its failure to take privacy more seriously, according to the experts. When individuals are unable to control information about themselves they become passive,' notes privacy lawyer Robert Belair. 'They sense that they're no longer participants in the world around them—just witnesses to it, under the thumb of decision-makers. And they stop being productive citizens.'

Everyone needs to be sensitized to the issues raised in this section. Teachers are in an ideal position to help prepare future generations of students so that they do not succumb to the machinations of those who would seek to control their lives.

4.3 Computing Inequities

Chapter 1 argued the case for using computer-based technology for teaching and learning. It examined the considerable body of research that has been carried out to determine the effectiveness of technology use in education. The conclusions, though tentative this early in the history of computer use in schools, argued strongly for the extension of the carefully considered incorporation of the computer into the curriculum. It will therefore be useful to consider how equitably this change is being carried out.

Education is not about the status quo; it is about change. Educators are leaders, charged to advance not only the minds of the children under their care, but also the society into which those children are being led. Educators should be model citizens, responsible for leading the nation's children by precept and by example. Commitment from teachers and school administrators is a prerequisite to equal opportunity for students in schools. This commitment to noble goals cannot come from an ignorant mind; nor can it come from an uncommitted heart.

Teachers and administrators should thus consider how well they understand the implications of the Equal Protection Clause of the Fourteenth Amendment to the Constitution. They also have a moral responsibility to examine how genuinely they support the goals of equal opportunity for all their students regardless of the students' race, color, or sex. Only teachers and administrators who support these goals should be permitted to work with children. The Do Something About It section at the end of this chapter provides the opportunity to examine where you stand on cross-cultural attitudes. After all, only educators with convictions in accord with the Constitution can be expected to fulfill their duty of providing the kind of education that will advance the state of the society which they serve.

4.3.1 Haves and Have-Nots: Rich versus Poor

"For computer-based knowledge to become an extension of a human mind, that mind must at least have access to the technology. The poor will not immediately have such access, placing them at a . . . disadvantage" (Madron, 1985). Piller (1992) describes "the creation of the technological underclass in America's public schools." "In 1984," he notes, "white children used computers in elementary and secondary schools at about twice the rate of African Americans and Hispanics." This corroborates the experience of Faflick (1982) who referenced a survey of Market Data Retrieval Inc. which found, in 1992, that "80% of the country's 2,000 largest and richest public high schools now have at least one micro[computer], while 60% of the 2,000 poorest schools have none."

However, if mere numbers representing investment in technology were useful indicators of actual, productive computer use in schools, it would appear that this situation has been largely corrected. "By 1989," Pillar writes, "according to the U.S. Bureau of Census, nearly the same percentages of those three groups [White, African American, and Hispanic] used computers in high schools. Elementary schools also made dramatic progress. And disparities between rich and poor and between public and private schools seemed to narrow just as sharply."

But Pillar was skeptical of the relevance of the United States Bureau of Census statistics and decided to see for himself what was going on in the schools. His findings were somewhat discouraging. "I visited inner-city, rural, and suburban schools in various parts of the country," he wrote, "and after discussions with scores of teachers, students, and school administrators, an inescapable conclusion emerged: Computer-based education in poor schools is in deep trouble." Not only did these schools lack the funds and skills to finance the maintenance of their computer hardware. They also lacked the training to make the best use of the machines. "In most cases," Pillar concluded, "computers simply perpetuate a two-tier system of education for rich and poor."

Right now there are pockets of privilege, so to speak, among the poorer school districts, where forward-looking parents, administrators, and teachers, sometimes sponsored by local business and/or by one or other of the major personal computer manufacturers, have taken on the challenge of providing the best possible educational opportunity for children. Usually, the key ingredient of success has been the driving force of significant individuals who have galvanized the community and done what is necessary, through grants and donations, to make computer-integrated teaching a reality in their schools. (For more on grant writing, see chapter 14.)

Unfortunately, however, there are still many school districts, even in the United States, where a half-hearted acceptance of the value of suitably integrated educational technology, tempered to some extent by economic realities, have resulted in children being denied the opportunity to share in the benefits enjoyed by the privileged few. Hardly a school in America today does not have computers for student use; every year the ratio of students to computers improves in the students' favor. Yet, as Pillar (1992) observed, many of the machines in the poorer schools are used "so rigidly and ineptly as to repel students."

A useful exercise would be to consider and discuss some of the special difficulties experienced by inner-city and rural school districts which result in underutilizing computer-based technology. The Do Something About It section at the end of the chapter invites you to brainstorm with colleagues or classmates to come up with ways in which these school districts can optimize their investment in the technology and overcome the difficulties under which such schools have to operate. One component of a solution might be to spend no more money on any more machines until adequate money has been appropriated for training the administrators and faculty, since they will be responsible for preparing the learning environments where the children can take advantage of the technology.

Figure 4.2

Girls should be given every encouragement to become skilled in the use of computer technology.
Photo courtesy of Jo Sanders

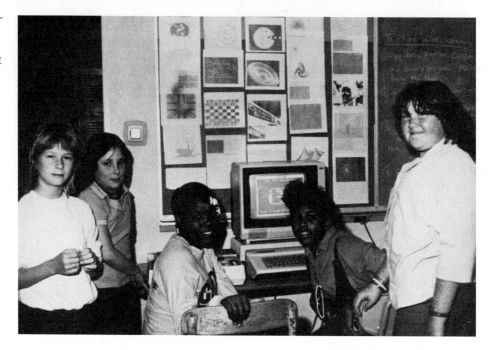

4.3.2 Haves and Have-Nots: Girls versus Boys

Women continue to suffer from stereotyping that casts them in the mold of the technologically inept. LaPlante (1992) speaks of the "entrenched high-tech sexism" that many women experience climbing the corporate ladder. She speaks of the glass ceiling, referring to the unseen but all-too-evident obstacles barring the promotion of women beyond male-determined levels in the corporate hierarchy. "Even women who make it through the glass ceiling still face a lot of obstacles—significant ones."

Noble (1992) reminds us that it is not just the glass ceiling that acts as a barrier to equal opportunity for women. Far more women are held back by the "sticky floor," a term coined by sociologist Catherine White Berheide to describe the millions of women paraprofessionals condemned to " 'women's work' . . . home health care aides and child support workers, and 'administrative support' or clerical staff." Unfortunately this "women's work" is low paying. It is also nontechnical in nature.

The problem pervades our social institutions, starting with the home and continuing in school. Sanders (1987) observed that "girls and boys use the computer equally when they are required to in class, but as soon as they're allowed a choice—such as after school or in elective computer courses—girls see that boys take advantage of the opportunity far more often than girls do. This reinforces the notion that computers are a male thing." Bill Arrigoni (1992), a teacher in a Washington State secondary school, reports that "a computer teacher in his school asked him if she could borrow his son's baseball card collection so that she could use them in a database lesson. Bill told her, "That's fine for the boys, but what about the girls?" The teacher said she had not thought about that, and decided to use cassette tapes for her lesson instead.

Unfortunately, as the foregoing illustrations suggest, women often stereotype themselves. For example, as recently as 1991, Ditchburn, writing in the London *Sunday Times* about women and careers in information technology (IT), implies that women are less likely than men to be "technically-qualified graduates" and that therefore women are not suited for technically oriented careers in IT. Condescendingly, the article concedes that there is a place in the IT industry for women "in sales and support." What is remarkable about the article is that it is written by a woman who is a member of Women into Information Technology (WIT), an advocacy group for women's rights.

All this belies the evidence from extensive research which strongly suggests that girls are at least equal to boys in tasks that involve communication skills and skills related to math and problem solving. A review of research into the effectiveness of microcomputers in education done between 1980 and 1987 showed no significant differences in ability between male and female students in any subject area or age group (Roblyer, 1988). Becker (1987) noted that boys and girls at the middle and high school levels were enrolled in programming courses in approximately equal numbers, but that girls were more likely to enroll in those programming classes that had higher math as a prerequisite. On the other hand, Choi (1987) found that males were more likely than females to retain knowledge accruing from scientific experiments. Johnson (1985b) goes further in concluding that "across all instructional conditions, boys performed better than girls on recognition and problem-solving questions."

Why is there such a discrepancy between the findings of one group of researchers and another? The answer may lie in the fact that both Choi and Johnson studied children of middle-school age, whereas the data examined by Roblyer and Becker was drawn from studies conducted with students of all age groups. Sanders (1986) found that girls in the middle and high school grades were less likely to take advantage of the opportunity to use computers in school. This is hardly surprising, according to Sanders, considering the male-oriented image of technology in general and computing in particular. Adolescent girls in particular shy away from being identified with what they have grown up to perceive as "masculine" activities.

Johnson (1985b) corroborates Sanders's findings, concluding that boys were "less individualistic and more competitive, felt more academic support from teachers, and believed the computer to be a male domain." Behaviors and attitudes such as these suggest that fundamental inequities are at work. There is plenty of evidence that girls are less likely than boys to be given the opportunity to gain advantage from the use of technology. This suggests that any solution to the problem of gender inequities will be most effective if applied from the very beginning of the educational process. Children, boys and girls, must be protected from the rigid stereotypes of masculinity/femininity that lead to inequities and abuse of all kinds. By the time we have grown to adulthood, much of the damage has been done and, while not irrevocable, is much more difficult to repair.

No problems, only solutions

Jo Sanders, now director of the Teacher Education Equity Project, was, until recently, director of the Women's Action Alliance, a nonprofit organization working to improve educational equity for girls and women. Funded by a grant from the United States Department of Education, the Alliance conducted a Computer Equity Training project between 1984 and 1986 to help teachers close the gender gap associated with computer use. Since

Figure 4.3
Girls must have the same opportunity as boys to learn about, enjoy, and benefit from computer-based technology.

Table 4.2	**The Principles of Computer Equity**
1. Focus specifically on girls.	
2. Target girls in groups.	
3. Design activities around girls' existing interests.	
4. Stress the usefulness of computers.	
5. Eliminate biased computer practices.	
6. Pay attention to your software.	
7. Let others know.	
8. Do it again next year.	

Courtesy Jo Sanders

then the Computer Equity Expert Project, sponsored by the National Science Foundation, IBM, American Express, Chevron, Hewlett Packard, Intel Foundation, Xerox Foundation, and The Westinghouse Foundation, has trained close to 200 educators throughout the United States to act as leaders in the program to increase girls' involvement with computers, math, and science.

It is beyond the scope of this book to itemize the 96 strategies for increasing girls' computer use recommended by Sanders and Stone (1986) in their book *The Neuter Computer: Computers for Girls and Boys.* Table 4.2 lists the Principles of Computer Equity defined by Jo Sanders. These principles should guide teachers when they are working to ensure that girls have the same opportunity as boys to learn about, enjoy, and benefit from computer-based technology.

The following are examples of the kinds of strategies that can help to overcome the stereotypes that perpetuate the computer gender gap.

Schedule computer use in your classroom or school. A first-come, first-served system tends to favor the boys. So reserve the computers for boys on Mondays and Wednesdays, for girls on Tuesdays and Thursdays, and have a free-for-all on Friday.

Use girls as computer lab assistants, or to demonstrate work that they have done on the computer. This seems like reverse inequity, giving preference to the girls, but it is necessary in order to break the stereotype.

Encourage homework done by computer. More and more schools provide adequate access to computers for it to be feasible, for example, to require students to complete writing assignments on the computer.

A very useful exercise would be for you to brainstorm with your colleagues or classmates to come up with strategies of your own. Then try them out, make a note of the most effective, and publish them in a booklet to share. This is one of the Do Something About It exercises recommended at the end of the chapter.

4.3.3 Haves and Have-Nots: Whites versus Minorities

It seems absurd to have to point out that the color of one's skin makes no difference whatsoever with regard to one's level of intelligence. My experience teaching in schools K–12 in Europe, Africa, the Middle East, and North America has proved that the range of intelligence among these diverse cultural and ethnic groups is identical. Those who believe otherwise should be helped to recognize one simple fact: that they are guilty of inexcusable prejudice born of unfortunate cultural bias.

Such bias continues to plague our social structures in general, and our educational institutions in particular. In much the same way as for girls, African Americans and Hispanics are not expected, and often do not expect themselves, to achieve success in technological fields such as those associated with computers. Much of the problem, unlike the gender inequities, is that children in these ethnic groups are more likely to come from families living below the poverty line, which translates into a lower likelihood that they will either attend schools in the wealthier, more technology-rich districts, attend school on a regular basis, or graduate from high school.

Statistics published by the United States Department of Education (1992) indicate that in 1990, 10.7% of white families were below the poverty level, while 28.1% and 31.9% of Hispanic and African-American families, respectively, lived below the poverty level. In 1991, 8.4% of white 14- to 34-year-olds had dropped out of school, compared to 36.9% and 13.3% of Hispanic and African-American 14- to 34-year-olds, respectively. In addition to dropping out, Hispanic, African-American and Native-American[5] students who attended school had the highest absentee rates as compared to white students. Finally, average SAT scores continued to bear out a correlation with poverty levels.

---

[5]Native-American data were not provided in the *Digest of Education Statistics* for most of the reports considered relevant for this analysis.

Average verbal and mathematical scores for whites in 1990–91 were 441 and 489, respectively; for Hispanics, 369 and 416; for African Americans, 351 and 385; and for Native Americans, 393 and 437.

The SAT scores confirm the inevitable outcome of a neglected K–12 education. What is the connection of all this with computing inequities? Sanders (1986) makes it clear that computing inequity "matters a lot—first, for educational reasons. Kids are simply better off with computer applications, computer-based instruction, and programming instruction." "Computer equity," she goes on to say, "matters for our role as citizens. Many people are concerned about what computers, lasers, robotics, and other high-technology will do to employment patterns, national security, privacy rights, crime, and our sense of ourselves as independent beings with control over our lives. While these are in part real issues, they are also in part exaggerated fears, fed by ignorance of the technology and our relation to it. . . . Finally," Sanders points out, "computer equity matters occupationally. Computers will figure in an increasing number of [relatively well-paying] jobs."

The solution?

With leadership and support from administration, teachers should employ strategies along the lines of those that have already proved effective in rectifying gender inequities. There is no doubt that a concerted effort must be made to help minorities because, as with girls, it is almost impossible for them to help themselves while they are children. Later, when they have the power that comes with adulthood, it is often too late for them to make up for a lost education.

4.3.4 Haves and Have-Nots: The Lack of Equal Access to Information

Since knowledge is power, and since not all children have equal access to information because of disparities in the funding and management of different school systems, it stands to reason that many children are at a serious disadvantage. All other things being equal, some students attend schools where they have access to libraries of electronic data in the form of interactive text and video,[6] with quality educational software to complement other forms of instruction, and with open lines of communication between themselves and students in other schools at home and abroad. Such privileged students are more likely to receive a more rounded and comprehensive educational experience than students attending less technologically endowed schools.

4.3.5 The Problems of the Haves and Have-Nots is Founded on More than Just Financial Inequities

Chapter 14, which deals with grant writing, will show that finance need have little to do with disadvantage. Money can always be raised when people are determined to provide for their children the best possible learning environment. Being aware of and caring about the lack of equity are the keys to overcoming the problems of inequities pertaining to educational opportunity. Administrators who care will make sure that their teachers have the training, the tools, and the time to perform both effectively and equitably in the classroom. This will build morale and foster good attitudes among teachers. For their part, teachers whose caring is thus endorsed by a good administration will be more likely to grow professionally, always looking to advance and update their teaching skills for the benefit of all children.

Parents and teachers have a huge responsibility for bringing about the kind of cultural change that alone can rectify the inequities described in this section. They are with the children from day to day. The children soak up adult ideas, attitudes, and prejudices with the characteristic receptiveness of young, unformed minds. Even what they learn from each other is learned indirectly from some adult role model. So often, we hear parents disavowing responsibility for the sexist or racist behavior the children "bring home from school." So often, we hear teachers explaining away a child's intellectual or physical inadequacy on the grounds of sex or race. Everyone blames everyone else, and no one takes responsibility for doing anything about it.

Teachers like to believe that they touch the future. If they really want to touch the future, they should take on themselves the responsibility to teach the whole child—not just the intellectual self of the child, but the cultural and moral self, too. This is a challenging responsibility because it means that the teacher must have come to terms with his or her own prejudices and set them aside. It also means that the teacher must be willing to make the

---

[6]Chapter 11 will discuss on-line database retrieval services such as DIALOG Information Services' *CLASSMATE*™ instruction program.

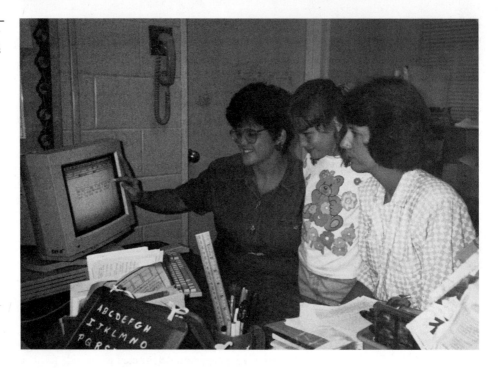

Figure 4.5
Parents and teachers have a huge responsibility for bringing about cultural change.
Courtesy Susan Giorgio Bond

effort to engage the support of parents or guardians if any success is to be achieved. This will not be possible unless teachers get support from school administrators. Indeed, in the end, it must be a community effort. But teachers can be the leaven in the bread, causing it to rise and take shape. The commitment to change must begin with the individual teacher.

There is great hope that computers and communications (C&C) will once and for all open wide the door to home–school communications, bringing the school into the community and the community into the school. Chapter 11 will explore this and other benefits of C&C.

■ Looking Back

The purpose of this chapter has been to argue the case for incorporating into school curricula the discussion with students of the computer-related ethical and legal issues that have been raised. There will always be a debate about the extent to which schools should become involved in such discussion. But it is difficult to see why taxpayers would not support the schools in their duty to prepare children to address ethical and legal problems, when ignorance of these issues will leave students vulnerable to victimization of the kinds described. As Sanders (1986) observed, we can restrict ourselves as teaching professionals to the narrow task of working within the framework of the narrow academic responsibilities that are assigned to us, or we can extend the scope of that commitment to include the parental/counseling/leadership roles that our students need more than ever today.

The Constitution demands the separation of church and state, not the separation of education from the development of a knowledgeable and responsible citizenry. Our students are getting an education in ethics one way or another—mostly from their peers, and unfortunately their peers need as much help as anyone.

To pretend that teachers are not responsible for sensitizing students to the issues raised is to behave like ostriches burying their heads in the sand. Times have changed. The family unit is not as reliable as it once was from a nurturing perspective. Survival in this late-20th-century, so-called developed society puts a strain on families that undermines the efforts of parents to provide the best environment for their children as they grow up. Indeed, many married couples are forgoing parenthood for this reason. So, schools must assume more responsibility than ever for the kind of child-raising that goes beyond the mere brokering of textbook knowledge.

As James Truslow Adams pointed out: "There are obviously two educations. One should teach us how to make a living, and the other how to live." Increasing students' sensitivity to the issues of computer-related privacy invasion and inequality will help them in respect to both of Adams's "educations." It will help them to make a living as well as teach them how to live. On the professional level, graduated students will function more effectively if they protect themselves against the unfair competition that comes with privacy invasion and against the unequal opportunity arising from a prejudicial conception that women lack technological competence. On the personal level, students will learn to be conscious of, and give due recognition to, the privacy and equal rights of others.

The question every teacher must address is this: Is it fair that just a few of today's children are already enjoying the advantages that computers, used appropriately, can bring? The objective of this book is to open a window into the classroom of tomorrow. This classroom is already available for a privileged few; we must ensure that it is available to all.

Looking Forward

The next chapter will conclude the discussion of the ethical issues related to computer use in today's information society. Software piracy is very prevalent and is often carried on by otherwise upstanding citizens, even though it is against the law. It will be useful to examine the issues involved with a view to appreciating why it should be discouraged in schools. The unethical activities of some hackers, experts in manipulating computer systems, is less likely to actively involve more than a small minority of students. But it will certainly involve all of us passively as victims of crimes perpetrated by such hackers. Knowledge will give students the power to protect themselves against the kind of activities in which unethical hackers engage.

Do Something About It: Exercises and Projects

1. What are some of the special difficulties experienced by inner-city and rural school districts that result in underutilizing computer-based technology? Brainstorm with colleagues or classmates to come up with ways in which these school districts can optimize their investment in the technology and overcome the difficulties under which such schools must operate.

2. "It is impossible to control invasion of one's privacy." Discuss the pros and cons of this argument. In what ways, other than those discussed in this chapter, can you protect your privacy? Is it important to raise this with students? Why?

3. Brainstorm with your colleagues or classmates to come up with further strategies for encouraging girls to get involved in computers, math, and science. Then try them out, make a note of the most effective, and publish them in a booklet.

4. Repeat exercise 3 with a focus on minority computing inequities.

Girls and technology

by Jo Sanders, Center for Advanced Study in Education, City University of New York Graduate Center, New York, New York.

We have known for years that many girls avoid computers. They tend not to take advanced computer courses, tend not to join after-school computer clubs, tend not to enter computer contests as much as boys do. We have known that computer avoidance is unhealthy for girls' future careers and lives.

Some of us have also known that girls decline computer opportunities because they feel that an interest in computers is not quite properly feminine—after all, they see that mostly boys and men use computers in school, at home, in the media, and elsewhere. This makes many girls bypass the computer room, which leads to the absence of their girlfriends, which reinforces the belief that technology is not appropriate for girls.

What we now know is how to make girls stop avoiding the computer. In the Computer Equity Expert Project[1] 200 educators, representing every state, became computer-equity trainers for faculty in their schools. One-fifth were men. After attending a week-long seminar, they taught two workshops on computer equity for girls and led teams of faculty and sometimes students as well in carrying out strategies aimed at increasing girls' participation in computer, math and science, both curricular and extracurricular.

Here is how three of the 200 computer-equity trainers and their faculty teams have had remarkable success with girls' involvement with computers in a year and a half.

Nancy Mahosky
Blackhawk High School
Beaver Falls, Pennsylvania

Strategies

- Nancy held a computer open house for parents at which all the student guides were girls. She showed a continuously running videotape on gender equity near the food. The program booklet described the school's computer-equity program.

- She talked with all the eighth- and ninth-grade girls in an assembly just for them about the importance of taking computer, math, and science classes.

- She invited girls and adult females of their choice to a computer brunch, with food donated by local businesses. The first two hours were spent at the computers, followed by brunch.

(continued)

Jo Sanders, author of the case study

The logo for the Computer Equity Expert Project
Courtesy Jo Sanders

[1]Funded by the National Science Foundation, IBM, Hewlett Packard, Intel, Xerox, American Express, Chevron and Westinghouse from 1990 to 1993.

Case Study 4 (continued)

- To make sure there would be girls in a new computer club for eighth and ninth graders, Nancy printed invitations that specifically mentioned girls. She also "went around to the homerooms and asked the teachers to pick out some good girls to encourage to come." As a result, the club is now half male and half female, and most of the eighth-grade girls go on to take computers in the ninth grade.

- Nancy specifically invites girls to come to the computer club for seniors, which used to be all boys, and to bring a friend. The club is now 30% female and has a female club officer.

- Nancy uses her turn for the teachers' "guest editorial" in the televised daily announcements by talking about the computer gender gap and encouraging girls to come to computer clubs and take computer electives.

- To prepare for the day a woman engineer came to school to speak, Nancy "went around to the homerooms and handed girls something to read about the woman and what we would be doing there—you know, to make it sound interesting." Twenty-five girls attended.

- Nancy arranged a lunch at which older girls tell younger ones about their advanced computer courses and career plans.

Results

In addition to the results above, the before-and-after female-enrollment figures are

Course	Pre-Program	Post-Program
Computer applications	45%	55%
BASIC	40%	52%
Pascal	30%	41%
Business Computer Club	53%	77%

Nancy is eager to see if next year's FORTRAN class, which in the past has been 100% male, will include girls.

Wanda Lindsey
Campus High School
Wichita, Kansas

Girls and computers go together.
Photo courtesy of Jo Sanders

Strategies

- Wanda puts technology-related articles, cartoons and statistics up in the hallway for girls to see.

- She set up an activity period during club meeting time when girls can meet with women speakers such as engineers and systems analysts.

- She takes girls to conferences on women in nontraditional careers.

- All counselors were required to meet with the computer teachers to learn more about what the classes involve and how to advise the students better.

- Wanda invited a woman engineer to talk to her programming and computer technology classes.

- She takes a minute at every faculty meeting to present a point, fact, or finding concerning computer equity for girls.

- At the awards banquet for senior girls, Wanda presented a certificate to a girl who had been an unusually active member of the computer-equity team, recruiting many girls to spend time on computers and take advanced courses.

- Wanda has individual conversations and writes notes to girls who show special promise, encouraging them to enroll in advanced computer courses.

(continued)

Case Study 4 (concluded)

Results

The before-and-after female-enrollment figures are:

Course	Pre-Program	Post-Program
Advanced programming	17%	56%
Computer technology	47%	67%
Pascal	0%	27%
Business Computer Club	53%	77%

Carolyn Reppert Sears
Fox Lane Middle School
Bedford, New York

Strategies

- Carrie started a Girls' Equity Committee that meets weekly for fifteen minutes of discussion and refreshments and then adjourns to the computer lab.

- Feeling that homeroom announcements of the Girls' Computer Marathon were not having enough impact, Carrie and the girls created invitations on the computer: "Have fun! Refreshments! Bring a friend!" Carrie handed them out in the halls (the middle-school-age girls were too embarrassed to do this themselves!). It worked: many girls attended.

- Carrie gave a presentation about computer equity for girls at a school assembly.

- She wrote an article about computer equity for a school publication distributed to all town residents in the early fall.

- She sends copies of the Girls' Equity Committee sign-in sheets to members of the faculty computer-equity team, letting them know whom to encourage to continue to participate.

- Carrie invites teachers to drop in at meetings of the Girls' Equity Committee, and to bring a couple of their female students with them.

- Among the special activities of the Girls' Equity Committee are conducting a survey of girls' favorite computer games and making jewelry with recycled computer parts.

Results

The computer lab, which formerly had a ratio of two girls to 25 boys during free-time access after school, now has a one-to-one ratio.

Talk About It

Topics for discussion based on the case study.

1. It is unusual for a school to carry out the sorts of gender equity efforts that Nancy Mahosky, Wanda Lindsey, and Carrie Sears carried out. Why is this so?

2. What was it about Nancy's, Wanda's, and Carrie's strategies that worked so well with the girls in their schools?

3. One-fifth of the trainers were male, and they were as successful as the female trainers in increasing girls' presence in computing. Nevertheless, male educators often mistakenly assume that gender equity in education is the concern of women alone. What would you say to a male educator to obtain his active participation in gender equity activities?

4. Using Nancy's, Wanda's, and Carrie's strategies as examples of the kind of things that can be done, what strategies can you devise for the following goals?

- Increase the awareness level of faculty members of the need for gender equity in computing.

- Increase the number of girls participating in a districtwide computing contest.

- Increase the awareness level of parents of the need for encouraging their daughters in computing.

- Use the assistance of girls now taking advanced computing to encourage younger ones to take these courses.

- Ensure that when middle-school girls continue on to high school, they will continue to receive encouragement in computing.

◾ References

Apple Computer, Inc. *The Impact of Computers on K–12 Education: A Resource for Decision-Makers.* Computer Software, 1990.

Becker, Henry Jay. "Using Computers for Instruction: The Results and Implications of a National Survey May Surprise You." *Byte,* vol. 12, no. 2, February 1987, pp. 149–62.

Burnham, David. *The Rise of the Computer State.* New York: Random House, 1983.

Choi, Byung-Soon, Eugene Gennaro. "The Effectiveness of Using Computer Simulated Experiments on Junior High Students' Understanding of the Volume Displacement Concept." *Journal of Research in Science Teaching,* vol. 24, no. 6, 1987, pp. 539–52. See Apple Computer Corporation, 1990.

ComputerWorld. *News item.* Edition c. 1986.

Dateline. *Interview with Reformed Computer Hacker.* NBC video, October 27.

Ditchburn, Rosalind. "Helping Women Take Part in IT." *London Sunday Times,* August 4, 1991, sect. 4, p. 9.

Faflick, Philip. "Peering into the Poverty Gap." *Time,* November 15, p. 69. Referenced in Johnson, 1985a.

Johnson, Deborah G., John W. Snapper. *Ethical Issues in the Use of Computers.* Belmont, CA: Wadsworth, 1985a.

Johnson, Roger T., David W. Johnson, Mary Beth Stanne. "Effects of Cooperative, Competitive, and Individualistic Goal Structures on Computer-Assisted Instruction." *Journal of Educational Psychology,* vol. 77, no. 6, 1985b, pp. 668–77.

LaPlante, Alice. "Women IS Professionals Battle Entrenched High-tech Sexism." *InfoWorld,* October 19, 1992, p. 60.

Mowshowitz, Abbe. *Conquest of the Will: Information Processing in Human Affairs.* Reading, MA: Addison-Wesley, 1976. Referenced in Johnson, 1985a.

Network World. Editorial: "Help Smother the FBI's Primal Scream." September 28, 1992, p. 5.

Neumann, Peter G. "Risks to the Public in Computers and Related Systems." *Software Engineering Notes,* vol. 17, no. 3, July 1992, pp. 5–7.

Noble, Barbara Presley. "And Now the 'Sticky Floor.' " *New York Times,* Sunday, November 22, 1992, p. 23.

Norton, Clark. "Absolutely NOT Confidential." *Hippocrates,* March/April 1989, pp. 52–59.

Orwell, George. *1984.* New York: Harcourt, Brace, Jovanovich, 1949.

Pillar, Charles. "Separate Realities: The Creation of the Technological Underclass in America's Schools." *MacWorld,* September 1992.

Postman, Neil. *Amusing Ourselves to Death.* Harmondsworth, Middlesex, England: Penguin Books, 1986.

Quinn, Jane Bryant. "Guarding Your Good Name." *Newsweek,* August 12, 1991.

Roblyer, M. D. "The Effectiveness of Microcomputers in Education: A Review of the Research from 1980–1987." *Technological Horizons in Education,* vol. 16, no. 2, September 1988, pp. 85–89.

Rothfeder, Jeffrey. "Taking a Byte Out of Privacy." *USA Weekend,* August 28–30, 1992, pp. 4–6.

Ruis, Nancy, Director, Johnstown Credit Bureau, Inc., 1992.

Sanders, Jo Shuchat, Antonia Stone. *The Neuter Computer: Computers for Girls and Boys.* New York: Neal-Schuman, 1986.

Sanders, Jo. "Closing the Computer Gender Gap." *Education Digest,* October, 1986, pp. 20–23.

Sanders, Jo. *Do Your Female Students Say "No, Thanks" to the Computer?* Flyer of the Women's Action Alliance, funded by Apple Computer Corporation, 1987.

Shanker, Albert. "Traditional Family Values . . ." *New York Times,* November 8, 1992, p. 7.

Tufte, Edward. *Envisioning Information.* Cheshire, CT: Graphics Press, 1990.

Turn, Rein, Willis H. Ware. "Privacy and Security Issues in Information Systems." *IEEE Transactions on Computers,* C-25, 12, December 1976. Referenced in Johnson, 1985a.

Computer Crime: Software Piracy and Hacking

Some are born good, some make good, some are caught with the goods.
Thomas Jefferson (1743–1826)

For every man there exists a bait which he cannot resist swallowing.
Friedrich Wilhelm Nietzsche (1844–1900)

A teacher who can arouse a feeling for one single good action, . . . accomplishes more than he who fills our memory with row on row of natural objects, classified with name and form.
Johann Wolfgang von Goethe (1749–1832)

Learning Outcomes

This chapter will focus on software piracy and hacking. The former comes close to home because theft of software is so easy, so little frowned on, and so common that few of us can honestly claim to have never been involved in it. Hacking involves the infiltration of computer systems, either for the fun of it, or for purposes of sabotage, damaging or stealing data, or embezzlement. It takes a special kind of skill and a certain obsessiveness, which limits the number of people likely to get actively involved. But we are all victims of hacking, whether we realize it or not. So it will be useful to familiarize ourselves with the ethical ins and outs and ethical rights and wrongs of these activities so that we can establish our own standards in their regard and help our students do the same.

Here is a breakdown of the topics that will be covered in this chapter:

- Software piracy
  - Theft of programs
  - Copyright law as applied to software
  - Public domain software versus shareware versus licensed software
  - Software protection
  - Steps schools should take to discourage software piracy
- Security: Hacking and cracking
  - Computer viruses and vaccines
  - Trespass of computer systems
  - Money theft (embezzlement)
  - Computer system security

5.1 Software Piracy

Everyone is directly or indirectly vulnerable to becoming a victim of computer crime. Many of us will also be tempted at one time or another to perpetrate the crime of stealing software. A very small minority of students, especially those who are more technically oriented, may find themselves involved in activities associated with hacking or, still worse, "cracking"—a once popular name for criminal hacking. The likelihood of students being involved in unauthorized infiltration of computer systems or in electronic theft of money is remote. Nonetheless, it is useful to know what is involved in each type of computer crime. It is also important that students discuss these issues, so that, on the one hand, they can be helped to make good ethical judgments about what is right and wrong in these matters, and, on the other hand, to help them avoid becoming victims of computer crime.

Needless to say, the teacher will need to decide what would be an appropriate time to bring up these issues with students. A useful brainstorming session (see the Do Something About It section at the end of the chapter) would be to join with a group of colleagues or classmates to come up with ideas on just when and how such a discussion might take place with students.

The remainder of this section will look briefly at one type of computer crime—software piracy—which is most likely to involve teachers in schools where policies are not well laid down and applied. Section 5.2 will deal with the unethical activities that come under the umbrella of hacking.

5.1.1 Theft of Programs

Teachers who use computers may not be aware of it, but it is quite possible that they are running pirated software on the systems they use at school or at home. Their students may be doing the same. On the other hand, they may be well aware of the existence of pirated software and know that it is, strictly speaking, stolen property. Their sense of guilt may not be strong enough to cause them to erase the unauthorized version from the computer system(s) they and their students use. At least one school associated with a bona fide religious group uses pirated software with the full approval of the school's administration! As if that is not bad enough, suit has been filed against no less an upholder of the law than the U.S. government's Department of Justice for theft of copyrighted software.

In 1990 alone, it is estimated that the software industry in the United States lost $2.4 billion to piracy—over 33% of its potential annual revenue. The good news is that the losses for 1991 represented a decrease of 41% from what they were in 1990, thanks in no small measure to the efforts of watchdog groups such as the **Software Publishers Association (SPA).** Worldwide estimated losses in 1992, however, are between $10 and $12 billion (Lewis, 1992).

Why is there so much blatant copying of software? Is it because computer software is intangible and therefore not real? Is it because it is so easy to get away with, and so we do not worry about getting caught? Is it because it is so easy to copy software that it just does not seem wrong to do so? Is it because we view software as a book we borrow from a library—intellectual property of which we feel we have unlimited use? Is it because we know that there is a lot of software (public domain software) that is free and so we question why we should have to pay for any of it? As Ken Wasch, executive director of the SPA observed: "It's ironic that people who would never think about stealing a candy bar from a drugstore seem to have no qualms about copying a $500 software package" (Lewis, 1992).

As one might expect in a democracy, there is an association called the Free Software Foundation which argues that it is wrong to make people pay for software. The foundation believes that, like other intellectual property such as library books, all software should be available free of charge. However, one problem the Free Software Foundation has not yet resolved is the fact that they do not have the law on their side—it is as simple as that.

Sometimes software piracy may be unintentional. A White Paper of the Software Publishers Association (SPA, 1992a) notes: "Copying software is easy to do and so difficult to control. Often piracy is unintentional and can be attributed to ignorance on the part of the end-users. Because copying software is so easy and because license agreements can be confusing, many people don't realize that they are breaking the law." That notwithstanding, most people do not usually need to be told it is wrong to take software they have not paid for—just as people do not usually need to be told it is wrong to shoplift.

5.1.2 Copyright Law as Applied to Software

What exactly does copyright law say?

Federal copyright law explains it thus: "It is illegal to make a copy of a piece of software for any reason other than as a back-up without the permission of the copyright holder." Copyright law has the same overall objective as patent law: "to promote the progress of science and useful arts." Why, after all, should software developers waste time and money inventing products of benefit to society if someone else can, with impunity, steal their ideas and get all the profit from them? Willett (1992) reports that the Software Copyright Protection Bill (1992), now Public Law 102–561, elevates copying software programs for "commercial advantage" or "private financial gain" from a misdemeanor offense to a felony. The law appears to be catching up with science.

The SPA has, since 1984, been the principal trade group of the PC software industry. One of its roles has been that of watchdog for the industry, maintaining an antipiracy hotline (1–800–388–7478) which accepts calls (as many as 30 per day) reporting software violations. According to its literature, SPA investigates these reports and, if there is solid evidence that an institution (including schools) has illegally duplicated large numbers of software programs, either works cooperatively with the offending institution to remedy the situation or petitions the federal court for a seizure order to force a supervised audit of the institution's software inventory. Funding to support any ensuing litigation is provided by SPA member companies, and according to Ken Wasch (1991), SPA executive director, "We are filing new lawsuits every few days."

The Software Publishers Association means business. By the end of 1992, the association had grown to a membership of over 1,000 representing the leading publishers in the business, consumer, and education software markets. Since 1988, SPA "has filed over 150 lawsuits on behalf of its members and obtained numerous search and seizure orders against businesses, computer dealers, bulletin board services, and educational institutions that have violated its members' copyrights" (SPA, 1992b) (emphasis added). As reported in *Information Week* (1991), the Business Software Alliance, a sister organization of SPA, investigates software piracy that takes place outside the United States, especially in countries where software is copied wholesale by bootleg operations and marketed at a fraction of the normal cost.

Schools are as likely to be targets as any other institution, as far as the SPA is concerned. On May 8, 1990, "over 600 copies of illegal software with a value of more than $250,000 were seized during a court ordered raid . . . on three locations of National Business Academy, a Los Angeles area computer training facility" (Pollock, 1990). The academy had routinely allowed students to make illegal copies of software to use at home. The suit also charged that the academy was responsible for illegally duplicating and distributing in excess of $2.5 million in copyrighted software.

In another case, the University of Oregon, charged with using pirated software, including Aldus *PageMaker* and Microsoft *Windows,* to teach adult education computer courses, agreed to pay $130,000 to SPA's Copyright Protection Fund. A further innovative penalty included in the settlement was for the university to "conduct an on-campus educational campaign about software copyright issues" and to run a national conference on "the copyright implications of software use in a modern computing environment" (Groner, 1992). The conference was held May 17–18, 1992.

Table 5.1	SPA Contact Data
	Software Publishers Association P.O. Box 79237 Baltimore, MD 21279–0237 or SPAudit Software Publishers Association 1730 M Street, NW Suite 700 Washington, DC 20036 Tel.: 202–452–1600 1–800–388–7478

Courtesy Software Publishers Association

In yet another case (January 1992), members of SPA filed a lawsuit against a Houston PC Learning Center run by Burnett Companies Consolidated, Inc., after receiving information that the Houston Center's computers were "loaded with unauthorized copies of SPA members' software" (Childs, 1992). The suit was settled out of court with Burnett paying a monetary settlement of $46,000 and agreeing to "purchase a sufficient number of licensed copies of software to ensure that all software in use by the company is licensed."

Figure 5.1 illustrates a question-and-answer sheet distributed by SPA which answers questions schools may have about software copyright law as it applies to them. The Do Something About It section at the end of the chapter invites you to discuss the details of this question and answer sheet.

The SPA has been proactive in its efforts to prevent software piracy. The association has prepared a number of resource materials with information about software use and the law. These resources include a video about software piracy, titled *Don't Copy That Floppy,* and a software management tool, *SPAudit,* which is a set of programs that will audit your hard disk and produce inventory reports summarizing the number and location of all applications. Both the video and *SPAudit* are free.

Make a note of the addresses and telephone numbers of the association (see table 5.1). SPA will be around in the foreseeable future and will prove an invaluable resource.

5.1.3 Public Domain Software versus Shareware versus Licensed Software

Public domain software

Public domain software is distributed free of charge. It is passed around from user to user, friend to friend, via disks or electronic-bulletin board systems. Countless examples of public domain software have been designed to handle most common computer applications,

Q. Is it okay for schools to copy software?

A. No, without the publisher's permission, it's not okay for schools to copy software. Software is protected by copyright law, which says that you can't make copies without the permission of the copyright holder. Copyright law is written this way to protect software programmers and publishers and the investment they've made in their products. The creative teams that develop the software — programmers, writers, graphic artists, content specialists, and others — all deserve fair compensation. Without the protection given by our copyright laws, they would be unable to produce the educational, entertainment and productivity software that adds so much to our daily lives.

Q. *What exactly does the law say about copying software?*

A. The law says that it is illegal to make or distribute copies of copyrighted material, including software, without authorization. If you do so, this is piracy, and you may face not only a civil suit, but also fines of up to $100,000 and jail terms of up to 5 years.

Q. *So I'm never allowed to copy software for any reason?*

A. If a backup copy was not included in the box with your original disk(s), you are permitted to make one copy in order to have both a working copy and a backup copy of the program. Copyright law prohibits you from making additional copies of the software for any other reason without the permission of the software company. If the publisher has authorized any exceptions to the copyright law, they will be stated in the license agreements that accompany all software products.

Q. *But aren't schools allowed to make copies for educational purposes?*

A. No. Like individuals and corporations, educational institutions are bound by the copyright law. Because of their unique position of influence, schools have a particular obligation to abide by the copyright law and educate students about their own responsibilities when using software. Just as it would be wrong to buy one textbook and photocopy it for use by many students, it is wrong for a school to duplicate software without the authorization of the publisher. This means that educators cannot make unauthorized copies for their students, either to use in school or to take home.

Q. *At our school, we share programs all the time. We assume this must be okay, since the school purchased the software in the first place.*

A. Many educators are not aware of how the copyright law applies to them. Without the publisher's authorization to make copies, your school needs to purchase as many copies of a program as you will use. However, many software firms do offer special sales arrangements to schools. These include reduced priced lab packs (a number of programs sold together) and site licenses (arrangements which permit schools to copy for a specific location at a fixed price). **Because these arrangements vary from publisher to publisher, it is essential that you read and understand the license agreement for each program before making any copies.**

Q. *We're planning to install a network for our students. How do we know how many copies of software we'll need to purchase?*

A. Remember that the installation of a network does not change your obligations with regard to the copyright law. When purchasing software for a network, be sure to ask the publisher what types of licensing arrangements are available for networks. Some software publishers allow schools to purchase a network license that authorizes the school to install stand-alone software on a network. In addition, many software publishers create special network versions that license the program to be run on the file server of a network. Because some publishers limit the number of workstations that are permitted to legally access the software on the network, it is very important to check the license agreement for any restrictions that may apply.

Q. *I've read the license agreement for one of the software packages purchased by our school. What if I'm not sure that I understand the arrangement correctly?*

A. If you have trouble understanding the license agreement, help is available. Your school district's media or computer specialist may be able to answer your questions. In addition, you can always contact the software publisher and ask for a clarification of the license agreement as it applies to your school. Finally, if you still have questions, contact the Software Publishers Association for more information about software and the copyright law.

Q. *I'll bet most of the people who copy software don't even know they're breaking the law.*

A. Because the software industry is relatively new and because copying software is so easy, many people are either unaware of the laws governing software use or choose to ignore them. It is the responsibility of each and every software user to read and understand the license agreements of the products they use and to be sure that their software use complies with copyright law. See what you can do to initiate a software use policy statement in your school that everyone respects. Finally, as an educator, help set an example for your students that responsible computer users should be "software legal."

If you have any questions about how the copyright law applies to you and your school, please contact the **Software Publishers Association at 202-452-1600.**

from games, to word processing, to data base management, and so on. The authors of this software have not forgone their right of copyright; they have simply given permission for anyone to make as many copies as they like.

But let the user beware! Public domain software is neither supported nor warranted by the author, and is generally not as well developed and tested as software that you pay for. In other words, you may regret using it for anything other than trivial applications. Indeed, even for trivial applications such as games, you may regret using it if it interferes with the operating system or with the data you have stored elsewhere on disks. Also, be warned that public domain software is a perfect vehicle for the infiltration of computer viruses onto computer systems. We will discuss this hazard in section 5.5.

Shareware is software which has been developed for sale and floated into the computer marketplace, often via electronic bulletin boards. The author relies on the honor system for payment. He or she allows users to make as many copies as they like, which they can then "share" with their friends. When the program is run, an introductory screen describes the conditions under which the software may be used. Typically, if you like the software and intend to continue using it, you are asked to make a contribution to the author of either a specified dollar amount or any sum of your choosing (presumably reflecting what you think the program is worth).

Shareware is more reliable than public domain software. Moreover, once you have made your contribution, the software is supported by the author, who will send you documentation explaining how to access the program's complete set of features. You will also be sent any updated versions of the software.

Licensed software is registered for your use and entitles you to full support from the company that sold you the product. The license agreement defines and controls the use of the software and specifies exactly how many copies may be made. If the license is for a single user, you are entitled to make one backup copy unless otherwise specified in the agreement. If the license is a site license, the exact nature of the site will have been negotiated between you and the company.

For example, if you purchase a site license for your middle school, the contract may specify that the software may be loaded only onto computers in the building that houses the middle school. You would not be able to use it on the high school computers next door—unless you want to receive a call from SPA! Nor would you be able to make copies of the software for use on your computer at home.

Some companies—Intellimation, for example—have started negotiating liberal site licenses that, apart from allowing purchasers to make multiple copies of the program for use solely at the site, also allow teachers and teachers' assistants of classes which use the programs to take one copy of each program home for preparation of class-related activities.

A software license is an agreement between you and the company supplying the software. You can often negotiate the terms of the license agreement. But once the negotiations are final, you are legally bound to the conditions.

5.1.4 Software Protection

Most of the money in the computer industry is made by the manufacturers of hardware. However, the software sells the hardware, since the machinery is useless without the programs that control its operations. As pointed out earlier, the software industry loses a far

MICROSOFT SOFTWARE LICENSE CARD

WORKS 3.00 MAC

This License Agreement is your proof of license.
Please treat it as valuable property.

Microsoft License Agreement

This is a legal agreement between you (either an individual or an entity), the end user, and Microsoft Corporation. If you do not agree to the terms of this Agreement, promptly return the disk package and accompanying items (including written materials and binders or other containers) to the place you obtained them for a full refund.

MICROSOFT SOFTWARE LICENSE

1. GRANT OF LICENSE. This Microsoft License Agreement ("License") permits you to use one copy of the specified version of the Microsoft software product identified above ("SOFTWARE") on any single computer, provided the SOFTWARE is in use on only one computer at any time. If you have multiple Licenses for the SOFTWARE, then at any time you may have as many copies of the SOFTWARE in use as you have Licenses. The SOFTWARE is "in use" on a computer when it is loaded into the temporary memory (i.e., RAM) or installed into the permanent memory (e.g., hard disk, CD-ROM, or other storage device) of that computer, except that a copy installed on a network server for the sole purpose of distribution to other computers is not "in use". If the anticipated number of users of the SOFTWARE will exceed the number of applicable Licenses, then you must have a reasonable mechanism or process in place to assure that the number of persons using the SOFTWARE concurrently does not exceed the number of Licenses. If the SOFTWARE is permanently installed on the hard disk or other storage device of a computer (other than a network server) and one person uses that computer more than 80% of the time it is in use, then that person may also use the SOFTWARE on a portable or home computer.

2. COPYRIGHT. The SOFTWARE is owned by Microsoft or its suppliers and is protected by United States copyright laws and international treaty provisions. Therefore, you must treat the SOFTWARE like any other copyrighted material (e.g., a book or musical recording) except that you may either (a) make one copy of the SOFTWARE solely for backup or archival purposes, or (b) transfer the SOFTWARE to a single hard disk provided you keep the original solely for backup or archival purposes. You may not copy the written materials accompanying the SOFTWARE.

3. OTHER RESTRICTIONS. This Microsoft License Agreement is your proof of license to exercise the rights granted herein and must be retained by you. You may not rent or lease the SOFTWARE, but you may transfer your rights under this Microsoft License Agreement on a permanent basis provided you transfer this License Agreement, the SOFTWARE, and all accompanying written materials and retain no copies, and the recipient agrees to the terms of this Agreement. You may not reverse engineer, decompile, or disassemble the SOFTWARE. Any transfer of the SOFTWARE must include the most recent update and all prior versions.

4. DUAL MEDIA SOFTWARE. If the SOFTWARE package contains both 3.5-inch and 5.25-inch disks, then you may use only the disks appropriate for your single designated computer or network server. You may not use the other disks on another computer or computer network, or loan, rent, lease, or transfer them to another user except as part of a transfer or other use as expressly permitted by this Microsoft License Agreement.

larger proportion of its revenues through unauthorized copying than does the hardware industry, simply because it is a lot easier to copy software than hardware. Software creators can protect their product against theft in two ways: (1) external protection in the form of legal prescription and (2) built-in protection using hardware and/or software safeguards.

The three kinds of legal protection are provided by patent law, copyright law, and trade-secret law. Of the three, only copyright law and trade-secret law offer any measure of practical protection (Gemignani, 1980). It is beyond the scope of this book to go into detail on why patent law is an impracticable solution to the problem of software piracy. Trade-secret law allows a company to require employees and others with whom the secret has been shared to sign a legally binding contract that includes a nondisclosure clause. This is a routine practice when hiring new employees or sharing technology between companies. Of course, proving in court that the secret was really a secret and applied to something not already known is a stumbling block that, more often than not, reduces the weight of trade-secret law to little more than an honor system. Even copyright law fails to adequately protect software developers, nothwithstanding the successful efforts of SPA.

It has always been possible to protect software against unauthorized copying. Various methods have, and still are, being used. The simplest is to build instructions into the program which will override any command from the operating system to complete a copy of files or disks pertaining to the program. The problem with this is that it is not difficult to create a program that gets around the copy protection. Often such programs are created by so-called hackers and are available free of charge in the public domain. (More about hackers in section 5.2.)

Another method of software protection involves setting a "time bomb" in the software which will go off after a certain period of time (days or weeks) if the user has not paid for an unauthorized copy. If the time bomb is triggered, the software may be programmed to erase itself, along with any files that have been created using the software.

Yet another method of protection used by computer manufacturers is to program the software so that it is linked to a serial number embedded in the chips on the logic board inside the system unit (Quinlan, 1991). The software would thus run only on the machine for which it had been purchased.

Fewer and fewer companies are using software protection methodologies such as those described because, in general, they penalize legitimate customers by limiting options for how they might use the software. Protection actually takes away from the perceived quality of the product and therefore adversely affects sales. Instead, software companies prefer to give a high profile to the pursuit and punishment of software copyright infringement through the efforts of associations such as SPA and the Business Software Alliance.

Companies also prefer to rely on people's sense of ethical responsibility. Software copyright infringement is theft; it is against the law. Teachers should unfailingly set an example to students and take time out with them to help them become sensitized to the ethical and legal implications of what they are doing when they copy software. Remember: the job of teachers is to guide children in their quest for the knowledge that will empower them to become responsible members of their local, national, and global communities.

COPY SOFTWARE ILLEGALLY AND YOU COULD GET THIS HARDWARE ABSOLUTELY FREE.

Software piracy isn't just a crime. It's a shame. Because most people who do it aren't even aware that it's illegal. If you copy software that's protected by copyright, you could lose your job, face a civil suit, pay a $250,000 fine and possibly be imprisoned.

So get the facts now. For more information about the legal use of software, contact the Software Publishers Association Piracy Hotline at 1-800-388-7478. Because in a court of law, ignorance is one thing you won't be able to plead.

Don't Copy That Floppy

5.1.5 Steps Schools Should Take to Discourage Software Piracy

The SPA (Lewis, 1992) has recommended that organizations such as schools initiate the following steps to discourage piracy:

- **"Appoint a software manager responsible for keeping records on purchases and software use."** Give the appointment a high profile in the school district so as to send a message that software theft is taken seriously. The software manager might ask for help from faculty representatives at each school in the district. The committee thus constituted would not only actively discourage piracy, but it might also act as a clearinghouse for the district in the purchase of software and negotiate sensible site licensing with a view to making piracy unnecessary.

- **"Develop a software code of ethics."** Figure 5.4 is an example of a code of ethics recommended by SPA. The software management committee would be responsible for giving this code a high profile, too.

- **"Keep a software log."** This would be another responsibility of the software manager. The log would include records of a program's date of purchase, user, and resident machine.

- **"Perform regular audits."** As already mentioned, SPA has developed and made available free of charge software that produces a list of all the software on a hard disk. The list can then be compared against purchasing records. This would be a simple process if a software manager has been appointed and keeps track of software purchase and use.

School districts that apply recommendations such as these not only protect themselves against liability, but they also help their students, through the faculty, to develop a sense of ethical responsibility that will overflow into other areas of their lives.

5.2 Security: Hacking and Cracking

Hacking generally describes the activity of computer afficionados who become absorbed with the challenge of pushing computer technology to the limits of its capabilities. The term *hacker* is not pejorative per se. Indeed, it started out as a term of endearment to describe lovable and often "nerdy" individuals who were recognized as benefactors to society because of the innovative computer-based solutions they created. In the mid-1970s, these benevolent hackers formed an informal association called the Home Brew Society, which included in its membership people like Steve Jobs and Steve Wozniak, who founded Apple Computer Inc. now the world's number one manufacturer of personal computers.

Today, hacking is generally frowned on because it has come to be associated with practices that involve individuals (usually males between the ages of 16 and 24) who use computer technology to break the law. The term that formerly described criminal hacking—**cracking**—was in vogue until "crack" and "crackers" became identified with other social ills not related to computing. In what follows, we will describe briefly the kind of criminal hacking of which teachers and their students should be aware. Few students will ever be guilty of criminal hacking, but many will be victims of it.

Figure 5.4
Sample software
code of ethics and
software policy
Courtesy Software
Publishers Association

Sample
Software Code Of Ethics

Purpose

This code of ethics states our organization's policy concerning software duplication. All employees shall use software only in accordance with its license agreement. Unless otherwise provided in the license, any duplication of copyrighted software, except for backup and archival purposes, is a violation of the law. Any unauthorized duplication of copyrighted computer software violates the law and is contrary to the organization's standards of conduct. The following points are to be followed to comply with software license agreements:

1. We will use all software in accordance with their license agreements.

2. Legitimate software will promptly be provided to all employees who   need it. No company employee will make any unauthorized copies of any software under any circumstances. Anyone found copying software other than for backup purposes is subject to termination.

3. We will not tolerate the use of any unauthorized copies of software in our company. Any person illegally reproducing software can be subject to civil and criminal penalties including fines and imprisonment. We do not condone illegal copying of software under any circumstances and anyone who makes, uses, or otherwise acquires unauthorized software shall be appropriately disciplined.

4. No employee shall give software to any outsiders including clients, customers and others.

5. Any employee who determines that there may be a misuse of software within the company shall notify their department manager or legal counsel.

6. All software used by the organization on company computers will be properly purchased through appropriate procedures.

I have read the company's software code of ethics. I am fully aware of our software policies and agree to abide by those policies.

_____   _____
Employee Signature   Date

a

Sample
Software Policy

Purpose

[Company] licenses the use of computer software from a variety of third parties. Such software is normally copyrighted by the software developer and, unless expressly authorized to do so, [company] has no right to make copies of the software except for backup or archival purposes. The purpose of this policy is to prevent copyright infringement and to protect the integrity of [company's] computer environment from viruses. This policy statement must be signed by all employees.

Policy Guidelines

1. **General Statement of Policy; Appointment of a Software Manager.** It is the policy of [company] to respect all computer software copyrights and to adhere to the terms of all software licenses to which the company is a party. [Name] is [company's] Software Manager and is charged with the responsibility for enforcing these guidelines.

   [Company] employees may not duplicate any licensed software or related documentation for use either on [company] premises or elsewhere unless [company] is expressly authorized to do so by agreement with the licensor. Unauthorized duplication of software may subject employees and/or the company to both civil and criminal penalties under the United States Copyright Act.

   Employees may not give software to any outsiders including clients, contractors, customers, and others. [Company] employees may use software on local area networks or on multiple machines only in accordance with applicable license agreements.

2. **Employee Education.** Each [company] employee must complete the one-hour software education program (to be crafted by the software manager; see page 10) described in this policy statement. Upon completion of the education program, employees shall be required to sign this software policy statement. New employees shall be provided the same education program within 10 days of the commencement of their employment.

b

5.2.1 Computer Viruses and Vaccines

Computer viruses are programs created by hackers. As their name implies, viruses infect other computer systems by attaching duplicate copies of themselves to other legitimate operating system or applications software with which they come into contact. They are carried from computer to computer either indirectly by way of disks or tapes, or directly by way of the communications media (cables or wireless transmission) that connect the machines that are part of computer networks.

Any computer virus should be taken seriously. Most viruses are designed to do some kind of damage to a system either by destroying data or otherwise compromising a system's operations in such a way as to make it unusable. Other viruses might appear harmless, perhaps causing data of no consequence to appear on the screen at some programmed date and time. But *harmless* is a relative term. Anything that interrupts normal computer operations is cause for alarm because there is no telling what else might be going on in the background, unseen on the computer screen.

Computer viruses are activated in various ways. Time bombs are so-called because they are programmed to "go off"—start doing the damage they have been programmed to do—at a certain time on a certain date (a popular date is Friday the 13th). Logic bombs, on the other hand, are usually less predictable because they are triggered when some specific set of switches (bits) inside the computer's memory become electronically set to a predetermined value.

A vaccine, as the name implies, is a program that counters the effects of a virus. It does this by watching out for viruses and warning the user when such a program is trying to infect a system. Once detected, the user can instruct the vaccine program to remove the virus if it is already on the system, or prevent the virus from getting onto the system in the first place.

Today, hundreds of decidedly harmful computer viruses are capable of anything from changing or destroying data, to slowing down or even immobilizing a system, to interfering with the system's interaction with peripheral devices such as the screen or printer.

Worms and Trojan horses

A special type of virus called a worm is designed to duplicate itself not only from machine to machine, but also within each machine, effectively overwhelming primary memory with copies of itself and leaving no room for any other programming activity. The most infamous worm in recent years was created by a graduate student at Cornell University and spread over the Internet academic network,[1] which connects colleges all over the world. Within hours, the virus was immobilizing computers as far away as Sydney, Australia. The student hacker was indicted by the FBI, found guilty, fined $10,000, and sentenced to three years probation and 400 hours of community service.

Here is a Monty Pythonesque—but nonetheless true—account of the exploits and subsequent fate of a hacker in the United Kingdom (Neumann, 1990). The story was printed under the headline "'Mad Hacker' jailed for computer war."

---

[1] See chapter 11 for a fuller description of this network.

The "Mad Hacker" in question, Nicholas Whiteley by name, who hailed from London, was sentenced to four months, with a further eight months suspended for the damage he perpetrated on university computer systems. Whiteley apparently wanted to become "Britain's top hacker" and he "wept in the dock and held his hands to his face as he walked to the cells to begin his sentence." As the newspaper report explained: "Whiteley declared war on computer experts, using a computer in his bedroom to swamp university computers with masses of useless material, including threats and boasts about his brilliance." In the spirit of Monty Python, one of his threats read: "Don't mess with me because I am extremely nutty."

Another specialized category of virus is the Trojan Horse, named after the innocent-looking, giant wooden horse built by the Greeks to gain covert entry inside the walls of Troy. The computer version of the Trojan Horse is a program that looks innocent enough—appearing, perhaps, as a computer game made available in the public domain—but which has code built into it which inflicts damage of one kind or another once installed on a computer system.

5.2.2 Trespass of Computer Systems

Trespassing is one of the seemingly innocuous yet potentially most devastating activities carried on by modern-day hackers. Using bulletin board systems (BBS) and other underground sources, hackers are able to obtain the access codes and passwords of institutional computer systems ranging from the local hospital or university to the Pentagon and beyond. The networked world is an open door to hackers determined and skilled enough to get around the various levels of security designed into the systems. Some hackers are motivated purely by the thrill of being able to gain access to these systems; they have no intention of damaging the data stored in them, and no particular interest in the data. But the activity is still illegal because it is trepass, an invasion of privacy, and an infringement of people's rights.

Other hackers go further, altering data, stealing data, destroying data, or adding data. Sometimes the objective is sabotage, sometimes espionage, sometimes thrill-seeking vandalism, as in the case of the 414s, a group of hackers from the 414 area code who joined together to infiltrate computer systems. Criminal prosecutions have been brought against a number of such hackers in the last few years.

When the hacker is working from a foreign base and infiltrating U.S. government computers via satellite, the potential for disaster is real. Such was the case in 1988, when a hacker in West Germany tapped into NASA computers. Fortunately, a NASA computer scientist discovered the intruder early on and, in order to track him down, set up elaborate monitoring procedures that kept NASA apprised of his every move. Eventually, the hacker was traced back to West Germany. No serious damage was done.

But it is not only outsiders that breach the security of networked computer systems. Kabay (1992) reminds us that "75% to 80% of all attacks on data confidentiality and integrity are by employees authorized to use the systems and networks they abuse." Much of this in-house hacking, even when detected, goes unreported because companies fear loss of reputation and credibility in the eyes of the public in much the same way that banks are loath to report that they have been victims of electronic embezzlement.

5.2.3 Money Theft (Embezzlement)

The bill paid by banks for electronic fraud runs into the billions of dollars per year. The banks, of course, pass the bill on to the consumer. If the bank goes under, the taxpayer picks up the tab. What Kabay (1992) has to say about network infiltration applies equally to electronic fraud: most of the theft involves company insiders—"white-collar criminals." In the past, the last thing the banks wanted was that their vulnerability to financial loss through credit card fraud and illegal transfers of funds should become public knowledge. Thus, much of this kind of crime went unreported. Today, however, electronic embezzlement is so rampant that financial institutions openly and diligently investigate cases when they are detected.

5.2.4 Computer System Security

As long as computer networks are vulnerable, hackers will attempt to breach them. The responsibility lies with the designers, builders, and managers of these systems to make them as secure as possible against unauthorized entry. This is a mammoth task because networks are communications systems; access is the key to their success. The only protection against hackers is vigilance. Networked organizations—including every school of the future—will have to implement the kind of steps recommended by Kabay (1992) in order to protect the rights of authorized users in schools who want to enjoy the benefits of communications-based education as described in chapter 11.

Here are Kabay's recommendations to network managers:

- Have a message at log-on that warns hackers that the system is for authorized users only and that intruders will be prosecuted.
- Have a written plan of network security procedures describing standard operating procedures including counter measures and defense plans for when the network is under attack.
- Make access controls and event logging (maintaining a record of all use of the network) part of this standard procedure.
- Regularly go over the procedures with personnel responsible for system security.

This might seem like overkill for many school teachers and administrators, especially in these early days of networked computing in schools K–12. However, computer managers at any college can relate a litany of horror stories that are the result of abuse of computer systems by that minority of students with a personal or societal ax to grind.

▪ Looking Back

Judicial systems worldwide are struggling to come to grips with the legal ramifications of computer-related activities that are injurious to the public welfare. Computers have been available for general, uncontrolled use for only about 20 years—since the advent of the first microcomputers. Before the mid-1970s, software piracy and hacking were relatively rare because there was little incentive for these activities. Systems were few in number, not nearly as openly networked as they are now, and software was almost entirely customized and therefore useful only on the systems, and in the context of the environments, for which it was developed. Today, the temptation to steal software and hack into computer systems is much greater. Stealing software is both easy to do and easy to get away with. Hacking is not so easy, but it presents an irresistible challenge to bright, determined, morally indifferent individuals who need the boost to their egos that comes with the exercise of the power that their computing skills puts at their fingertips. Unfortunately, they do not feel constrained by a code of ethics that respects the security and privacy rights of others.

The more we understand the realities of the computerized world, the more fully we will be able to function in it. We have discussed software piracy and hacking in some depth not simply because they are interesting to learn about. It is part of a teacher's role to make students aware, on the one hand, of the constraints on their freedom dictated by the rights of others and, on the other hand, of the extent to which their own rights can be infringed on by the kind of unethical and illegal activities described.

Software piracy and hacking are two examples of antisocial activity which our students are not likely to learn about at home. Students will almost certainly be direct or indirect victims of hacking. They may well be among the few who find these activities "bait which [they find difficult to] resist swallowing." The knowledge that teachers help them acquire will give them the power to minimize the impact of these unethical activities on their lives.

▪ Looking Forward

This concludes our discussion of the broad sweep of computing against the backdrop of society in general and schools in particular. It is time to narrow the focus onto the computer hardware and software itself. This will be the subject matter of part II.

If you have been using the Microsoft-*Works* tutorials, which optionally accompany this text, you will by now be familiar with using the computer and ready to learn more about the technical aspects of the machine's construction, management, and maintenance. Chapter 6 will examine the hardware, including both the computer itself and the various machines, called peripheral devices, which make up the computer system. Then, in chapter 7, we will discuss the different types of software necessary to take advantage of the power that the computer puts into our hands.

▪ Do Something About It: Exercises and Projects

1. There is an appropriate time to bring up specific ethical and legal issues with students. Brainstorm with your colleagues or classmates to define just when and how such a discussion might arise with students, and how it might best be conducted.

2. Examine the details of a typical software license agreement and determine to what extent the agreement tallies with copyright law.

3. Invite a guest "expert" from a local software company to your class to discuss the negative effects of unauthorized copying on the software industry. During the class, students should take notes, and afterward, write a newspaper style article about the visit.

4. List examples of your own intellectual property which you would not like to have copied without permission or given to others without receiving credit. Examples might include: homework assignments; drawings or pictures you have created; creative writings.

School piracy: A case study
by Christopher B. Hopkins, Software Publishers Association, Washington, D.C.

The Scenario

It should have been another normal school day. The principal at Central High School was busy grading yesterday's computer assignments when a secretary delivered an unusual Federal Express package. "The Software Publishers Association," he muttered suspiciously as he opened the letter.

"I am writing on behalf of the Software Publishers Association (SPA), which is the principal trade group of the PC software industry. Our more than 1,000 members count on us to help stop the unauthorized duplication of their products. We have received information that your organization may be making and using unauthorized copies of our members' software in violation of the Federal Copyright Law. From the information we have obtained, the software involved is published by. . . ."

As he finished the letter, he let it drop on the desk. His eyes went to the shelf with two copies of the school's standard word processor on it and then he gazed to the computer room beyond it. It was full of students writing English assignments on thirty computers with the illegally copied software.

"What are we going to do?" he thought. Central High had a special task force on ethical decision making that promoted ethics in the curriculum and behavior. The student body had a computer network team that founded the school's Council on Ethics, which focused

on ethical issues in technology. The head of that team had presented a program on computer ethics at a recent education conference. "Yet we still copied software illegally to cut corners," he said to himself. "And now we've been caught."

Despite its awareness of the ethical issues involved in using unauthorized software, the school had no program in place to ensure compliance with federal **(continued)**

Christopher B. Hopkins, author of the case study

■ References

Childs, Terri, and Ilene Rosenthal. "Settlement Announced in Copyright Infringement Suit Against Burnett Companies Consolidated, Inc. of Houston." News Release of the Software Publishers Association, April 14, 1992.

Gemignani, Michael C. *Rutgers Journal of Computers, Technology, and the Law 7.* 1980, pp. 269–312.

Groner, Jonathan. "Swatting Back at Software Pirates." *Legal Times,* June 1992.

Information Week. "The Long Arm of the Software Industry." *Information Week,* June 17, 1991.

Kabay, Michel. "Send Hackers a Strong Message by Reporting Security Breaches." *Network World,* September 1992, p. 95.

Lewis, Peter H. "As Piracy Grows, the Software Industry Counterattacks." *New York Times,* Nov. 8, 1992, p. 12.

Neumann, Peter G. "Risks to the Public in Computers and Related Systems." *Software Engineering Notes,* vol. 17, no. 3, July 1992, pp. 5–7.

Case Study 5 (concluded)

copyright laws. The SPA's letter plainly pointed out the school's violation and even knew the illegally copied programs they were using. Clearly, SPA had received a tip from a student or teacher from inside the school. The request was simple: destroy the illegal copies of the software, buy legal copies, and inform SPA within two weeks that this has been accomplished. *Or face legal alternatives,* SPA warned. From the enclosed brochures and news clippings, several referring to SPA as the "Software Police," one could obviously see that the group meant business.

What Has Happened

Such a scenario is not uncommon. Central High is like many schools across the country. The computer labs are often filled with illegally duplicated software instead of having legal copies on each machine. The administration is aware of the violation but still illegally copies the software. The school was under fiscal constraints and chose to spend elsewhere the funds that were needed to purchase software.

The SPA was contacted via their piracy hotline (1–800–388–7478), which receives 20–30 calls a day from employees, students, and temp workers. A computer instructor from the high school called the SPA hotline to file a report. He had urged the administration to purchase legal copies of software over the past several months, it had refused. Faced with a moral dilemma, he contacted SPA as a last resort.

The SPA has reported that, in 1991, the software industry lost more than $1.2 billion in the United States. As the principal trade organization of the personal computer industry, SPA has an obligation to follow up on all tips regarding piracy activities. The organization is also actively involved in educating users, especially in schools and corporations. Through the "Don't Copy That Floppy" campaign, SPA teaches users that computer piracy hurts software users as well as manufacturers and that it is against the law. For more information or for free educational materials, call SPA at 1–800–388–7478.

Talk About It

Topics for discussion based on the case study.

1. What are intellectual properties? What protection do they deserve in comparison to physical properties?

2. How does *fairness* fit in with computer software piracy? What effects does piracy have on the industry?

3. What are several methods of protecting intellectual properties and what are the ramifications? How do those methods compare with federal and state laws?

4. Identify businesses, industries, and jobs for which protecting intellectual property is important (for example, photography, music publishing). For each business, industry, or job, describe the kinds of intellectual property that might need protection.

Pollock, Jodi. "Software Publishers Raid Software Training Facility." *SPA News Release,* May 23, 1990.

Quinlan, Tom. "Apple Declares War On Software Piracy." *InfoWorld,* August 12, 1991, p. 8.

Software Publishers Association. *White Paper: Software Piracy.* 1992. (a)

Software Publishers Association. News release, April 14, 1992. (b)

Wasch, Ken, Executive Director, SPA. *Conduct a Software Audit: Protect Your Clients.* Draft of SPA news release, undated.

Wasch, Ken. "Estimated Loss to Piracy in US Exceeds $2.4 Billion in '90." News release of the Software Publisher's Association, August 6, 1991.

Willett, Shawn. "Mixed Reaction to Software Copyright Law." *InfoWorld,* October 19, 1992, p. 17.

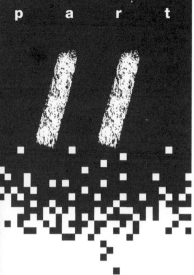

Computing
Fundamentals

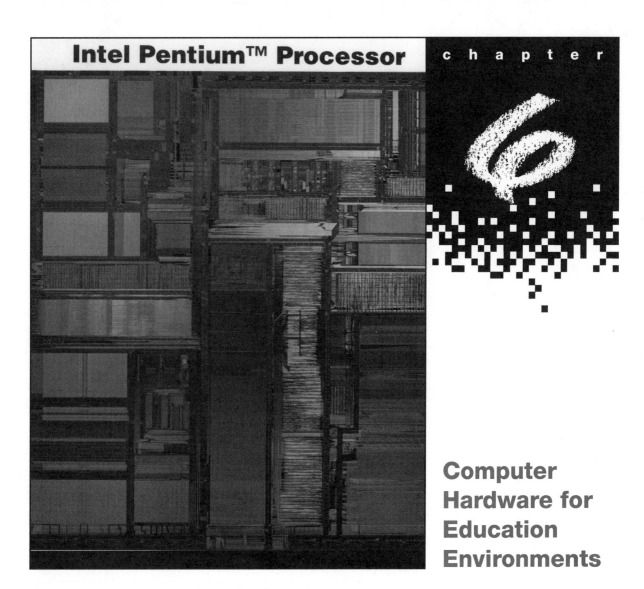

Intel Pentium™ Processor

6

Computer Hardware for Education Environments

What we have not yet done is only what we have not yet attempted to do.
Alexis de Tocqueville (1805–1859)

Good tools do not make an excellent teacher, but an excellent teacher makes good use of tools.
Eleanor L. Doan (1918–)

This chapter discusses the **hardware** components of the type of computer systems most used in K–12 educational environments. *Hardware* is the term used to describe those parts of a system that one can see and touch—machinery in the *solid* sense of the word. Another type of machinery, **software,** is based on sets of logical instructions. These latter machines are "complex operating systems"[1] crafted into programs that control the functioning of the hardware. When one uses the computer, one cannot see the software. One sees only the effects of the software as manifested in the behavior of the hardware. The next chapter will consider the two basic types of software—operating systems software and applications software. Later, in chapter 13, we will investigate how teachers might go about building software systems themselves for use in the classroom.

After briefly discussing the growing presence of computers in K–12 schools, we will focus on the hardware common to all desktop computer systems. Notwithstanding superficial variations, there is little fundamental difference between one make of computer and another, just as automobiles all basically look alike and function in a more or less predictable fashion.

We will also focus on the specialized hardware required for multimedia systems. These systems are becoming more popular in schools as costs come down on the components that enable the computer to easily handle video and sound on an interactive basis. We will revisit the important subject of multimedia in part III, chapter 12, when we examine in more depth the ways in which the specialized hardware technologies involved in multimedia systems can be integrated into the curriculum.

We will conclude this chapter with a discussion of specific issues with regard to taking care of computer system hardware. In a later chapter (part III, chapter 8) we will discuss the broader issue of management of educational computing environments.

The topics that will be addressed here include:

■ The components of a basic computer system

■ The components of a multimedia educational computing system

■ The maintenance of your computer system

    ■ General dos and don'ts

    ■ Dos and don'ts regarding particular devices

■■ 6.1 Electronic Computers Were Invented to Meet Educational Needs

Earlier, in chapters 2 and 3, you were introduced to John Vincent Atanasoff, who in 1938 was professor of Physics at Iowa State University and was determined to build a machine that would take the drudgery out of the number-crunching research required of his Ph.D. students. He was not the first to express frustration at the time wasted doing relatively menial, manual calculations. The time line at the beginning of chapter 2 identified some of the "giants" in the history of computers on whose shoulders Atanasoff stood. One of these giants, in particular, Wilhelm Gottfried Von Leibnitz, whose life spanned the 17th

---

[1]This is the *Random House Webster's College Dictionary* (1991 ed.) definition of a machine.

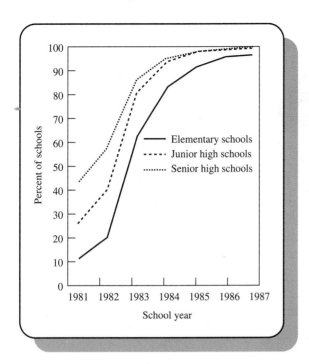

Figure 6.1
U.S. public schools
with at least one
computer by grade
level, 1981-87
Source: Office of
Technology Assessment,
based on data from Market
Data Retrieval, Inc., 1988.

and 18th centuries, had this to say about computation and its automation: "It is unworthy of excellent men to lose hours like slaves in the labor of calculation which could safely be relegated to anything else if machines were used" (Shurkin, 1985).

As early as the 1960s, high school students, usually of a mathematical bent, would accompany their instructor on field trips to local-company computer installations, where they would program the early monolithic machines. Looking back, those students must have initially felt a little like they were entering the twilight zone, so awe-inspiring must those early machines have been. Human nature being what it is, however, no doubt they quickly adjusted. The humdrum, limited nature of the machines would have become apparent as the novelty wore off. The thirst for more powerful machines capable of handling richer problems at faster speeds would have been as insatiable then as it is today.

In the late 1970s, following the 1971 invention of the microprocessor by Intel Corporation, microcomputers first began to appear in schools. As noted in chapter 2, most of those early machines—Commodore Pets, Radio Shack TRS-80s, early versions of the Apple II—are still around and still in use. But they are relatively few in number. According to the report of the Office of Technology Assessment (1988), 90% of elementary schools and 60% of high schools in the U.S. were unable to boast of owning even one computer in 1981. (See figure 6.1.) By 1987, that number had increased to close to 100% for all grade levels. In fact, by 1988, the ratio of computers to students in all schools was approximately one computer for every 40 students. (See figure 6.2.)

This is not a particularly positive ratio—less than one computer per class of students—nonetheless, it represents a massive investment in computer technology over the seven-year period from 1981 to 1988.

Figure 6.2
Distribution of
computers in U.S.
public schools, 1988.
Source: Office of
Technology Assessment,
based on data from Market
Data Retrieval, Inc., 1988.

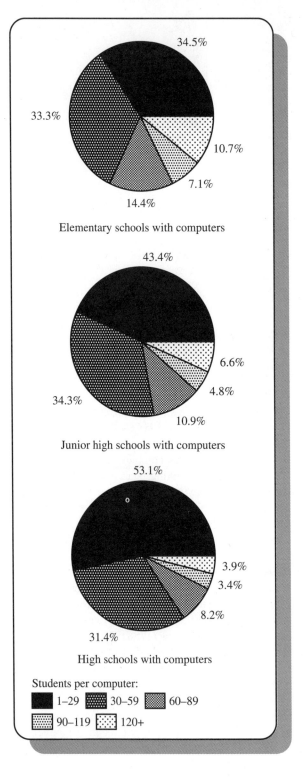

34.5%

33.3%

10.7%

7.1%

14.4%

Elementary schools with computers

43.4%

6.6%

4.8%

34.3%

10.9%

Junior high schools with computers

53.1%

3.9%

3.4%

8.2%

31.4%

High schools with computers

Students per computer:

1–29   30–59   60–89

90–119   120+

The bulk of the machines purchased between 1981 and 1991 have been Apple IIs (especially IIe and IIGS) and IBM PCs or compatible machines. Commodore Computer Corporation generated a flurry of purchasing activity when the company introduced the Commodore-64 in 1982. Its price (less than half as much as the Apple/IBM competition) and performance (it had double the memory capacity of competing machines) made it hard to resist, and quite a few school districts that had been waiting on the sidelines with regard to computer technology opted to jump in at this point. Unfortunately, relatively little educational software was developed for the Commodore-64, and its initially vaunted performance was soon surpassed by machines from Apple and IBM. Aggressive marketing by these two companies has meant, in the U.S. at least, that the successor to the Commodore-64, the Commodore Amiga, has remained a distant third in the educational computing stakes.

Students K–12 no longer need to make a field trip to use a computer. The desktop computer is proliferating in classrooms worldwide. In many school districts, computers are electronically linked throughout the district so that children can communicate across age groups and over wide areas. They are also able to hook into the large computers at local universities. This gives them the ability to establish contacts worldwide via the public access networks that link the academic community. This is no twilight zone; this is reality, at least for those students who are fortunate enough to be already participating in an educational environment where computing technology has been woven into the curriculum.

■■ 6.2 The Components of a Basic Computer System

Section 6.2 examines the components of a basic computer—the minimum requirements of a useful system. Computer systems for use in the classroom can also include a wide range of other computer-controlled devices, especially where multimedia systems are concerned. Section 6.3 therefore looks at the kind of equipment needed to incorporate sound, video, graphics and text in a multimedia learning environment.

Superficial features, dictated by hardware and software design, make one computer system appear different from another. These superficial variations may intimidate you. Many people find it difficult to master one type of computer, let alone two or more. If the technology seems off-putting, remember that the diversity is illusory, that the differences are really minor. The skills learned in the mastery of one computing environment will transfer to any of the others.

Today, even these superficial differences are melting away as computer manufacturers adopt common standards. One machine may be more powerful than another and have more features, but otherwise there will be few surprises in the way they function. Remember that you are learning these computing skills so that you can include them in your set of teaching tools. The appropriately programmed and integrated computer is perhaps the most effective tool for learning yet devised. The time and energy teachers invest in mastering the tool will yield a return that will benefit not only them, but also those they teach.

Readers will find it easiest to follow this section if they are sitting in front of a computer system as they read along. Figure 6.3 illustrates a typical setup for desktop computer systems found in schools.

Those who are already familiar with the hardware components of a computer system such as those illustrated in figure 6.3 can skip to the next section (6.3 The Components of a Multimedia Educational Computing System). Those who are not might like a brief description of what each component does. Let us take them one by one. Use figure 6.3 to visually verify the descriptions that follow.

6.2.1 The Monitor

Those who have not spent much time with computers may not be familiar with the term *monitor*. In fact, the monitor is much like the televisions in our homes. It is also described as a VDT (video display terminal) or a CRT (cathode ray tube).

The monitor is used to display what is going on in the system unit of the computer. The display on a monitor is called soft copy in computerese.[2] The monitor displays the results of any processing carried out by the computer. This is necessary because it keeps us in touch with what is going on in the computer itself. What we see on the monitor reassures us that the system is behaving sensibly. Those with an Apple II or a Macintosh LC or a late model IBM PC, P5/2, or compatible machine probably have a color monitor. Others may have what is called a monochrome monitor. A monochrome monitor basically uses two colors: usually black for the background, and some other color (green, white, orange) for the text.

---

[2]An important objective of this text is to introduce readers to computerese. Like anything in life, there is an extensive vocabulary associated with computers which needs to be learned and which, once learned, helps to remove the mystery from these high-tech machines.

ELFs

One warning about monitors and extremely low frequency electromagnetic emissions (ELFs). The jury is still out on whether or not it is dangerous to be exposed to ELFs from monitors. Research indicates that there are potentially hazardous effects from ELFs. In particular, there appears to be an increased incidence of miscarriage among pregnant women who work for long hours in front of certain computer screens. Some monitors (larger color monitors) emit more ELF emissions than others. Shielding devices that reduce the emissions do offer protection, but they add significantly to the cost of the monitor. In a cut-throat marketplace, some manufacturers are afraid of pricing their product out of the market even though the shielding is necessary to protect the consumer.

Inevitably, ELF emission shielding will eventually be mandated by law in the U.S., as is already the case in some European countries. In the meantime, the best protection against them is to keep your distance. Do not sit closer than an arm's length to the monitor—an adult arm's length. Set up school computers so that children are encouraged to keep their distance, too. We will return to this subject when discussing educational computing environments in chapter 8.

6.2.2 The System Unit

Figure 6.4 is an annotated illustration of the internal components of the system unit of the IBM PS/2. The system unit, which usually sits underneath the monitor, contains the computer chips[3] on which are etched the tiny electronic components that enable the computer to do its job. We can think of it like a miniaturized cityscape. Buildings are everywhere (in the form of different kinds of silicon chips) and between the buildings are electronic highways (called buses) that link them together.

Let us take a closer look at the key components of this system unit one by one.

The Central Processing Unit (CPU)

The most important chip, called the microprocessor, contains the electronic circuitry that makes up the central processing unit (CPU), which controls everything the computer does. Data travel along the buses under the control of the CPU. The CPU knows where everything is because every location, every device controlled by the CPU, has an address just as in a city. Figure 6.5 illustrates the different components of the CPU in the context of the basic components of a computer system.

Specifically, the CPU has a control unit which, as its name implies, literally controls (manages) the execution of every single instruction carried out by the computer. The control unit is connected by a bus to another unit designed to handle arithmetic and logic (it is called the A/LU for short). As one might expect, the arithmetic unit carries out all the mathematical processing—addition, subtraction, multiplication, division, and so on.

---

[3]The chips described here are fingernail-size devices that can hold several million electronic components etched onto a wafer of silicon. They are often referred to as "silicon chips." In the mid-1960s, a new industry grew up around the manufacture of these chips in a valley just south of San Francisco which is now popularly called Silicon Valley. The industry of the valley used to be fruit farming, which is possibly the origin of the name of one of the most successful computer corporations born in this valley— Apple Computer, Inc.

Figure 6.4
An actual photo of the
internal components
of the system unit
Photo courtesy IBM
Corporation

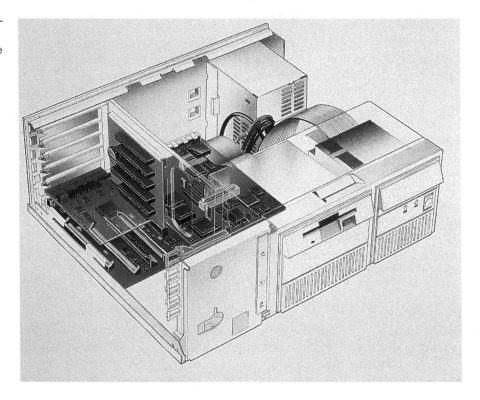

The logic unit's job is not so obvious. Logic has to do with whether or not statements are true or false. The logic unit examines relations between data on the basis of whether, say, one item of data is greater than, or less than, or equal to some other item of data. For example, one might ask the computer to select all the students in a class who scored less than 70% on a test. The instruction to the computer would be something like: If test score < (less than) 70%, then write student's name on the screen. The "if" tells the computer it is dealing with a logic instruction. If a score is less than 70%, the logic unit will return the answer *true* to the control unit, and the student's name will be printed on the screen. If, on the other hand, the student's score is equal to, or greater than, 70%, the logic unit will return the answer *false,* and the name will be ignored.

Random Access Memory (RAM)

The system unit also contains the internal memory chips known as random access memory (**RAM,** for short). These memory chips, which are connected to the CPU by another bus, are highlighted in figure 6.5. If you look at a RAM chip with a magnifying glass, you can just about make out that it is made up of row upon tiny row of places to store data. The computer needs RAM to store the programs and data that will be used during processing. For example, when you want to do any word processing, you must first load the word processor program into RAM. Then, as you enter your text (the data) the computer stores the characters you type in RAM, too.

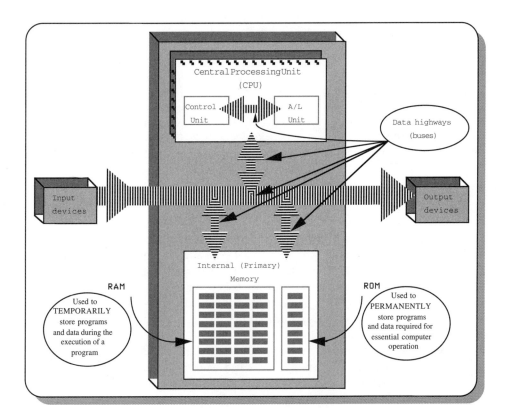

Figure 6.5
The central
processing unit
(CPU) in the context
of a computer's basic
components

The size of RAM is measured in terms of how many bytes of data it can store. A **byte** is a unit of memory capable of storing the equivalent of one character (such as a letter of the alphabet). Later in this chapter, we will learn more about how the computer represents data. For now, remember that the more bytes there are in RAM, the faster and more flexible the computer. It is not unusual today for the RAM of a desktop computer to have in megabytes of memory (a megabyte is a little over 1 million bytes).

One problem with RAM is that it is a **volatile** storage medium. A good definition of the word *volatile* is the definition that applies when the same word is used to describe gases: "dangerously unstable." RAM depends on a steady supply of electric current in order to store data. If the power supply is turned off, the data are lost. This is why we need disk drives. The disk is a **nonvolatile** storage medium, capable of storing data after the system has been turned off or when the disk has been removed from the system.

Those who are new to computing will sooner or later discover the difference between volatile and nonvolatile memory when they lose their work because they forgot to save it on the disk as they went along. One of the problems with computers is that they can accidentally get turned off (power cuts and so forth), so users will find themselves becoming very conscientious about saving to disk at regular intervals while in the process of completing the task at hand.

Table 6.1	The Differences between RAM and ROM	
RAM		**ROM**
Volatile: needs a steady supply of electricity to keep the data in memory.		*Non volatile:* data and programs (firmware) stay in memory after the power is turned off.
RAM is the user's workspace. Data and programs are constantly changing.		ROM contains a fixed library of programs used by the system in its operations.

Read Only Memory (ROM)

The system unit also needs special internal memory chips that, like disk storage, are nonvolatile—the contents of these chips are retained even after the power is turned off. These are called **ROM** chips (ROM stands for read only memory). Their purpose is primarily to store programs and data that the computer needs in order to start itself up. When we turn on a computer and hear stirrings of electronic life, like the disk drives spinning and images appearing on the screen, the instructions that trigger that life are stored permanently in ROM.

ROM is nonvolatile because the instructions are "hardwired" onto the chips. The chips are actually built with the programs etched onto them. As such the programs are physically, and therefore permanently, part of the hardware. For this reason these programs are called **firmware** to distinguish them from software that is not permanently etched onto a chip's surface.

Table 6.1 illustrates the differences between RAM and ROM.

We do not need to know any more about the electronics involved in the system unit of a computer. Just be aware that if the system unit goes down, everything goes down!

6.2.3 The Keyboard

With most computer systems, the keyboard is the most common means of getting data into the system to be processed. Other input devices include the mouse, joystick, graphics pad, a microphone for voice input, and so forth. We can also input commands to some computers by touching appropriate areas on the screen. Such touch-screen devices are common for systems used exclusively for accessing information—such as those used in shopping malls or tourist welcome centers. But it is likely that they will become more common in classrooms, too, to simplify children's interaction with multimedia databases and other learning systems.

The table that follows (table 6.2) lists some of the less familiar keys on a keyboard, along with their typical uses with programs. Bear in mind that not all keyboards will have all of the keys listed.

Table 6.2	Special Keys on the Computer Keyboard
Key	**Function**
Return/Enter	Tells computer to accept data you have entered, or to perform a task you have selected.
ESC	Switches back to a previous state or screen, or backs one out of changes.
Delete/Backspace	Removes unwanted characters or lines or other blocks of data.
Tab	Skips across the screen several characters at a time.
Function keys	Keys that may be programmed to carry out specific functions.
Special purpose keys (Control, Option, Command, etc.)	Used extensively in conjunction with other keys to carry out specific functions.

6.2.4 The Disk Drive(s)

RAM and ROM are examples of internal, or primary, memory. However, we must be able to store data outside the system unit for two reasons: (1) internal memory is volatile—when the power is turned off memory is erased; so a long-term memory is essential; (2) the amount of memory in RAM and ROM is limited by the size of the machine, so an unlimited data storage medium is also essential.

The memory outside the system unit is called secondary memory. The four most common media for secondary memory are:

- punched cards (used from the very beginnings of the electronic computer in 1939)
- magnetic tape (used since the late 1950s)
- magnetic disk (also used since the late 1950s)
- optical discs (introduced in the 1980s)

Potentially, the supply of secondary memory is infinite; one can simply add disks or tape or punch cards as needed.

Magnetic disk is the most common medium for secondary storage of data. Magnetic tape and punched cards are rarely used at all with educational computing systems. Early microcomputers used magnetic cassette tape, but magnetic disk is universally used today because of its speed and ease of data access. **Optical discs** (CD-ROM, **WORM,** and **interactive videodisc**), which will be described later in the context of multimedia systems, are becoming more and more popular as we shall see.

The drives that are used to make the data on the disks accessible to the computer are described as either **floppy** or **hard** disk drives. The floppy drive uses a disk that is flexible; inside the outer protective case is a thin, circular sheet of mylar plastic which has

Figure 6.6
Computers today
commonly use both
3½″ and 5¼″ disks for
secondary storage.

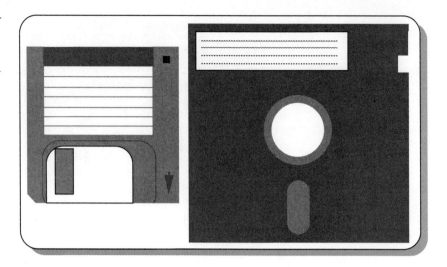

been coated with a thin film of magnetizable metal oxide. Data are stored on the disk by way of magnetized spots on the metal oxide surface, as we shall see.[4] A hard disk drive, on the other hand, uses a rigid, metallic disk.

The advantage of a hard disk is twofold:

1. A hard, or fixed, disk can store data more densely than a floppy disk—this is because the hard disk is fixed in place and therefore less likely to be damaged, which means that the parts can be manufactured to much finer tolerances than with removable and flexible floppy disks.

2. The data can be accessed much more quickly from a hard disk.

It is normal for a new system today to come with a hard disk, since processing is so slow and cumbersome without one. Of course, a hard disk drive can usually be added to computer systems that do not already have one.

Figure 6.6 illustrates the two most popular types of floppy disk. The Apple Plus, IIe, and IIc invariably use a 5¼″ floppy disk. The Macintosh Plus, SE, and Classic use only 3½″ disks. The Apple IIGS and the Apple Macintosh LC, on the other hand, typically use both 3½″ disks and 5¼″ disks.

IBM and Commodore systems now also come configured (designed) with both 3½″ and 5¼″ disk drives. Eventually, however, the 5¼″ disk will be completely re-placed by the more recent, more reliable, and convenient 3½″ format. The 3½″ disk is housed in a more rigid casing, none of the disk is exposed, and its smaller size enables it to fit nicely in a coat or shirt pocket.

Later, in section 6.4, we will learn the ins and outs of taking care of disks, along with the other components of computer systems.

Does your computer system have two disk drives? Is one disk drive bigger than the other? If so, the smaller of the two drives is for the 3½″ disks.

---

[4]A magnetized spot represents a 1; a nonmagnetized spot, 0. Data are encoded in 1s and 0s, as explained later.

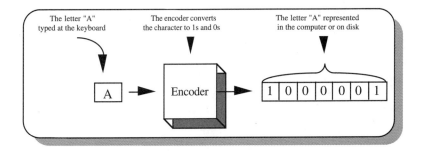

Figure 6.7
Data are represented
in the computer as
1s and 0s

If you have only one disk drive, you can still run many older, less complex programs because you can store your files on the same disk as the program. But, it is much more convenient to work with at least two drives—either two floppy disk drives, or one floppy disk drive and a hard disk drive. If there are two disk drives on the system that you will be using, you would put the program disk in one drive (on the hard disk if you have one), and your data disk in the second drive. This dual drive arrangement means that you will not find yourself constantly swapping disks in and out of one drive.

Remember: The disks are categorized as secondary (or external) memory. This is different from RAM, which we already discussed. RAM, also called primary (or internal) memory, is part of the system unit of the computer. RAM is capable of storing data only when the power is turned on. If you want to keep files after you turn off the computer, it is essential that you use secondary memory such as disks.

Data are stored on the disk using magnetized spots to represent the characters that make up the data that we want to save. Each spot can have a positive or negative charge—a positive charge typically represents a 1 and a negative charge represents a 0 (zero). One might find it easiest to think of these magnetized spots like switches. When the switch is turned on, it represents a 1; when the switch is turned off, it represents a 0.

The 1s and 0s are the basic units of the binary (base 2) number system, which is the language computers understand. Everything in a computer—the instructions that tell the computer what to do as well as the data that it manipulates—must be represented in 1s and 0s. (See figure 6.7.)

Special codes have been devised to enable a computer to store the data that we understand in our human language (letters of the alphabet, names, numbers, text in general) in the language of 1s and 0s. The most commonly used code today is **ASCII.**[5] For example, the capital letter *A* is represented in this code as follows: 1000001. (See figure 6.7.) The encoder is part of the computer's system unit, and it has the job of converting everything either typed at the keyboard or entered by other means into the binary coded equivalent. Each 1 or 0 is called a **bit** (bit is an acronym for binary digit), and all seven or eight bits together are called a **byte.** One byte is equivalent to one character on a keyboard—a punctuation mark, a letter of the alphabet, a digit, and so forth.

Appendix A contains the complete set of ASCII codes for all the characters that we use in the electronic storage and exchange of data (Information Interchange). Using

---

[5] American Standard Code for Information Interchange

ASCII code, you could easily write out your name in 1s and 0s. You could also write a secret message to a friend—provided your friend knew the code, too! Think of the 1s and 0s of machine language as if they were the characters of any other foreign language—a means of communication that needs to be translated from one language to the other before it can be understood and acted on.

There is no mystery here. All you need to remember is that a computer can allow us to capture, represent, store, and manipulate literally anything, as long as we can come up with a way of converting everything to 1s and 0s. This is true of images and sound, not just characters in a language. For example, a black and white picture can be divided up into tiny dots or segments. (See figure 6.8.) Think of the grid in figure 6.8a as if it were made up of row upon row of electronic switches, or magnetizable spots. Wherever part of the image of the face crosses a square in the grid, the switch is turned on in that square. (See figure 6.8b.) This would be equivalent to the binary value 1 in the computer or on the disk (colored black when printed on the screen or on paper). Wherever a square is empty, the switch is turned off. This, of course, would be equivalent to the binary value 0 in the computer or on the disk (colored white on the screen or on paper).

The process of converting a regular image, say one drawn by hand, to the 1s and 0s of the computer-based version is called **digitizing**—storing an image or a sound in digits (1s and 0s). The dots (small squares) in figure 6.8 are called **pixels** in graphics (pixel being short for picture element). Wherever there is a black dot, the computer would store it as a 1 in memory. The white dots would be represented as a 0. Shades of grey would depend on how closely the black dots are packed together. The more dots there are to play with, the better the picture. Figure 6.8 is made up on a grid of only about 40 pixels by 40 pixels. That is just 1,600 dots to play around with. This is considered very **low resolution**, as you can see for yourself. The fewer the pixels used to capture the image, the lower the resolution. The low resolution digitized version of the face is quite a distortion of the original (even though the original is not exactly a work of art!).

It is not unusual today to display images on the screens of **high resolution** computer monitors that have the capability of representing the images on a grid comprised of 1,000 pixels by 1,000 pixels. That is over 600 times better resolution than the image in figure 6.8b. The illustration of the smiley face in figure 6.8a could be digitally reproduced much more faithfully on such a monitor.

Sound, as you probably know, travels in waves through the air and can be represented on paper as wavy lines. These, too, can be converted into 1s and 0s and stored on a disk or in the computer's memory. Just as images such as our smiley face can be more faithfully rendered the more bits (pixels) we use, so the more bits (1s and 0s) we use to capture the sound wave, the more accurately we can represent it in the computer or on disk. We simply need a method for converting the digitized signals back into a form that can be reproduced as sound through an amplifier. This is more or less how compact discs (CDs) work. We will look at this technology when we examine the special components that are added to make up a multimedia educational computing system.

6.2.5 The Printer

The most common printer still used with computers in schools today is the dot matrix printer (such as Apple's Imagewriter II™). "Dot matrix" means that a character that is

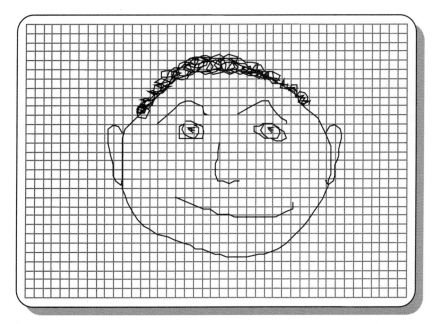

a

Figure 6.8
(*a*) Undigitized
image; (*b*) digitized
image.

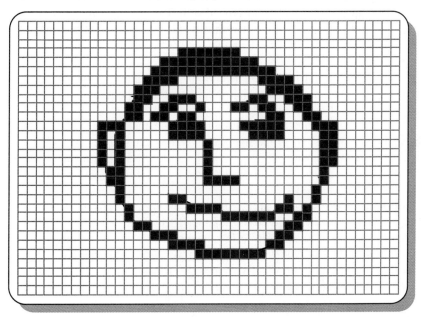

b

printed on the paper is formed by a set of pins (a matrix of pins) organized into the shape of the character that is then smacked against the printer's ribbon and thence imprinted onto the paper.

Unfortunately, dot matrix printers have several disadvantages. They are slow, noisy, and produce output that is not of the highest quality. Laser printers, on the other hand, are relatively fast and quiet, and produce output that is close to printshop quality.

Until recently, the best thing about dot matrix printers has been their price as compared to laser printers. This is why most of the printers you will find in the school are of the dot matrix variety. In the late 1970s and early 1980s, laser printers were priced in the tens of thousands of dollars. Only businesses were able to justify the expense involved. Today, however, laser printers have become a superior and financially viable alternative to dot matrix printers. The print quality of laser printers is invariably superb as long as you have a good supply of toner (ink) and everything is in good working order. The cost of laser printers has fallen to the $500 range.

Dot matrix printers usually have buttons that allow control of the quality of the output they produce. Later in this chapter (6.3 Maintaining Your Computer System), we will examine some of the routines necessary to maintain in optimal working condition printers and other vulnerable, computer-driven devices.

6.2.6 The Mouse

In the next chapter, we will learn about operating systems. These are the sets of software that, among other functions, allow us to use a mouse to give directions to the computer and to make selections among prompts that are displayed on the screen. The mouse, in terms of hardware, is the palm-size critter that sits on the desktop next to the computer. It has a tail, of course, that snakes its way to the plug at the back of the system unit, and is designed to run around on the desk (under our control, of course!). It has a couple of moving parts: a track ball underneath, which controls the movement of the cursor on the screen, and one or more buttons on top, which are clicked to carry out the tasks pointed at on the screen by the arrow-shaped cursor.

An Apple IIGS or Macintosh LC will have a mouse with the machine. The same will probably be true for later versions of the IBM PC or compatible systems. The IBM PS/1 and PS/2 also come with a mouse. All the software developed for the Macintosh is designed to use the mouse for interaction with the system. Software developed for the Apple II or IBM PC, however, does not necessarily take advantage of the mouse. Most software constructed today assumes that the mouse is an integral component of a computer system, so one will need to get used to "pointing," "clicking," and "dragging."

If you are not already accustomed to using the mouse and you know that you have one with your computer system, you would do well to work your way through the on-line tutorial prepared for your machine. Find your copy of this software, put it in the disk drive, and turn on your computer. Then just follow along with the tutorial. You will enjoy the ride!

Now that you have read about them, take a moment to identify the components of your system. Check off each of the components (table 6.3) after you recognize it as part of your basic computer setup.

Table 6.3	Computer System Hardware	
	Component	**Check**
	The system unit	——
	The keyboard	——
	The monitor	——
	The disk drive(s)	——
	The printer	——
	The mouse	——

6.3 The Components of a Multimedia Educational Computing System

Multimedia computing systems are slowly spreading in schools. In part III, chapter 12, the place of these exciting systems in the classroom is discussed at length, especially in regard to the software needed to drive the technology and which enable teachers and students to author their own interactive learning experiences.

The hardware required consists of the basic computer system already described plus secondary memory devices that include an optical disc[6] drive such as a CD-ROM drive and/or an interactive videodisc player and remote control device. Multimedia is most effective if there is also either a large, high-resolution color monitor or a good-quality color LCD panel to go along with the overhead projector. High-quality speakers will take care of sound output. Finally, a scanner for capturing still images adds a useful capability to the system. Figure 6.9 illustrates the components of the *IMPAC•T*™ multimedia system developed by Multimedia Design Corporation. Let us examine these components one by one.

6.3.1 Optical Disc Drives

There are two kinds of discs that use laser technology to store data: CD-ROM drives which use 5¼″ discs, and interactive videodisc (also called laserdisc) players that use 12″ discs. Typically, the CD-ROM disc can store the equivalent of about 800 high-density floppy disks or 1,500, 5¼″ floppy disks. A 12″ videodisc can store roughly the equivalent of 5,000 high density floppy disks!

The numbers are not important. What *is* important is to understand that laser-based storage technology can store data much more compactly than magnetic storage technology. This is critical when it comes to video images because so much data is needed to represent each image (remember those pixels we talked about earlier in this chapter?). A moving video sequence needs to be "refreshed" on the screen at a rate of 30 frames per second and each frame has to be captured on the disk. Magnetic disks simply cannot handle this kind of storage density, at least for the time being. As it is, the 12″ videodisc can store only one hour's worth of video programming, 30 minutes on each side of the disc.

---

[6] Notice the spelling of *disc* when referring to optical discs. Magnetic disks are spelled with a "k"; optical discs with a "c."

Figure 6.9
The components of a
multimedia system
(annotated)
Illustration courtesy
Multimedia Design
Corporation

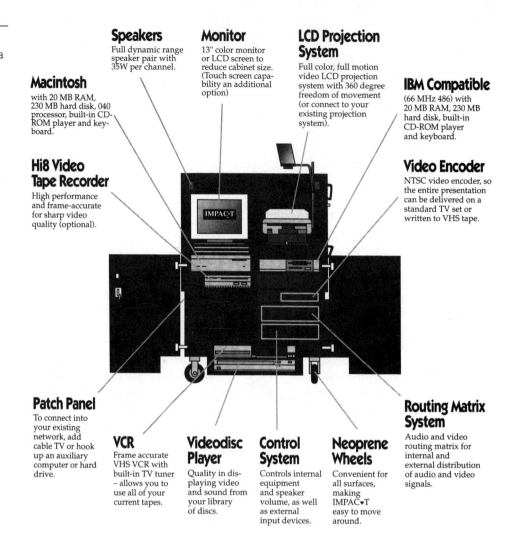

Speakers
Full dynamic range
speaker pair with
35W per channel.

Monitor
13" color monitor
or LCD screen to
reduce cabinet size.
(Touch screen capa-
bility an additional
option)

**LCD Projection
System**
Full color, full motion
video LCD projection
system with 360 degree
freedom of movement
(or connect to your
existing projection
system).

Macintosh
with 20 MB RAM,
230 MB hard disk, 040
processor, built-in CD-
ROM player and key-
board.

IBM Compatible
(66 MHz 486) with
20 MB RAM, 230 MB
hard disk, built-in
CD-ROM player
and keyboard.

**Hi8 Video
Tape Recorder**
High performance
and frame-accurate
for sharp video
quality (optional).

Video Encoder
NTSC video encoder, so
the entire presentation
can be delivered on a
standard TV set or
written to VHS tape.

Patch Panel
To connect into
your existing
network, add
cable TV or hook
up an auxiliary
computer or hard
drive.

VCR
Frame accurate
VHS VCR with
built-in TV tuner
– allows you to
use all of your
current tapes.

**Videodisc
Player**
Quality in dis-
playing video
and sound from
your library
of discs.

**Control
System**
Controls internal
equipment
and speaker
volume, as well
as external
input devices.

**Neoprene
Wheels**
Convenient for
all surfaces,
making
IMPAC▾T
easy to move
around.

**Routing Matrix
System**
Audio and video
routing matrix for
internal and
external distribution
of audio and video
signals.

Laser technology is often referred to as optical technology because beams or pulses of light (optics) are used to transmit the data from place to place, from disk to computer, from computer to computer, and so on. Data are usually stored on the surface of the optical disc using microscopic "pits," or indentations, that are burned into the platter by a laser beam. Data on CD-ROM discs are represented in 1s and 0s on the tracks that spiral[7] around the disk's surface. A pit is used to store a 1 on the disc's surface; where there is no pit, the system interprets that as a 0. It is as simple as that.

---

[7] The track into which the pits are burned is actually a continuous path that starts near the center of the disc and spirals its way toward the outer edge. The tracks on a magnetic disk, by contrast, are concentric—each track is independent of the others.

When read from the disc, data must be decoded into magnetic form so that it can be processed in the computer on its way to being displayed on the monitor or amplified over the speakers. Researchers are currently refining the technology which allows computers to process data in the form of pulses of light. Such laser computers will operate considerably faster than the current electromagnetic machines.

6.3.2 Display and Audio Devices

Today, multimedia places a great deal of emphasis on video and graphic images as a stimulating dimension to inquiry learning. Along with the availability of whole libraries of on-line textual material, there is an ever-increasing abundance of magnificent still and motion picture material that multimedia systems typically tap into.

Clearly, the display technology is a critical component of a visually oriented, information delivery system. This is especially true when the material is to be presented to larger groups such as a class of children. So, a large screen, high-resolution display device is almost a necessity. Alternatively, a good-quality LCD panel can capture the images from the computer screen and display them on a large screen using the overhead projection system.

6.3.3 Scanners

A scanner is a device that converts images into digital format by reducing them to a matrix of dots (pixels) as illustrated earlier. (See figure 6.8.) Each dot has a binary value made up of 1s and 0s that captures the exact characteristics of the dot. If the image is black and white, just one bit (1 = black; 0 = white) is sufficient to describe the dot. If, on the other hand, the image is rich in color, more bits are required depending on the range of colors the system is designed to handle.

Commodore Computer Corporation led the personal computer industry when the company offered a palette of 16 million different colors from which to choose when displaying images on the monitor of its Amiga personal computer. The Apple Macintosh II and IBM PS/2 quickly followed suit. In these machines, the characteristics of *each* pixel are captured and represented in memory using 16 bits.

Fax machines, which create a digitized version of an image and then transmit it, bit by bit, over telephone lines to some other location are no more than glorified scanners connected by **modem** to the local and wide area networks that make up the data communications system. We will learn more about modems and local and wide area networks in part III, chapter 11.

■ 6.4 Maintaining Your Computer System

This section will deal with some of the dos and don'ts of taking care of a computer system. Ideally, the computers in the schools will get a great deal of use from children. You should, therefore, be aware of problems that can arise with different parts of a computer system, and how to avoid them, so that you can instill in your students appropriate behavior around the machines. The following compendium of correct practice will go from the general to the particular, focusing first on the classroom or laboratory environment in which computers are found, and then on the specific components of a system.

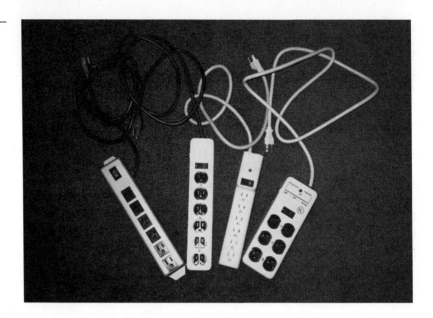

6.4.1 General Dos and Don'ts

- **Don't smoke around the equipment, and keep it covered when not in use.** Dust and smoke can damage the tiny components of various devices, especially disk drives. Covering the computer would be especially important in a classroom. There is often a chalkboard, and there are always children! Even "dustless" chalk creates fine-grain dust, and children bring in and kick up their fair share of airborne particulates.

- **Use a surge protecting power strip to plug in the various components of the system.** Unusual "spikes" in the electrical power supply can "fry" the circuits on the computer chips. Surge protection devices can be purchased at little expense and will save you hundreds, if not thousands, of dollars worth of damage.

- **Keep food and drink away from the equipment.** This is a difficult one for children and adults alike. Crumbs and sticky liquids can gum up the works.

- **Dust down the various machines using a *damp* cloth** so that the dirt is carried away from the machine. If the keyboard is separate from the system unit, hold it upside down while you clean it.

6.4.2 Taking Care of Disks

It might not seem important to cover this topic, and you might be tempted to skim through it, especially if you have already held a disk in your hand and it looks robust enough. The fact is, however, that more grief is caused through careless handling and use of disks, especially the 5¼″ disks still commonly associated with the Apple II or IBM PC systems, than any other component of a computer system. Even if you think you know all there is to know about disks, read on to see if there are one or two tips that will help ensure you trouble-free use of computers in the future. This section will also be useful when you are teaching your students to use computers.

Disks are damaged more easily than you think

As figure 6.11 illustrates, there are five parts to the 5¼″ disks you use. Figure 6.12 illustrates that the 3½″ disk, because of its rigid case and metal flange, does not need the protective sleeve.

Check off on the list in table 6.4 each of the parts as you recognize them on one of your own disks.

You should understand that data stored on disks should be cared for at least as much as we take care of data stored on paper. The computer disk that is used to store programs and/or data can take a certain amount of punishment. Here, however, are some of the things that can happen to cause damage to the disk, and therefore loss (accidentally, of course!) of any data that might be stored on it:

- *The disk may be crumpled.* One fold anywhere can be enough to make it unreadable.
- *The disk may become stuck in its protective cover.* This can happen if you put books on top of the disk, or if you keep it inside a book that then gets stacked under other books. You can imagine how readily such a scenario might occur.
- *Sticky food or drink may be spilled on the disk's surface.* How easy it is to innocently put a disk down on a table only to discover that someone (never you!) has not cleaned up coffee or fruit juice that was spilled before your arrival.
- *The disk may get overheated* by being left in a car on a sunny day. Extreme cold can also cause a disk to become unreadable, though this is less likely—unless you live in Alaska!
- *You may damage the disk by pressing too hard with a ballpoint pen* when writing on the identification label.
- *Any magnetic field* (such as the ones on the refrigerator door) *brought into close proximity with the disk will erase the contents* since the data are stored in electromagnetic form.

The simple protection against such hazards?

- **Make a backup copy of all your disks,** no matter how unimportant you might think they are. This takes a little extra time at the end of sessions during which you have been working at the computer, but the payoff in peace of mind is well worth the effort.
- **When not in the disk drive, the diskette should always be kept in its protective sleeve.** This sleeve, as well as the protective cover, is specially coated to protect the diskette from static electricity and the like.
- **Identify your diskettes by writing your name and the contents on a sticker attached to the disk.** Usually you will write the name of a disk on the sticker label *before* you attach the label. If you write on the label after you have stuck it on the disk, always do so with a soft, felt-tip marker.

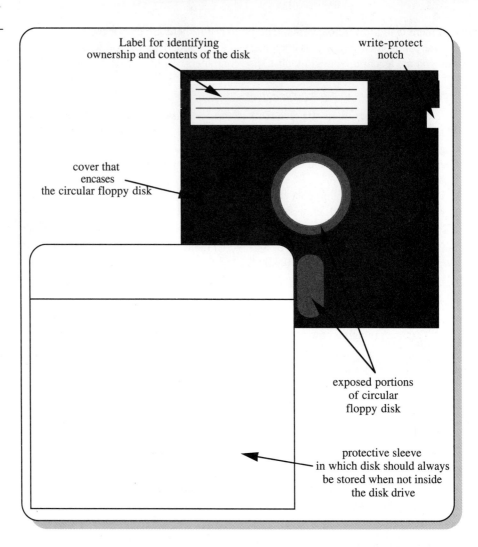

Figure 6.11
The components of a 5¼″ disk

Label for identifying ownership and contents of the disk

write-protect notch

cover that encases the circular floppy disk

exposed portions of circular floppy disk

protective sleeve in which disk should always be stored when not inside the disk drive

Table 6.4	**Component Parts of Floppy Disks**	
	Component	**Check**
1.	**The protective sleeve** used to store the disk when not in use in order to protect the exposed read/write opening (5¼″ disks only).	——
2.	**The cover** that encases the actual circular floppy disk on which the data are stored.	——
3.	**The write-protect notch** that can be covered to prevent the disk from being written to ("written to" is more computerese. It describes the process whereby data is saved on, i.e. transferred to, a disk).	——
4.	**The floppy disk itself,** circular and made of mylar plastic coated with metal oxide.	——
5.	**The label** used to identify the disk.	——

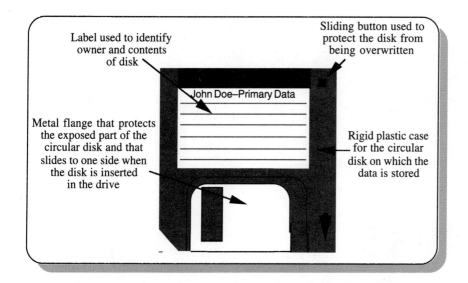

Figure 6.12
The components of a
3½″ disk

Label used to identify
owner and contents
of disk

Sliding button used to
protect the disk from
being overwritten

John Doe–Primary Data

Metal flange that protects
the exposed part of the
circular disk and that
slides to one side when
the disk is inserted
in the drive

Rigid plastic case
for the circular
disk on which the
data is stored

- **Disks should be carried around in a container** such as those illustrated in figure 6.13. The more you use computers, the more loose disks you will have around. You should set up a system for storing them carefully at home or in the office. Larger containers can hold as many as 50 disks at a time. You can attach labels to different sections and thus catalog them so that it is easy to retrieve the one you need at any particular time. It is surprising, otherwise, how easy it is to lose track of the data that you have collected after you have been using your computer for more than a few months.
- **Do not leave disks lying around, even in the office.** The risk of loss, damage, or vandalism is obvious. Consider how important the data stored on those disks is to you, and take appropriate security measures to safeguard its integrity.

The key is to always handle disks with care. You will thus avoid the grief that comes to those who lose hours of work.

Handling disks

Figure 6.14 illustrates the proper way to hold a 5¼″ disk. When you remove the 5¼″ disk from its protective sleeve, you will notice that there is a small area cut away (fig. 6.11) which exposes the specially coated plastic disk on which the data is actually stored. Be careful not to touch this one small exposed area, since you could otherwise destroy the data on the disk.

Figure 6.15 illustrates the correct and incorrect orientation of a 5¼″ disk when placed into the disk drive. If you examine the disk, you will see that one side (the reverse side) has folds along the edges where the outer casing of the disk has been stuck down. The other side of the disk is entirely smooth along the edges. The smooth side is the front side, and should always be facing up when you put the disk into the drive.

Loading the disk into the disk drive

This activity depends on whether you are using a 5¼″ drive or a 3½″ drive.

Figure 6.13
Containers for
carrying disks

Figure 6.14
Handling a 5¼" disk

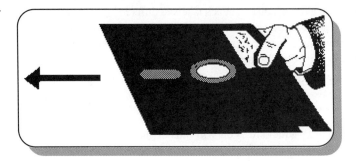

If you are using a 5¼" disk drive . . .

In the 5¼" drives, there is a latch, or door as it is also called, that closes over the slot in the disk drive. This latch should be open when you put the disk into the drive. Holding the disk as illustrated in figure 6.14, gently slide it into the disk drive. Never force the disk into place. Once the disk is fully inserted into the drive, carefully close the latch. To remove the disk, open the door by raising the latch, and carefully slide out the disk.

If you have a 3½" disk drive . . .

Loading a disk into the 3½" disk drive is a simpler process. Hold the disk as illustrated in figure 6.16 and slide it into the slot in the front of the drive. After you

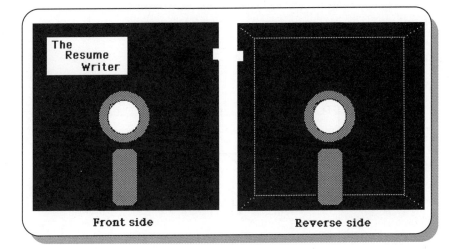

Figure 6.15
Front and reverse
sides of a 5¼″ disk

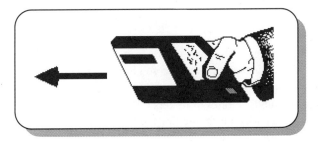

Figure 6.16
The correct way to
hold the 3½″ disk

have pushed the disk most of the way in, the drive will "grab" it and complete the loading process for you. Unlike the 5¼″ drives, there is no latch or lever to close once the disk is inserted.

To remove the disk from an external 3½″ drive (off to one side and connected to the system unit by a cable), press the small button to the right of the slot. If the disk is in an internal drive (underneath the monitor), use the mouse to drag the disk down to the trash can on the screen. The system will then automatically eject the disk.

Organizing your data on disk

This is a task usually given far less attention than it deserves. If you are new to computing, you will be amazed how easily you can lose track of the work you have stored on disk. If you are not new to computing you are no doubt nodding your head in agreement! Two simple strategies can solve this problem:

- **Always give your files meaningful names.** If it is a file about grades, call it Grades. If it is a file about field trips, call it Field Trips—unless you are using a program that does not allow you to use more than eight characters for a file name, in which case

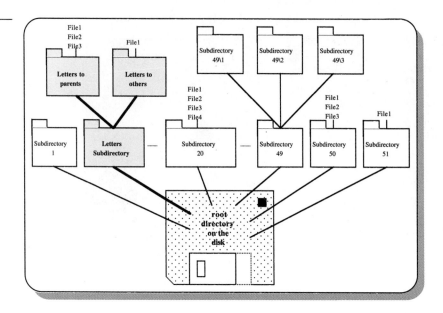

Figure 6.17
Directories and subdirectories (folders)

call it Trips, or FldTrips. Notice that even the abbreviation is at least a mnemonic. Do not use a name that will be meaningless to you once you have forgotten why you used it in the first place (Stuff, Junk, XYZ).

- Learn how to create and manage subdirectories or folders on your system. Subdirectories (called folders on the Macintosh) are like the drawers in a filing cabinet: they enable you to store your files according to categories of your choosing. After a while, you may have a collection of letters saved on your disk; put them all in a subdirectory called Letters. You may have different types of letters, some to parents, some to others; create one subdirectory inside the Letters subdirectory called Parents and another subdirectory called Other. (See figure 6.17.) And so on. This way, when you look at the list of subdirectories and files in your top level (root) directory, you will easily be able to find whatever you are looking for.

6.4.3 Printers

The appearance of your printed output (called hard copy in computerese) ultimately depends on the quality of your printer. The appearance of your printed output also depends on how well your printer has been cared for. Of course, if you have a low-quality printer, you can hardly expect to get anything other than low-quality results. But often a printer can be made to look cheap because it is not cared for and also because it is not used correctly.

On dot matrix printers such as Apple's Imagewriter or the Epson FX series of printers, the ribbon is the easiest component to control. For a few dollars, the purchase of a new ribbon will greatly improve the definition of the type on the printed page. To get the best use out of a ribbon, it is also important to make sure it is housed correctly on the machine. This may mean pressing harder than you expect when installing a new ribbon. It must click firmly into place; otherwise only part of the ribbon will be used, thus shortening its useful life.

If you have an impact printer such as a dot matrix printer or a daisy wheel printer,[8] you may have to worry about noise, especially if you expect the printer to be used in the classroom while other activities are taking place. To cut down the noise you can buy, or rig up, a cover to act as a muffler for the sound.

Nonimpact printers, such as laser printers, have fewer moving parts than impact printers, and therefore tend to be more reliable. They also make a minimal amount of noise, and print much faster than the kind of impact printers you are likely to see connected to microcomputers. Just as you must change ribbons on impact printers to maintain the best quality output, so you must replace the ink cartridges in laser printers. If the output from a laser printer is uneven, it usually means the ink supply is running low in the cartridge, but it does not necessarily mean that you have to replace the cartridge yet. You can often eke out a worthwhile number of extra pages by taking the ink cartridge out of the printer and shaking it to spread the remaining ink evenly in the drum.

The disks, disk drives, printer, and keyboard are the parts of a microcomputer system that need the most care because they have more moving parts and are therefore more vulnerable to damage. Normal care will significantly prolong the life of the machinery, giving you and your students the benefit of more trouble-free hours of productive use.

■ Looking Back

The material in this chapter has been included for the benefit of the newcomer to computer technology. As such, it may also be useful for teachers who are already familiar with the computer but who have not yet actually taught computer use to children. For this latter group, there may well be material in this chapter that will be of value in the classroom: ideas for how to explain certain aspects of the technology, useful tips for system maintenance, and so on.

Although technology may not interest you per se, you should try to understand at least the basics of what makes machines work. In general, it is true that the more you understand the mechanics of a tool, the more effectively you will be able to use it.

■ Looking Forward

Chapter 7 will examine the different types of software necessary to control and take advantage of a computer's capabilities. The software is the key to a computer system's usefulness. We buy computers so that we can use the software for a wide variety of data processing tasks. There are two types of software: system software and applications software. The system software is necessary so that you can use the applications software. Good system software enables you to use the computer without your being aware of the complexities of the machine. Good system software allows you to concentrate on the application, the task you want to complete, using the computer as the tool to that end.

■ Do Something About It: Exercises and Projects

1. Prepare a lesson plan having your students use an on-line encyclopedia to help them learn about Martin Luther King, Jr. Have them memorize his "I have a dream" speech. Make sure they use the available audio and visual help.

2. Using software such as PC USA or PC Globe, prepare a lesson plan for your students to ascertain various facts and statistics about the state or country in which they were born. Make sure they use all available functions of the software.

3. Prepare weekly reference questions for your students, who will find the answers by using an on-line encyclopedia.

4. Have your students identify, describe, and understand all the parts of a computer system.

---

[8]A daisy wheel printer uses a fixed head for the type font, unlike the dot matrix printer, which uses a matrix of pins to form the character on the paper. The name "daisy wheel" comes from the fact that the characters are set on the end of spokes radiating from the center of the print head. The wheel rotates until the required character is in position, then the hammer hits the character at the end of the spoke against the ribbon and thence onto the paper.

Interactive multimedia in the media center
by Susan Bond, Skyline Elementary School, Cape Coral, Florida

Skyline Elementary School, serving 1,150 students from kindergarten through fifth grade, has a Tandy (IBM PC compatible) computer in the media center. The children use any one of several available compact discs to do research, hear a tiger roar, or see an elbow joint move.

The students already are quite comfortable working on computers as they routinely visit the Apple IIe and Mac LC II computer labs with their classes and use the four Apple IIe and Mac LC II computers in the media center individually throughout the day. Also each classroom at Skyline has five Mac LC IIs.

When the students viewed the Tandy computer's arrival, they thought it was "just another computer" on which to play such learning games as MECC's *Oregon Trail, Number Munchers,* and so forth. They were in for a surprise!

All the classes together with their teachers received an orientation for the Tandy multimedia PC. They soon came to realize that it is one of the neatest things to come along in a while. Not only can they browse through an entire encyclopedia, dictionary, atlases, and animal database for pure enjoyment, but also they have discovered how quickly they can find answers to questions for homework or research projects.

One of the compact discs the students use is the Compton's *Multimedia Encyclopedia* ("Bringing you the world on a disc!"). Access from the main menu to the encyclopaedia is by keyboard or mouse. Most students find the mouse exceptionally easy to use. In the encyclopedia, the student has a choice between Topic Tree, U.S. History Timeline, Picture Explorer, Science Feature Articles, Atlas, and Idea Search.

For example, the student may need information for a report on volcanoes. By selecting Idea Search and then typing in the key word *volcano,* the student calls up the entire article from the encyclopedia onto the screen. The left-hand margin displays various icons on which the student can click with the mouse. A headset indicates a human voice, a motion picture camera presents a moving picture, a camera displays a still picture and so on. Upon clicking on any underlined word in the article, the student will hear the word pronounced and a definition

will be displayed on the screen in a box superimposed on the article. Any word not underlined in the article on which one clicks will have its definition given.

If, while strolling through the article, the student cares to take notes, she simply clicks on the toolbox icon in the bottom margin and she can type in and save her own notes to be printed out later. Of course, the entire article can be printed, too, if needed. The student may click on the motion picture icon and actually watch a volcano erupt!

Another student may choose the U.S. History Timeline to view a chronological history of events from 1492 to the present, stopping now and then to hear Lincoln's Gettysburg Address, John F. Kennedy's inaugural speech, or Neil Armstrong's first words as he stepped onto the moon. History literally comes alive. From the Timeline, one can call up any article about a person or event listed.

The younger students especially enjoy calling up a seemingly never-ending variation of the best pictures **(continued)**

Susan Bond, author of the case study

in the encyclopedia by using the function called The Picture Explorer. Or, if they need to see a picture of a certain animal, place, or thing, they simply type the entire word or a truncated version of that word to bring up a color picture of what they would like to view.

If it is geography one needs, the Atlas zooms in and out of places on the whole earth, adds latitude or longitude lines, and gives geographical details in specific places. The world literally rotates in front of the students as they travel from place to place, focusing on the areas of interest. The student can call up all sorts of statistics about the different places or the entire relevant encyclopedia article without leaving the Atlas.

The Tandy PC at Skyline also has two other atlases, PC Globe and PC USA, from which very detailed maps may be printed. Students also can scan through statistics about the chosen location or even hear the state song of each U.S. state!

If animals are the subject of interest, one simply pops in the National Geographic Mammals disk. With simple icons, the student can bring up information on any mammal in the world. They will see moving pictures of a tiger racing towards them or hungry lions stalking, then eating, their prey. If one wants to know the specific call of an orangutan, one clicks on the headset icon showing at the bottom of the screen underneath the orangutan and the sound comes through loud and clear.

Like students everywhere, those at Skyline are very comfortable using the new technology and do not appear intimidated in any way by it. They use the PC for research reports, to get answers to reference questions, and just for fun.

Skyline teachers often use the computer in their classrooms connected to an LCD display panel. In this way, they can use the overhead projector to display whatever is on the computer's screen—very useful for whole-group instruction. The teachers use the PC to teach research skills, to view science experiments, and to help the students comprehend spatial geographical relationships.

Another feature available on the Tandy and unique to the Lee County School District is the county's movie, video, and instructional television (ITV) catalog. Teachers select the catalog from the computer's main menu. Then they search for their title or subject from one of seven subject areas (Science, Literature, Home Economics, and so forth). The search is made based on an exact title or a key word since every title is annotated!

For example, a teacher might want all available audiovisuals on dinosaurs. By first selecting Science from the menu, then typing *dinosaur,* the teacher almost immediately sees a countdown of every science title (approximately 10,000) being searched with the number of "hits" for dinosaur also displayed.

(continued)

Students using Compton's multimedia Encyclopedia

Skyline teacher doing an ITV on-line catalog search

Case Study 6 (concluded)

After the search is completed, the 40-plus dinosaur titles are listed with the format (movie, video, ITV program), audience (KPIJSA), date of publication, and length. Selection of any of these titles produces an annotation. The teacher can then print out any or all of the dinosaur titles for ease in ordering over the telephone and also to incorporate the printout in her lesson plans.

The only problem now seems to be that with so many teachers and students using the Tandy multimedia PC, Skyline could use a few more!

Talk About It

Topics for discussion based on the case study.

1. Having read the case study, how would you suggest leading an orientation for teachers on using the Tandy PC?

2. How do you think the on-line encyclopedia and other CD programs could aid your lesson preparation and learning for your students?

3. What new skills can your students gain by using a computer for research? Which skills possibly could be weakened by using a computer for research?

4. Suggest some activities for primary students using the picture capabilities of the various CD-based software systems.

5. How could you convince a reluctant teacher or student that using an on-line computer for research would be helpful to them?

References

Shurkin, Joel, *Engines of the Mind.* New York: Washington Square Press, 1985.

U.S. Congress, Office of Technology Assessment, *Power On! New Tools for Teaching and Learning,* OTA-SET-379. Washington, DC: U.S. Government Printing Office, September 1988.

Software
Systems for
Microcomputers

Those who educate children well are more to be
honored than those who produce them; for these only
gave them life, those the art of living well.

Aristotle (384–322 B.C.E.)

There is no short cut in the quest for perfection.

Ben Hogan (1912–   )

Learning Outcomes

In the previous chapter we learned about the hardware, the machinery, of educational computing systems. We also learned about one particular part of the hardware called ROM—read only memory. You may recall that ROM is comprised of computer chips on which are etched programs used by the central processing unit (CPU) at start-up to bring the system to life, so to speak. This is called **booting** or **bootstrapping**—the CPU reaches down into the ROM chips to get the instructions that enable it to receive further instructions from other parts of the system. Turning on the power switch acts as a wake-up call for the computer to go through this bootstrap routine. Without it the computer would be useless.

Bootstrapping is part of the **operating system** of a computer. In this chapter we will learn more about the functions of operating systems. We will also learn about two other types of software that depend on the operating system and that are essential to productive use of the computer. These are the **user-interface** software and **applications** software.

It is beyond the scope of this book to present the ins and outs of any specific operating system, user interface, or application. If, however, you are working your way through one of the set of tutorials that optionally accompany this text you will have a hands-on opportunity to discover many facets of the software that has been developed to run on the machine for which the tutorials have been designed.

This chapter will introduce key features of the three types of software, with special focus on the operating system and the user interface. Later, chapters 8 through 12 will focus on the wide range of applications software that has proved effective in the classroom when carefully integrated into the K–12 curriculum. Specifically, this chapter addresses the following topics:

- The layers of software
- The operating system
    - What is an operating system?
    - Operating systems most commonly found in schools
    - Utilities
    - Functions common to operating systems for popular educational computing systems
    - Useful user-controlled operating system functions
- The Graphical User Interface (GUI)
    - The problem of non-standard user interfaces
    - Standardization through integrated software
    - GUIs and educational psychology
- Applications software

7.1 Layers of Software

At the heart of any computer system is the hardware, discussed in the previous chapter. Layered onto the hardware are the different types of software that allow us, the users, to carry out useful tasks with the hardware. Figure 7.1 illustrates this idea. An operating

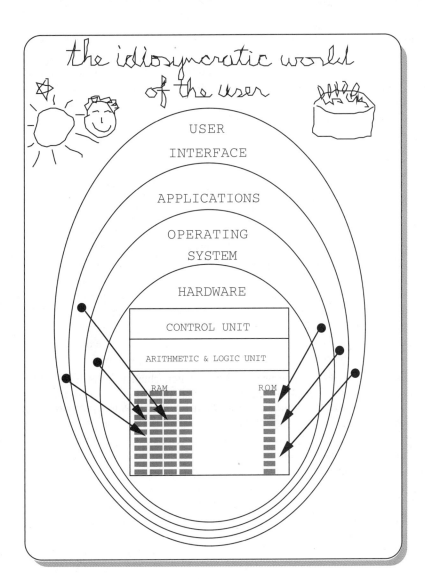

Figure 7.1
The operating system
is one of three layers
of software.

system is often represented as the inner of the three layers of software that make the power of computing machinery available to the user. As you can see, the operating system, comprised of a set of programs, comes between the hardware and the applications software. It makes it possible for us to work (the applications) on the computer without having to worry more than absolutely necessary about the machinery involved.

The user interface is the set of programs that controls the way in which the computer system presents itself to the world of the user. Notice the idiosyncratic nature of the user's world. The handwriting symbolizes the infinite variability of people's needs, wants, emotional state, personality and genetic constitution. A well-designed user interface will go a long way to accommodating this diverse world of users.

The user interface consists, on the one hand, of the software that controls how we interact with the computer system, whether by typing at the keyboard, or by pointing and clicking with the mouse, or by issuing voice commands, or by touching the screen. On the other hand, it consists of the software that controls how the computer interacts with us, whether by displaying text on the monitor or on a printer, or by speaking back to us, beeping, and so on.

7.1.1 Software that Is Part of the Computer's Hardware

The arrows pointing to RAM and ROM in figure 7.1 indicate that the programs that make up the operating system, the application, or the user interface must be stored in primary memory on one or the other of the sets of chips that constitute RAM and ROM. You may recall from chapter 6 that ROM contains at the very least the programs that the system needs to set itself up and make itself available to carry out the tasks delineated in other software. In the IBM PC family of computers, this basic set of programs is called the basic input/output system—*BIOS,* for short.

As computers become more powerful, more and more of the operating system is *hardwired* onto the ROM chips in the form of firmware. The advantage of this is Speed with a capital *S!* The system can access data much more quickly from primary memory than from secondary memory. Thus, as you can see in figure 7.1, some of the software that makes up the user interface may also be part of the firmware on the ROM chips along with key operating system programs. On a few systems, even applications programs such as simple word processors have been etched as firmware onto the ROM chips.

Firmware is thus software that has been hardwired onto the chips that are part of the computer's hardware. Until the 1980s and 1990s, firmware was a relatively precious commodity because the density with which the electronic components (switches and circuits and so forth) could be packed onto the surface of the chips was not great. However, there have been breathtaking advances in chip technology since the integrated circuit was invented in 1958.

In general, the more circuits that can be packed onto the surface of a computer chip the more powerful the machine at a cheaper price. It is projected that, by the year 2000, it will be possible to store about 100 million electronic components (**bits,** as they are called) onto a single chip no bigger than your little finger nail. You need 8 bits to store one character, and, on a printed page, you have about 3,000 characters. By the year 2000, one chip will be able to store about 33,000 pages of text—that is about sixty 500 page books!

Such chips will make it viable to increase the number of programs etched as firmware onto the ROM chips. This is already opening up a whole new industry based on the production of what have been called software ICs—computer chips (containing *Int*egrated *C*ircuits) that have prepackaged programs printed on them. It is a distinct possibility that by the year 2000, you will buy a computer with options packages, just like you buy a car. The vendor will simply plug into the logic board inside the computer the chips you need for specific applications such as word processing and so forth.

But that is in the future. For the time being, most software is still loaded into RAM from secondary storage. The computers used in schools have either magnetic or optical disks for this purpose, and it is the operating system that takes care of the humdrum tasks involved in running the software on the system. This is the subject of the next section.

7.2 The Operating System

The primary goal of this section is to encourage you to learn about the operating system of any computer you use because to do so elevates you to the level of a power user of that system. A very high percentage of computer users, understandably to some extent, learn only what they think they need to know about a computer to run a particular application such as a word processor. They never discover the many useful, built-in functions of modern, microcomputer operating systems such as sorting, merging, backup, use of subdirectories (folders on the Apple Macintosh), copying files and disks, multitasking, and on and on. As a result, even the little use they make of the computer is inefficient, often disorganized, and sometimes disastrous, as when data is lost because of failure to backup files. Familiarity with your computer's operating system gives you a higher level of control, which translates into power and peace of mind.

A secondary goal of this section is to help you appreciate the value of an operating system. Using a computer would be a nightmare if you had to manage all the computer's resources for yourself—which is what the computer pioneers had to do before they cottoned on to software-based operating systems. The job of computer operator used to involve responsible and reasonably well-paid work. One could take an associate degree in computer operations. That was before systems programmers wrote the software that allows a computer to take care of itself, thus relieving people of this responsibility.

7.2.1 What Is an Operating System?

We should begin by answering the question: What is an operating system? Then we will briefly examine each of the operating systems most likely to be encountered in schools. It is beyond the scope of this book to present all the features of all the operating systems. Our emphasis will be to show the similarities between them rather than the differences. Operating systems all behave in much the same way. The differences are the result of idiosyncrasies built into them by their creators.

A definition of a traditional operating system

An operating system consists of a set of programs that give added value to the computer by making available to the user the full resources of the computer hardware for which the operating system has been designed.

An operating system not only allows a computer to manage its operations and resources, but it also makes them available to you, the user, so that you can carry out the various applications that you had in mind when you bought your computer. An operating system makes it possible for you to get the utmost out of the computer's various control, input, output, and communications components. Davis (1978) puts it this way: "A well-designed operating system is not concerned with just hardware or just software or just data management, but with optimizing the way in which all of these resources work together."

The quotation from Aristotle at the opening of this chapter was not chosen simply to make you feel good about your choice of teaching as a profession. It also has some analogous relevance to operating systems. Without stretching the analogy too far, one might say that an operating system is to a computer what an education system is to a child. An understanding of this idea might deepen your appreciation of the role of an operating system.

Much of the behavior of a human being is determined by innate capabilities, genetics if you will, about which you learn a great deal in your education classes at college. These innate capabilities are akin to the characteristics of a computer that are built into the machinery, hardwired onto the chips in the CPU and ROM. You do not have too much choice about them. You are who you are, just as a computer is whatever model of computer it is.

As children grow, they are exposed to life. One way or another, they are educated. This process of education (nurture in the broadest sense) further individuates a person, ideally for the better—hence, the crucial role of good parenting and of good teachers. Aristotle is implying, of course, that the best parents are also good teachers. Continuing the parallel between a person's education and a computer's operating system, we might say that the operating system gives the computer an extra layer of individuation or character, if you will forgive the anthropomorphism. An operating system thus gives added value to the computer, just as education aims to increase the potential of the human being.

A definition of a modern operating system

Today we can refine our definition of an operating system by adding one ingredient that is having a dramatic impact on computer use. The ingredient is accessibility, and we can rewrite the definition as follows: A modern operating system consists of a set of programs that gives added value to the computer by making available to the general user in an easily accessible way the full resources of the computer hardware for which the operating system has been designed.

The ingredient of general accessibility was a side issue for the first thirty years or so of operating system design, largely because it was too expensive to implement. At first, the hardware technology was not powerful enough to handle the processing involved in carrying out computational tasks and at the same time present a comfortable, user-friendly face to the world. Also, the early users of computers were invariably techie types who relished the challenge of figuring out how to make a computer do what they wanted. However, once the machinery of computing became capable of handling the interactive display of colorful, high-quality graphics, a few insightful individuals, whom we will introduce shortly, wrote the programs that transformed the computer into a machine that *invites* use even by "ordinary" people like you and me!

A good operating system does its job in such a way that you are barely aware of the complex activity that has to go on in the background. When you or your students use the computer to do some word processing or practice math skills or engage in any one of the myriad applications designed for computers, you should not have to worry about how the computer manages the cursor on the monitor screen, or how the system finds the data on the disk in the disk drives, or how files are copied, or how the system switches from one process to another. The full capabilities of the machinery should be easily accessible to you.

7.2.2 Operating Systems Most Commonly Found in Schools

It is time to briefly identify the operating systems created for the computers most used in schools. As we shall see, some computers have better operating systems than others.

You will recall from chapter 2 that, in the United States, the most popular educational computer systems are supplied by either the Apple, IBM, or Commodore Computer Corporations. Apple supplies the Apple II and Macintosh families of machines. The IBM PC has established a reasonably strong foothold in the educational arena largely because of clone makers—companies licensed by IBM to market copies of the PC—who sold their machines at prices that significantly undercut those of Apple and IBM. Finally, Commodore has achieved limited success with its Amiga computer, which is more popular outside the United States, especially in Europe.

The Disk Operating System (DOS)

The acronym *DOS* (disk operating system) has been used to describe the relatively limited operating systems for microcomputers such as the Apple II (*DOS 3.3* and *ProDOS*) and IBM PC (*PC-DOS/MS-DOS*[1]) families of machines. The Apple IIGS, the last of the Apple II line, needed an operating system of its own (**GS OS**) since it was modeled after the Apple Macintosh (more affectionately called the Mac). The Mac, as we will see, represented a radical departure from traditional operating systems, especially in regard to the way the user interacts with the computer. The Mac's operating system programs that are not already built into the ROM chips are mostly captured into what is called the system folder.

For IBM and compatible systems, Microsoft *Windows* has become the user interface of choice for machines which use the *MS-DOS* operating system. More recently, a new Microsoft operating system, called *Windows NT,* has been released. *Windows NT* (NT stands for new technology) will eventually replace *MS-DOS* as the operating system for the more powerful desktop machines currently available in the IBM and compatible range of systems.

The IBM PS/2, like the Mac, has an operating system (*OS/2*) that is more akin to the powerful counterparts in the workstation, minicomputer and mainframe worlds. The Commodore Amiga, another popular machine in schools, also has a sophisticated operating system that has many of the capabilities of larger computers. But the name of the Amiga's operating system (*AmigaDOS*) harks back to the time when it was still customary to use the DOS acronym.

Typically, all these operating systems are supported by special-purpose programs called **utilities,** which we will discuss next.

7.2.3 Utilities

A utility is a program extension of an operating system. Think of a utility as a tool on a workbench.[2] It helps you make more efficient use of your computer. A widely known set of utilities for personal computers is Norton *Utilities.* This package of utilities provides tools to "restore, manage, and accelerate access to data. . . . You can diagnose and recover crashed or accidentally formatted hard disks, recover files that have been trashed, optimize the organization of your disks, and much more" (Norton, 1990).

---

[1]*MS-DOS* is short for Microsoft disk operating system.

[2]The operating system for the Commodore Amiga actually used the name *workbench* for its graphical user interface (see later section in this chapter), and the available utilities are called tools.

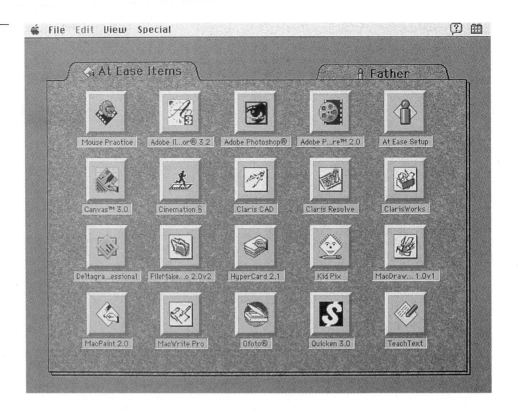

A utility also helps you accomplish certain tasks that extend the capability of the computer. For example, the Apple Macintosh and Commodore Amiga have built-in calculators; all the computers have clocks, some more accessible than others; the Amiga has a notepad (for to-do lists, memos, reminders, and other jottings) as part of the built-in set of tools; the Mac has a scrapbook, very useful for cutting and pasting, and gaining ready access to your favorite graphic images; all systems now have utilities for protection against viruses, a subject discussed in chapter 5.

Another important utility for computers in schools is one that protects files on hard disk drives against unauthorized access and inadvertent damage or loss. Apple Computer's *At Ease™,* for example, hides the operating system from the Macintosh user, allowing the user access only to selected documents and programs. The system administrator—media coordinator, classroom teacher, parent—decides which documents and programs the children can use.

The screen presents an attractive set of enlarged icons representing the accessible documents and programs. The term **icon** is just another word for a picture or image. Instead of listing just the name of a program on the screen, *At Ease* displays a different picture for each program, and the picture (icon) is large enough for even a small child to easily point at it with the mouse and click on it to open the program. Not only does this simplify the children's interaction with the computer; it also protects the programs from being trashed or renamed or otherwise disturbed.

The number of utilities available today is too large to list here. As you become more and more familiar with your computer, and as you exchange ideas about computing with your colleagues and students, you will discover those utilities that are most useful to you.

7.2.4 Functions Common to Operating Systems for Popular Educational Computing Systems

Here is a list of functions typically taken care of by the operating system of a modern microcomputer; the operating system must

- manage the transfer of data between primary storage (RAM) and secondary storage devices;
- manage the secondary storage medium itself along with the data stored on it;
- manage the transfer of data between peripheral devices and RAM;
- manage computer interaction with communications devices and provide support for communications networks;
- manage the allocation of storage space in RAM to several applications (multitasking).

Let us look at each of these in a little more detail.

Managing the transfer of data between primary storage (RAM) and secondary storage devices

Typical secondary storage devices on microcomputers are hard and floppy magnetic disk drives and optical disc drives. These devices were described in some detail in the previous chapter on hardware. Several tasks are involved in this data transfer function. If data are being transferred ("input") from secondary storage to RAM, the operating system must locate the correct data in the correct file on the disk in the correct drive. This may mean following a trail of pointers if the file is split into sections on different parts of the disk. As the data are transferred into RAM, they must be stored in memory locations on the computer chips that have not already been taken up by other instructions and data. And when the file is stored back on the disk the operating system will have to find free space on the disk if the file has been enlarged as a result of the updating process.

When data are input by the user from some device such as a keyboard, they are initially stored in the computer's primary memory (RAM). If these same data are transferred ("output" or "saved") from RAM to secondary storage, they have to find their way to the correct file on the correct disk in the correct drive. The operating system is also responsible for informing the user if any problems occurred in the whole process, problems such as damage to a disk or a nonexistent file, and so forth.

Managing the secondary storage medium itself along with the data stored on it

An important operating system utility is called disk optimization. This utility involves telling the operating system to reorganize the files stored on a disk so that they are not split into sections that are scattered over the surface of the disk. Imagine how long it would take to gather together the contents of a book in a library if each chapter were stored on a different shelf! Likewise it takes the computer longer to find the contents of a file when the file is not all together in one place.

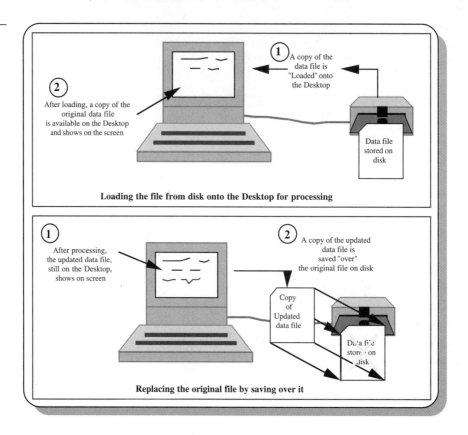

Figure 7.3
Loading, updating, and replacing a file

① A copy of the data file is "Loaded" onto the Desktop

② After loading, a copy of the original data file is available on the Desktop and shows on the screen

Data file stored on disk

Loading the file from disk onto the Desktop for processing

① After processing, the updated data file, still on the Desktop, shows on screen

② A copy of the updated data file is saved "over" the original file on disk

Copy of Updated data file

Data file stored on disk

Replacing the original file by saving over it

So, disk optimization is the process whereby the operating system gathers together the scattered parts of each file. The benefit of this process is not just a saving in time; it also saves space because it frees up sections of the disk that had become unusable because they were too small. Again, imagine if, in a library, there were lots of small gaps between the books. Each of the gaps would be too small to take a book, but if you were to push all the books up together you would free up large blocks of space into which you could then store more books.

Not all microcomputer operating systems include the program to optimize the file storage on disks in this way. But other disk management tasks are essential, and therefore common to all modern operating systems. These include:

- formatting a disk in preparation for storing data files;
- listing the contents of a disk (often called the directory);
- organizing the files into logical groups of files called subdirectories or folders;
- renaming a file;
- locking and unlocking a file to protect the data by preventing it from being accidentally written over;
- backing up (copying) the contents of a file or an entire disk;
- displaying the contents of a file;
- deleting files.

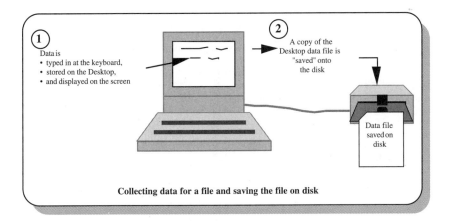

Figure 7.4
Gathering data and
saving to a file on
disk

Collecting data for a file and saving the file on disk

Managing the transfer of data between peripheral devices and RAM

A computer system, as you know, has a wide range of peripheral devices such as keyboards, monitors, printers, scanners, and so forth. These are items of hardware that are usually hooked up directly to the system unit of the computer and are therefore under the computer's control. They are usually located in the periphery of (near or around) the system unit, which is why they are called peripheral devices. In and of themselves they are not essential to a computer's operations. In the very early history of electronic computers, there were no peripheral devices. All data were input and output using secondary storage media, which in the 1940s was exclusively punched cards. It was not long, however, before other devices such as keyboards, monitors and printers were added so as to increase the system's flexibility.

Today, there is a growing range of such peripheral hardware which, while it is not part of the system unit of the computer, is nonetheless under its control. The invention and manufacture of such peripheral devices has spawned an enormous new industry worldwide. Many of these peripherals are used to input data to the computer's primary memory (RAM). Input devices include machines such as the keyboard, the mouse, joy sticks, a graphics pad, a scanner (including bar code scanners in stores), a voice recognition device, a touch screen, and the like.

As illustrated in figure 7.5, another extensive range of peripheral devices is devoted to displaying data that are output from RAM. These include the monitor, the printer, voice synthesizers, overhead projection systems, sound amplification systems, holographic devices that produce laser-based images, ultrasound imaging systems, and so forth.

Notice that these peripheral devices do not include secondary storage devices such as disk drives, cassette tape drives, or CD-ROM drives. As already pointed out, secondary storage is essential to a computer system; peripheral devices are extremely useful, but a computer can manage without them.

Applications programs rely on the basic input/output capability of an operating system whenever it is necessary for the computer to interact with any of these peripheral devices. Thanks to the operating system, the applications programmer's job is much easier since the instructions to read data *from* input devices, and to write data *to* output devices is largely taken care of by the operating system.

Figure 7.5
Typical peripheral
devices controlled by
the CPU

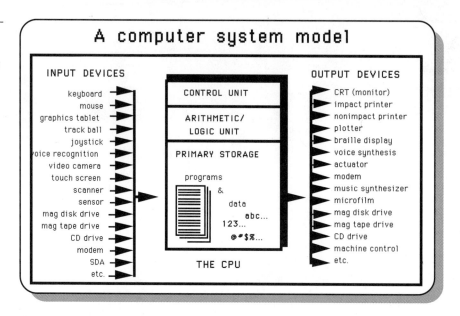

Managing computer interaction with communications devices
and providing support for communications networks

Advances in computer and communications technology have given rise to a new perception of the computer as a tool for gaining rapid access to people and data over local and wide area networks. In some schools, for example, students are collaborating on projects using e-mail (electronic mail) over a local area network. Students are also using wide area networks based on the telephone system to log into electronic bulletin boards, which enable them to communicate with other students all over the world. Networks are also useful for more mundane tasks such as allowing several computers to share a printer.

Communications hardware and software take care of the various rules of the road (called protocols) that have to be observed in order to make a successful connection between different machines in a network. The software to do this is often part of the operating system of a computer and is designed to allow the user to send and receive data, specify such things as protocols—data transfer speeds—and so forth, and ensure that the data is as error-free as possible.

The growing use of networked learning environments will be discussed at length in chapter 11 when we focus on specialized communications technologies.

Managing the allocation of storage space in RAM to several applications (Multitasking)

Many of the utilities available for your computer system are designed to run in the background while you are busy with other work such as word processing or recording your grades or designing some graphical materials for class. This ability of a computer to handle several programs at the same time is one aspect of what is called multitasking.

Other utilities (or applications for that matter) can be co-resident in memory, available at the touch of a function key or the click of the mouse button. In other words, you can have several programs open at the same time. The operating system divides RAM up

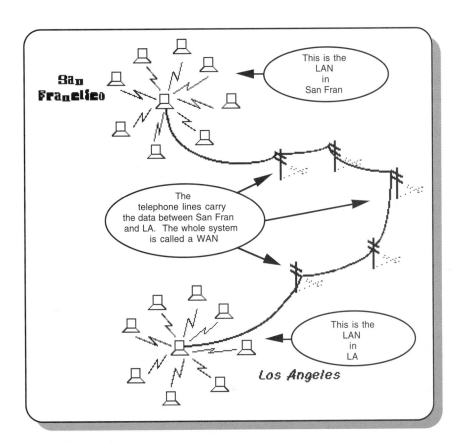

The telephone lines carry the data between San Fran and LA. The whole system is called a WAN

This is the LAN in San Fran

This is the LAN in LA

San Francisco

Los Angeles

Figure 7.6
Local and wide area networks

Figure 7.7
A computer lab networked to a shared printer
Photo courtesy Susan Giorgio Bond

Figure 7.8
Multitasking

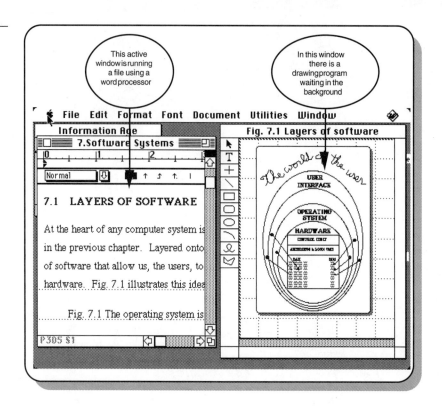

into sections, one program per section, and makes sure that the different programs don't interfere with each other as you switch back and forth between them. The computer actually works on only one program at a time.

Multitasking is an important feature of an operating system and it is becoming more and more the norm on all computers today. The Apple Macintosh, IBM PS/2 and Commodore Amiga, for example, have multitasking operating systems that give them the flexibility and potential for productivity that was the proud preserve of mainframe and minicomputer systems just a few years ago.

When we first learn to use a computer, we might be impressed by the speed at which things gets done. But it is surprising how soon we adjust to this speed, take it for granted, and then become impatient when the computer makes us wait a few minutes, even a few seconds, as it completes a process that might previously have taken us hours without the computer!

As Piaget (1970) pointed out: "the notion of time is an intellectual construction." We all know how much longer it takes for a kettle to boil when we stand there and watch it. But if we have something else to keep us busy, the kettle boils in no time at all! Likewise, when we use a computer, we might become impatient when a printer seems slow, for example. With a multitasking operating system, we can overcome this notion of slowness by being able to get on with another job on the computer while it completes some other process in the background, such as sending a file to the printer or recalculating a large spreadsheet.

Table 7.1	Comparison of Tasks Common to Microcomputer Operating Systems			
Task	**DOS 3.3**	**ProDOS**	**MS/PC-DOS**	**Graphic OS**
Format a disk	INIT HELLO	Choose "F" for FORMAT A VOLUME from VOLUME COMMANDS menu	FORMAT name of drive in which new disk is placed	Depends on the system. Mac automatically prompts user if new disk is in the drive
List the contents of a disk	CATALOG	CATALOG	DIR	Double click on the disk icon
Load a program from disk	LOAD program name	LOAD program name	Type the name of the executable file	Double click on the program name
Execute a program	RUN	RUN	Type the name of the executable file	Double click on the program name
Copy a file	LOAD and SAVE	Choose "C" for COPY FILES from FILE COMMANDS menu	COPY \pathname of file(s) to be copied\ \pathname of new file(s)\	Use mouse to drag file to new folder or drawer on same disk or on another disk
Rename a file	RENAME oldname, newname	Choose "R" for RENAME FILES from FILE COMMANDS menu	REN \pathname of file to be renamed\ \pathname of renamed file\	Depends on system. On Mac you highlight the name and retype it

7.2.5 Useful User-Controlled Operating System Functions

For the most part, the operating system takes care of the management tasks described in the previous section without your needing to be aware of what is going on. There are, of course, many jobs that you may want to do on an ad hoc basis related to the files on your disks, or with the way your computer is set up (called the configuration of the system), or, more and more today, with the way you interact with the computer via the graphical user interface. Table 7.1 shows how the operating systems for the most popular computers used in schools handle a few of these management tasks. Notice, for the most part, the similarities between the different systems. Emphasizing these similarities is very important. There is no doubt that learning the ins and outs of one operating system will help you make the transition to another.

7.3 The Graphical User Interface (GUI)

7.3.1 The Problem of Nonstandard User Interfaces

Until recently, the way software behaved toward the user had little or nothing to do with the operating system. Whoever wrote the program—the word processor, the game, the course scheduler, and so on—also had to design and write the instructions to control how the user interacted with the computer. There was no standard method or style of interaction. For every new piece of software that came along, the user had to learn the language of the interface: How do I save files with this software? How do I load a file from disk? How do I name a new file? How do I change a name? How do I tell the computer to do this, that or the other?

Programs designed to run under early operating systems such as Apple's DOS 3.3 or Microsoft's MS-DOS behave very differently even when they are designed for the same operating system. Baudville's *Award Maker Plus™,* for example, is like a foreign land compared to, say, a program such as Brøderbund's *Print Shop™.* Both are excellent software tools, but one would never know by looking at them that they were designed for the same operating system running on the same machine. One would almost experience a kind of culture shock when making the transition from one software package to another, and the learning curve would be much steeper than necessary.

Those brave souls who have taken the plunge and mastered the basics of one or two applications such as word processing (the most commonly used application) and a graphics program often have not progressed beyond this level of computer competency. The steep learning curve has quickly exhausted whatever motivation they may have started out with.

And those are the brave souls. The fact is that an inordinately high proportion of teachers have taken one look at what is involved in learning to use these traditional computer systems and, not surprisingly, they have run a mile rather than get involved. School administrators who have recognized the importance of the computer in the educational process and who have invested in computer hardware for the schools have had to factor in the added expense of extensive in-service training for the teachers just so they could learn how to use the machines—let alone incorporate the technology into the curriculum. Where such training has not been available, the machinery has all too often remained idle in classrooms and computer laboratories.

Until recently, this lack of standardization with regard to the user interface has been a major factor in inhibiting many teachers from accepting computer technology. Fortunately, two innovations have helped significantly in reducing people's phobias: integrated software and the graphical user interface.

7.3.2 Standardization through Integrated Software

To get around the problem of nonstandard user interfaces, some software, called **integrated software,** combines into one program several of the most useful types of application. Claris Corporation's *AppleWorks™,* long the flagship in this regard, combines a word processor, a file manager (database), and a spreadsheet. It is still very popular in those schools where the Apple II is the predominant machine. Integrated software designed for more powerful machines such as the Apple Macintosh, the IBM PS/2 or the Commodore Amiga include graphics (charting, painting and drawing) and communications components along with the word processor, database, and spreadsheet. Microsoft Corporation's Microsoft *Works™* and Claris Corporation's *ClarisWorks™* are currently the leading products that have this extra functionality. Tutorials to help you become productive as teachers using the Microsoft *Works* integrated package are included as optional supplements to this text (Poole, 1994).

The user interface for integrated software has few surprises because the different applications are woven into the same program. Commands to copy, delete, move, find, or

Command	Table 7.2 Examples of Common Commands in *AppleWorks* Integrated Software		
	Word Processor	**Data base**	**Spreadsheet**
open apple-**C**	Copy text	Copy records	Copy cells
open apple-**D**	Delete block of text	Delete records	Delete cells
open apple-**E**	Switch between insert and overstrike cursors	Switch between insert and overstrike cursors	Switch between insert and overstrike cursors
open apple-**F**	Find text	Find records	Find cell or text
open apple-**M**	Move text	Move records	Move cells
open apple-**N**	Change filename	Change filename or category names	Change filename
open apple-**P**	Print text	Print reports	Print worksheet
open apple-**S**	Save file	Save file	Save file
open apple-**Y**	Delete ("Y"ank text) to end of line	Delete category entry to end of line	Delete cell entry to end of line
open apple-**Z**	Zoom/display printer options	Zoom between single and multiple record layouts	Zoom/display formulas
open apple-**1. . . 9**	Move proportionally within the text file	Move proportionally within the file of data base records	Move proportionally within the worksheet
open apple-**?**	Call up help screen	Call up help screen	Call up help screen

save data are the same whether one is manipulating text in the word processor, entries in the data base, or values in the spreadsheet. Cutting and pasting data between the different components is also greatly simplified. Consequently, the effort invested in learning to use the software is rewarded with easy access to several applications designed to increase productivity. Table 7.2 lists a selection of *AppleWorks* commands. Notice that the same command has an identical or similar effect in each of the three components of the software. This is typical of integrated software in general, and makes the applications easier to learn and use.

7.3.3 Standardization through Graphical User Interfaces

Integrated software is one approach to standardization, but the standardization is still limited to a specific software package. *AppleWorks* does not look like *ClarisWorks,* for example. An experienced *AppleWorks* user would need to make a significant adjustment to learn to use *ClarisWorks* and of course the reverse is also true. Each computing environment—the Apple II and the Apple Macintosh respectively—is quite different. But the graphical user interface—or GUI, as it is called—is changing all that.

As illustrated in figure 7.9, the key features of GUIs are the images represented by pull-down menus, windows, and icons. Using the mouse or keyboard commands, the user is able to interact with the computer through these screen-based images, which can be selected, opened, closed, browsed, moved around, overlapped, scrolled, and otherwise manipulated. Once one has learned the basic set of interaction skills, the computer as machine becomes transparent to the user and the mind is set free to explore data and

Figure 7.9
The Apple Macintosh
graphical user
interface

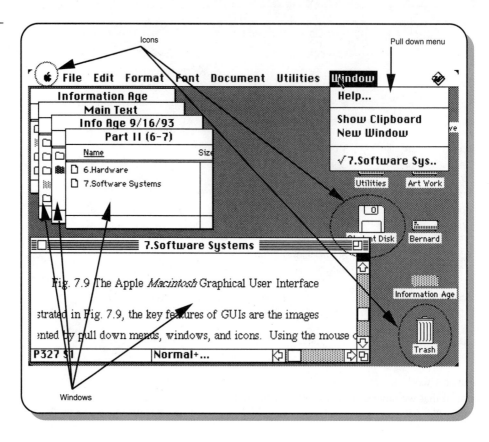

applications. Unlike with traditional command-based systems, when one uses a GUI-based system the computer no longer gets in the way. Quite the contrary, the GUI invites use with its attractive and consistent mode of interaction.

As Metcalfe (1992) reminds us, early GUIs were pioneered in the 1960s by Doug Englebart at Science Research International (SRI). Englebart developed and experimented with the original mouse-based, interactive computing environments and his research was taken up in the 1970s by Bill English and Ron Rider at the Xerox Palo Alto Research Center (Xerox PARC). The GUI that has set the tone for the industry, however, was that designed for the Apple Lisa, introduced in 1983. The Lisa was superseded a year later by Apple's Macintosh. This GUI was the brainchild of Alan Kay who had also conducted initial research at Xerox PARC and is now a research fellow at Apple Computer, Inc.

On systems such as the Apple Macintosh, the user interface is dictated by the operating system. It is *part of* the operating system. Anyone who writes applications for the Mac is constrained to follow the standard conventions (guidelines, as they are called) laid down by the system's designers at Apple Computer, Inc. So all the software for the Mac looks alike; it behaves in a predictable way.

The success of the Mac in the marketplace has not gone unnoticed by the other computer manufacturers, especially IBM and the makers of IBM-compatible machines.

Several GUIs that reflect the look and feel of the Mac have been developed since 1984. Larger computers—mainframes, minicomputers, and work stations—have adopted *XWindows™ Motif™*, GUIs that acted as front ends to the *UNIX™* operating system. Microsoft Corporation's *Windows* product, which was designed as a user interface for IBM PCs, has beaten out other GUIs such as *TopView™* and *Presentation Manager™*[3] and is now the user interface of choice for the more powerful IBM-compatible PCs.

7.3.4 GUIs and Educational Psychology

As a student of education, you will perhaps be interested to learn something of the research, based on a study of the process whereby humans learn, that led to the development of the GUI for the Apple Macintosh.

Dr. Alan Kay (1990) was convinced that "whatever user interface design might be, it was solidly intertwined with learning." He acknowledged his debt to the work of many individuals for the ideas that led to the Mac GUI. But he singled out three in particular because they helped him define the philosophy that drove his design of the Macintosh computer system: Jean Piaget, surely among the epistemologists best known to students majoring in Education; Seymour Papert, creator of the Logo programming language and disciple of Piaget; and Jerome Bruner, whose learning theory was also much influenced by the work of Piaget.

We will take a closer look at the work of these and other scholars at various points on our journey through this text. The paradigm that Kay formulated, based especially on Bruner's work, is what concerns us here as we study operating systems. Bruner (1966) noticed that we have different modes of thought—"multiple separate mentalities," as Kay calls them. The many different ways in which we learn are closely related to the various stages of cognitive development identified by Piaget. Three of these mentalities—called *enactive, iconic,* and *symbolic* by Bruner—Kay interpreted as doing, image, and symbolic mentalities, respectively, from which he formulated his model: "Doing with images makes symbols."

When we interact with the Macintosh computer, or with any computer that enables the user to interact via a GUI, we are actively ("doing") pointing and clicking with the mouse to select from pictures called icons ("images" on the screen representing objects and operations) in order to carry out some intellectual ("symbolic") activity that extends our mental capabilities.

Today, the GUI à la Mac is becoming the norm on all computer systems, including IBM and compatible machines. It means that we can look forward to being able to learn new systems and new applications without the trauma that once accompanied what was called the migration from one computer system to another, even from one application to another on the same system.

We should be thankful to people like Doug Englebart, Alan Kay, and friends, along with the "giants on whose shoulders they stood,"[4] for taking computing out of the exclusive hands of technicians and making it available to the rest of us.

---

[3]Both *TopView* and *Presentation Manager* were developed by IBM.

[4]Sir Isaac Newton is credited with the quote "If I have seen farther than others, it is because I have stood on the shoulders of giants."

⬝⬝ 7.4 Applications Software

As observed earlier in this chapter in the discussion of integrated software, five types of computerized applications are widely used in all professions, all walks of life. These include word processing, file or database management, spreadsheets, graphics, and communications. When they are sensibly integrated into the work environment by well-trained and experienced users, these applications are powerful productivity tools. This is as true for the teacher and student in the school as it is for those involved in other professions.

Of course, there are literally hundreds of thousands of other applications—programs designed to help the user use the computer to accomplish some task or other. A growing army of programmers worldwide, many teachers among them, are working alone or in teams developing new applications in response to the demand for software. The potential is simply boundless because of the nature of the computer as a **Universal Machine.** There is no end in sight to the ways in which the computer can be applied to solve problems and help us complete jobs more efficiently.

In the context of the classroom, applications have been developed to help the teacher teach and the student learn. The term *computer assisted instruction* (CAI) was coined to described such systems. Here is a partial listing of different applications of CAI used in schools today.

- **Drill and practice,** which has great value for remedial learning.
- **Tutorials,** which enable students to learn new material at their own pace.
- **Simulations** where students experience "real" life in the "virtual" reality of programmed worlds.
- **Microcomputer-based laboratories (MBLs)** in which children conduct science experiments where the computer is a key tool in the collection and visualization of data.
- **Collaborative learning** where students use the computer to coordinate their efforts as a team towards some educational goal.
- **Distance learning** where networks of computers linked by telephone communications allow students to attend classes from remote sites distributed around a region or even around the globe.
- **Multimedia** applications where students and teachers use interactive video, sound, graphics and text combined in a symphony of modalities to produce learning environments that are rich in intellectual stimulation.
- **Computer managed instruction** where the teacher uses the computer as a tool to keep close track of the process of educational growth as it is experienced by each individual student in the class.

In chapters 9 through 12, we will examine each of these application areas in more detail.

Looking Back

Part II has covered the fundamentals of computing. Think of this material on hardware and software as the foundation for what is to follow. The better you understand these fundamentals, the more control you will have over the mechanics of computer use. This will free you to take better advantage of the computer as a tool for teaching and learning.

There is a culture that surrounds the use of computers. Those who have become acculturated tend to save their work more frequently; they hesitate before pressing certain keys, depending on the software they are using; they handle disks carefully; they exit from software by closing files and shutting down the program before turning off the machine; they are not unduly surprised when software fails; and so forth. They have learned to accommodate the idiosyncrasies of computers, which are just dumb machines, after all. The software that controls them is only as good as the people who created it and the people who use it.

Looking Forward

It will be useful to examine the key features of each of the different types of applications software overviewed in this chapter, and at the same time discuss how each can be effectively integrated into the learning process. This will be the subject of chapters 8 through 12 in part III.

We will begin in chapter 8 by discussing different strategies for setting up educational computing environments. Then, in chapter 9, we will examine software that is useful to the teacher for the purpose of managing the instructional process. Chapters 10 and 11 will survey the various types of software designed with the student's learning needs in mind, software for productivity, drill and practice, tutorials, and simulations. Chapter 12 is all about computer-based multimedia. We will discuss learning systems that have emerged in the last few years which take advantage of the integration of audiovisual materials with computer control.

Later, in chapter 13, we will discuss software development. The challenge of creating quality software applications is not for the fainthearted, but understanding the nature of that challenge will help you appreciate the talent of the people who create the software that you use. Perhaps you will even be bitten by the programming bug yourself.

Computer technology is expensive, as is training in its use. Many school districts cannot raise the funds to pay for more than token support of technology-based education. Chapter 14, therefore, discusses the topic of grants: *Where* to apply for money, *how* to apply for it, and *what* to do with a grant once it has been won.

One of the most promising benefits of computer-based learning is that it gives children control of their own learning. The pedagogical implications of this will be discussed in chapter 15 against the backdrop of educational theory.

Do Something About It: Exercises and Projects

1. With a partner, brainstorm ways that computers might be used to enhance a school's operations.

2. Using computer magazines or software catalogs develop a price list of software that would be most useful to a school. Prioritize the list.

3. Make a list of different documents that a school might choose to have professionally printed.

4. Focusing on a particular school, list the different types of employees who would have to be hired and how each could use a computer.

5. The process of computerization is typically as difficult for teachers as it is for employees in a company. Develop a training plan so that teachers who intend to use the computer will feel comfortable with their new assignments.

6. Once a school has nearly every teacher using computers, what is next in terms of computer use? Develop one unheard of computer application for a particular school that would make that school state-of-the art while still improving efficiency and efficacy.

7. With a partner, develop a showcase portfolio that incorporates all of the ideas and software knowledge that you have acquired in your study and practice of teaching. Include computerized examples of projects and plans that would be necessary to manage the kind of computerized classroom that you would create.

Simulated corporate success
by Carolyn Cornish, Berlin BrothersValley School District, Berlin, Pennsylvania

Change is inevitable in the field of education. The inclusion of technology into a broad range of new and once familiar careers has dictated a rethinking of curricula in general and of the computer curriculum in particular.

Students who are mathematically inclined, who enjoy the invaluable problem-solving activities of programming, can still find their niche in the mastery of a variety of programming languages. However, there is a need to provide meaningful computer experiences for students who are not so inclined. For these students, we share an equally powerful problem-solving tool—simulation.

Ours is not a prepackaged simulation bought from an educational software supply company, but one created by our own students. Our classroom projects into corporate America, where budding young executives, armed with a variety of computer tools, contemplate decisions that could eventually earn them the status of success.

At Berlin BrothersValley School District, in Berlin, Pennsylvania, our high school students participate in an elective entitled "Simulated Corporate Success."[1] The goal of this year-long venture is to allow each student to become the CEO in a business of his or her choice. Students gather background information pertinent to a career area and participate in a corporate management simulation where computers, peripherals, and software packages become the tools of the trade.

The initial focus for the program is that of career selection. Students involve family members, community people, and school personnel in search of background information on their chosen career. These findings, which often include advertising ideas, information flow-charts, memos, application examples, payroll considerations, employee structure, budgets, board agendas, and so on, are collected as part of a working portfolio.

Since this is an introductory course in computers, the students' technical skills must be honed to ensure computer competence at a functional level. It is for this reason that all students participate in large group, guided instruction related to a variety of hardware and software applications.

The most popular software packages are selected and include word processing, database management, spreadsheets, presentation software, graphics packages, communications software, and desktop publishing.

(continued)

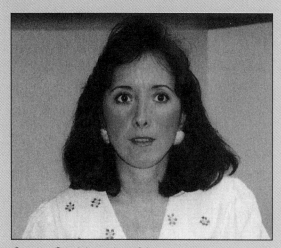

Carolyn Cornish, author of the case study
Photo courtesy Hilary Englebert

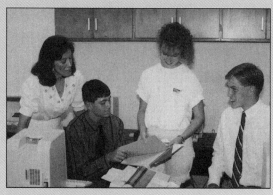

Students get down to business.
Photo courtesy Hilary Englebert

[1]Carolyn Cornish won a 1990 Classroom Computer Learning's Teacher of the Year award for her design and implementation of this winning computer curriculum.

Case Study 7 (concluded)

As the instructor presents an overview of each application along with hands-on activities, students are shown the relationship of each to a business situation. They must then, in their turn, analyze that relationship vis-à-vis the actual business that they plan to develop and run. Calling cards, budgets, floor plans, flowcharts, travel schedules, and agendas are just a sampling of the many wonderful connections that the students realize.

The most valuable portion of the course takes shape once this groundwork has been laid. As the role of the teacher changes from disseminator of information to facilitator of information acquisition, so too does the mood of the class. Students become corporate executive officers with a sound working knowledge of both business objectives and technological tools. As students rotate through a variety of peer-initiated activities, they are guided by evaluation sheets, project schedules, and timelines approved by the president of the board, the teacher. Throughout the plan a review of each project is completed and credit is awarded accordingly.

At the conclusion of all company work, the students prepare to share their individual corporate portfolios with their peers and a select audience of invited guests. For the entire class, this becomes a rewarding culmination to an overwhelming effort.

Computer literacy is a term that most educators recognize from the 1980s, when computing was in its infancy in schools. The curriculum for a course with such a title typically focused on computer history, computer vocabulary, hardware architecture, programming in BASIC, and a selection of software examples. For the decade of the 1990s, a new vision for computer use has surfaced in which "computer integration" seems to be the popular buzz phrase. This integration is an attempt to make computer use a more meaningful activity while eliminating one more requirement from an overburdened course load.

A major problem with this goal is that many teachers have not been trained in computer applications. They find it threatening to incorporate computers as part of their written curriculum. This project helps to bridge the gap between educational computing curricula of the 1980s and 1990s.

We struggle each year with new paradigms in education. Perhaps the computer integration that is proposed in this Case Study should not be viewed as an integration of this tool into traditional course offerings. Instead, it should be an integration of these traditional topics into a new information age curriculum—one that better prepares our students for success in times such as these.

It was John Dewey who stated that "education, properly so-called, is closely associated with change—is always fitting man for higher things, and unfitting him for things as they are." As educators, we must alter our thinking about computer integration as well.

Talk About It

Topics for discussion based on the case study.

1. Talk about how local businesses are using computers.
2. How do the computer needs of a small business differ from those of a large business?
3. What are the advantages and disadvantages of computerizing a business?
4. What kinds of information does one need to gather before the process of computerizing a business can begin?
5. Discuss how the status of computerization within a company would impact the employees.

■ References

Bruner, Jerome S., R. R. Olver, P. M. Greenfield et al. *Studies in Cognitive Growth.* New York: John Wiley & Sons, 1966.

Davis, William S. *Operating Systems: A Systematic View.* Reading, MA: Addison-Wesley, 1978.

Kay, Alan. *"User Interface: A Personal View."* In Laurel, Brenda, ed., *The Art of Human-Computer Interface Design.* Reading, MA: Addison-Wesley, 1990, pp. 191-207.

Metcalfe, Bob. *"Reverse Pied Piper of Mice Has Senses Working Overtime." InfoWorld,* November 9, 1992, p. 65.

Norton. *The Norton Utilities for the Macintosh: User's Guide and Reference Manual.* Cupertino, CA: Symantec, 1990.

Piaget, Jean. *Genetic Epistemology.* New York: Columbia University Press, 1970.

Poole, Bernard John, Susan Giorgio Bond. *Essential Microsoft Works: Tutorials for Teachers.* Madison, WI: Brown & Benchmark, 1994.

Computers in the Classroom

Educational Computing Environments

Go to the place where the thing you wish to know is native; your best teacher is there. Where the thing you wish to know is so dominant that you must breathe its very atmosphere, there teaching is most thorough, and learning is most easy. You acquire a language most readily in the country where it is spoken; you study mineralogy best among miners; and so with everything else.

Johann Wolfgang von Goethe (1749–1832)

Learning Outcomes

A common mistake made by educational institutions from elementary school through college is to give little consideration to pedagogical matters when installing computer-based technology in classrooms or laboratories. Decisions about where and how to place monitors, what types of computers to buy, how to situate them in a room, what software to use, whether to network the computers together, and how to configure a networked environment are made too quickly and without concern for the effectiveness on learning outcomes of the installation plan. As a result, much potentially exciting change is stillborn and further initiatives discouraged.

Expediency is often the primary rationale for decision making. How many electrical outlets are in the proposed computer laboratory? Where are the electrical outlets? How many children will need to be accommodated in the room at one time? How many tables and chairs will therefore be needed in the room? How many computers can fit on the tables in the room where the lab is to be set up? These are questions that recognize the understandable need for compliance with constraints. But constraints should not control design. Good design works around constraints to achieve a system's goals.

"Here is the room, here are the electrical outlets, here is the number of children we need to be able to get in there at any one time—can the room be used for the proposed laboratory?"

"Sure. No Problem."

"Then get on with it."

Often, the needs of administration come first; the needs of teachers and children are an afterthought. It is almost as if the policy says: "We'll do everything we can to provide a quality education for our children provided it's convenient." But teachers should always be involved in decisions about the learning environment since their training and experience qualifies them better than most others to understand children's learning needs.

Certainly, it is important to plan for optimal use of computer-based technology. The best planning draws on knowledge and experience. It makes sense for the people who have had training or experience in the use of technology to make decisions about its use. This brings us back to the fundamental importance of career-long training for teachers and administrators, especially in today's world where, as Toffler (1970) pointed out, change is occurring at an accelerating rate. Just as any other institution, schools must be prepared to adapt in response to the needs of a changing world.

This chapter examines the criteria that should govern the introduction and design of environments for computer-based teaching and learning. In particular we will focus on the following topics.

- First things first: training for the teachers
    - ISTE foundational skills and concepts
- Safety first: computers and health
    - Extremely low frequency (ELF) electronic emissions
    - Carpal tunnel syndrome (CTS)
    - Other ergonomics-related considerations
    - Summary of safety and ergonomics recommendations

8.1 Introduction

The best teachers establish an environment in which expected outcomes occur spontaneously. John Dewey made much of the importance of child-centered learning, where education comes about through discovery of knowledge from within the experience of doing—whether the doing be artistic, scientific, or athletic. The success of Montessori schools, too, relies on what Dr. Montessori called the "prepared environment" (Standing, 1962).

Dr. Maria Montessori discovered the effectiveness of a school that has been set up as *"a prepared environment* in which the child, set free from unique adult intervention, can live its life according to the laws of its development" (Standing, 1962). Directors of Montessori schools worldwide attest to the fact that children have a spontaneous interest in purposeful mental and physical activity when the appropriate environment is offered to them, including the set of didactic materials designed by Dr. Montessori to stimulate "the spontaneous interest of the children as the mainspring of their work" (Standing, 1962). The task of teaching is thus to supply and maintain that "appropriate environment" that will function as fertile ground for childrens' growth as fully rounded individuals.

Dewey and Montessori, among other educationists, anticipated the constructivist philosophy of learning, which Nickerson (1988) defined thus: "Learning is best described not as a process of assimilating knowledge but as one of constructing mental models. The learner's role is seen as necessarily an active one. It is questionable whether there is such a thing as passive learning. If new information is to be retained it must be related to existing knowledge *actively* in an integrative way" (emphasis added). Merrill (1990) further strengthens the link to Montessori methodology by emphasizing that "the most adaptive teachers are those who have previously prepared a wide variety of alternative learning activities that they can call upon when evidence of misunderstanding appears."

The Montessori model, though not recognized as mainstream, has been successfully applied, knowingly or unknowingly, in many ostensibly traditional schools. Good teachers, often in spite of straightened circumstances in the classroom, go out of their way to individualize instruction. Good teachers give their students the freedom to discover knowledge by preparing classes that will stimulate curiosity, capture attention, and promote a love of learning.

Good teachers are also those most likely to recognize intuitively the power of well-designed and integrated computer-based teaching and learning. As Denise Ryan observes (see case study), the computer is in and of itself "another manipulative" for helping students learn. Merrill (1990), speaking of computer-based interactive learning, also recognizes the advantages of technology in education when observing "that interactive environments can be made even more adaptive because a wider range of alternatives can be made available, and a more individual and systematic assessment of misunderstanding is possible."

Dewey (1956) reinforces this idea when he describes the experience of a child discovering through doing.

"If wishes were horses, beggars would ride." Since they are not, since really to satisfy an impulse or interest means to work it out, and working it out involves running up against obstacles, becoming acquainted with materials, exercising ingenuity, patience, persistence, alertness, it of necessity involves discipline—ordering or power—and supplies knowledge. Take the example of the little child who wants to make a box. If he stops short with the imagination or wish, he certainly will not get discipline. But when he attempts to realize his impulse, it is a question of making his idea definite, making it into a plan, of taking the right kind of wood, measuring the parts needed, giving them the necessary proportions, etc. There is involved the preparation of materials, the sawing, planing, the sandpapering, making all the edges and corners to fit. Knowledge of tools and processes is inevitable. If the child realizes his instinct and makes the box, there is plenty of opportunity to gain discipline and perseverance, to exercise effort in overcoming obstacles, and to attain as well a great deal of information.

The computer is a useful medium for putting the child into an artificial world where experimentation can take place, limited only by the availability of the appropriate software and hardware. "Everything that we do on a computer is a simulation," observes Dr. Alan Kay (Elmer-Dewitt, 1991), whose impact on modern computing was profiled earlier (see chapter 7). In fact, the computer can be programmed to simulate virtually any reality, hence the growing interest in virtual reality systems.

As such, it seems reasonable that computer-based learning systems should simulate and extend the set of didactic materials designed by such great educationists as Maria Montessori. Imagine a lesson about volcanoes where the teacher's own knowledge and experience are reinforced by the child's ability to read and talk about the lesson, all in the context of an interactive simulation of volcanic activity using multimedia. Imagine a lesson on the romantic poets where the teacher's own knowledge and experience are reinforced by reading the poetry and discussing it, all in the context of video clips from films based on the lives of Wordsworth or Keats set in the context of 19th century England. None of these ideas is new. Since time immemorial, teachers have been innovative in making learning exciting. Computer-based technology is one more tool in such teachers' hands.

8.2 First Things First: Training for Teachers

Training is important throughout a teacher's career. This is no less true today, when teaching appears to be on the brink of radical transformation as a result of the infusion of computing technology into schools. The task of making the transition from traditional teaching to teaching with technology is much tougher than it seems. This is because the transition is as much a cultural one as one of mere methodologies. It involves a shift in teaching paradigms, a shift in the way of thinking about teaching. This shift, away from the teacher as imparter of learning to the teacher as facilitator of learning, demands a great deal of curriculum rethinking and redesign as well as the learning of new methodologies vi-à-vis the use of computer-based technologies in the classroom. One teacher put it this way: "We're all philosophically committed to this, but it has involved so much work, we're barely keeping our heads above water. We have spent a massive amount of time in rethinking things and rewriting courses."

8.2.1 ISTE Foundational Skills and Concepts

Exactly which technology skills and concepts is a teacher expected to have learned to be able to operate effectively in schools today? The International Society for Technology in Education (ISTE) is the largest not-for-profit professional organization supporting computer-using educators in the world. ISTE endorses the belief that "computer-related technology must become a tool that students and teachers use routinely if students are to be adequately prepared for adult citizenship in our Information Age society" (ISTE, 1992). For this reason, the society has drawn up a set of Curriculum Guidelines for Accreditation of Educational Computing and Technology Programs "to provide guidance to teacher preparation institutions that are developing programs in educational computing and technology and to assist them in preparing folios for the National Council for Accreditation of Teacher Education (NCATE) program evaluation."

ISTE's Curriculum Guidelines[1] include a listing of the set of "fundamental concepts and skills for applying information technology in educational settings" (table 8.1). These concepts and skills should form a foundation for the studies that prepare teachers to teach in the modern computerized classroom. Teachers cannot be expected to use computer-based learning systems effectively unless they acquire these skills and assimilate these concepts. It will be useful to examine these skills and concepts more closely.

1. **Teachers must demonstrate ability to operate a computer system in order to successfully utilize software.**

   The use of computer-based systems should become second nature for teachers, much like using the chalkboard. Today, teachers have more opportunities to use computers in the classroom than they did 10 years ago. Systems are much easier to use because of improved operating environments that shield the user from much of the technical detail. We discussed graphical user interfaces (GUIs) in chapter 7. GUIs such as those integral to the Apple Macintosh and Commodore Amiga computers are now also available to IBM users since the introduction of Microsoft *Windows* and *Windows NT*. The major advantage of GUIs is standardization; users can quickly learn how to use all the new software because much of the interaction is common across applications. There are few surprises; however, for the beginner, there is still much to learn in order to arrive at the point where the use of computer-based technology can be integrated into curriculum and lesson planning.

2. **Teachers must be able to evaluate and use computers and other related technologies to support the instructional process.**

   Evaluation involves keeping current with state-of-the-art hardware useful in educational computing. It is important for teachers to know what is going on, because otherwise they are at the mercy of suppliers. They may not be getting the

---

[1]The society's publications—*ISTE Update, The Computing Teacher,* and *Journal of Research on Computing in Education*—are listed as recommended reading in appendix B.

Table 8.1	ISTE Fundamental Teacher Skills and Concepts
Skill or Concept	

1. Demonstrate ability to operate a computer system in order to successfully utilize software.
2. Evaluate and use computers and related technologies to support the instructional process.
3. Apply current instructional principles, research, and appropriate assessment practices to the use of computers and related technologies.
4. Explore, evaluate, and use computer/technology-based materials, including applications, educational software, and associated documentation.
5. Demonstrate knowledge of uses of computers for problem-solving, data collection, information management, communications, presentations, and decision making.
6. Design and develop student learning activities that integrate computing and technology for a variety of student grouping strategies and for diverse student populations.
7. Evaluate, select, and integrate computer/technology-based instruction in the curriculum of one's subject area(s) and/or grade levels.
8. Demonstrate knowledge of uses of multimedia, hypermedia, and telecommunications to support instruction.
9. Demonstrate skill in using productivity tools for professional and personal use, including word processing, database, spreadsheet, and print/graphic utilities.
10. Demonstrate knowledge of equity, ethical, legal, and human issues of computing and technology use as they relate to society, and model appropriate behaviors.
11. Identify resources for staying current in applications of computing and related technologies in education.
12. Use computer-based technologies to access information to enhance personal and professional productivity.
13. Apply computers and related technologies to facilitate emerging roles of the learner and the educator.

best value for money or the appropriate equipment to meet their needs. Some of the best ways to keep current are to subscribe to magazines and journals, attend conferences where systems are demonstrated by other users and vendors, and join professional organizations.

Appendix B lists many such publications, conferences, and professional organizations. Several publications are free of charge to qualified subscribers. If you have any responsibility at all for computer hardware or software selection, purchase, and use, you will usually qualify. That includes almost every teacher who uses a computer. Usually, your school will subscribe to such publications, but if not, you should initiate this. The advantage of receiving your own personal copy, delivered to your door at home, is that you will be more likely to read it.

The best school districts will support teachers to attend courses and seminars related to computer use in education. Another successful way to keep current with regard to methodologies, research, and assessment practices is to set up an electronic bulletin-board system (BBS) in the district or statewide, as is the case in some parts of the United States. This would allow teachers unrestricted exchange of ideas.

3. **Teachers should learn to apply current instructional principles, research, and appropriate assessment practices to the use of computers and related technologies.**

This is another reason to subscribe to publications, attend conferences, and join professional organizations. Teachers should be familiar with changing philosophies of education, especially as they apply to using the computer in the classroom. They should also know how to evaluate the impact of methodologies that involve computer-based technology. One of the deceptive dangers of using computers in the classroom is that children enjoy using computers whether they are learning anything or not. So teachers must be discerning about the educational benefits accruing from the use of specific learning systems.

4. **Teachers should take time to explore, evaluate, and use computer/technology-based materials, including applications, educational software and associated documentation.**

This is a time-consuming, but nonetheless essential, task. Once again, well-managed school districts will set aside, on an ongoing basis, adequate time for all teachers to examine new learning systems, whether individually or in groups. Teacher-computerists should preview all technology-based materials, sifting out the good from the garbage, so that the other teachers do not have to waste time filtering the plethora of systems flooding the market. If acceptance of technology for teaching and learning has been halfhearted in the past, it has been at least in part because teachers have not been given a fair chance to find out what is available and to learn how best to incorporate the technology into the curriculum.

5. **Teachers should be able to demonstrate knowledge of uses of computers for problem-solving, data collection, information management, communications, presentations, and decision-making.**

Teachers should use computers to manage the whole instructional process from lesson planning to delivery to evaluation. Courses and workshops are useful only if they lead to application of what has been learned. Teachers have spent untold hours attending such courses and workshops without experiencing a transfer of skills into their professional lives. Why is this? In some cases, the hardware and software that the teachers have learned about are either not available in their schools or classrooms, or are available in inadequate numbers and with inadequate support. It is true that teachers must be trained before they can adopt the new teaching technologies, but it makes sense to provide them with the logistical support once they have taken the trouble to learn how to use the systems. What currently happens in too many school districts is equivalent to training soldiers in armed combat—introducing them to all the latest weaponry, and then sending them into the battlefield with bows and arrows.

6. **Teachers should be able to design and develop student learning activities that integrate computing and technology for a variety of student grouping strategies and for diverse student populations.**

This skill will follow naturally when the technological skills are acquired. Once you know how to use the machinery and run the software, your training as a teacher and your natural abilities will stand you in good stead as you apply the skills you have learned in preparing lessons and activities that incorporate the technology. You will also get many ideas from your colleagues, and from your reading of current literature.

7. **Teachers should be able to evaluate, select, and integrate computer/technology-based instruction in the curriculum of one's subject area(s) and/or grade levels.**

   This skill also depends on acquiring the other skills and concepts and follows naturally from them. In fact, you should be most creative when applying the technology in your own areas of expertise, and be able to share your ideas with others. For example, math teachers will be best at identifying appropriate applications in the math classroom.

8. **Teachers should demonstrate knowledge of multimedia, hypermedia, and telecommunications to support instruction.**

   We looked briefly at the components of multimedia in chapter 6. The term **hypermedia** describes systems that enable the user to follow links between data of all types—text, film, still images, and sound—in pursuit of the information they need. Thus, knowledge acquisition is multidimensional and associational—like a voyage of discovery. For example, a child might have some interest in learning about some species of animal. The search for information will lead back and forth from text, to video clips, to photos, and back to text.

   To some extent, these technologies involve rethinking the whole learning process. As we will discuss in chapters 11 and 12, classrooms are being redefined around the broader concept of interactive learning that becomes possible with multimedia and hypermedia technology. Students, individually or in groups, should be able to interact with hypermedia databases, whether within the confines of the classroom or beyond. In a world aptly defined as the "global village," the best schools will also make sure that their students have the opportunity to experience cultures other than their own. What better way to do this than to enable children to interact over local and wide area networks both verbally and, eventually, visually.

9. **Teachers must be able to demonstrate skill in using productivity tools for professional and personal use, including word processing, database, spreadsheet, and print/graphic utilities.**

   Chapter 9 will describe the ways in which computers can be used to manage the classroom. Naturally enough, teachers who learn to use the computer to organize their working day will also be more likely to use the computer at home. Ideally, every teacher and every student would have at home a computer system that is compatible with those they use at school. The teaching and learning activities that take place during the scheduled school day are but a prelude to the teaching and learning activities that take place at home. The computer is thus one of the parts that make up the educational whole: the harmonious *Gestalt*[2] that unites every dimension of the learning process. Many schools are finding out that the combined computer-phone is a still more powerful part of that *Gestalt* (Bauch, 1990). We will examine this idea more closely in chapter 11.

   ---

   [2]A school of psychology based on the concept of the "wholeness" of experience. "The essential idea behind *Gestalt* is that *parts* have no identity independent of their place, role, function in the *whole*" (Linskie, 1977).

10. **Teachers should demonstrate knowledge of equity, ethical, legal, and human issues of computing and technology use as they relate to society, and model appropriate behaviors.**

Computers are changing our world. As explained in chapters 4 and 5, many moral dilemmas have arisen as a result of the rapid spread of computer-based technology throughout society. Teachers do have some measure of responsibility for the moral well-being of the children with whom they work. Some would say that this responsibility is more important today than ever before. Good teachers care about their students' education beyond the mere learning of the subject matter. Teachers need to know about these equity, ethical, legal, and human issues so that they can prepare their students for a world where such knowledge will itself give them power to function successfully and morally.

11. **Teachers should be able to identify resources for staying current in applications of computing and related technologies in education.**

Here again, reading, attending conferences and workshops, and belonging to professional organizations will ensure that one's teaching methodologies are kept up-to-date. Appendixes B and C list many of these resources. Of course, teachers can be expected to keep current only if their school districts provide them with the environment in which to apply newly acquired skills. Why become an expert in using technology in the classroom if there is no technology available in the school?

12. **Teachers should know how to use computer-based technologies to access information to enhance personal and professional productivity.**

This involves learning to use database searching techniques and telecommunications to update knowledge and skills related to one's teaching and learning. National and international networks enable teachers to interact with others in their discipline or profession. Many universities now offer distance learning courses, mass-media-based home study, and so forth. Libraries now have on-line catalogs and access to special on-line databases of research materials in all academic areas including, of course, pedagogy, educational psychology, methodology, and other teaching-related disciplines. As Edward Albert Filene observed: "If a man's education is finished, he is finished." An educational system, after all, can be only as good as its teachers.

13. **Teachers should be able to apply computers and related technologies to facilitate emerging roles of the learner and the educator.**

Inevitably, teachers who master and apply all the skills and concepts detailed above will transform education even as they transform themselves in terms of their teaching skills and abilities. This may not happen overnight, but it will happen because the technology itself will cause reconsideration of the ways in which learning is delivered and received. The medium *is* the message, as McLuhan observed.

Courses in educational technology for undergraduate education majors should introduce all these skills and concepts. An interesting discussion would be to consider whether or not your preparation for teaching, or in-service training, covered these skills and concepts. This is a recommendation in the Do Something About It section at the end of the chapter.

◆ 8.3 Safety First: Computers and Health

Information about the threat that computers present to health is important for all those involved in education—administrators, teachers, and students. Obviously, administrators and teachers need to know because they control how the technology is set up and used. But students should also be taught correct use of technology because they will be using it throughout their working lives. Health issues are especially significant. Computer and related electronic systems can cause debilitating, even life-threatening, illness when used incorrectly. These issues are being discussed more and more in the media as we become aware of the cumulative effects of long-term exposure to, or use of, the machinery.

8.3.1 Extremely Low Frequency (ELF) Electronic Emissions

All electrical devices emit electromagnetic radiation. These **extremely low frequency (ELF)** emissions are for the most part harmless. Extensive research has turned up no significant adverse effects from normal exposure to ELF emissions, such as those that are produced by most electronic equipment in the home. Display terminals—(televisions, computer monitors, video display terminals (VDTs), or cathode ray tubes (CRTs)—are a different story, notwithstanding the conclusions of the Center for Office Technology referenced in Hagar (1991).

Although no conclusive connection has yet been established between ELF emissions and various side effects harmful to health, several U.S. and European studies offer support for some level of concern, according to Branscum (1991) and O'Connor (1991). Suspected side effects of ELF emissions are leukemia, breast cancer (male and female), testicular cancer (especially in the case of troopers who have been accustomed to resting radar speed-detection devices in their laps when on traffic duty), and miscarriage in pregnant women. Branscum cites an Office of Technology Assessment report that "suggests taking a 'prudent avoidance' strategy to minimize any potential risk."

In the interests of safety, the following recommendations should be implemented in any school, home, or office computing environment:

- Position computer monitors so that users can sit at least an adult arm's length (two to three feet) from the screen.
- Maintain similarly adequate distance from the sides and back of other adjacent computing machines.

The standard recommended depth for computer tables, by the way, is 30 inches (Apple Computer, 1991). A table with a depth of less than 30 inches or so cannot allow adequate distance between the user and the monitor screen and still allow for a comfortable position at the keyboard. In a well-designed computing environment, these recommendations may well be implemented anyway because the user needs desk space for work in front, and at the sides, of the computer equipment. Later, we will return to these issues as they relate to educational computing.

Figure 8.1
Optimal positioning of
a user in relation to a
computer monitor
Photo courtesy Rick
Povich

8.3.2 Carpal Tunnel Syndrome (CTS)

Carpal tunnel syndrome (CTS) is a type of **repetitive stress injury (RSI)** that affects at least the hand, wrist, and forearm as a result of an inflamed ligament that presses on a nerve in the wrist, where the carpal bones are located. Pain, numbness, and/or tingling sensations occur in the thumb and fingers and can also shoot up the forearm. In some cases, the pain can extend to the upper arm, shoulder, and upper back. It can be debilitating, to say the least.

One cause of CTS is relentless repetition of work at a keyboard (or mouse). It is more likely to occur when using a computer as opposed to a typewriter because it is not unusual to work continuously at a computer keyboard without changing the basic position of the hands; the fingers just hammer away for hours. At least with an old-fashioned typewriter, the user had to stop typing at the end of every line to return the carriage and again every few minutes in order to change the paper. Of course, even typists used to fall victim to CTS. But since they were mostly women, no one paid attention to the suffering they had to endure. Some say that it is only since men started using computers during their workday that CTS has been recognized as a problem at all!

The computer has brought about changes in the nature of people's jobs. An increasingly large percentage of workers use a computer keyboard for a significant proportion of their workday. Many take their work home, and continue to type there. It is not surprising that there has been a consequent increase in the reported cases of RSI, mostly attributable

Figure 8.2
Carpal tunnel
syndrome can be
debilitating, to say the
least.

to the increase in CTS. According to U.S. Department of Labor statistics, in 1992, half of all workplace injuries were related to RSI as compared to only one-fifth in 1980 (Adler, 1992).

Ergonomics to the rescue

Ergonomics is "an applied science that coordinates the design of devices, systems, and physical working conditions with the capacities and requirements of the worker" (Webster's, 1991). Another name for this science is human factors engineering. Human factors are becoming more critical for students as computer use in schools increases. It is quite possible in the near future that students will spend a large part of a school day at a computer workstation. For this reason, health and safety considerations related to ergonomics will have to be factored into the design of the educational workplace.

There are several ways to prevent keyboarding-induced CTS. Adler (1992) profiles some revolutionary alternative keyboard designs that enable the hands to assume a more natural, unstrained position while typing. One design, for example, literally breaks the keyboard in two so that it takes on the shape of a shallow "V" (see figure 8.3). Using this keyboard the hands can maintain a more natural position. But it will be a long time before such devices replace the traditional keyboard—unless the law gets in on the act.

Gannett (1992) reports that "U.S. District Court Judge Jack Weinstein of New York has consolidated 44 lawsuits against AT&T, Apple Computer, IBM, Northern Telecom and other technology companies" because of what are claimed to be design flaws in computer keyboards that are responsible for hand injuries such as CTS. Whether the lawsuits will prosper need not concern us here. The ideal situation is for one to avoid the injury in the first place, and this is possible with the application of elementary ergonomic adjustments to furniture and to one's work routines.

Figure 8.3
Apple's ergonomic
keyboard
Photo courtesy Apple
Computer, Inc.

Take a break

Since CTS is caused by relentless repetitive activity over long periods of time, breaks from the keyboard should be taken frequently, at least every hour or two. Utility programs have been developed to address this need. The software, which runs in the background while the user is busy at some computer-related task, makes an audible beep and puts a message on the screen every half hour or so to remind the user to take a break. With speech synthesizers built into more and more computers, there is no reason why the computer could not be programmed to put the reminder into words: "Why don't you take a break, my friend?"

Support the wrist

The wrist should be supported in some way or another. Figure 8.4 illustrates an example of an adjustable wrist rest which helps to maintain correct wrist position.

Share jobs

A further measure might be to assign workers (and students) to a variety of tasks to break up the day with different types of work. Activities should be rotated among a group or team of people so that no one individual has to work at the keyboard for days or weeks on end. Today, more than ever because of the proliferation of computers in the workplace (and soon in schools, too), many people are chained to a keyboard five or six days a week, fifty weeks a year, for their entire careers. No wonder there is a dramatic increase in the number of reported cases of CTS.

8.3.3 Other Ergonomics-Related Recommendations

Keep work habits flexible and varied

Ergonomics has as much to do with the culture of the workplace (or study place) as with physical comfort. When people talk about ergonomics, they most often refer to physical things such as the design of furniture, the levels and type of lighting, or the levels of noise in an environment. These are extremely important considerations when designing working conditions in which people can be maximally productive, and we will examine them more closely. But as Hagar (1991) points out, people's behavior patterns when using machinery, for computing or otherwise, also contribute to people's physical and emotional problems on the job.

The human body does not react well to extended periods in a fixed position. The computer is an unusual machine in the sense that it demands relatively little overall body movement. At the same time, the activity on the computer monitor tends to focus concentration to such an extent that the user does not notice the passage of time. Hours become condensed into what seem like minutes. Turkle (1984) reminds us of this "holding power" of the computer. This is most likely to happen when the mind is at the same time engaged in a high level of concentration. In this respect a computer is not unlike a car. During a long, unbroken stretch of driving we do not notice that our body is getting stiff until we stop and try to slide gracefully out of the vehicle!

When we work at computers, we should do what sensible people do on a long trip: stop frequently, stretch our legs, get some fresh air. At one time, we made fun of the Japanese because they would be shown doing calisthenics in the office during the work-day. Now we know that they had more sense than we were prepared to give them credit for. More and more American companies encourage workers to vary their working patterns. Some companies even provide exercise facilities for aerobics and so forth. These cultural changes are predicated on the belief that a sound body and a healthy mind lead to greater physical and intellectual productivity.

Create the right ambience

Ambience covers everything from lighting, to noise, colors, wall coverings, and space. Computer labs are often cold, cluttered spaces. A few simple alterations can significantly improve the comfort of users and increase their productivity.

Lighting should be subdued and localized so as to cut down on eyestrain and headache-inducing glare from the computer screen. The computer screen should be tilted if necessary in order to reduce glare. Noise should be muted by sound-absorbing floor, wall, and ceiling materials. Colors of walls and ceilings should be neutral (light pastel shades). All surfaces should be nonreflective.

The more space for movement around a classroom the better. This reduces stress, both physically and psychologically. People also work better when they have room to breathe. Usually, very little consideration is given to how to optimize the space in a room so that open space is maximized. It is surprising how much space can be gained through careful placement of furniture. The simplest technique is to use scaled-down, cut-out shapes of all the furniture that will go in the room. Then, on a similarly scaled-down floor plan, try any number of options until the maximum amount of open space is made available. Applying this idea will help avoid stereotypical layouts. A nice team-building idea is to make a competition out of designing the best layouts for classrooms or computer labs.

Use ergonomics when setting up standard computer equipment

The footprint of a machine is the amount of space it takes up on a tabletop or floor. Ideally, the footprint of the standard components of a computer system—not including the printer, but including the system unit, hard and floppy disk drives, CD-ROM drive, and monitor—should take up no more space than the footprint of the monitor. The monitor should also be adjustable to tilt so that, if necessary, the user can reduce glare from reflected light.

Printers should not be located on the workstation tabletop. Sometimes they are stacked above the monitor, on a stand, but this arrangement usually makes access difficult when it is necessary to adjust printer settings and insert and remove paper, especially for small children. Ideally, the printer—especially if it is a noisy dot-matrix printer—should be located somewhere out of the way. This is important in a lab environment where desktop space is at a premium. Modern networked environments need only one or two relatively inexpensive and quiet, high-speed laser printers to serve the needs of a labful of users.

The keyboard, which is usually connected by a cable to the system unit, should be capable of being moved around independently of the system unit. A wireless keyboard and mouse would be the ideal since there would be no wiring straggling across the surface of the workstation tabletop and getting caught up in other equipment. Very few computers are yet designed with wireless keyboards and mice (mouses?), but it is only a matter of time before this becomes a standard configuration. Whether or not wireless mice become standard in schools remains to be seen. After all, they would more easily "run away" if not tethered to the machine!

Figure 8.5
Andrew looks
comfortable using his
computer.
Photo courtesy Susan
Giorgio Bond

The special extra equipment for multimedia systems—scanners, laser disc players, CD-ROM drives, large-screen high-resolution monitors—should also be mounted on a mobile unit so that it can be shuttled from classroom to classroom or, if it belongs in one room, so that it can be moved to the location in the room where it will be used by the students or the teacher. We will discuss multimedia equipment in more detail in chapter 12.

Select or adapt furniture to fit the user

Workstation tables and chairs should fit the person using them, which means they should come in different heights and also be adjustable.

Tables   The table should include an adjustable keyboard shelf and should be large enough to accommodate the computer while leaving room for ample workspace on one side of the computer.

Figure 8.6
Ergonomically
designed
workstations with
embedded
computers
Photo courtesy Nova
Office Furniture, Inc.

Ankrum (1993) presents research spanning the last 50 years which shows that eye-strain caused by extended work at a computer can be reduced significantly if one sits at an optimal distance (about 30 inches—or about an average adult arm's length) from the computer screen and if the screen itself is in a relatively low position compared to what is normally the case when computer monitors are placed on tabletops. Ankrum makes a strong case for embedding the computer monitor below the glass surface of the table or desk. This configuration is common today in television studios, where the announcers sit at desks that have embedded monitors. Ankrum (Nova, 1993) points out that this design is not only ergonomic, but it is also more effective in several other ways. It saves space by freeing up the tabletop for work; it simplifies the management of wires, which do not have to be tracked away from the tabletop and can more easily be concealed both from view and from accidental damage; and it helps secure privacy by concealing the screen from prying eyes.

Chairs Chairs that are adjustable for height will enable the user to sit in such a way that the computer monitor is positioned below eye level. But chairs should be adjustable for more than just height. The back rest should also be adjustable so that it can support the lower and middle back and help the user maintain a relaxed, upright

Figure 8.7
Unsatisfactory work
environment
Photo courtesy Susan
Giorgio Bond

position. An adjustable footrest would also be useful, especially when small children use desks that are too high for them. The legs should not be allowed to dangle unsupported for long periods since, over time, this can lead to injury to the back of the knees and elsewhere. The lad in figure 8.7 may not complain about the oversized work environment he is putting up with, but that does not mean it is acceptable.

When using the mouse, all of the wrist and much of the forearm should be able to rest on the table top so that the upper arm hangs naturally close to the side of the body on which the mouse is used (not excessively off to one side or reaching out in front of the body). This will reduce strain on the upper arm, shoulder, and upper back. Usually, the mouse pad is positioned just to the left or right of the keyboard. Figure 8.8 illustrates the ideal configuration for the keyboard and the mouse.

Notice, however, that the student is sitting too close to the monitor's screen. Fortunately, the monitor in this case is manufactured by Apple Computer, Inc. and Apple has for several years worked to develop screens that are designed in such a way as to significantly reduce the ELF magnetic emissions (O'Connor, 1991). Nonetheless, teachers

Figure 8.8
Recommended
ergonomic desktop
setup for mouse-
based computing
Photo courtesy Susan
Giorgio Bond

should warn their students to keep their distance, and schools should provide furniture that will allow students to do this without compromising their comfort while working at the computer.

Discomfort, perhaps even chronic pain, will result when the only room for the mouse pad is either too far to one side or on the edge of the table next to the keyboard. In either configuration, the upper arm, shoulder, and upper back will soon feel the strain.

8.3.4 Summary of Safety and Ergonomics Recommendations

Our focus in this book is on the computer, so the following are some inexpensive and highly effective recommendations for maintaining ergonomically-correct computing environments in schools. Some of the recommendations are adapted from Hagar (1991).

- Provide chairs that can be adjusted for height so that users can position the computer monitor at, or slightly below, eye level. This encourages users to hold the head in a comfortable upright position, thus taking pressure off the neck and upper back.
- The chairs should also have adjustable back rests to support the lower and middle back.
- If possible, set the controls for computer screens so that the background color is white. This reduces eye strain.
- Tilt the screen (with wedges if necessary) to cut glare from light sources, natural or otherwise.

Figure 8.9
Folded-up toweling
makes an adequate
wrist rest.
Photo courtesy Susan
Giorgio Bond

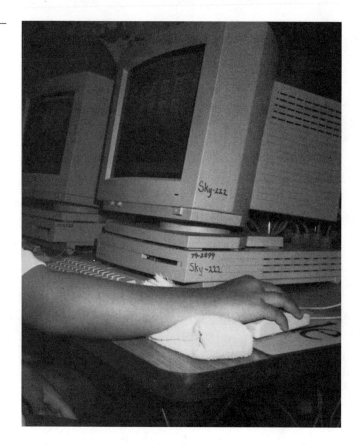

- Computer keyboards should be detachable so that the user can sit back from the monitor and also adjust the orientation of the keyboard for maximum comfort.
- Keyboards should also be adjustable for height to fit the position of the wrist, which will vary from person to person.
- Put some kind of padding in front of the keyboard and the mouse, on which the user's wrists can rest. Folded-up toweling will do.

  Alternatively, consider padded wristbands. This way the wrist rest goes wherever the wrist goes, from the keyboard to the mouse and back again. Figure 8.10 illustrates a wristband designed for the author by Anne Giorgio.
- Use tables that are deep enough to allow the user to be at least an adult arm's length from the computer monitor. This reduces the risk of side effects from ELF emissions.
- The tables should also be large enough to provide adequate work space for writing and other activities.
- Use nonreflective and sound-proofed materials for all surfaces in the room to cut down on glare and noise.
- Use neutral colors for surfaces and equipment to create a restful ambience for the eyes.

Figure 8.10
Prototype wristband
designed by Anne
Giorgio

8.4 Considerations for Computer Setup

How computers are introduced into the learning environment is critical to their effectiveness. Selfe (1992) points out that the introduction of computers in schools through the 1980s and early 1990s was often poorly planned, without consideration for pedagogical and logistical problems. Her immediate concern is the retrograde effect this has on the teaching of writing, but the problems apply across the curriculum.

Selfe notes that computer labs, especially those with sound-proofed study carrels arranged in rows, make it difficult for students to collaborate on tasks and share information. Instead, Selfe recommends, among other things, that computers be arranged in clusters or pods to facilitate discussion and sharing of work and ideas.

Let us examine several other issues that are often overlooked when introducing computers into the learning environment, whether that environment be the classroom, the computer lab, or the home.

8.4.1 Computers in the Classroom

Every school at one time or another has debated whether to put computers in classrooms or in labs. Arguments against computers in the classroom are that they are expensive resources that are underutilized. When they are clustered in a laboratory setting, they can be scheduled for use by all classes, and actually are used in many cases all day, every day of the week.

The remainder of this section will focus on the setup for computers in the classroom. Section 8.4.2 will consider issues that arise when setting up and maintaining a computer lab.

Figure 8.11
Computer system set
up on mobile cart
Photo courtesy Susan
Giorgio Bond

One computer, one classroom

The safety-first recommendations discussed earlier in this chapter should be applied whenever possible, no matter what the computing environment. If they cannot all be applied, students should at least be told about them. They are an important aspect of computer literacy which is often neglected. Use the computer to make posters displaying the relevant safety and ergonomics-related recommendations, and periodically go over them with students. Better yet, each year, start out with a project where students make up new posters covering all the ergonomics and safety-first bases surrounding the installation and use of technology in the classroom.

The following strategies will optimize the use of a computer in the one-computer classroom:

■ Set up the computer equipment on a mobile table so that it can be moved easily from one part of the room to another. Sometimes you may want to use it in a front, central location in conjunction with an overhead LCD[3] panel. Other times you may want to put it at the back of the class where a project group can work on it while you are busy with the rest of the class. You should be careful to stow the LCD panel with its cable in a safe place after use.

---

[3]LCD: liquid crystal display. The same type of display is used in most digital watches and calculators.

LOK•SMITH™

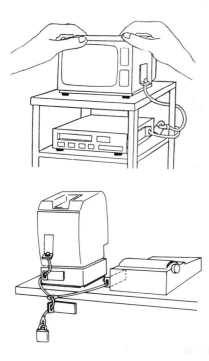

Figure 8.12
D&D Security's
Lok•Smith™ antitheft
system
Illustrations courtesy D&D
Enterprises

- Secure the computer equipment against theft. Most insurance companies will not insure equipment such as computers and peripherals unless they are secured in some way that makes them difficult to steal. The Apple Macintosh, for example, has a security slot on the back for attaching cables so that the computer can be padlocked to the table. A company called D&D Security has an antitheft device called Lok•Smith™, which is easy to install because it requires no modification of the equipment, such as drilling holes. The system consists of heavy-duty steel plates, cables, and padlocks. A steel plate is bonded to the surface of each piece of equipment to be secured. The cable connects the equipment together through the eyes on each of the steel plates and the padlock is used to secure the set of connected equipment to the table or cart on which it sits (see figure 8.12).

- The more you use the computer, the better. A computer suffers from lack of use, like any machine. When not in use, it should be covered to keep out dust. Appoint a student for this task.

- Shalvey (1987) reminds us of an excellent idea, which is to use a splitter cable (a "T" or "Y" adapter) to enable the output from the computer to be displayed simultaneously on the computer screen and on the large overhead television screen. If you have a computer, but you do not have a large-screen television in your classroom, you should think about getting one!

Figure 8.13
You would be
surprised at how easy
it is to turn off a
power switch or
dislodge a plug with
your foot.
Photo courtesy of Susan
Giorgio Bond

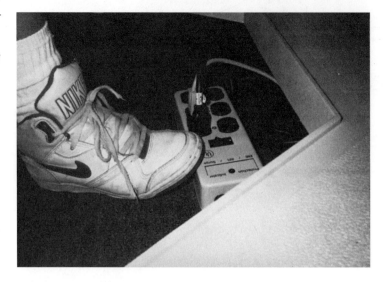

- Electronic devices should be plugged into a surge suppressor to protect the components against "spikes" in the power supply. Otherwise the chips might get "fried"! This is especially important if you live in a part of the country which is more vulnerable to blackouts or brownouts. Be sure to locate the surge suppressor in a place where the power switch cannot be accidentally turned off. The worst place to put it is on the floor. Usually a surge protector strip comes with recessed hanger holes, which allow it to be hung from screws located in some out-of-the-way spot (on the underside of a table, at the back of a desk, or on the wall).

- Display rules of correct computer use close to where the computer is located, and occasionally go over the rules in order to foster computer literacy. Figure 8.14 illustrates a whimsical set of rules drawn up by one lab assistant—presumably on a quiet day.

- Handicapped students will want to use the computer, too. In the interests of equity, you may need to acquire special devices for data input and display for special-needs students. Voice recognition, touch-screen overlays, and braille keyboards and screens are examples of the many adaptive devices available. Students in wheelchairs should have recessed tables.

  It is beyond our scope to dwell in more detail on this important topic. Appendix B includes titles of publications that deal specifically with the computing needs of the disabled. Local foundations (the Rotary Club, Lions, March of Dimes, for example) can be approached for funding for workstations adapted for the disabled (Apple Computer, 1991).

- Keep food and drink away from the machinery. We discussed this in chapter 6 in the context of taking care of disks and disk drives.

- Each computer in a school *must* have antiviral software such as Symantec Corporation's *SAM* virus protection package installed on the hard drive. You will recall our discussion of viruses and vaccines in chapter 5.

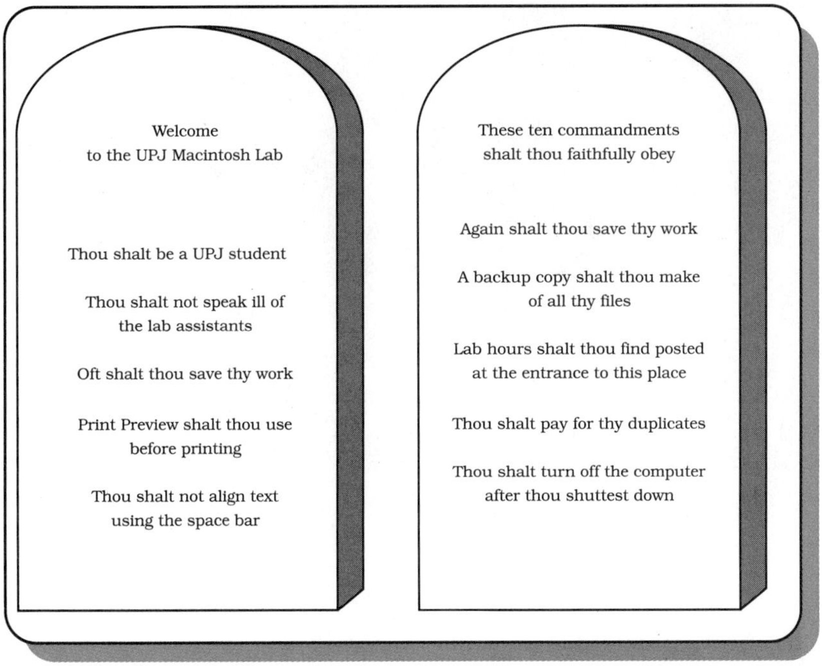

Figure 8.14
The ten
commandments of
computer use
Courtesy Paul Durem,
University of Pittsburgh at
Johnstown

A computer pod or cluster

Your classroom may contain several computers. At least one computer should be set up independently and on a mobile cart so that you can use it for group presentation purposes. The setup for the other computers will vary from room to room depending on the age group, and on the size and shape of the room itself. Do not hide computers behind carrels. Visibility and open setup encourages collaborative use, which often results in the best outcomes. An interesting arrangement of computers is a pod, as illustrated in figure 8.16.

8.4.2 The Planning, Design, and Management of the Computer Lab or Multiple-Computer Classroom

Once again, all the safety and ergonomics-related recommendations should be applied as far as possible in the computer lab. The layout of the lab will vary depending on the size and configuration of the room. At the end of the chapter, in Do Something About It, you will have the opportunity to further discuss lab design. Any layout should be carefully thought through to make the most of the conditions.

Methodology for planning the lab

The classic approach to problem solving devised by Polya (1945) applies equally well to planning the layout for a computer lab. Let us say that you have been given the task of designing the layout for a new computer lab. Here are the steps you should take to help guarantee that your design will be the best possible, given the circumstances and constraints under which you will have to work.

Figure 8.15
How to ruin a
perfectly good
computer system.
Keep food and drink
away from the
machinery.
Photo courtesy Susan
Giorgio Bond

Step 1: Understand the problem

Plan ahead, and start planning as early as possible.

Consider the physical setup of the room. How many electrical wall outlets are there? Where are they located? Will you need more? What kind of lighting is there? Will it need to be changed? What is the minimum recommended distance between machines (Apple recommends three feet)? How many computers can reasonably be accommodated in the room?

Consider the hardware and software that will be used. How many computers will need to be accommodated? What type of computers will the lab house? Will the computers be stand-alone or networked? Will they need to be networked to some other local site (in the school building) or remote site? Will there be one printer per machine, or will the computers be hooked up to two or three high-speed printers?

Consider the expected users of the lab and their needs. Who will use the lab? What furniture will need to be acquired (tables, chairs, cabinets, shelves)? Will the lab be used as a classroom? If so, what extra equipment should be available? What ergonomic features should be considered to enhance the users' comfort and productivity?

Consider security. What type of antitheft devices will be needed? How will they be installed? What other security measures will be necessary (lab supervision, shutdown procedures, lockup, and so on)?

Figure 8.16
Several computers can be arranged in an open pod or cluster.
Photo courtesy Bretford Manufacturing, Inc., Schiller Park, IL

Consider protection against power fluctuations or outages. Is the school located in an area of the country where such fluctuations or outages justify an uninterruptible power supply (UPS)? If so, what kind of UPS will serve your needs: standby or on-line?[4]

Produce a report (some call it a proposal) specifying the requirements for the lab, including a statement of the objectives for the lab, with answers to questions such as those raised above.

Discuss the report with all interested parties: students, teachers, and administrators. Visit labs in other schools. Do not rely only on your own resources. You will be surprised what good ideas other people have. Once a lab is set up, its layout becomes chiseled in stone, difficult to change. You want to do your utmost to get it right the first time.

Step 2: Devise a plan

Map out the lab on a scaled-down floor plan as recommended earlier. Make sure all the requirements drawn up in Step 1 are taken into account in your design. The

---

[4]An on-line UPS routes the AC power supply from the wall outlet through a DC power supply (battery) to the machine. In so doing, the battery is constantly charged, which means that it will always be fully charged when the AC power supply fails. A standby UPS routes the AC power supply from the wall outlet directly to the machine, bypassing the battery. Each time a power failure occurs, the battery power is drawn down—and not automatically recharged, which means that the UPS will eventually fail unless the battery is regularly checked and recharged (Eisner, 1992).

purpose of the requirements is to make sure you do not overlook anything. Remember, the later you discover problems, the more difficult they will be to fix.

Step 3: Carry out the plan

This should be fun if you have done a conscientious job in Steps 1 and 2. There will probably still be surprises, but there will be far fewer than if you neglected the planning.

Step 4: Look back

Once the lab is installed and in use, monitor its use and abuse. Learn from experience with an eye on future lab installations. Make any modifications as they become necessary. Careful management, constant maintenance with attention to detail, and frequent evaluation will significantly prolong the life of the lab.

8.4.3 Recommendations for Lab Management

Many of the recommendations for computer use in the classroom spelled out above apply equally in the computer lab. The following recommendations should also be considered.

- Every lab should have full time technical support. Heavily used computer equipment needs constant maintenance. Students will also need support for hardware and software use. The best people to take care of the latter are trained and supervised student volunteers who acquire valuable social and leadership skills in such roles.
- Do not forget about students with disabilities, a subject we already touched on.
- If you have a choice, connect the computers in the lab to one or two high-speed laser printers. This will work out much better than having one printer per machine. It is much easier to maintain and support one or two printers rather than 30 or 40, and the noise level of a laser printer is minimal.
- Think about an uninterruptible power supply (UPS). This is no longer too expensive an outlay, and can save much grief, especially in areas of the country where power outages are frequent. It takes only a fraction of a second to lose hours of work. You may need to think about installing this UPS option in the lab. You should still display recommendations for correct computer use as recommended (see figure 8.14), including the all-important recommendation to remind students to back up their work regularly.
- Route cables and outlet boxes so that they are concealed and unlikely to be accidentally disturbed. There is already enough danger of loss of power without leaving cables to be tripped over and plugs disconnected.
- Do not allow eating, drinking, or rowdiness in the lab. Children (and adults, too, for that matter) must be reminded often. Do not just post a notice and expect instant acquiescence. Children have no problem obeying rules as long as they know what the rules are and know that they will be applied consistently.
- Encourage collaborative learning. Do not use carrels. Have enough extra chairs so that two or three students can work together at a station. Provide comfortable seating.

Figure 8.17
A possible layout for
a multiple-computer
classroom or
computer lab
Photo courtesy Bretford
Manufacturing, Inc.,
Schiller Park, IL

Figure 8.17 illustrates an attractive layout for a multiple-computer classroom or computer lab.

It is beyond our scope here to cover in more depth the planning, design, and management of a computer lab or multiple-computer classroom. Fortunately, there are many published sources for this kind of material, and the best resource is often the company that supplies the equipment for the lab. For example, Apple Computer (1991) offers an excellent review of the factors involved in establishing and maintaining a computer lab in the publication *Apple Technology in Support of Learning,* which is distributed free of charge to educational institutions. Some of the recommendations in this chapter are drawn from that publication.

Looking Back

The moral of Aesop's fable about the bundle of sticks is that unity gives strength. The computerized classroom will become a reality when all facets of the structure are identified and combined into a unified whole. Just as there must be a continuity between the child's life at school and the child's life at home—the child must be ready for school, and the school must be ready for the child—there must also be continuity within the school between the various parts of the educational process. There is more to creating a computerized classroom than simply adding a computer system to the educational mix. Teachers must be trained, the technology must be supported, and the environment must be carefully prepared.

We have examined the skills that should be acquired, and the concepts that should be assimilated, by the teacher who wishes to effectively incorporate the computer into the curriculum. We have also examined the aspects of the physical setup of the computerized classroom. Appropriate training and a prepared environment are prerequisites to effective education. With a clear understanding of both, we can proceed to look at the ways in which computer technology—hardware and software—can be used to enhance the process of education.

Looking Forward

Schools today recognize that they must change. In this chapter, we have examined the fundamentals of that change, the training of teachers, and the physical and ergonomic infrastructure of computing environments.

The remaining chapters of part III will examine the many technologies, both hardware and software, that have been developed for classroom use, along with the methodologies that have developed around computer-integrated teaching and learning. Ideally, you will have the opportunity to use a variety of learning systems while you are studying the chapters that follow, because hands-on experience is the only way to acquire the skills necessary for competent computer use.

Do Something About It: Exercises and Projects

1. Courses in educational technology for undergraduate education majors should introduce all the skills and concepts drawn up by ISTE, and itemized in section 8.2. An interesting discussion would be whether or not your preparation for teaching, or in-service training, covered these skills and concepts. Prepare a paper or a presentation that reviews your teacher training in the light of the ISTE recommendations.

2. Many companies apply the techniques of quality circles or total quality management, where teams are recognized rather than individuals, where cooperation rather than competition is encouraged in the pursuit of quality, and where small, incremental improvements are constantly identified and made. How might this be applied to the teaching profession in general, and to the creation of quality working environments for the students and teachers in our schools? Document your findings.

3. You are given the assignment of designing the lab layout for a rectangular room 40 feet long by 25 feet wide. What would be the maximum number of computers that would fit into the room and still satisfy all the safety, ergonomic, and logistical recommendations made in this chapter? Develop different plans (designs) for arranging the computers and printer(s) if the lab (a) were to be used as a classroom for lectures that incorporated use of the computers; (b) were not to be used as a classroom, but simply as a computing resource area.

Planning the computer lab at Cornell Middle School
by Jodi Tims, University of Pittsburgh, Johnstown, Pennsylvania

Background

The Pennsylvania Higher Education Assistance Agency (PHEAA) sponsored a program called ITEC (Information Technology for the Commonwealth) aimed at bringing computers and other state-of-the-art technology into the classrooms of Pennsylvania's elementary and secondary schools.

This goal is being accomplished in two ways. The first is by offering a tuition-free, graduate-level course for teachers certified in Pennsylvania to provide experience with using computers, selecting and evaluating software, and integrating the computer into lesson plans. The second is by awarding several grants each year to school districts that wish to introduce or enhance the use of technology in their curriculum. Both programs have played a central role in the development of a computer lab for learning disabled and at-risk students in the Cornell Middle School of the McKeesport School District just outside of Pittsburgh.

Pat Kelm was a student in the ITEC course I was teaching in the fall semester of 1988. Pat already had some experience using computers in her classroom but hoped to gain additional knowledge on how computers could be used more effectively and on a larger scale than she was using them. After completing the course, Pat asked me if I would be willing to sponsor her in an independent study project during the next term, in which she would design a computer lab to be used for enrichment purposes with the learning disabled students she taught at Cornell. I agreed to supervise the project.

Planning

During the next four months, Pat spent considerable time planning the details of the lab. She identified the kind of technology she would like to have in the laboratory. She decided on the ideal arrangement of the computers, peripherals and furniture, taking into account logistical as well as pedagogical criteria for successful design. She even specified where all the wall outlets would be placed in the room. The result was a report that outlined in detail every aspect of the proposed lab.

Funding

By this time, Pat's work was receiving attention from the administration of her school. They encouraged her

Jodi Tims, author of the case study
Photo courtesy Bernie Poole

to consider submitting her plan as a proposal for an ITEC grant. With the aid of a colleague, Gwen Clarke, Pat wrote the grant proposal and submitted it to PHEAA. In March 1990, word was received that the Cornell Middle School would be awarded monies for development of the proposed lab.

Implementation

Summer 1990 was spent setting up the lab. Twenty Apple IIGS computers were purchased along with a laserdisc player. During the first year, the focus of the lab would be the mathematics, science, and social studies curriculum for the fifth- and sixth-grade students. A software and laserdisc library was assembled to address those areas. The second year would involve expansion of the program to include the seventh-grade students. In the third year, the program was to be expanded to include the eighth graders.

Evaluation

The computer lab serves an enrichment role for the students involved. They receive their main instruction in a traditional classroom setting. Pat works with the classroom teacher to come up with a plan to correlate available software with the lesson plans drawn up by the **(continued)**

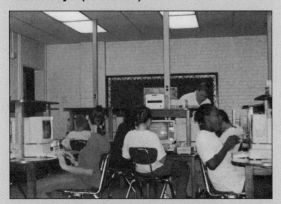

The computers are arranged in clusters to encourage collaborative learning.
Photo courtesy Pat Kelm

This "traditional" classroom setting includes laserdisc audiovisual technology.
Photo courtesy Pat Kelm

classroom teacher. Students primarily receive individual attention in the computer lab; however, some small-group work is also done. The students have a computer lab period five of every ten school days.

So far, the program shows much promise for the students involved. Pat reports that students are excited about working with the computers. They seem willing to work at a subject longer when the computer is used than if traditional pencil-and-paper work is required. Some students have even begun coming in during their study hall and lunch periods to work. Although no hard statistics are yet available, preliminary data indicate an improvement in achievement test scores and attendance for the at-risk students.

The technology has also had an influence on Pat as she teaches. She observes, "It has given me a whole new way of teaching these students. I am no longer there just to lecture and give information. I now feel I am a learning resource for my students and that it is now possible to make learning interesting for them."

The combination of computers and laserdisc technology has also opened up new teaching techniques for Pat. She has successfully interfaced the laserdisc with the computer, allowing her to develop entire lessons where the computer controls the laserdisc to display the appropriate information at the appropriate time. In addition, Pat finds that the laserdisc makes it easier to introduce ideas related to the main topic which may be of interest to her students.

Perhaps the most exciting outcome of the computer lab is the interest that it has sparked in other teachers in the building. They are beginning to ask questions about

how they can use computers in their classrooms, too. Ultimately, the goal of the ITEC program is being realized. Technology is having an impact in the classroom today with a promise of even more in the future.

Talk About It

Topics for discussion based on the case study

1. If you were to design a computer lab from scratch, what criteria would you establish for the lab? Be sure to consider not only computer hardware and software, but also things such as furniture, lighting, power supply, and so on.

2. Your school has just been awarded a $30,000 grant for computer enhancement. What arguments could be made for spending the money to equip a centralized lab? What are the advantages to distributing the equipment among individual classrooms?

3. Given the same $30,000, how much of it should be allocated to purchasing software versus hardware? Justify your response.

4. If a computer resource lab (including laserdisc technology) were suddenly available for your use, what impact would that have on the way you teach? Why?

5. Technological advancement often renders computer equipment "obsolete" before it ever hits the marketplace. How does this realization affect the planning of a computer lab?

■ References

Adler, Jerry, Elizabeth Ann Leonard, Tessa Manuth, Mary Hager. *"Typing Without Keys." Newsweek,* December 7, 1992, pp. 63–64.

Ankrum, Dennis R. *"Viewing Angle and Distance in Computer Workstations."* In preparation for publication, 1993.

Apple Computer. *Apple Technology in Support of Learning: Creating and Managing an Academic Computer Lab.* Sunnyvale, CA: PUBLIX Information Products, 1991.

Bauch, Jerold P. *"The TransParent School: A Partnership for Parent Involvement." Educational Horizons,* summer 1990, pp. 187–89.

Branscum, Deborah. *"Electromagnetic Update: The Controversy—and Research Continues." MacWorld,* October 1991, pp. 65–69.

Dewey, John. *The Child and the Curriculum and The School and Society.* Chicago: Phoenix Books, The University of Chicago Press, 1956.

Eisner, Andrew, et al. *"When Lightning Strikes: Power Protection." MacUser,* February 1992.

Elmer-Dewitt, Philip. *"The Revolution That Fizzled." Time,* May 20, 1991.

Gannett. *"Battle Looming Over Hand Injuries." News-Press,* Cape Coral, Florida, June 20, 1992, p. 7A.

Hagar, Laura. *"Office Ergonomics: Don't Let Computers Cramp Your Style." Communication Arts,* September/October, 1991, pp. 62–65.

ISTE. *Curriculum Guidelines for Accreditation of Educational Computing and Technology Programs.* Eugene, OR: International Society for Technology in Education, 1992.

Linskie, Rosella. *The Learning Process: Theory and Practice.* New York: D. Van Nostrand, 1977.

Merrill, David M., Zhongmin Li, Mark K. Jones. *ID_2 and Constructivist Theory. Educational Technology,* December 1990, pp. 52–55.

Nickerson, R. S. *Technology in Education in 2020: Thinking About the Non-Distant Future.* In R. S. Nickerson and P. P. Zodhiates, eds., *Technology in Education: Looking Toward 2020.* Hillsdale, NJ: Lawrence Erlbaum Associates, 1988.

Nova. *Workstation Handbook.* Effingham, IL: Nova Solutions, 1993.

O'Connor, Rory J. *"Seeking ELF Relief." MacWorld,* October 1991, pp. 124–29.

Polya, G. Gyorgy. *How To Solve It: A New Aspect of Mathematical Method.* Princeton, NJ: Princeton University Press, 1945.

Selfe, Cynthia. *"The Humanization of Computers: Forget Technology, Remember Literacy."* In Jeffrey Carroll, ed., *Dialogs: Reading and Writing in the Disciplines,* New York: Macmillan, 1992.

Shalvey, Donald H. *"How To Get Comfortable With 32 Kids and One Computer." Learning,* May/June, 1987, pp. 33–36.

Standing, E. M. *Maria Montessori: Her Life and Work.* Fresno, CA: New American Library of World Literature, 1962.

Toffler, Alvin. *Future Shock.* New York: Random House, 1970.

Turkle, Sherry. *The Second Self: Computers and the Human Spirit.* New York: Simon & Schuster, 1984.

Webster's Dictionary. *Random House Webster's College Dictionary.* New York: Random House, 1991.

Computer-Managed Instruction (CMI)

Upon the subject of education. . . . I can only say that I view it as the most important subject which we, as a people, can be engaged in.

Abraham Lincoln (1809–1865)

It takes a lot of preparation to teach just a little.

Eleanor L. Doan (1918–   )

Much of what a teacher does goes unnoticed. Teachers devote a great deal of time to remote and immediate class preparation and follow-up. Unfortunately, K–12 teachers can rarely find time for this preparation during the school day, let alone immediately before or immediately after each class. There are two reasons for this.

- First, one class is often immediately followed by another during the school day, especially in the K–12 environment. So most of a K–12 teacher's "immediate" preparation for class takes place at home, in the evenings and on weekends.

- Second, remote preparation, by definition, takes place outside the context of specific class-related concerns. Remote preparation takes place during the semester on a catch-as-catch-can basis and as time and energy allow. Many K–12 teachers also attend conferences and take courses during the summer months.

Thus, any help teachers can get with preparation, evaluation, and follow-up is a great help. The computer can play an important role. "Good tools," quipped Eleanor Doan, "do not make an excellent teacher, but an excellent teacher makes good use of tools." **Computer-managed instruction (CMI)** is designed to help with that broad range of classroom administrative tasks that are such a time-consuming responsibility for individual teachers. This chapter will examine ways in which the computer can be used to assist in the general management of education, at both classroom and administrative levels.

Here are the topics that will be covered:

- Using productivity software
  - The word processor
  - The database
  - The spreadsheet
  - Drawing software
  - Communications software
  - Useful utilities
- Other CMI applications
  - Using electronic templates
  - Preparing and maintaining curricula and syllabi
  - Planning lessons
  - Preparing learning materials
  - Generating and evaluating tests
  - Computerizing audiovisual support
  - Managing, assessing, and guiding students
  - Communicating between home and school

■ 9.1 Introduction

9.1.1 People, Not Computers, Increase Productivity

A recurring dream is shared by members of administrative bodies in all walks of life. They dream that to achieve the objective of increasing productivity and improving efficiency, all one needs is technology. So, they buy computers, put them on people's desks, and think the objective will somehow magically be achieved. As all too many have found out, the objective often remains a dream, and sometimes becomes a nightmare.

Computers are just dumb machines. They are only as efficient and productive as the people using them. These people must be given the time, ongoing training, and support to use the technology effectively. In this chapter, we will discuss ways in which the computer can help teachers and administrators manage their operations in such a way as to save time and increase efficiency. Success, however, depends entirely on the people using the systems that are introduced.

9.1.2 Success with Computers Has Not Come Easily

Conscientious teachers[1] at all levels of education devote time and energy above and beyond the call of duty in order to be effective in the classroom. This is especially true of teachers K–12. The report of the National Commission on Excellence in Education titled *A Nation at Risk* (1984) noted this "dedication, against all odds, that keeps teachers serving in schools and colleges, even as the rewards diminish." Against all the odds, many teachers have learned to use computers and have successfully incorporated them into their curricula.

Unfortunately, this is not true of all K–12 teachers. In fact, one can understand a reluctance to make the effort to master computing skills when, as one teacher put it, "I've been too busy teaching to integrate the computers" (Bulkeley, 1988). Teachers do need help. This is one of the *raisons d'être*[2] of the National Faculty, an organization of college liberal-arts professors which sends faculty to work with teachers in elementary and secondary schools. The idea is "to give teachers time to reflect on their own teaching and make changes in it," says Professor Benjamin Ladner, one National Faculty member. "Teachers usually cannot take that time because they are so overworked" (Nicklin, 1992).

Perhaps more teachers would be motivated to embrace technology if they could see that it not only improves the effectiveness of their teaching, but that it can also save time and effort. With this in mind, let us examine practical steps that teachers can take to reduce the class management burden, thus allowing them to devote more time and energy to doing what they do best: teach. The following sections present some of the

---

[1] Cynical viewpoints notwithstanding, the great majority of teachers are conscientious and do credit to their profession. All professions have their share of individuals who are not conscientious. The teaching profession is no exception; however, it is in the nature of teaching that, like other care-oriented professions, it attracts a higher proportion of caring and conscientious individuals.

[2] French for "reasons for being in existence."

Figure 9.1
Teachers use
computers to
organize their work
with children.
Photo courtesy Charlene
Potochar

applications that teachers are already using in schools. The case study at the end of the chapter presents further class management applications made possible by computer mediated communications (CMC).

9.2 Teachers and Productivity Software

Productivity software describes computer applications that have become the staple set of data-processing tools used in administrative environments. These applications include word processing for tasks that involve writing or publication, database management for general purpose record keeping, spreadsheets for numerical record keeping, charting and data analysis, drawing tools for graphic design, and communications software for establishing and maintaining links to other people and systems.

Each of these tools has myriad applications in the classroom. In the next chapter, we will focus on their application for purposes of instruction. Here we are concerned only with their value for class managements tasks. It is beyond the scope of this book to explain in detail the features of these productivity tools. If you are using the tutorials for *MS-Works* (Poole, 1994), which optionally accompany this text, you will be learning about them in the best way possible: hands-on. If you are not using the tutorials, it is assumed that your studies include an opportunity to work with productivity software. You cannot learn to use the computer without actually using it, any more than you can learn to ride a bike without riding one.

Figure 9.2
A word-processed
form letter with place
holders for data
merged from a
student roster
database (created
using Microsoft
Works 2.0)

Hillsdale Elementary School
Birmingham, AL 11798
October 25, 1994

Roster:HomeContact
Roster:Address 1
Roster:City , Roster:State Roster:Zip

Dear Roster:HomeContact :

I would like to take this opportunity to introduce myself to you. I am
Roster:First Name 's home room teacher this year. You will be pleased
to know that the class has settled down well and the children are already
making excellent progress on the whole.

I am writing to report to you about Roster:First Name 's participation in
school this first half of the current session. I'm sure you appreciate how
important it is for you to be aware of how Roster:First Name is doing,
especially in regard to class grades and attendance.

Roster:First Name 's current grade is Temp Merge DB:Grade . So far
this session Roster:First Name has missed Temp Merge DB:ATD days,
which is Temp Merge DB:Comment .

Please feel free to call me anytime to arrange a conference, especially if the
grade or attendance data above are not what you expected. I can be
contacted at school between the hours of 7:30 am and 4:00 pm, Monday
through Friday. My telephone extension is 2923.

Yours very sincerely,

Isabelle Gordon
Home Room Teacher, Grade 4

9.2.1 The Word Processor

The **word processor**[3] is the most efficient writing tool yet invented. While it has all the
advantages of a typewriter, it also has memory and programmability, which make text infinitely malleable. A word processor can handle a far wider range of publishing tasks
than a traditional typewriter. Examples of these tasks include graphics, cutting and pasting between and within documents, pagination, font and style selection, indexing, automatic tabulation, and so on.

---

[3]The modern typewriter that comes with built-in memory is an albeit limited type of word processor.

Figure 9.3
Student record drawn
from a database of
records (created
using Microsoft
Works 2.0)

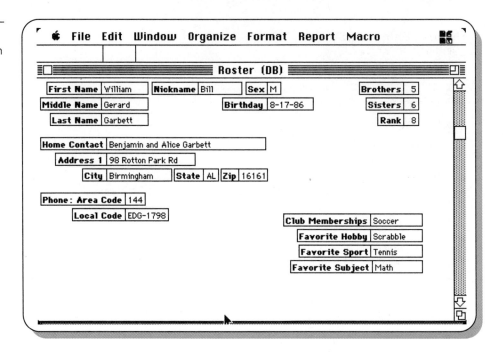

In the next section of this chapter (section 9.3 Applications of CMI), we will examine some specific uses of the word processor for class management. The word processor not only improves the mechanical process of writing by enhancing the appearance of documents. As research has shown, it also improves the quality of one's writing by encouraging rereading and revision of one's work. Changing and moving text is so simple that one is more inclined to produce one's best work.

9.2.2 The Database

The electronic **database** is designed to store data and make that data available to the user in as simple and flexible a manner as possible. Even small databases can store thousands of records. Those records—let us say they are student records—can be sorted in any order, selected (accessed) individually or in groupings determined by the user, and displayed as reports on the screen or on paper.

Many schools now keep student records in an electronic database. Some schools have set up a computer on every teacher's desk and networked every system to a central computer called a host or server. The server controls access to the database of student records by enforcing the use of access codes and passwords in order to protect privileged data. But teachers often have a need to know data about their students, and schools that make this data easily available to teachers are fostering the educational process. The more teachers know about their students, the better they can attend to individual needs.

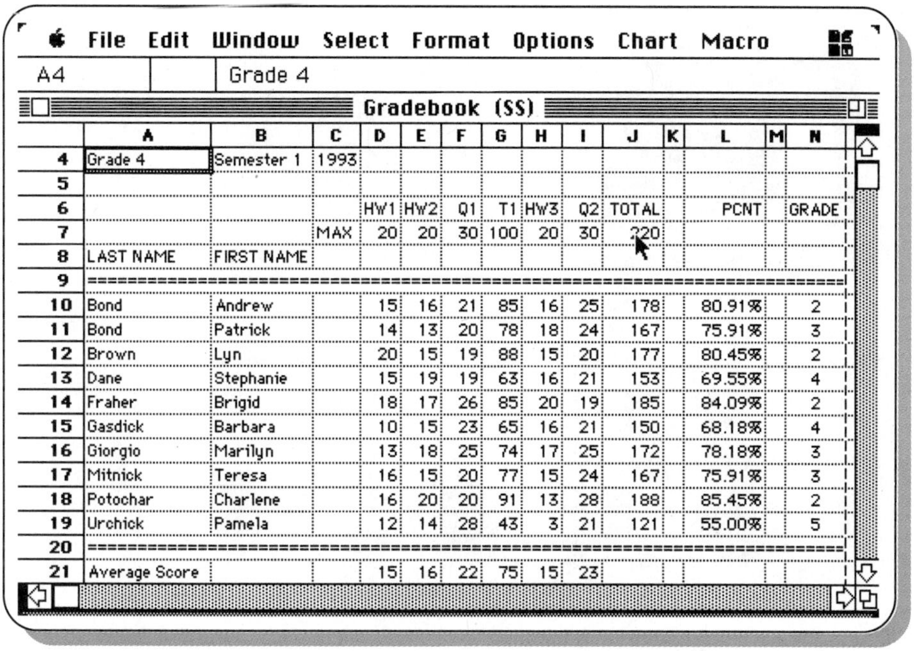

	A	B	C	D	E	F	G	H	I	J	K	L	M	N
4	Grade 4	Semester 1	1993											
5														
6				HW1	HW2	Q1	T1	HW3	Q2	TOTAL		PCNT		GRADE
7			MAX	20	20	30	100	20	30	220				
8	LAST NAME	FIRST NAME												
9	==========													
10	Bond	Andrew		15	16	21	85	16	25	178		80.91%		2
11	Bond	Patrick		14	13	20	78	18	24	167		75.91%		3
12	Brown	Lyn		20	15	19	88	15	20	177		80.45%		2
13	Dane	Stephanie		15	19	19	63	16	21	153		69.55%		4
14	Fraher	Brigid		18	17	26	85	20	19	185		84.09%		2
15	Gasdick	Barbara		10	15	23	65	16	21	150		68.18%		4
16	Giorgio	Marilyn		13	18	25	74	17	25	172		78.18%		3
17	Mitnick	Teresa		16	15	20	77	15	24	167		75.91%		3
18	Potochar	Charlene		16	20	20	91	13	28	188		85.45%		2
19	Urchick	Pamela		12	14	28	43	3	21	121		55.00%		5
20	==========													
21	Average Score			15	16	22	75	15	23					

Figure 9.4
A set of student grades in a spreadsheet (created using Microsoft *Works* 2.0)

9.2.3 The Spreadsheet

A **spreadsheet** is a tool for handling numerical data of all kinds. It started out in the late 1970s as a tool for accounting applications, but it was adopted quickly by number crunchers in all walks of life, including teaching. The typical application of spreadsheets for purposes of class management is for recording and weighting scores for assignments, quizzes, and tests, and for calculating averages and grades.

The typical spreadsheet has a selection of built-in mathematical functions (also called formulas) and graphing capabilities which greatly simplify the manipulation of the numerical data. Fig. 9.4 illustrates a gradesheet. Notice the boxes (called cells in spreadsheet parlance) in which a formula has been set up to carry out a calculation based on a set of scores, such as the total score for one student, or the average score for a class.

9.2.4 Drawing Software

Drawing software is useful for creating visual aids and learning materials in general. Today's bit-mapped,[4] high resolution monitors and printers have encouraged the development of highly sophisticated drawing tools such as Adobe *Illustrator,* Deneba *Canvas,* and Corel *CORELDRAW.* These tools enable skilled artists to produce high-quality graphic art. But the real beauty of these tools is that they enable relatively unsophisticated users to produce artwork that they would have considered daunting if they had to produce the same work by hand.

[4]*Bit-mapped* means that the image or text on the monitor's screen or the printer's page is mapped dot for dot with the bits on the memory chips inside the computer's system unit. This idea was discussed in chapter 6 when we examined computer hardware.

CORELDRAW

CORELCHART

CORELPHOTO•PAINT

CORELSHOW

CORELMOVE

CORELMOSAIC

9.2.5 Communications Software

The subject of communications involves the use of local and remote (wide) area networks to link people and computers for the purpose of data and information exchange.[5]

Communication is the lifeblood of education. The more that schools cultivate opportunities for their students to communicate—both within the school and with the larger community of the school district, the county, the country, or the world,—the better. Such communication is the best means to break down prejudice and barriers between people.

---

[5]You may recall the discussion of the difference between data and information in chapter 3, data being the raw material of information, information being the mind-enriching experience once data have been transmitted, processed, understood, and assimilated by the human brain.

Communication is a key class-management tool when it comes to establishing and maintaining close contact between parents and the school. Such contact is vital to an educational institution's success. Children who are aware of the collaboration between their parent(s) and the school are much more likely to gain the maximum benefit from the educational experience. We will return to this subject later in this chapter (section 9.3.8 Communicating between Home and School) and again in chapter 11 when we discuss computers and communications (C&C).

9.2.6 Useful Utilities

Teachers who have a computer on their desk can take advantage of several useful time-management utilities such as on-line calendars and scheduling software. Once again, this kind of software is only as organized as the people using it. Because on-line calendars come with perpetual calendars, one need only enter the year; the system works out which day of the week January 1 falls on, and whether or not it is a leap year. On the screen, one can display a full month, like a hard-copy calendar, and enter data into each day's box. One can add details to an entry by opening up the box for a single day and typing in more extensive notes. For example, say you have a department meeting scheduled for March 10. You would enter the time of the meeting in the box for March 10, then open up the box to add notes about what to bring up at the meeting. Another useful feature of most on-line calendars is an alarm that can be set to correspond with a time set on a certain date. For example, you could have the computer remind you at 3:00 P.M. that you have a department meeting scheduled for 3:30 P.M. on March 10. Of course the computer will do this only if you are using it on March 10!

Another useful utility is an on-line notepad for memos. This is easy to set up, especially if one is using a modern operating system such as *Multifinder* on the Apple Macintosh, Microsoft *Windows* or *Windows NT,* or IBM's *OS/2* for IBM or compatible machines, or *Workbench* for the Commodore Amiga. These operating systems enable you to have several files open at the same time[6] on the screen.

One of these files could be a word processor file called Notepad, which would be permanently available in the background, ready to receive notes in the form of memos, reminders, ideas, dates, to-do lists, even shopping lists! At the end of the day, before shutting down the computer, one would run off a copy of the notepad, if necessary, or save it for future use.

Desktop computers also come with built-in utilities such as a calculator, an alarm clock, or a file finder. A file finder is useful if you have dozens of poorly organized files on disk and you cannot remember where you saved the file you need or, even worse, you can not remember the name of the file. The utility will help you search all the files on a disk on a trial-and-error basis, using a subset of the name you think you might have used.

---

[6]In computerese, this is called concurrent processing.

Figure 9.6
Multitasking on the
IBM PS/2

Photo courtesy IBM
Corporation

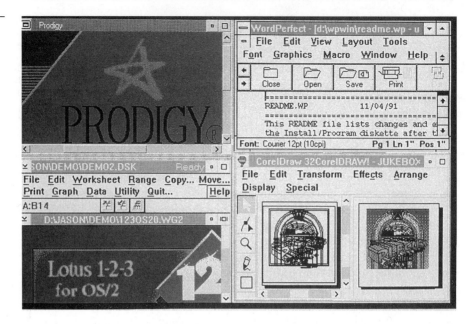

◗ 9.3 Other CMI Applications

9.3.1 Using Electronic Templates

If you have been using the set of *MS-Works* tutorials that optionally accompany this text, you will be familiar with the concept of **templates,** which are also known as stationery documents or forms. To a great extent, much of the paperwork that we use both in and out of the classroom is standardized. This is true whether the paperwork is something as simple as a personal letterhead or a permission slip, or something relatively complex such as a deficiency report or a medical treatment form.

Usually, schools develop templates or forms for these purposes, with fill-in-the-blanks spaces for data entry, as illustrated in figure 9.7.

There are at least two problems with paper-based templates:

- It is necessary to produce multiple copies and store them somewhere where they can be easily accessed in anticipation of need—so they waste paper and take up space.
- Once they are printed (usually in large quantities!), they cannot be easily changed—so if it is necessary to update the forms, the old ones have to be scrapped (they usually become memo pads if one side is unused).

Electronic templates, on the other hand, have neither disadvantage. Once they have been designed and saved on disk, they can be easily duplicated and shared with the rest of the administration and/or faculty. Where faculty members have their own computer, the set of templates useful for instructional or class management purposes would be downloaded into a subdirectory or folder on their hard disks or stored on a floppy disk designated for templates.

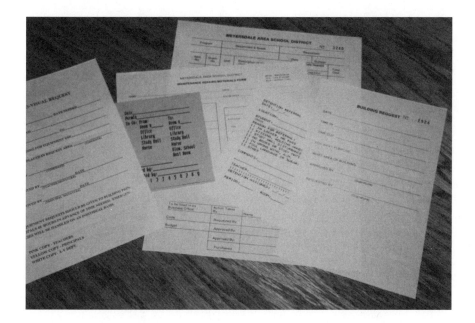

Figure 9.7
Typical templates
(forms) used in
schools
Photo courtesy Charlene
Potochar

This arrangement would not work for critical templates that would suffer from arbitrary change—for example, templates for medical treatment forms used to supply information and permissions should a student be injured or taken ill while at school. Assuming that all the teachers have their own computers, and assuming that every teacher knows how to use the word processor or other software that was used to create the template, how would one control changes to critical templates if they were not centrally located? As soon as they were distributed onto multiple machines, it would be possible (Murphy's law says it would be more than likely) that advertent or inadvertent changes would creep into them.

Of course, the ideal situation is for every faculty or administrative computer to be networked together. One computer, called a server, would be centrally controlled and managed. Anyone with a computer on the network would have different levels of access to different sets of files or data. Certain files such as student records would be available for read-only access by faculty; they could read the data, but they could not change it or add to it. Likewise, certain templates would be available only from the central repository on the server. In this way, the format and content of these critical templates would be less likely to be arbitrarily corrupted.

Other templates, such as letterheads or ditto masters and so forth, would be stored on each faculty member's machine so that they could be customized to serve that faculty member's needs. Many of these templates would be shared among faculty. Indeed, a well-organized school would make some individual—a computer coordinator, perhaps—responsible for setting up a system whereby this sharing was formalized and encouraged.

A useful exercise would be for you to get together with a few classmates or colleagues and brainstorm to come up with a list of as many template possibilities as you can think of. Then go through the resulting list to separate critical from noncritical templates. The next step would be to go ahead and create the templates, save them on disk, and share them. This is one of the recommended exercises in the Do Something About It section at the end of the chapter.

9.3.2 Preparing and Maintaining Curricula and Syllabi

A syllabus is part of the content of a curriculum. As Zais (1976) reminds us, the word *curriculum* comes from the Latin for "racecourse." Zais goes on to point out that many confuse the curriculum with the program of studies followed by students in their race toward graduation. Other interpretations define curriculum as course content, planned learning experiences, a structured series of intended learning outcomes, a written plan of action, even a "hidden" entity defining the unspoken outcomes of a specific educational experience. The concept of "curriculum" is, in fact, as diverse a concept as "educational goals" because the curriculum is, in the end, whatever an educational institution establishes to promote in its students. The curriculum can be painted with broad brush strokes describing overall goals of the institution; it can be painted with fine brush strokes describing the detailed specification of learning experiences and methodologies that are used in practice to achieve the goals of the institution; or it can be painted with any degree of precision in between.

If we think of curriculum at the subject level, we can talk of the math curriculum, the language arts curriculum, the social studies curriculum, and so on. Each curriculum would be promoted by a series of courses, and each course would be described by a syllabus detailing its content and learning outcomes.

A curriculum is not static; nor is a syllabus—though a syllabus will change more frequently than a curriculum. This is because a syllabus tends to reflect the current realities of a discipline even though its primary objective is to promote the long-range goals of the curriculum. For example, the syllabus for a geography course in the social studies curriculum will naturally be subject to frequent change in order to reflect current thinking in the field and, if it is contemporary geography, current world affairs. If it does not, there is a problem with the administration of the course: the course content will become progressively out of date. Although this is not true of all courses (for example, courses that offer instruction in the unchanging fundamentals of a subject such as mathematics), it is true of most.

The realities of change, the rate of which is constantly accelerating, can be avoided less today than ever before. This is why teachers are encouraged to keep abreast of their discipline. We all know how easy it is to get by on old knowledge, especially in the teaching profession, where accountability is not nearly as stringent as in a business environment. But it is unethical to do so, because students will suffer from such neglect. Assuming, therefore, that teachers are keeping current in their fields of expertise, it follows that syllabi and curricula will be refined frequently.

Now, as the classical Latin scholar Publilius Syrus observed in his Moral Sayings: "It's a bad plan that can't be changed." Curricula and syllabi that are drawn up and saved in electronic (soft copy) form will be more likely to remain current than those that are produced only on paper (hard copy). This is because it is easier to change an electronic file. When doing advance preparation for a new school year or a new course, a teacher

Figure 9.8
A team of teachers
plans lessons around
computer-based
learning.
Photo courtesy Rick
Povich

who has only a hard-copy version of a syllabus will be less inclined to update it because it may mean rewriting the whole thing. The teacher with the electronic version knows that the syllabus can be quickly updated to reflect new topics, methodologies, and so forth.

9.3.3 Planning Lessons

Lesson plans are drawn up as part of the immediate preparation for a class. Most school districts require that teachers not only prepare written plans for every lesson, but expect them to be available for inspection, too. Aside from the obvious practical necessity of having something laid down for a substitute teacher to follow, lesson plans are crucial to the process of achieving educational goals. Another classical philosopher, Seneca, had this to say about plans: "Our plans miscarry when they have no aim. When a man does not know what harbor he is making for, no wind is the right wind."

Lesson plans are more prone to change than syllabi or curricula. It is difficult to predict much ahead of time what will be covered on any particular day. Lesson plans from previous offerings of a course are useful, of course, but they may need to be rearranged, moved forward, moved back, updated with regard to content, and so on. Fortunately, more and more school districts are accepting lesson plans that have been prepared on the computer instead of using preprinted lesson-plan books. This is another application of the templates we discussed in the previous section. It is easy to prepare a template that maps into the model used in a school district's lesson plan book. This template can then be made available to any teachers who want to use the computer for their plans. The plans, once prepared, can be printed out and collected into a ring binder for inspection and use.

Advantages to using the computer for lesson plans include:

- The plans are easy to read because they are not handwritten.
- The plans are more likely to be detailed since it is quicker and less tiring to key in data than to write it by hand (even for people who are slow at the keyboard—though perhaps not for snails!).
- Plans that have been used before can be easily modified if necessary and reused.
- Computerized lesson plans are more flexible. They can be easily rearranged, resequenced, added to, or deleted. This is true both for short-term and long-term planning. Some schools insist on teachers using bound lesson-plan booklets, which has definite disadvantages. Others also provide booklets for this purpose but allow teachers the option of using a format of their own design, such as customized printed sheets in a loose-leaf binder or, of course, computerized lesson plans. If a teacher decides in the middle of the week that a lesson prepared the previous weekend is not going to work for some reason, the lesson can simply be replaced. This would be more difficult to do if the plan had been handwritten in a bound booklet. In addition, a bound booklet does not allow for idiosyncrasy with regard to different approaches to class preparation.

9.3.4 Preparing Learning Materials

Ditto masters, illustrations involving graphics in general or graphs and charts in particular, seating plans, style sheets, word lists, questionnaires, quizzes, assignment specifications, summary sheets, handouts of all kinds: these are the bread and butter of the teaching profession. Not only is a picture worth a thousand words; directions are more likely to be followed if they are written down, and concepts are more likely to be digested if time is allowed for them to be mulled over.

It stands to reason that the computer is the best tool to use to prepare this kind of material. Even illustrations that might take extra effort using a computer, as compared with preparing them freehand, will benefit in the long run because of the increased flexibility afforded by the computer. If some detail of a design needs to be changed, this can be accomplished easily on the computer, whereas a freehand drawing might need to be completely redone.

Drawing tools

The computer can transform anyone's artwork. Straight lines, jagged lines, smoothly curved lines, circles, ellipses, and shapes of all sorts are a snap to draw, move into position, and fill with a wide range of patterns and colors (even if you do not have a color monitor—but you need a color printer, of course). When you want to include an illustration that might be difficult for a nonartist to create—like a picture of a ship, or a map of the world, or a sports figure—you can use a collection of clip art. **Clip art** is the term used for sets of predrawn images saved in electronic form on disk, which one can copy into other documents such as newsletters, posters, and so forth. Figure 9.9 illustrates this concept.

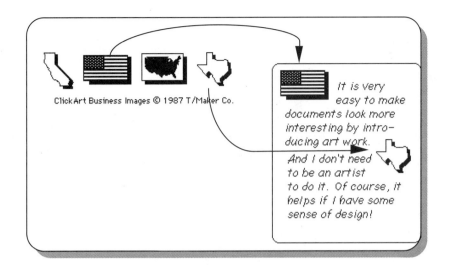

Figure 9.9
Cutting and pasting
with "clip" art

ClickArt Business Images © 1987 T/Maker Co.

It is very easy to make documents look more interesting by introducing art work.
And I don't need to be an artist to do it. Of course, it helps if I have some sense of design!

The computer also saves time when producing charts, especially ones that are based on numerical data. Most spreadsheets today, including those that are integrated with other software in packages such as Claris Corporation's *ClarisWorks* or Microsoft *Works,* have charting functions built into them. The user indicates which set of figures is to be charted, then instructs the computer to go ahead and produce either a bar chart, a pie chart, a line chart, or some combination of charts. The process is simple, and the impact in the classroom is significant.

Desktop Publishing

The latest versions of word processors such as *WordPerfect* and Microsoft *Word* incorporate more and more features that originally characterized desktop publishing (DP) software such as Aldus *PageMaker.* Teachers who use these modern word processors can easily create columns of text and tables, along with the usual page-layout features expected of word processors. Also, today it is easy to use different fonts (character styles) in a wide range of font sizes. Producing professional-looking documents for distribution to students, parents, or colleagues is well within everyone's capabilities.

9.3.5 Generating and Evaluating Tests

Assessment is integral to the learning process. It includes self-assessment by both the teacher and the student. It includes teacher assessment of each student, of groups of students engaged in collaborative work, and of the class as a whole. It includes student assessment of each other, and of the teacher, too.

Assessment is both formal and informal. Informal assessment is frequent (several times a day) and takes one of two forms: self-questioning about one's immediate and longer-range personal and academic objectives, activities in pursuit of those objectives,

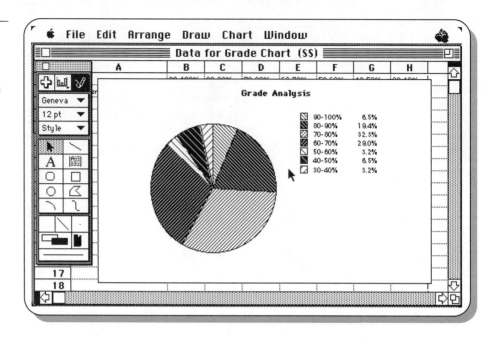

Figure 9.11
Log sheets, planning
sheets, and ditto
masters
Photo courtesy Susan
Giorgio Bond

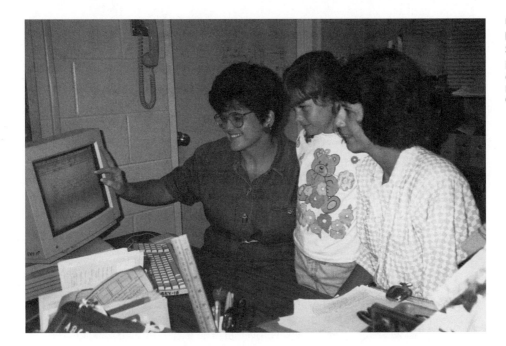

Figure 9.12
Student, teacher, and
parents reviewing the
child's portfolio
Photo courtesy Susan
Giorgio Bond

and accomplishments; and questioning about the progress being made by others. In business it is called taking stock. Good teachers create an environment where students are encouraged to be conscientious about conducting this kind of informal assessment, thus taking much of the weight off formal tests and other standardized measures of progress or achievement.

Portfolios

Good teachers assess their students on the basis of portfolios of work gathered over time, rather than relying predominantly on snapshots of progress captured periodically. Portfolios are especially important in assessing the objective value of a student's work, regardless of what other students may be doing. No two students are equally capable or gifted. Using computer-based tools, students can access data of all kinds, make sense of it, and organize it in such a manner as to demonstrate understanding and assimilation of the knowledge learned or the experience gained. The materials that are the outcomes of their studies are gathered into portfolios that allow the teacher to assess not how smart the children are, but rather, more appropriately, how they are smart!

Are formal tests necessary?

It is beyond the scope of this book to dwell on the arguments for and against formal testing. Some would argue that tests are necessary because it is naive to expect that all students (and all teachers, for that matter) will conscientiously conduct useful self-assessment. Others argue that fundamental change is needed in the way schools are organized and managed if we want to do away with formal assessment techniques.

Some schools of thought would do away with formal testing altogether. But for the time being, at least, formal tests are necessary for two reasons:

- Those that pay for the education system need some commonly agreed upon guideline for assessing the effectiveness of the schools, which usually takes the form of scores on tests.

- There is a tradition of formal testing in schools, a tradition with an inertia of its own. Where this is the case, formal testing actually dictates to some extent the academic ethos of the school, in regards both to teaching styles and student study habits. Many teachers rely on testing as an important component of their methodology.

Using the computer to generate tests

The computer can help with the generation of tests in at least three ways:

- Many textbooks come packaged with computerized test-generation tools. The software gives the teacher the ability to create new tests, revise old tests, and save multiple versions of tests with questions ordered differently to discourage cheating in classrooms where children sit closely together. The package usually includes a database of test questions prepared by the author of the textbook. A good test bank is made up of different types of questions: short essay, multiple choice, true/false, fill in the blanks, and matching, for example.

- Using the word processor, teachers can set up test templates, including all the formatting and page layout features. These templates can be made available for other teachers to use. Devising and entering the questions would be the only time-consuming activity. An alternative to using the word processor is test-generation software such as *MakeTest,* offered by Mountain Lake Software. This package is not affiliated with any particular text. Its four modules help a teacher create a question file (including graphics, if desired), then create a test, organize the test, and print it out. Once again, the only time-consuming activity is devising and entering the questions.

- There are many reasons why a teacher should involve students in building tests. In the spirit of encouraging students to assess each other and themselves, a teacher can set up the word processor for students to submit their own questions for tests. For example, if there are 25 students, each would be given the assignment of designing two questions, say, and handing them in by a certain date to a student assigned to enter them into a predetermined word-processor file. On the due date, the file would be checked by the teacher. Errors would be removed and, if necessary, more questions added, to make sure all aspects of the material have been covered. A copy of the questions would be run off and duplicated so that each student would have a study sheet as a guide in studying for the test. Finally, the teacher would select items from the set of questions for the test, cut and paste them into a file of their own, run off the test, and give it on the designated date.

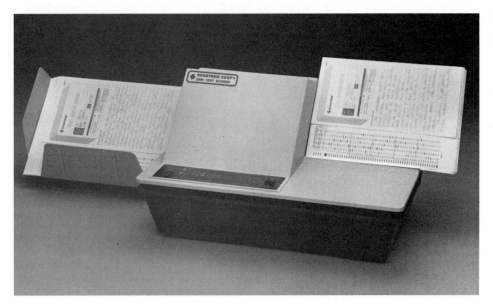

Grading tests

Optical mark recognition (OMR) is a well-established scanning technology that comes in handy in schools for many forms-based tasks such as attendance-data gathering, questionnaire analysis, test scoring and assessment, checklists, and so forth. The computer recognizes marks made on the printed page and is programmed to interpret them according to a predetermined set of criteria. Figure 9.13 illustrates a typical OMR form and a mark reader.

Tests that consist of one-option answers (multiple choice, true/false, matching) can be scored in a few seconds, depending on the size of the class. Typically, an optical scanner can process from 50 to more than 150 sheets per minute.

The forms can be purchased from the company that supplies the mark reader. Alternatively, one can develop forms in-house using software such as *Forms on Demand* by Systems Factor, Inc. or *DB*FORMAKER* by Data Blocks. The latter software, however, has more application at the school-district administrative level, where there may be a need to process large numbers of forms for data collection and analysis.

The Test Banking Service

At least one school, albeit at the college level, has developed a computerized system that coordinates the generation and evaluation of tests collegewide. This system, described in Watkins (1991), "stockpiles instructors' test questions in a data bank, creates examinations and scores them, and enters students' marks in a grade book." The system, located at Miami-Dade County Community College's Medical Center, takes care of security since tests are controlled at a central location; it also saves secretarial time. As one might expect, a system such as this requires a significant amount of planning and support.

Six years of development have led to the Test Banking Service, which enables instructors to store questions and select questions for tests from printouts from the test bank. The service then makes up the test (up to four versions of scrambled questions) from the instructor's work order. OMR answer sheets are supplied with the tests. Essay questions are graded by the instructor, of course. All other questions are scored by the OMR scanner. Finally, the system sends the instructor a breakdown of the results with a list that can be posted for the students.

Outcomes of the Test Banking Service

About 60% of the faculty members now use the service. The most interesting outcome has been a renewed interest in testing per se, and in innovative testing methodologies. For example, some faculty members give their students two versions of the same test, the first (10 minutes to complete) to test what they know "off the top of their heads," and the other (20 minutes) to test "what they know when they have time to think about it."

When the computer is used to handle time-consuming overhead, creativity is given freer rein and interesting possibilities become viable. Could a system such as this be implemented in schools K–12? That is a question for discussion in the Do Something About It section at the end of the chapter.

9.3.6 Computerizing Audiovisual Support

Computers have significantly increased the number of options available to teachers for using audiovisual aids to increase the impact of their lessons. Technology such as record players, tape recorders, film and slide projectors, overhead projectors, and videocassette recorders (VCRs) are still part of the armory of audiovisual equipment at most schools. But computers and related equipment that are powerful enough and at the same time cheap enough to eventually replace most of these machines are now proliferating in schools.

Computer-coordinated A-V

In the classroom, the computer can be used with other technologies to coordinate the incorporation of audiovisual material into lesson plans. In chapter 12, we will look more closely at the subject of multimedia. Scanners, for example, can be used to digitize[7] and capture illustrations on disk. Once in electronic form, they can be sequenced and called up on large-screen televisions or projected directly onto an overhead screen using an LCD panel and an overhead projector. CD-ROM discs and interactive videodiscs packed with computer-accessible audiovisual material such as still pictures and video clips with multilingual sound tracks are at the heart of multimedia systems.

Companies such as Optical Data Corporation, National Geographic, IBM, and Computer Curriculum Corporation are among a growing number of companies that have developed magnificent multimedia systems. A useful exercise for teachers would

---

[7]You will recall that the process of digitizing reduces a physical entity such as an image or a sound to the binary 1s and 0s that can be handled by computers.

Figure 9.14
Students developing
a project using IBM's
Ultimedia ™
Photo courtesy IBM
Corporation

be to discuss the myriad ways in which a multimedia system could be used in the K–12 classroom. This will be one of the exercises in the Do Something About It section at the end of the chapter.

Teachers who have multimedia systems in their classrooms will find that they will make much more use of them than of the traditional audiovisual equipment. This is because, as we will see in chapter 12, these systems greatly simplify the incorporation of audiovisual materials into lesson plans. More important, multimedia systems lend themselves naturally to student-directed use for the development of research-related projects and portfolios of all kinds and for all age groups.

If a classroom has a computer, an overhead projector, and an LCD panel, software-driven applications will enable the teacher to call on interactive audiovisual aids during the course of a presentation to reinforce, and add interest to, what is being studied. Such applications are available in all subject areas. A history lesson, for example, gains focus from the display of maps, contemporary fashions, architecture, time lines, and so on. History teachers have always appreciated the need to use audiovisual materials such as these.

The difference a computer makes is largely logistical: it streamlines the integration of a variety of audiovisual materials by reducing them to a single digital format. This reduces the clutter and handling otherwise involved with paper, slides, transparencies, film, records, audio and video cassette tapes, and other traditional media.

We are still in the early stages of computer use in schools, but it does not take much imagination to foresee a future where this technology will transform the way teachers teach. Chapter 12 will provide an opportunity to learn more about this exciting technology.

9.3.7 Managing, Assessing, and Guiding Students

Managing students

Keeping track of students is another time-consuming task. Keeping grades, taking attendance, checking on irregular attendance, following up with communication with the home, keeping notes on each child's attitudes, behavior, health, and home background— these are just a few of the responsibilities that teachers are supposed to take in their stride along with their other responsibilities. Of course, teachers cannot do all this as thoroughly as they would like. After all, they also have to teach!

It would help if there were software to manage tasks such as these. *Teacher's Pet*™, published by Classroom Data Systems, is a program designed to run on the computer on a teacher's desk. The heart of the program is a computerized seating chart that connects students' names with their records. Student records are modified by positioning the cursor on the "seat" occupied by a particular student and entering data about the student, such as an *A* for absent, a *T* for tardy, and so forth. If a student is marked absent, his or her name blinks or changes color so that it will stand out in the chart. Should the student arrive late, the teacher simply types a *T,* with the cursor positioned on the name. The student record is automatically updated to record the absent or tardy status. Also recorded with a tardy status is the time the student arrived in class.

Recording of grades and behavior is done in a similar manner. Several reports may be printed by the system based on the student records in the database.

- A list of students, by period, marked absent today.
- A list and total of students enrolled in each period.
- Complete attendance records for all classes.
- A grade report by test or assignment, including averages.
- A grade report by individual student.
- Attendance report by individual student.
- Behavior report by individual student.
- A printout of all notes in the notepad utility.
- A seating chart for each period.

Teacher's Pet also has several utilities that are useful for class management purposes. There is a calendar program for keeping track of meetings and appointments. There is an on-screen scientific calculator. The notepad utility is for keeping free-form memos of all kinds. The address book keeps track of names, addresses, and telephone numbers. A reminder system displays preset messages on the screen at a specific time, say, at the beginning of a particular period. A birthday reminder pops up on the screen a list of any students in a particular class period whose birthdays are on that day. Finally, a backup utility copies files from the hard disk drive to floppy disks.

Assessing and guiding students

Systems such as *Teacher's Pet* can come in handy when the teacher is in the role of guidance counselor. We discussed assessment earlier when reviewing the subject of testing. Another aspect of assessment relates to less easily measured skills such as social skills, study skills, and creative skills—skills that are more generally related to character and personality. A person's character might be defined as the set of basic traits that make up that person's nature, and personality describes the way that character is projected and perceived by others.[8]

One of the greatest difficulties facing teachers today, perhaps more than ever, is the need to help children who are not "ready" for school. Problems at home, in particular, and pressures in the social milieu as well, can mean that a student may be physically present in class but mentally unable to participate to the best of his or her abilities. Even children from relatively stable family and social backgrounds will bring to the learning process ways of being that demand special consideration. Every child is different, and deserves individual attention.

Teachers are most effective with the children whom they come to know well. Some understanding of a student's character and personality and a familiarity with a student's home background and academic history are important in terms of providing the best learning experience. An experienced and empathetic teacher may be skilled at recognizing character and personality traits by interacting with a student. But the only way to learn about the same student's home background and academic history is to ask. This is where the computer is a useful tool.

Schools that have established computerized databases of student records are more likely to keep teachers apprised of important student data. This is simply because it is easier to do so. Manual collections of data stored in filing cabinets are more cumbersome to get at and more time-consuming to search through. Teachers are human; the more difficult it is to get something done, the less likely it is that the effort will be made. Because it is important to know one's students well, data about students should be readily available to those who need it.

9.3.8 Communicating between Home and School

An important part of any teacher's job at the K–12 level is to hold conferences with parents, either at school or in the home. This interaction is vital to the quality of the educational process, notwithstanding the fact that it is often neglected. Unfortunately, as reported by the National Education Association and the National Parent Teacher Association, it is estimated that only about half of all parents have ever visited their child's school (Bauch, 1990). When the responsibility for interacting with parents is taken on by teachers, it must either be scheduled during lunch hours, in the evenings, or on weekends, both because of the teacher's heavy class schedule and because parents are not usually available during the day.

---

[8]Random House *Webster's College Dictionary,* 1991 ed.

In some schools, interaction between the school and the home is coordinated by counselors—or "domestic mediators," as they are sometimes called. This arrangement works especially well when teachers are involved in developing those precious links to the students' homes. The domestic mediator, apart from having the benefit of training and experience, can bring objectivity to the three-way relationship between the parent, the child, and the teacher. Objectivity is especially important whenever, as is often the case, the reason prompting the interaction is some shortfall in the child's performance—for example, poor attendance, unruly behavior, or substandard academic performance.

In several areas, computer technology can foster this extra dimension to education by bringing the home into the school and the school into the home. The telephone system combined with computer technology gives schools the capability of maintaining close contact with the students' homes. The computerized functions already available in the regular telephone system are being used in many school districts to maintain this open, two-way communication. Parents can dial in to a teacher's classroom and listen to a message from the teacher describing the homework that has been assigned or any other information they need to know. The school can use the autodial function to have the computer send memos to one or all parents. This is useful to follow up on absences, or to notify groups of students that their bus has been delayed, and so forth (Bauch, 1990). Eventually, powerful systems for interactive, two-way communication between the home and the school will become available once the computer is in most, if not all, homes.

Since these technologies come under the umbrella of C&C, we will discuss them in detail in chapter 11. We should recognize for now that the classroom is an extension of the home. Using computer technology and the telephone system with the features just described, teachers can establish and maintain close and highly effective 24-hour links between the home and the school.

■ Looking Back

K–12 teachers make money the old-fashioned way; they earn it! Learning to use computers effectively in the classroom takes a good deal of effort and, for those who are understandably frightened by the technology, it takes a good measure of determination as well. Those who have become skilled in using computers as a tool for teaching and learning will attest to the fact that CMI can be an effective ally to the teacher in the task of preparing and managing an environment in which children will feel encouraged to open up to knowledge. This chapter has identified various features of CMI, showing how technology can add a new dimension to a teacher's work with students.

Unfortunately, the computer does not make the job of teaching any easier in the long run. It can, however, make it more effective when used with quality software in a conscientiously prepared learning environment. When teachers are given the opportunity to learn the new methodologies associated with computer use, and when they are given the ongoing support that must accompany the hardware and software tools, they have shown themselves capable of transforming the way they teach and the way their students learn. The end result is more effective teaching and more time for interaction with students, which brings its own reward. As Henry Adams reminds us: "Teachers affect eternity; no one can tell where their influence stops."

■ Looking Forward

Computer-assisted instruction (CAI) is a growing field with enormous potential. Learning systems that are available today are laying the groundwork for future, more standardized, and comprehensive learning environments. We are learning what works and what does not, evaluation of CAI being an important task for all teachers who use it in their classes.

In the next chapter, we will look at the broad range of CAI available today. We will look at different types of CAI, and at specific applications designed for specific subject areas. We also will examine different software-evaluation instruments. Finally, we will look into the crystal ball and try to predict future directions for CAI. It is an exciting prospect.

Charles Babbage, the "Father of Computers"; Alan Turing, who posited the theory of the Universal Machine; and John Vincent Atanasoff, who invented the first working electronic digital computer—along with the countless other individuals who made small and large contributions to the development of this amazing machine—deserve the gratitude of society in general and of children in particular. Haltingly, step by step, the state of the art in educational computing is advancing. It is up to teachers to help maintain the momentum, for "all that is human must retrograde if it does not advance."[9]

■ Do Something About It: Exercises and Projects

1. It would be interesting to visit a school one hundred years from now to see teaching and learning take place. Although skeptics would say that schools have not changed much over the last 500 years, there is little doubt that the computer as a catalyst for change has already transformed a few schools that have committed to innovative teaching methodologies and learning systems. Will these become the norm? What will be the future in schools? Get together with a group of classmates or colleagues to discuss and document these issues.

2. A useful exercise would be for you to get together with a few classmates or colleagues and brainstorm to come up with a list of as many computerized template possibilities as you can think of. Then go through the resulting list to separate critical from noncritical templates. The next step, of course, is to go ahead and create the templates, save them on disk, and share them.

3. In section 9.3.5, three ideas are presented for generating tests using the computer. Discuss other ways in which the computer can help with assessment which may not involve formal testing. Draw up a description of each idea you can come up with. Assess the merits of each idea.

4. Could the Test Banking Service described in section 9.3.5 be applied at the elementary or secondary levels of education?

■ References

Bauch, Jerold P. Touch 1 for Improved Parent-Teacher Contact. *School Safety,* spring 1990, pp. 25–27.

Bulkeley, William M. Computers Failing As Teaching Aids. *Wall Street Journal,* 1988.

Nicklin, Julie L. "Guerrilla" Army Finds Professors to Help Schools. *Chronicle of Higher Education,* December 2, 1992, p. A5.

Poole, Bernard J. and Susan Giorgio Bond. *Essential Microsoft Works: Tutorials For Teachers.* Madison, WI: Brown & Benchmark, 1994.

The National Commission on Excellence in Education. *A Nation At Risk: The Full Account.* Cambridge, MA: USA Research, 1984.

Watkins, Beverley T. Test Questions Stockpiled and Exams Created and Scored by Computer System at Miami-Dade Medical Campus. *Chronicle of Higher Education,* October 16, 1991, pp. 25, 39.

Zais, Robert S. *Curriculum: Principles and Foundations.* New York: Harper & Row, 1976.

---

[9]Edward Gibbon, *The History of the Decline and Fall of the Roman Empire,* 1776.

Computer mediated communications can increase teacher productivity
by David Popp, Pennsylvania State University, State College, Pennsylvania

What Is CMC?

Although the term *computer-mediated communications* (CMC) may be new, the use of computers as a communication medium has been with us for some time. A simple example of CMC is connecting two personal computers with a cable attached to their serial ports and using software to pass information through the cable from one computer to another. A more sophisticated example is to use a third computer (called a host computer) as the storage medium for the information. The third computer typically runs software which manages the information by providing each user with an address and storage space on the host computer.

This electronic mail (or e-mail) provides instantaneous delivery of the information to anyone who is connected to the system, whether locally or globally. It can be a valuable means of communication among teachers who often find themselves unavailable at different times of the day.

The power of e-mail and its preference over other means of communication increases when one person wishes to communicate with many. A message can be sent to ten people as quickly as to one. The software on the intermediate computer, or host, places a copy of the message in the mailbox of each recipient.

E-mail communication can thus be either private or public. It is private when it is one-to-one, public when it is one-to-many. Public communication with e-mail is accomplished by addressing the mail to a mailbox accessible to a designated group of individuals who have access to the host.

What contribution has CMC made?

CMC has spawned a number of education-related activities that have not previously been possible. CMC has made it possible to link classes from different regions or even nations. Students using these systems have an opportunity to examine issues from different cultural perspectives. CMC has been used to support contests among schools, access to mentors or experts in a field, joint newsletters, the sharing of scientific data, and sharing of lesson plans.

Another use of CMC, which is similar to lesson-plan sharing, is for collaboration and professional growth among teachers by facilitating the exchange of ideas. A common work space uses the conferencing ability of a host computer and its storage capacity to create a place where teachers can systematically approach a problem, discuss it, reach a consensus on how the problem should be approached, divide the task among the group, and combine the results of each member's work to create a product available to all.

To date, the idea of common electronic work space has not been used in the K–12 arena, but it is only a matter of time before it becomes a reality, especially in those school districts where every teacher has a computer networked for CMC.

Much of the work teachers do is the same from school to school and is repeated from day to day. Each day, thousands of teachers write lesson plans, courses of study, and tests; create worksheets; and look for teaching resources. How much teacher time can be saved if lesson plans, courses of study, tests, worksheets, and resources are made available in a common workspace?
(continued)

David Popp, author of the case study

A teacher can take from the common workspace that which suits his or her philosophy of teaching and create materials that are not otherwise available. Newly created materials are contributed to the workspace. The amount of available material as well as the number of ideas and opinions about the teaching of a topic would grow. Why should these thousands of teachers literally reinvent the wheel each day?

Physhare

An example of a project that will examine these issues is being piloted through the joint efforts of the ITEC (Information Technology Education for the Commonwealth) Center at Penn State, the Center for Academic Computing at Penn State, and the Pennsylvania Science Teacher Education Program (PA STEP). The Center for Academic Computing provides computer accounts to physics teachers involved in the project on Penn State's mainframe computer. The Center has also created an information distribution list called *physhare*. The computer accounts provide the teachers with electronic mail capabilities and access to a computer program that supports *physhare*. The program supports public messages, a form of electronic bulletin board, and provides a method for distributing files to members. Physics teachers send messages to *physhare* which are automatically distributed to all of the teachers who belong to the mailing list. Files of information are stored on the Penn State mainframe and distributed through *physhare*. Teachers can request a file by sending an electronic mail message to the computer program that manages *physhare*. The program automatically sends the file to the teacher.

One example of this capacity is the sharing of a physics test-question database. Physics test questions are collected from physics teachers, classified into topic groups, assigned catalog numbers, and typed into files according to topic. The files are stored on the mainframe. A program has been written in BASIC which enables teachers to compose tests from the files. Teachers do this by entering the catalog numbers of the questions to be included on the test. The files are dynamic; they are constantly being updated. A teacher can access the most recent file by sending an electronic mail message

to the computer program that operates *physhare*. The program searches the electronic message for commands and responds to them. If a teacher requests a certain file, the program sends the file to the teacher as electronic mail. The mail file can be transferred from the mainframe to a floppy disk, which the teacher can then use with the BASIC program to compose tests.

This physics test-question database thus serves as an example of how teachers can contribute their work to an electronic pool, and at the same time share in the work of many other contributors.

Physhare: The Road Ahead

There are several advantages to using a large computer system to operate *physhare*. The greatest is the fact that university computers and many others are connected and can pass electronic mail and other information through an international network called Internet. Teachers with accounts at Penn State can use *physhare* to communicate with teachers who have accounts at the University of Pittsburgh, Lehigh University, Susquehanna University, Drexel University, Carnegie Mellon University, or any other Pennsylvania institution. State departments of education are beginning to establish computer networks for their teachers which are connected to the Internet. With the passage of the National Supercomputing bill in December 1991, K–12 access to Internet will increase. This will give teachers nationwide access to *physhare* and other programs that have been designed to promote information access and communications among the K–12 community.

A unique opportunity exists in Pennsylvania to test the use of *physhare* as a common workspace. The Pennsylvania State Board of Education is in the process of revising the regulations under which schools develop and measure the success of their curricula. The passage of new regulations will require all school districts to reevaluate how their courses are taught and assessed. Teachers who have been trained to use *physhare* will have this resource available to collaborate in the development of new courses for Pennsylvania's students.

(continued)

Case Study 9 (concluded)

Use of a program such as *physhare* cannot succeed without training. PA STEP has provided funding for training of physics teachers at the ITEC Center at Penn State. The physics teachers learned how to use their personal computers to connect to the Penn State mainframe, how to send and receive electronic mail, how to operate *physhare,* and how to transfer information from the mainframe to their own computers. Once the teachers were trained, *physhare* was made available as a forum for the discussion of the issues related to the new curriculum regulations. The system also enabled the discussion of effective teaching strategies, and helped collect and disseminate the results of those discussions. *Physhare* is an experiment in progress.

More information can be obtained by contacting:

David Popp
(jdp115@psuvm.bitnet
or
jdp115@psuvm.psu.edu)
ITEC Center at Penn State
Rider Building II, 2nd Floor
227 West Beaver Avenue
University Park, PA 16801
(814) 863–2427

Talk About It

Topics for discussion based on the case study

1. Discuss the concept of e-mail in the context of its value in an educational setting. As a teacher, how might you use e-mail in a K–12 setting?

2. The various applications of CMC are discussed in the case study. Which of these applications do you see yourself using, and why?

3. Many teachers feel uncomfortable using other teachers' materials: test databases, lesson plans, and so forth. Why? Do you think the case study presents a convincing argument for CMC (using *physhare,* for example) as a way to overcome the problems inherent in sharing materials.

4. The case study makes a strong argument in favor of teachers learning to use Internet so that they can exchange information and share materials. Discuss ways, other than those presented, in which Internet can serve the needs of teachers.

Computer-Assisted Instruction (CAI)

It is the supreme art of the teacher to awaken joy in creative expression and knowledge.

Albert Einstein (1879–1955)

If a student flunks once, he is out; but an inventor is almost always failing—he tries and fails maybe a thousand times. . . . Our biggest job is to teach how to fail intelligently . . . to keep on trying, and failing, and trying.

Charles Franklin Kettering (1876–1958)

Learning Outcomes

The term **computer-assisted instruction (CAI)** describes computer hardware and software that is designed to assist both teacher and student in the learning process. As such, it includes several types of systems that are tailored to different teaching methodologies. In this chapter, we will examine the various types of CAI with a view to broadening our awareness of what is available in the way of computer-based tools for educational applications.

The reader should bear in mind, as pointed out in the introduction, that it is beyond the scope of this book to profile in more than cursory fashion specific CAI applications. We are concerned here with concepts, rather than keystrokes. The ideal accompaniment to the study of the material in this chapter, and in the book as a whole, would be hands-on review of as wide a range as possible of CAI software.

This chapter will also look at the process of software evaluation. Teachers must not only evaluate learning materials before incorporating them into lessons plans; they must evaluate the effectiveness of those materials *while* students are using them as well as after their use in order to determine whether or not they should be used again. This evaluation should be shared with other teachers. Computer technology can help with this task in various ways.

The following topics will therefore be dealt with in this chapter.

- Students and productivity software
  - "Word processing to learn"
  - Database management
  - Spreadsheets
  - Charting and drawing
  - Communications
- Classifications of CAI
  - Software for drill and practice
  - Software for tutorials
  - Software for simulations
  - Microcomputer-based laboratories
  - Programming and problem solving
  - Integrated learning systems
- Software evaluation
  - Criteria for software selection
  - Evaluation checklists
  - The process of evaluation

10.1 Introduction

The French writer and educator Anatole France once wrote: "Let our teaching be full of ideas. Hitherto it has been stuffed only with facts. . . . The whole art of teaching is only the art of awakening the natural curiosity of young minds for the purpose of satisfying it afterwards." Learning *is* more likely to take place if natural curiosity is awakened. As any teacher knows, children can be coerced into the kind of academic achievement that is measured by scores on standardized tests. But knowledge acquired out of inherent interest in the subject matter is much more likely to persist than that acquired purely for the purpose of passing tests. Inherent interest in the subject matter of a discipline also provides a surer foundation for lifelong learning.

10.1.1 Children Want to Learn

A Nation at Risk (The National Commission on Excellence in Education, 1984) recognized "the natural abilities of the young that cry out to be developed and the undiminished concern of parents for the well-being of their children." The report's recommendations "are based on the belief that everyone can learn, that everyone is born with an *urge* to learn which can be nurtured, that solid high school education is within the reach of virtually all, and that life-long learning will equip people with the skills required for new careers and for citizenship."

The teacher's task is therefore to nurture the student's innate "*urge* to learn." In this chapter, we will look at the various ways in which computer assisted instruction (CAI) can be a tool, but by no means the only tool, for accomplishing this objective.

10.2 Students and Productivity Software

Ralph Waldo Emerson observed: "The person who can make the hard things easy is the educator." Before we examine what are generally regarded as categories of CAI, it will be interesting to discuss how the tools of data processing can be used by students to further their educational endeavors.

As already noted in chapter 9, teachers as well as students can be more productive by using productivity software for word processing, database management, spreadsheets, graphics, and communications. The term *productivity* is used because these tasks, which are the workhorses of any organization, are made less onerous when the computer is used to assist in them, thus enabling teachers to get more done in less time. There is no reason why they should not also be the workhorses for the students in a computerized classroom.

10.2.1 Productivity Software Is a Platform for CAI

Productivity software provides study tools for all aspects of learning. Chapter 1 showed how learning in the language arts, math, science, and social studies can be enhanced by the incorporating of computers into the curriculum. For the most part, what the computer does is free up the student to concentrate on the important aspects of an area of study. In writing, as in fine arts, the area of study is the generation and written expression of creative ideas; in math, it is the acquisition of the foundations for logical thought; in science, it is the investigation and analysis of the physical or material world; in social studies, it is the kaleidoscope of culture. As Smith (1957) put it: "Without a culture there could be no society, and without a society there could be no culture."

In all areas of study, students need to be able to access the database of human experience that has contributed to a field of knowledge. The easier and more enjoyable

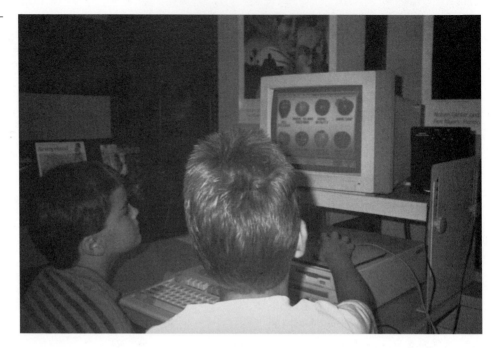

Figure 10.1
Students running *Picture Explorer*™ on Compton's on-line *Encyclopedia*
Photo Courtesy Susan Giorgio Bond

this access, the more likely that students will discover the learning for themselves. The computer can contribute to this process through the availability of productivity tools such as on-line encyclopedias and general-purpose databases.

The computer has become one of the most important tools of research, regardless of the academic discipline or level. Students use databases and spreadsheets to capture, manipulate, and organize data. They use word processors to write about the data. They use graphics tools to design presentation materials to accompany their written and/or spoken descriptions of what they have learned.

This process of capturing, manipulating, organizing, and presenting is a profound learning experience, especially when facilitated by a teacher who knows how to stimulate inquiry, who understands when to leave students alone to discover knowledge by themselves, and who is ready to step in with ideas and guidance of an enriching nature that will redirect and reinvigorate flagging research.

For example, children often need help with oral and written presentations. Teachers have training and experience to help students develop their communication skills so that the lack of those skills does not become a barrier to academic advancement or a pall on motivation. Equally often, children may need help with regard to the direction they should take in their search for some aspect of knowledge related to a subject of interest. A good teacher will draw on a wide range of ideas and experience to *e-ducere*[1]—to lead the students out of their apparent intellectual impasse by pointing them down fruitful paths of inquiry.

---

[1] The word *educate* has a Latin root, "e-ducere," which means "to lead out or forward."

As another example, a student might be working on a paper and might want to include in a database or spreadsheet some data that have been collected. He or she might also want to add some graphic material, perhaps generated from data in a spreadsheet, or created freehand with drawing tools, or even scanned from original artwork.

Until the introduction of modern, multitasking operating systems, integrated software was the only easy way to do this kind of work, especially when using microcomputers.

Without integrated software, cutting and pasting between applications might have meant opening up a temporary file to store the set of data to be pasted to another document. The format of the data had to be prespecified, and once pasted to the destination document, the same data would have had to be reformatted. If one knew what one was doing, it was still much quicker than rekeying all the data, but it was sufficiently tricky to discourage the majority of computer users from trying.

Today, however, computers that use a common interface for all software have greatly simplified this, and most other, tasks. This is true of computers such as the Commodore Amiga series from Commodore International, the IBM PS/2 series running the *OS/2* operating system, IBM compatible computers running software for Microsoft *Windows* and *Windows NT,* and the Apple Macintosh computers.

It is beyond our scope here to dwell more than superficially on the various functions of integrated software. Readers should note, however, the set of tutorials for Microsoft *Works™* which optionally accompanies this text (Poole, 1994). The tutorials introduce the user to the essential features of the software using examples that are appropriate for the classroom.

A valuable exercise for preservice and in-service teachers would be to get together and discuss the ways in which productivity software could be used to further learning. This is recommended as an exercise in the Do Something About It section at the end of the chapter.

The next five sections will examine the features of each of the components of productivity software. Many schools have invested in integrated software packages such as Claris Corporation's *AppleWorks™* or *ClarisWorks™*, and Microsoft *Works,* which enable the user to easily work concurrently with several productivity applications.

10.2.2 Word Processing

The word processor is the software that accompanies almost any computer system today and it can be the most effective example of CAI. In an information age, an individual's ability to communicate effectively both orally and in writing is a key ingredient of success, even of economic survival. An important goal of education, therefore, is to help students develop good communication skills. Teachers are role models, whether they like it or not. Students look to them for example and direction. Teachers owe it to themselves and to their students to improve their own speech and writing skills. Those who regard themselves as teachers in the best sense of the word cannot shirk this responsibility.

A good place to start might be to take more advantage of the word processor as the most fundamental of all computer applications. Chapter 1 made the case that the word processor as a tool for learning will inevitably revolutionize the teaching of writing in elementary and secondary schools where computers are made available to all students. Modern word-processing systems are not difficult to learn and use, and children quickly

Figure 10.2
ClarisWorks word-
processor document
window

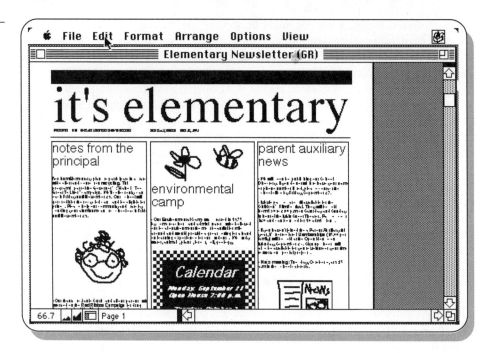

get beyond the technical barrier represented by the interface presented by the software. This is true whether interaction with the system be via a keyboard and mouse along with a graphical user interface (GUI)—such as is the case for most software developed today—or via a less friendly and increasingly anachronistic, command-based interface such as Apple's *DOS* or Microsoft's *MS-DOS* for the IBM PC and clones. Figure 10.2 illustrates a typical word-processor document, with some graphics included to demonstrate the versatility of the modern word processor.

Children prefer writing at a computer because of the ease of text modification and because of the improved appearance of the final product. The net result of this is that the children are motivated to write more, and this alone leads to improved writing skills, especially when they are working with teachers who provide that "prepared environment" where spontaneous intellectual growth can flourish. Not only are children more likely to become better writers when they use a word processor; they are also more likely to blossom in all areas of academic life.

Myers (1984) makes a powerful case for Writing to Learn across the Curriculum. "Writing to learn," he writes, "is based on a growing body of research into the writing process that suggests that writing can be a powerful strategy for learning content. The student who participates in a writing to learn program is likely to learn more content, understand it better, and retain it longer. As a bonus, writing skills are also likely to improve through use." Myers goes on to say: "Writing should be an integral part of any instructional program. It is unfortunate that, outside the English classroom, most teachers provide only limited writing opportunities for their students, usually in the form of note-taking or an occasional essay question on an exam. Writing can do much more. Properly used, *it can become the single most powerful tool a teacher can employ.*" (Emphasis added)

Figure 10.3
Class newspapers
and ditto masters
Photo courtesy Susan
Giorgio Bond

There are already teachers who, along with other applications of computers across the curriculum, also expect their students to use the word processor for writing, no matter what the academic discipline involved. They routinely work with students to revise word-processed writing assignments until they are of an acceptably high standard. Such revision is naturally difficult to realize when assignments are handwritten; by contrast, such revision is difficult to *avoid* when assignments are word processed.

"Ideally," as Myers recommends, "writing to learn in the content areas is complemented by an effective learning to write program in the English classroom. The result of the two is synergistic—the sum of the two parts working together is greater than either working alone. Writing to learn and learning to write are two sides of the same coin. . . . They are both important."

If we use computers for no other purpose than to actively promote writing across the curriculum, we will have already taken a huge step toward improving the overall quality of the educational experience. If we also put those word processing systems on local and wide area computer networks, as discussed in the next chapter, we can foster collaborative writing in, and between, more and more schools.

An excellent ongoing assignment for students is managing the production of a class magazine. Such a whole-language exercise serves as a focus for all the learning activities in which the children are engaged. It also provides an opportunity to reinforce and develop a wide range of intellectual and social skills. Many teachers have been so convinced of the value of this kind of assignment that they have organized it even without the help of a computer, which has usually meant an enormous amount of extra work for the teacher because of the coordination involved at the end of the process, to bring everything together.

Figure 10.4
ClarisWorks database
data-entry form
window

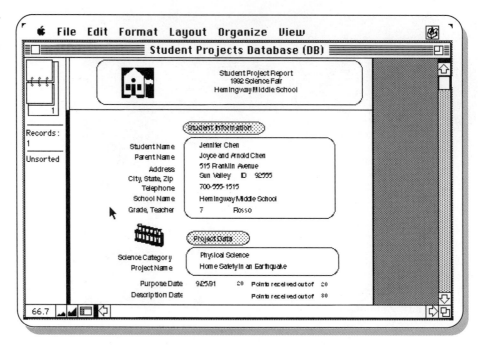

Today's desktop computers are powerful enough to handle multipage files of mixed text and graphics, and are easy for students to use. There is no reason why they (the students) should not do most, if not all, of the work. Indeed, the last thing a teacher wants to do is to get in the way while the students are learning so much from the experience—and having so much fun!

10.2.3 Database Management

A database package is designed to help the user create files containing perhaps thousands of records, capture the data, store it on disk, rearrange it, sort it on specific fields, select subsets of records and of fields within records, and produce reports. The package is able to handle any character-based data, whether text or numbers. Figure 10.4 illustrates a typical database data-entry form.

Although modern databases are designed to carry out mathematical operations on numbers, for the most part, the database is best at handling everything as plain text. The spreadsheet is a more appropriate tool for the mathematical manipulation of numeric data. The database component of integrated software is relatively easy to use once the user has mastered the concept of database management. This means practice.

One of the best services teachers can provide to students is to teach them—or, even better, let them teach each other—how to use a database. Give them year-long team projects in which they research a subject, design a database to capture the data, assemble the data, produce reports using the database package and the word processor, and make a presentation based on their findings. Children of all ages can do this, probably even in first

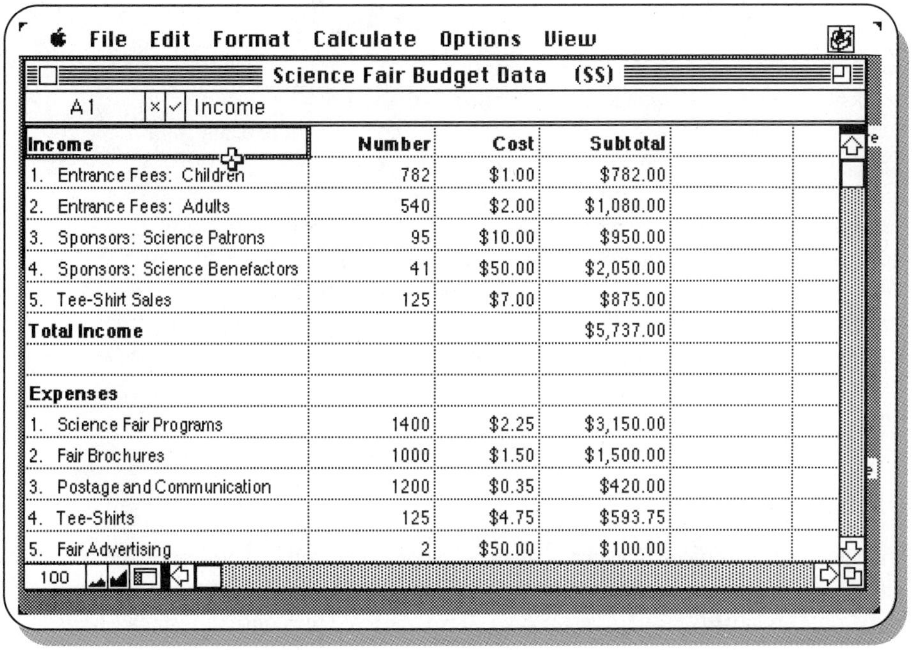

Income	Number	Cost	Subtotal
1. Entrance Fees: Children	782	$1.00	$782.00
2. Entrance Fees: Adults	540	$2.00	$1,080.00
3. Sponsors: Science Patrons	95	$10.00	$950.00
4. Sponsors: Science Benefactors	41	$50.00	$2,050.00
5. Tee-Shirt Sales	125	$7.00	$875.00
Total Income			$5,737.00
Expenses			
1. Science Fair Programs	1400	$2.25	$3,150.00
2. Fair Brochures	1000	$1.50	$1,500.00
3. Postage and Communication	1200	$0.35	$420.00
4. Tee-Shirts	125	$4.75	$593.75
5. Fair Advertising	2	$50.00	$100.00

Figure 10.5 *ClarisWorks* spreadsheet

grade. At the kindergarten level, the teacher will probably have to do most of the data entry; but, as kindergarten teachers and the developers of the IBM *Writing To Read* program know, you would be surprised what children in kindergarten can do.

10.2.4 Spreadsheets

A spreadsheet, like a database, is a powerful tool for gathering data, manipulating it, and presenting it in various ways. The difference is that a spreadsheet is designed primarily to handle numeric data, whereas a database is best for handling plain text. A spreadsheet file consists of a grid of rows and columns. At the intersections of rows and columns are cells into which the data is entered.

The strengths of spreadsheets are their functions and their graphing capability. Functions are mathematical formulas (such as *Sum all the values in such and such a column*) that direct the spreadsheet in some otherwise time-consuming and error-prone mathematical calculations. Many of these functions are built in, such as the *sum* function or the *average* function. But users can also create their own functions, if they like. Table 10.1 lists some of the more commonly used built-in functions of a spreadsheet.

Most spreadsheets today have useful graphing functions. This means that the user can specify a set of values in the spreadsheet—say, all the values in a column—and press a few keys to tell the spreadsheet to draw a pie chart, bar chart, line chart, or a

Table 10.1	Commonly Used Spreadsheet Functions
Function	**Effect**
Random ( )	Produces random number between 0 and 1
Round ( )	Rounds the specified number to specified number of digits
Sqrt ( )	Produces the square root of the specified number
Average ( )	Averages the specified set of numbers
Count ( )	Produces how many values there are in a set of values
Max ( )	Finds the largest value in the specified set of values
Min ( )	Finds the smallest value in the specified set of values
Stndev ( )	Calculates the standard deviation for the specified set of values
Sum ( )	Adds up the values in the specified set of values
Date ( )	Produces today's date
Time ( )	Produces the current time

combination of chart types. The chart can then be combined with a word-processed document, a set of data from the database, and so forth. As with the word processor and the database, a spreadsheet is relatively easy to use once you have mastered the concept of spreadsheets.

When you have learned to use a spreadsheet, you can teach it to your students. The electronic spreadsheet was, in fact, originally designed for accounting applications,[2] so it is a natural tool for business students. But there are many uses for spreadsheets as vehicles for learning concepts related to math, statistics, and problem solving in general. Students of all ages who are involved in projects that are number intensive—counts of entities that are the subject of research, for example—can use the spreadsheet as a useful tool for analyzing the data and producing graphs and charts.

10.2.5 Charting and Drawing

Many excellent drawing packages are available for today's powerful microcomputers. Applications such as Scholastic's *SuperPrint*™, Computer Associates' *Cricket Draw*™, Deneba Software's *Canvas*™, Aldus *Freehand*™, and Corel Systems Corporation's *CORELDRAW*™, can make students who do not think they are artistic feel like birds released from a cage. Students who *are* artistic may feel inhibited, initially at least, by the constraints imposed by software, which obviously limits freedom of artistic expression. But these same artistic students will, because of their special talents, make the software sing. All students will come to appreciate drawing software as a timesaving tool.

Other software drawing tools, such as Claris Corporation's *MacDraw II*™ and *MacDraw Pro*™, offer simpler drawing and charting features.[3] Brøderbund's *Kid Pix*™ program is beautifully designed to allow the youngest children to create artwork in an enjoyable, on-screen environment.

---

[2]By Dan Bricklin and Robert Franston in 1978 while they were graduate students at the Harvard School of Business.

[3]These programs have now been discontinued and replaced with the more powerful *ClarisDraw,* which can run on both Apple Mac and Microsoft *Windows*-based PCs.

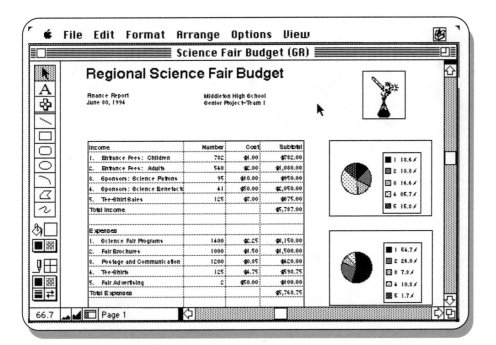

Figure 10.6
Charts are produced easily from spreadsheet data.

Another product from Brøderbund, *The New Print Shop*™, has been a staple graphics program for many years. In fact, it was one of the first graphics utility programs available on microcomputers. It is useful for creating attractive, personalized greetings cards, notices, banners, letterheads, calendars, and so forth. The software will even create posters as big as a garage door—just what every school needs.

Drawing software typically provides freehand drawing tools as well as charting and presentation graphics tools. It also includes a more or less extensive selection of clip art. With the advent of GUIs many of the tools—palettes of shape icons, using the mouse to create and manipulate figures on the screen, selecting colors and shades, sizing shapes, and so on—are much the same for all the different programs, thus making the software much easier to learn and use.

Hinze (1989) and Tufte (1990) remind us of the power of graphics to convey meaning. In combination with the database and spreadsheet, large sets of data can be reduced to graphs of various kinds. These graphs can then be incorporated into word-processed reports, along with other computer-generated illustrations.

Most integrated software packages today have a drawing component that includes tools for easy manipulation of shapes, shades, colors, and text.

Figure 10.7
Brøderbund's *Kid Pix*
Photo courtesy
Brøderbund

Figure 10.8
Brøderbund's *The New Print Shop*
Photo Courtesy
Brøderbund

10.2.6 Communications

A computer, a telephone, and a modem[4] are all that are necessary to connect a student with the rest of the world. Strictly speaking, a telephone can be a useful tool for teaching since it puts students in touch with students elsewhere and also acts as a vital link between the school and the home. But it has several disadvantages that remove it from consideration as a teaching tool *in its own right* (apart from cost per call, a problem shared no matter what communications technology is used).

First, telephones invite telephone tag; there is no guarantee that the party to be communicated with is available at the end of the line. Second, the telephone has no respect for time zones; a student's telefriend in Vladivostok would not appreciate being roused for a cross-cultural chat at two o'clock in the morning. But when a modem is used to connect a computer to the telephone system, interesting educational opportunities open up.

In this regard, the world of K–12 education is slowly catching up with its big brother at the college level, and with the rest of the computerized world. In a growing number of K–12 schools, students are afforded the opportunity for cross-cultural interaction over telephone networks with students in other communities at home and abroad. Learning in these schools is taking on a reach that extends beyond the school into the local and global community. Computers and communications (C&C) technology is thus extending a student's educational experience. It can bring the home into the school and the school into the home, making possible a synergy that has been shown to have a significant impact on the quality of the educational process (Bauch, 1990).

In the next chapter, we will look more closely at the contribution that C&C can make to our students' educational experience. The software that manages the complex processing involved, and mercifully hides that complexity from the user, is usually included as one of the components of integrated software. Many stand-alone, communications software products range in price from fifty to several thousand dollars. But workable software can also be acquired free of charge since there are public domain products such as *Kermit* which can handle all the basic communications functions.

10.3 Classifications of CAI

Basically, the computer can be used to foster learning in six ways, each of which is appropriate under different instructional circumstances and therefore takes a different pedagogical approach. The following sections clarify the unique characteristics that have made them popular examples of CAI.

10.3.1 Software for Drill and Practice

Drill and practice, which is a learning methodology used to reinforce familiar knowledge, is a type of CAI that, in recent years, has received a certain amount of bad press. The criticism in some cases stems more from disparagement of drill and practice as a CAI genre than from dissatisfaction with the methodology. It is less exotic than other forms of CAI, such as simulation, for example. Other criticism comes from a belief that

---

[4]A modem is a device for connecting a computer to the telephone system.

the methodology itself is flawed and basically ineffective in terms of higher-level learning. As Bigge (1982) points out, ever since Edward L. Thorndike in the early 1900s debunked mental discipline as a working hypothesis for learning, there has been a rejection of the idea that the mind can be exercised with a view to strengthening its intellectual capabilities. Drill and practice, Thorndike would say, is not the way to nurture ideas.

Some mental abilities involve skills (remembering a list of items, manipulating numbers mathematically) rather than concepts, and in these cases drill and practice ("mental gymnastics") is clearly an appropriate learning methodology. It can also be argued that drill and practice is, indirectly, as fundamental to the learning of intellectual concepts as it is to the acquisition of mental and physical skills.

For example, mathematicians have no choice but to be thoroughly familiar with the fundamentals of their discipline—all the way from the two-times table to the rules of calculus and beyond. These fundamentals must become second nature before mathematicians can venture into the realms of more-creative problem solving. What is more, they have to stay versed in math—applying the basic skills on the way to completing calculations or proving theories—in order to maintain their edge of excellence. "Use it or lose it," as they say. This is true of many disciplines, in the arts as well as the sciences. As long as one remains versed in a discipline, the need for rote learning recedes. But becoming versed can benefit significantly from the kind of rote learning provided by drill and practice.

In this sense, intellectual skills may differ from physical skills.[5] With regard to physical skills, one must use drill and practice (that is, constantly refresh basic skills) even when one has become an expert, as any golfer, carpenter, or music instrumentalist knows. The brilliance shown by a skilled sports player, craftsperson, dancer, or instrumentalist is founded on constantly honed basic skills.

Reinforcing basic skills

So, drill and practice is an important learning technique for building basic knowledge and for honing the myriad, basic intellectual skills (such as number manipulation, vocabulary, spelling, sentence construction, following the steps in problem solving, and so on) that are the foundation for higher-level intellectual activity. This is not to say that the computer is always the best vehicle for mental drill-and-practice activity. It depends on the discipline, the circumstances, and the individual student.

Computers do lend themselves to fruitful drill and practice activity. Research appears to bear this out. Roblyer (1988), in his review of the research from 1980 to 1987, found that using drill and practice programs to reinforce basic skills was one of the "areas to emphasize" when computers are involved in the learning process. Good drill-and-practice software provides the user with an enjoyable opportunity for repetitive interaction and immediate feedback on the accuracy of responses. It will monitor those responses, moving the user forward if the lesson appears to be well learned, and backward if responses indicate that the user is over his or her head.

---

[5]One could probably argue that even intellectual skills benefit from frequent rehearsal of basic skills and refreshment of basic knowledge.

Figure 10.9
MECC's *Super Munchers*™
Photo courtesy of MECC

MECC uses a game format for its *Muncher* series of drill and practice programs. This game format masks the real learning that goes on when children match their math, language, and general knowledge skills at a variety of difficulty levels against Muncher-menacing Troggles.

10.3.2 Software for Tutorials

Drill and practice software is designed to reinforce known skills, whereas tutorial software is designed to introduce the learner to new skills. Samson et al. (1986), in their review of 43 research studies, concluded among other things that "the effect of drill and practice using computers on student achievement is relatively small when compared to the effect of computer-based tutoring."

Tutorials take many forms. Students may sit with tutors (persons) who will help them learn a body of knowledge. Or, students may work with a book that steps them through the exercise of acquiring a body of knowledge. We are interested here in computerized tutorials where a conceptual or skill-based body of knowledge is presented to the user on screen, followed by opportunities to validate the user's comprehension of the concept or acquisition of the skill. The software monitors progress on the basis of the results of validation, taking the user on to new material or back over old material in the same way as a sensitive human tutor would.

Figure 10.10
Intellimation's
Exploring Languages,
Word for Word School
Series
Picture courtesy Kathryn
Downing, Touchstone
Computer Learning Center

A good tutorial presents the goal up front; is enjoyable, thorough, and sensitive to the user's capabilities; and provides immediate and appropriate feedback. Interactivity is key to user involvement and perseverance. An excellent example of tutorial software is Intellimation's *Exploring Languages*™ series, which tutors English-speaking students in the learning of Spanish, French, or German. Students use the "discovery mode" to learn meanings and pronunciation interactively by clicking on objects in scenes that depict everyday life. The computer sounds out words and phrases in both English and the target language. The system also includes drill and practice components—a necessary adjunct of language learning. (See figure 10.10.)

In the classroom environment, a teacher will incorporate software such as *Exploring Languages* into a curriculum that includes many other language-learning activities—conversation, drama, reading, writing, recitation, dictation, and so forth. The computer-based tutorials form a piece of the puzzle that is the learning process.

10.3.3 Software for Simulations

Simulations are powerful tools for learning. They involve the learner in a vicarious experience of events or processes, a kind of "trial run on reality" (Bruner et al., 1966). As such, they marry nicely into a constructivist philosophy of teaching in that students experience life vicariously through the simulation, constructing knowledge about the world from that experience. Such simulations may be designed specifically for educational

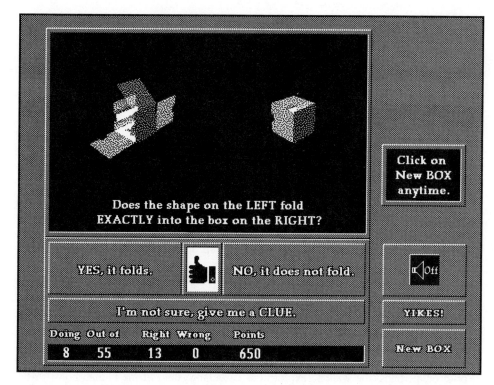

Figure 10.11
Intellimation's *Folding Boxes*™ spatial-reasoning simulation software
Photo courtesy Nelson Greene. Published by Intellimation, 130 Cremona Dr., Santa Barbara, CA 93117, 1–800–346–8355

Within the figure:

Does the shape on the LEFT fold EXACTLY into the box on the RIGHT?

Click on New BOX anytime.

YES, it folds.   NO, it does not fold.

I'm not sure, give me a CLUE.   YIKES!

Doing	Out of	Right	Wrong	Points
8	55	13	0	650

New BOX

purposes, such as the *Oregon Trail* system published by MECC, or they may be only indirectly educational, such as the Maxis *Sim* series—*SimCity, SimEarth,* and *SimAnt*—and the growing number of virtual reality systems being developed today.

Simulation takes many forms. When we capture in writing an imaginary or real experience, we use symbols (words) to create a verbal simulation of the experience. A literature teacher might bring to life a scene from a play by having a class of students act it out. Another example occurs every four years in the United States, when students simulate the presidential election in order to develop a sense of civic responsibility.

Another interesting computer-based simulation has been designed into the manufacture of an automobile that, when driven, simulates the effects of being driven by a drunk driver (in controlled circumstances, of course!). Simulations such as these can be accompanied by rich learning experiences.

Simulations, computerized or not, are excellent learning tools when they put students into an interactive discovery mode; they are most effective when a realistic range of feedback accompanies the interaction. The CAI simulations that are commonly available suffer from the weakness of being somewhat removed from reality by the limitations of a relatively unsophisticated computing environment. But students, nonetheless, have little difficulty suspending disbelief and often become engrossed with software that steps them through a science experiment, or a historical sequence of events, and, along the way, prompts them for feedback to monitor understanding and point the way to deeper learning.

Multimedia systems, using interactive videodisc to access high-quality video and still images and sound recordings, make it possible for students and teachers to create their own simulations. We will discuss these systems in chapter 12.

Virtual reality

As mentioned above, another technology called **virtual reality** promises to bring simulation into real time. The user in a virtual reality simulation usually dons headgear that enables a set of monitor screens to be suspended in front of the eyes. Computer-generated images of some predetermined simulation (such as a voyage to the bottom of the ocean) are displayed on the screens, and a tiny camera inside the hood of the headgear tracks the user's eyes as they look around the scene as it unfolds. The computer pans across the scene in response to the user's eye movements, thus creating the illusion that the user is immersed in the scene as if really there—"virtually" there. To add to the illusion, the user wears a pair of gloves that are wired to the system. This allows the user to reach out into the simulation displayed inside the headset, pick up objects to examine them, or otherwise interact with the scene.

There is no doubt that educational computing has barely scratched the surface of potential applications for rich learning experience of a simulated nature. But virtual reality systems are expensive, and, for the time being, they will not be seen in many, if any, schools. Once the technology—hardware and software—has been refined and adapted for educational applications, it should attract considerable interest. Imagine, if you will, becoming a sailor in the crew of the Santa Maria accompanying Columbus to the New World; or, perhaps you want to explore the vascular system of the human body by becoming a cell in the bloodstream. Virtual reality systems enable you to be immersed in the simulated scene.

10.3.4 Microcomputer-Based Laboratories

Probes, sensors, and similar data-capture devices have long been essential components of instruments used in scientific experimentation. Their purpose has been to augment our highly sophisticated, inbuilt instruments represented by the five human senses. The scientific method, whereby "a problem is identified, relevant data are gathered, a hypothesis is formulated, and the hypothesis is empirically tested" (Webster's, 1991), is applied differently depending on the discipline, but, at its core, it is concerned with the measurement of phenomena and experimentation or repeated observation.[6]

Science naturally depends a great deal on instrumentation, as much for purposes of precise measurement as for recording the results of experiments and repeated observation. Natural phenomena, too, are often recorded as measures on some kind of scale (such as a voltmeter for measuring flow of electricity) or as marks or traces on paper or some other suitable medium, such as gels (as in the chemical analysis involved in chromatography). The measures, marks, or traces are then painstakingly analyzed and the results of the analysis recorded, often in numeric form. These numbers might then be graphed for

---

[6]*Encyclopaedia Britannica*, 1974.

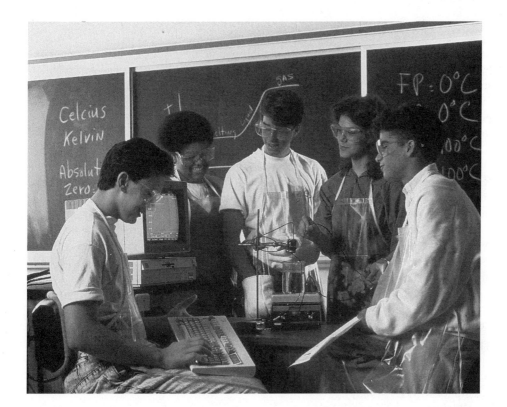

Figure 10.12
Students at work in
an MBL
Photo courtesy IBM
Corporation

purposes of scientific visualization. The whole process can take days, weeks, even years of effort before hypotheses about the natural world can be demonstrated to be true or false based on the experimentation.

Scientists quickly recognized the value of the **computer-based laboratory (MBL)** to research and, as touched on in chapter 2, have developed hardware and software systems that have enabled them to automate the process of gathering data from experiments, conducting relevant analysis, and producing meaningful reports.

Schools K–12 are using computers to involve even the youngest students in projects that require the capture and analysis of considerable volumes of data. Scientific experiments are linked to microcomputers in laboratories to automate the process of recording the results of experiments. As a result, far more experimental data can be generated. Before microcomputer-based labs were introduced, canned experimentation in schools produced a small sampling of data that could be used only as corroboration of results already known. But the most valuable aspect of MBLs is the real time-graphing of data as they are captured in an experiment. Complete data sets can be stored in secondary memory for further analysis. Summary data are produced as text and in a graphed format.

The case study at the end of the chapter will be of special interest since it focuses on MBL applications in the K–12 classroom.

10.3.5 Programming and Problem Solving

Several interesting discussions have been published on the issue of whether or not computer programming (in Logo, BASIC, or Pascal, for example) helps develop problem-solving skills (Papert, 1980; Turkle, 1984; OTA, 1988; Capper, 1988; Apple Computer, 1990; Kearsley, 1992—to mention a few). The consensus is that the practice of computer programming does not necessarily help when it comes either to learning mathematics or to teaching mathematics to others.

Turkle (1984), in the context of child programmers, asks the question: "Do computers change the way children think?" Turkle's answer is another question: "What do different kinds of children make of the computer?" The implication, of course, is that the computer can tell us more about the nature of children (through their mode of interaction) than in itself affect that nature.[7]

Computer literacy in general is very important from the perspective of employability, but programming per se will be useful to only about 2% of the workforce (OTA, 1988), especially in the future, when computer applications will be developed using very-high-level systems, which will require planning skills beyond what are traditionally considered computer programming skills.

Logo

There appears to be support for the Logo programming language as a medium for developing nonverbal cognitive skills such as creativity, independent learning, "the ability to monitor and evaluate one's own thinking processes," and the "ability to provide accurate descriptions" (OTA, 1988).

You may recall from chapter 1 that Logo, developed by Seymour Papert, was a by-product of his association with Jean Piaget, the famous Swiss psychologist, with whom he studied. Logo's graphics-based interface, which uses a simulated "turtle" as a vehicle for programmed instructions, is both motivational and enjoyable for children (Kearsley, 1992). This facilitates early introduction to relatively advanced programming concepts such as recursion (procedures or functions that call themselves), and indirectly motivates the student to think independently along conceptual lines that lead to the acquisition of geometric and other problem-solving skills (Turkle, 1984). Figure 10.13 illustrates Logo's "turtle"-based programming interface.

Once again, it is beyond our scope here to examine Logo more closely. But there are many excellent Logo tutorials should the reader wish to pursue this topic further.

10.3.6 Integrated Learning Systems

The truly integrated learning system would be "a system for learning [which] would make available a variety of appropriate activities, well-integrated and well-suited to a learner's interests and capabilities" (Komoski, 1990). About the only integrated learning system that fits this description is a good school. Such a system is too complex to be captured in toto and delivered within the constraints of a computer-based system. In practice,

---

[7]This brings to mind the common reflection of sports coaches who say that the best place to learn about children's personalities is on the playing field.

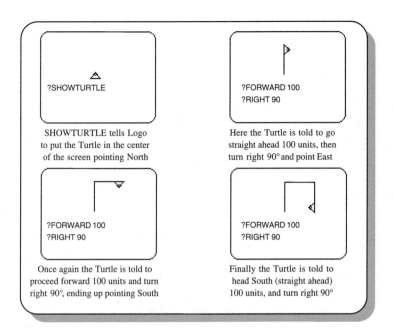

Figure 10.13
Logo programming
interface (annotated)

therefore, an **integrated learning systems (ILS)** is a comprehensive, networked instructional system composed of software that is integrated with any textbook a school requests, along with standardized and nonstandardized student-assessment vehicles with built-in individual and group student-progress reporting functions.

As Sherry (1992) notes, a good ILS includes courseware for a broad range of learning experiences, including simulations and on-line vehicles for research, such as productivity software and reference tools. The ILS is more comprehensively integrated as far as teaching objectives, textbooks, and courseware are concerned, and is often customized around a school's existing, traditional nonelectronic learning systems in terms of curriculum and assessment methods.

A growing number of companies offer ILS software for this burgeoning market, of which Computer Curriculum Corporation (CCC) is the oldest, according to Sherry (1992). Here, however, we will profile the products of two other companies: Jostens Learning Corporation, the largest ILS vendor, and Apple Computer, Inc., a relative newcomer to ILSs.

Jostens Learning First™

Among the most comprehensive integrated learning systems are those offered by Jostens Learning Corporation. The company, which stands by the philosophy that "every student has the ability to learn" (Jostens, 1993), has designed ILSs for every age group from K through 12. Indeed, Jostens offers ILSs for preschoolers and adults as well. Their individual systems, such as *InterActiveMedia*™ and *Learning First*™, are more complete than most others in regard to hardware, software, and support materials supplied.

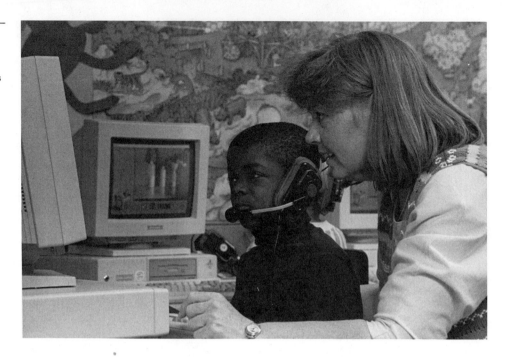

In terms of computer hardware, Jostens systems run on the more recent Apple and IBM platforms. In addition, the company, which entered the computer hardware market itself in 1992 in partnership with Dell Computer Corporation, supplies its own machines. On the software front, like Apple with its *Early Language Connections*™, Jostens has entered into partnerships with many of the most well-established developers of quality software and multimedia systems for education. Included are companies such as Optical Data Corporation, Davidson and Associates, The Learning Company, Encyclopaedia Brittanica, and World Book Encyclopaedia, to name but a few. Finally, Jostens systems include customizable software (courseware) along with computer-based tools for student evaluation and for management of the instructional process—test creation, productivity tools, and the like.

Jostens *Learning First,* for example, comprises modules for the early learner (for children from preschool age to grade 3), the elementary learner (for grades K through 6), the middle school learner (for grades 6 through 9), the secondary learner (grades 9 through 12), and for the bilingual learner of all ages. Echoing the words of the well-known educationist Ted Sizer (in Goldberg, 1993), Jostens recognizes that no two schools are the same. The company goes to great lengths to customize the ILS to suit the local environment, working closely with the administration, teachers, and parents in the difficult process of integrating the ILS with existing curricula.

Apple Early Language Connections

Another interesting ILS for the early years of schooling is *Apple Early Language Connections,* developed by Apple Computer, Inc. Simpler than the Jostens *Learning First*

Figure 10.15
Components of the *Apple Early Language Connections* learning system
Photo courtesy Apple Computer, Inc.

system, the *Apple Early Language Connections* program is designed for single-classroom implementation and supports a literature-based approach to teaching language arts in grades K–2. The system is based on a balanced curriculum that supports the development of the four basic communication skills: reading, writing, listening, and speaking. Books are included with the package (over 350 by well-known children's authors, including some on CD-ROM, such as *The Mud Puddle* by Robert Munsch), along with audiotapes, detailed lesson plans, and the computers themselves (Macintosh LCs and other hardware such as scanners and touch screens). The computers come already loaded with the set of software programs that the children need. When the children use CD-ROM to read the *Discis Books* from Discis Knowledge Research, Inc., they can call up voices, music, and sound effects to enhance their understanding.

Apple Early Language Connections includes seven 4-week thematic units—two for each grade K–2, with an additional 4-week unit for kindergarten. The lesson plans include activities for literature, music, math, art, and science. The CAI software packaged with the system may be run in either Spanish mode or English mode,[8] and includes the following titles:

- *Kid Works 2*™ from Davidson & Associates, Inc.
- *Scholastic Superprint*™ from Scholastic, Inc.
- *Reading Magic Library*™: *Jack and the Beanstalk*™, from Tom Snyder Productions.
- *Muppets on Stage*™ from WINGS for Learning, Inc.

---

[8]The entire interface—menus, directions, spoken and written interactions—switches to the selected language.

- *ReadingMaze*™ from Great Wave Software.
- *Word Munchers* from MECC.

Apple Early Language Connections also includes some management tools for the teacher, as well as on-site training. The individual components of the system, such as the books and the software listed above, have already been well received in the classroom environment. What is impressive about the system is the way these separate components have been integrated to form the backbone of an entire K–2 curriculum.

As Mageau (1992) points out, however, ILSs such as those described are very difficult to implement in the school. First, teachers must be trained to use computers. Next, they must be trained to use computers for instructional purposes, and only then are they ready to be trained *again* in the use of an ILS. Although most teachers, given the opportunity, will take advantage of an ILS by incorporating aspects of the system into the curriculum, only those with considerable computer background will take full advantage. It is not surprising that Dr. Henry Becker, who has conducted considerable research in ILS, observed that the most effective users of ILSs were teachers who "knew the most about the system, knew the most about what the kids were doing in the lab, and went back to the classroom and made decisions about what to do based on that information" (Mageau, 1990).

As with so much computer-based teaching and learning, these integrated learning systems have much to offer, but there is still a way to go before they can be incorporated seamlessly into the K–12 curriculum. However, more than any other development in the use of technology in schools, ILSs may well be the catalyst that brings on fundamental change in the structure of education, the kind of change (reduced teacher–pupil ratios, increased allocation of time for teachers to work with the technology, distance learning, closer parental involvement in education, and so forth) that has been discussed in this book.

■■ 10.4 Software Evaluation

It is important that teachers be able to evaluate the effectiveness of the CAI material that they plan to use in their lessons, even if it has already been evaluated by others. The stamp of approval that someone else puts on an application should encourage teachers to carry out their own evaluations, not replace them. Often, the best such evaluation will have been done by a colleague or by a fellow teacher from another school who has used the system in a real learning situation and recommended it. Teachers may read reviews of a learning system in a journal; but as pointed out in OTA (1988), journal reviews tend to be positive, if only because they rely on advertising revenue for their survival. Teachers may read sales literature written by the publisher of the system: but this also has the problem of subjectivity. Thus, no matter what the source of an evaluation, it cannot compare to the evaluation that teachers conduct themselves.

Teachers know their students, their backgrounds, their capabilities, their learning needs; thus, teachers can best decide what methodologies will work with students. Teachers must take upon themselves the responsibility to evaluate the CAI they decide to use. Having done so and, in the process, tried out the systems with students, teachers have a responsibility to share their experiences with others—immediate colleagues or, in the broader forum, with colleagues in classrooms everywhere.

10.4.1 Characteristics of Quality CAI Software

A software evaluation checklist is a prerequisite to the selection of the best from among the rapidly expanding database of available educational software. As with all teaching materials, educational software selection will be affected by the characteristics of the population for which it is intended. For this reason, a software evaluation checklist should be drawn up locally with the help of local teachers and students. In this way, software that is selected will more likely be appropriate to local needs. Software vendors, too, will have a guideline to help them when they are developing new applications or customizing existing software for specific teaching and learning needs.

The U.S. Congress Office of Technology Assessment (OTA) (1988) assembled a comprehensive list of educational software-evaluation criteria from evaluation instruments used by 36 public, private, and governmental software-evaluation agencies. Table 10.2 summarizes the criteria recommended by selected teachers, software publishers, university professors, and private consultants. It will be a valuable exercise for you to work through the entire list, selecting the criteria that you consider most important in the context of your school.

Try not to let the length of the list overwhelm you. If nothing else, it should impress you that so much work goes into producing quality educational software. Every educational environment is different, and in the next section, we will discuss what goes into the design of a useful, tailor-made, software evaluation instrument. The table will also be relevant in chapter 13, where we will discuss the production of educational software.

10.4.2 The Design of Effective Software-Evaluation Instruments

A software evaluation instrument is essentially a data entry form. As such, its design should reflect the known human factors characteristic of effective data-entry instruments. The following set of guidelines will help in the design of an evaluation instrument appropriate to local needs. Some of the recommendations are from Bailey (1989). At the end of the list is an evaluation format that applies these design guidelines (see figure 10.16).

Figure 10.16
Software evaluation
form
This form is slightly
reduced in size for
purposes of publication.
Adapted from one
developed for Trinity Area
School District,
Washington, PA

TRINITY AREA SCHOOL DISTRICT

COURSEWARE EVALUATION FORM

Program Title: _____

_____

Product Number: _____

Cost (if known): $ _____

Publisher: _____

Address: _____

_____

Phone: (_____)_____ – _____

System Requirements:

Computer: _____

Memory (RAM) needed: _____

Type of system:

    Standalone: ____ Networkable: ____

Disk type:

    Magnetic disk: ____ CD-ROM: ____

Disk size (if magnetic):

    5 1/4": ____ 3 1/2": ____

Operating system: _____

Other system data (if any): _____

For administrative use only

Vendor: _____

Address: _____

_____

_____

Phone: (_____)_____ – _____

Recommendation (please check):

Highly recommend purchase   _____

Recommend purchase   _____

Do not recommend purchase   _____

Rating Criteria:

Number of stars from back   _____

Product Application:

This product is applicable to the following planned course(s) (Please specify by course, unit, and objective):

_____

_____

_____

The following signatures are required:

Reviewer(s): _____ Date: _____

Department Chairperson: _____ Date: _____

Principal: _____ Date: _____

>>>Please continue on the back>>>

page 1 of 2

Directions: The items listed below should be present to ensure an effective program. When evaluating courseware, review all **general** guidelines first, then review **specific category** guidelines. Mark + (the plus sign) for each item present and adequate. Thank you.

General Guidelines

1. Documentation:
   ___ Clear Instructions
   ___ Manual included
   ___ Clear goals and specific objectives
___ 2. Program meets stated goals and objectives
___ 3. Easy to use
___ 4. Visually appealing
___ 5. Can control sound
___ 6. Can enter or exit at any state of program
___ 7. Versatile (able to enter specific data related to curriculum)
___ 8. Accurate information
___ 9. Instructional objectives clearly stated
___ 10. Easily used in existing curriculum

Specific Courseware Categories

Drill and Practice:

___ 1. Personalized (relates to user)
___ 2. Reinforces/rewards user
___ 3. Student-controlled pace
___ 4. Interest maintained
___ 5. Level of difficulty
   ___ Student choice
   ___ Continuum (easy to hard)
___ 6. Cumulative score presented

Tutorial:

___ 1. Introduction of material is complete and understandable
___ 2. Includes Pretest for placement
___ 3. Frequent testing
___ 4. Limited number of retries on error
___ 5. Reteaches when established number of errors accumulate
___ 6. Properly sequenced tasks
___ 7. Program can branch

Simulation:

___ 1. Directions clear
___ 2. Interest maintained
___ 3. Realistic
___ 4. Graphics:
   ___ Present
   ___ Appropriate
___ 5. Level of difficulty:
   ___ Student choice
   ___ Continuum (easy to hard)

Management tools:

___ 1. Help commands on page/screen
___ 2. Flexible entry and retrieval
___ 3. Adequate storage
___ 4. Security measures adequate
___ 5. User prompts given
___ 6. Performance speed
___ 7. Flexible report formatting

Rating Criteria: Count the number of + (plus) signs for both general and specific category guidelines. Mark the box on the front of the form with the number of stars corresponding to the criteria legend as follows:

15 + signs or more:	****
12–14 + signs:	***
9–11 + signs:	**
8 or fewer + signs:	*

Comments:

_____
_____

| Table 10.2 | Characteristics Considered in Evaluating Educational Software |

INSTRUCTIONAL QUALITY

General

- Program is useful in a school-based instructional setting.
- Program avoids potentially controversial, nonstandard teaching methodologies.
- Program allows completion of a lesson in one class period (approximately 30 minutes).
- Instruction is integrated with previous student experience.
- Program will more quickly convey the subject matter for both student and teacher.

Content

- Content is appropriate for intended student population.
- Content is accurate.
- Content is current.
- Content breadth is reasonable, focusing on neither too little nor too much in one session.
- Information and skills learned apply in other domains of knowledge and experience.
- Content is free of grammar, spelling, punctuation, and usage errors.
- Content is free of bias or stereotyping.
- Content supports the school curriculum and is relevant to the subject field.
- Definitions are provided when necessary.
- There is continuity between the information presented and prerequisite skills required.
- Content avoids taking a side on potentially controversial moral or social issues.
- There is a need for better than the standard treatment of this topic in the curriculum.

Appropriateness

- Application is well suited to computer use.
- The pedagogic approach is superior to what is available elsewhere.
- Readability level and tone of address are appropriate for the intended student population.
- The means of response is appropriate to the intended student population.
- Prerequisite skills are appropriate for the intended student population.
- Time required for use by typical student does not exceed student's attention span.
- Multiple levels of instruction are available.
- Sufficient exposure and practice are provided to master skills.
- Sufficient information is presented for intended learning to occur.

Questioning techniques

- Questions are appropriate to the content and effectively measure student mastery.
- Questions incorrectly answered can be repeated later in the lesson/exercise.
- The number of trials is reasonable and appropriate before correct answer is given.
- Calculation can be accomplished easily on-screen when appropriate.

Approach/Motivation

- Approach is appropriate for the intended student population.
- Format is varied, and overall tenor of interaction is helpful.
- Student is an active participant in the learning process.

Table 10.2	*Continued*

Evaluator's field-test results

- Student understands on-screen presentation and can proceed without confusion/frustration.
- Student enjoys using the program.
- Student retains a positive attitude about using the program.
- Student retains the desire to use the program again, or to pursue the topic in other ways.
- Program involves students in competition in a positive way.
- Program fosters cooperation among students.

Creativity

- Program challenges and stimulates creativity.
- Pedagogy is innovative.
- Program allows the student as many decisions as possible.
- Program provides opportunities to answer open-ended questions and provides evaluative criteria to assess responses.
- Program demonstrates a creative way of using knowledge.
- Program challenges the student to alter an underlying model, or design an alternative model.

Learner control

- Learner can alter program sequence and pace and review instructions and previous frames.
- Learner can end activity any time and return to main menu.
- Learner can enter program at different points.
- Learner can stop in the midst of an activity and, at a later session, begin at that stopping point with the previous record of progress intact.
- Help is available at likely points of need.

Learning objectives, goals, and outcomes

- Learner objectives are stated and purpose is well defined.
- Steps are taken to make learning generalizable to other situations.
- For programs requiring use over several days, learning outcomes are worth the time invested.

Feedback

- Feedback is positive.
- Feedback is appropriate to intended student population and does not threaten or inadvertently reward incorrect responses.
- Feedback is relevant to student responses.
- Feedback is timely.
- Feedback is informative.
- Feedback is corrective when appropriate.
- Feedback remediates and/or explains when appropriate.
- Feedback employs a variety of responses to student input, and avoids being boring or unnecessarily detailed.

Table 10.2	*Continued*

- Feedback remains on the screen for an appropriate amount of time.
- Branching is used effectively to remediate.
- Program uses branching to automatically adjust difficulty levels or sequence according to student performance.

Simulations

- Simulation model is valid and neither too complex nor too simple for intended student population.
- Variables used in the simulation are the most relevant.
- Variables in the simulation interact and produce results approximating real life.
- Assumptions are adequately identified.
- Program simulates activities that can be too difficult, dangerous, or expensive to demonstrate in reality.
- Time needed to complete both a step and the entire simulation is reasonable and effective.
- The simulation encourages decision making or calculation rather than guessing.

TEACHER MODIFIABILITY

- Teacher can easily change or add content.
- Teacher can easily regulate parameters (e.g., numbers of problems, rate of presentation, percentage correct needed for mastery) for each class using the program.
- Teacher can easily regulate parameters for each student.
- Parameter setups can be bypassed (e.g., default settings are available).

EVALUATION AND RECORDKEEPING

- Program provides an adequate means of evaluating student mastery of the content.
- If tests are included, criteria for success are appropriate for the ability/skills of the intended student population.
- Scorekeeping and performance reports are provided, where appropriate.
- Useful information about student performance is stored for future retrieval.
- Useful diagnostic pretest or placement test is provided, where appropriate.
- Useful diagnostic or prescriptive analysis of student performance is available to teacher.
- Student performance information is easily accessible to the teacher.
- Management system includes adequate security.
- Program allows printout and screen display of student records.
- Program can hold multiple performance records of a single class (35 to 50 students).
- Program can hold multiple, separate performance records of up to five classes.

DOCUMENTATION AND SUPPORT MATERIALS

- Quality of packaging is durable and appropriate for student use at a computer station.
- Student, parent, or teacher guides and materials are clearly identified as such.
- Technical and operational explanations for implementation are clear and complete.
- If appropriate, "quick start-up" section is included.
- Useful, reproducible student worksheets are provided.
- Other valuable support materials are provided (e.g., wall charts).
- Sample screen-by-screen printouts of the program are provided.

Table 10.2	*Continued*

- Teacher support materials can be separated from student materials.
- Useful suggestions are provided for introductory classroom activities.
- Useful suggestions are provided for classroom activities during use of program.
- Useful suggestions are provided for follow-up activities.
- Useful suggestions are given for classroom logistics in a variety of hardware situations (e.g., single or multiple machines) and student groupings.
- Useful suggestions are provided on how to integrate program with regular curriculum.
- If program is open-ended, subject-specific suggestions are included.
- Clear explanations of the differences between the various difficulty levels are provided.
- Prerequisite skills are clearly stated.
- Accurate and clear description of instructional activities are provided.
- Accurate and clear descriptions of content topics are provided.
- Where appropriate, there is a description of how the material correlates to standard textbook.
- Necessary information can be found quickly and easily (contents, index, etc.).
- Quick reference card for program use is included, where appropriate.
- Printed text is clear and readable.
- Printed graphics are clear and readable.
- Printed text is free of errors in spelling, grammar, punctuation, and usage.

TECHNICAL QUALITY

General

- Audio can be adjusted (up, down, or off).
- Audio is clear and used effectively.
- Character sets used in text display are clear, appropriate, and visually interesting.
- Graphics are acceptable on a monochrome monitor.
- Graphics are clear and can be easily interpreted.
- Program is "crash-proof."
- Program runs consistently under all normal conditions and is "bug-free."
- Program runs without undue delays.
- The transitions between screen displays (e.g., text changes) are effective.
- Program guards against multiple key presses advancing the student past next screen.
- Program avoids unnecessary or inappropriate moving back and forth between screens.
- Special features (e.g., flash, inverse, scrolling) are used appropriately and effectively.
- Program requires a minimal amount of typing (except typing programs).
- Random generation or selection is used when appropriate (e.g., to allow repeated use by varying problems or data presented).
- Program judges responses accurately and accounts for minor variations in format of input.
- Program allows user to correct answer before being accepted by the program.
- Program accepts partial answers as correct whenever appropriate.
- Where students must input responses, inappropriate keys are disabled.
- Control keys are used consistently.
- Students need minimum amount of teacher supervision when using program as appropriate.

Table 10.2	*Continued*

- Computer (and peripheral) operation does not interfere with concentration on activity.
- Program makes effective use of devices other than keyboard for input modes.
- Program considers a previously unexplored potential of the computer or greatly expands on existing capability (e.g., new animation techniques, digitized speech).
- Program uses other technologies (audiotape, videodisc) to enhance learning, as appropriate.
- Printing is easy, and simple to accomplish with a variety of popular printers.

Clarity

- Procedural and instructional statements are clear.
- On-screen prompts clearly indicate where user should focus attention.
- Frame formatting is clear, uncluttered, and consistent from screen to screen.
- Presentation of each discrete content topic is logical.
- Sequence of content topics and instruction is logical and in appropriate steps.
- Sequence of menu items is logical.
- Prompts and cues are clear and consistently and logically applied.
- Hints are clear and not misleading (e.g., length of spaces for fill-in-the-blanks).
- Demonstrations and examples are clear and available, when appropriate.
- Interface is simple enough to be used with little or no reading of the documentation.
- Program makes clear where the user is in the program (e.g., question number, etc.).
- User-computer communication is consistent and logical.
- Prompts to save work are given when appropriate.

Start-up and implementation

For the teacher:
- Software code modifications or unusual manipulations of disks not required.
- Start-up time for teacher implementation is not excessive.
- Teacher needs a minimum of computer competencies to operate program.

For the student:
- Start-up time for student implementation is brief enough to permit completion of a lesson.
- Students need a minimum of computer competencies to operate program.

Graphics and audio

- Graphics and audio are used to motivate.
- Graphics and audio are appropriate for the intended student population.
- Graphics, audio, and color enhance the instructional process.
- Graphics help focus attention on appropriate content and are not distracting.

Probeware and peripherals included in the software package

- Probes or peripherals are durable.
- Probes or peripherals are sensitive.
- Audio and/or graphic quality are effective.
- Probes or peripherals are easy to install.
- Calibration is accurate and easy.
- Data displays are flexible (e.g., can be scaled, redrawn).
- Data analysis is useful.

Table 10.2	*Continued*
Hardware and marketing issues	

- Potential usefulness of program justifies its price in comparison to other similar products.
- Peripherals (not included in package) that are difficult to acquire or too expensive are not required.
- Producer field-test data are available.
- Field-test data indicate that students learned more or better, or had a better attitude toward the subject matter, as a result of using the program.
- Preview copies are available.
- Backup copies are provided.
- Adequate warranty is provided.
- Telephone support is available.
- If allowable, multiple loading is possible.
- Site license is available.
- Network versions are available.
- Multiple copies discount is available.

Source OTA, Power On! New Tools for Teaching and Learning (1988, 2)

- **Keep it simple**

  Explain technical terms, if necessary. Use familiar words, even local dialect, to make the form easier to read. Keep questions brief. Short sentences are easier to follow than long ones. Make the form easy to fill out; the user should not have to write sentences in response to anything, except, perhaps, for the final open-ended, freeform question "Any other comments?"

- **Keep it brief**

  The evaluation should be no longer than two sides of a single sheet of paper.

- **Make it easy to follow**

  Include summary evaluation data at the top of the form to assist in first-pass selection—a star rating (with legend), subject area, appropriate age group.

  Break up evaluation criteria into categories and use topic headings to guide the user.

  Use dots or the underscore character to visually align the space allocated for responses with questions. This response space should *not* be boxed; it should be lined up with other responses, and should be as close to the end of the question as is convenient for easy reading.

- **Make it attractive**

  Use plenty of white space on the page, especially between sections and between lines. Handwriting needs a minimum ¼″ of vertical height. Regardless of the font (typeface) you use, do not use a point size (the height of the characters) less than 12. Try not to crowd the questions. Top, bottom, left, and right margins should be a minimum ½″.

Figure 10.17
Serif and sans serif
fonts

The serifs are the little extra lines (circled) that complete the letters

sans serifs

Use no more than two fonts. *Serif* fonts (fonts with smaller lines added to finish off a main stroke of a letter (see figure 10.17)) are easier to read than *sans serif* fonts. The model form in figure 10.16 uses a *sans serif* font for headings, and a *serif* font for the rest.

Do not use all uppercase characters, except perhaps for headings.

- **Make it available**

  Hard copy (paper) is more convenient than soft copy for data collection, so prepare a set of forms on paper and make them available to teachers and students. Have a box nearby that is large enough to receive 8½″ by 11″ paper. Because the evaluation records should be amendable, accessible, and capable of easy categorization, set up an on-line database for easy referral. A student volunteer can be responsible for updating and maintaining the database.

10.4.3 The Process of CAI System Evaluation and Purchase

Here are a few recommendations to guide you in the process of software evaluation and/or software purchase. Some of these ideas are drawn from Apple Macintosh (1990).

- Plan ahead. Draw up a list of needs: What is the age group and subject area for which the software is required? What criteria may be necessary to fit your teaching style? What kind of CAI software do you prefer for your students? Will it be used in a classroom or lab setting? What hardware must it run on?

- Be a "review worm." Subscribe to journals (computer or otherwise) relevant to your responsibilities and interests in the education field. Scan them from cover to cover. Read reviews of products that might meet your needs.

- Always try to preview software before buying it. Most companies will have an unconditional return policy on unwanted products. If you have no opportunity to try out a package, you probably should not buy it.

- Weed out software that is inappropriate (racist, sexist, or otherwise unacceptable).

- *Always* preview software before using it in class. Run through the software at least once yourself. Fill out the evaluation form. Then, if you still like it, have other teachers or students run it, too, and get their feedback by having them fill out an evaluation form.

- Check the license agreement. More companies today are agreeing to let teachers have a copy for use at home as well as at school. Site licenses are also well worth negotiating.

- Negotiate for the lowest price possible. Multiple copies should be discounted. The recommended retail price is rarely the going rate.

Looking Back

In this chapter, we have examined many aspects of CAI. It is beyond the scope of this book to profile even a tiny proportion of the ever-growing base of CAI applications that are being used to supplement education in our schools. The fact that it is available for integration into the curriculum does not automatically make it appropriate or effective. Teachers have the responsibility to determine what, if any, applications will be appropriate for their classes. Of course, they cannot do this unless they give the technology a chance.

This and the previous chapter have tried to present the characteristics of CAI, along with tools for software evaluation and recommendations for successful incorporation of the technology into the teaching and learning process. But the real work begins when teachers get their hands on the technology and start to "learn by doing." Such an opportunity should be integral to any teacher-education program, and it is hoped that it is part of yours.

Looking Forward

Chapters 11 and 12 will continue to examine practical aspects of computerized teaching and learning. The focus in chapter 11 will be computers and communications (C&C) and its impact on schools, today and in the future. Chapter 12 will examine all aspects of multimedia. As will be seen, we have barely begun to scratch the surface of the methodologies for instructional delivery systems enabled by C&C and multimedia technology. Fred D'Ignazio (Bruder, 1992) reminds us that "education is a faddish profession" (like any other), but there are times when it is reasonable to predict that some fads will endure longer than others. Computer technology in the classroom is one of these and, like computer technology in the other professions, it will transform education in ways that may seem beyond our wildest dreams.

Successful innovation in schools cannot happen without strong and enlightened leadership. The best leaders involve everyone—teachers, parents, administrators, and students—in the process of change and renewal. As noted in Joyce (1993): "Two extremely important dimensions of strong leadership" are the ability to generate a collaborative community, along with the ability to diagnose the essence of problems, solve them, and lead others "to find needs and create solutions." Schools and school districts are almost totally dependent on the quality of their leadership. Superintendents and principals with true leadership skills have shown again and again that ordinary schools can triumph over the most difficult circumstances and compete effectively with the most privileged schools in the world.

Do Something About It: Exercises and Projects

1. Get together with a group of your colleagues or classmates and discuss all the ways in which productivity software could be used to further learning. Start by examining appropriate uses of each type of productivity software one by one, then recommend integrated applications.

2. Section 10.4 includes a complete listing of the criteria used for educational software evaluation as published by the U.S. Congress Office of Technology Assessment (1988). Brainstorm with a group of classmates or colleagues to come up with a reduced list including only those criteria that you consider important when evaluating software for use in your school. Feel free to add new criteria that address your specific needs. Design the evaluation instrument along the lines laid down in the chapter (section 10.4.2). Ideally, you will want to produce a list that will easily fit on, at most, two sides of a single sheet of paper. The briefer the evaluation instrument, the more likely that it will be used.

3. There are innumerable ways in which computers can help integrate educationally disadvantaged students into the general school system. Discuss some of these applications.

4. "The computer is the most versatile writing implement yet invented." Do you agree with this statement? What is meant by the concept "writing to learn"? Do you think the author makes an adequate case for the use of the word processor in schools? Draw up a list of ways in which the computer as a writing instrument can benefit the learning process across the curriculum.

5. Is it fair to say that much educational software is "dubiously educational"? What do you understand by this? Is it always advantageous to incorporate the computer into the curriculum? Develop a document defining the pros and cons of computer use in education.

Microcomputer-based laboratories: Sound ideas for science

by James Stringfield and Donna Verdini,
University of Pittsburgh, Johnstown, Pennsylvania

One promising development in the use of computers in science classrooms has been the arrival of the micro-computer-based laboratory (MBL). MBLs use micro-computers to collect and analyze data during real experiments; probes and software are used to measure physical quantities such as sound, light, temperature, and pressure.

Microcomputer-Based Laboratories: An Effective Tool for Hands-On Elementary Science

The third-grade students at Rachel Hill Elementary School in Richland, Pennsylvania, received a "sound thrashing" in science when they were exposed to an MBL as a supplement to their normal hands-on science activities.

Primary-age children typically have difficulty grasping the concepts of pitch and frequency as well as intensity and amplitude when relating sound concepts to sound waves. With *HRM Sound,* a commercially available MBL program, the students used a microphone to collect sound data, which was immediately graphed on the computer monitor. A wide variety of experiments can be conducted as sound waves become more real for students.

The activities typically used in the elementary schools to teach sound concepts—varying the length of the column will produce different pitches (wavelengths) and changing the intensity of the vibration will produce different amplitudes of sound—were shown visually to the third graders using *HRM Sound.*

Activity 1: Seeing is believing!

For this activity, children were given eight soda bottles filled with colored water to replicate the eight notes of a scale in music. The third graders repeatedly tapped the eight bottles and watched the sound wave being produced by *HRM Sound.*

Activity 2: See no wave, hear no sound!

This activity involved the children singing a favorite song ("John Jacob Jingle Himer Schmidt") during which they went from singing loudly to singing softly, almost whispering while watching the sound waves being produced on the computer monitor.

Activity 3: Hear ye! Hear ye!

For this activity, the children observed the sound waves produced by several tuning forks of different pitches and the sound waves produced by blowing into a whistle.

(continued)

James Stringfield and Donna Verdini, authors of the case study
Photo courtesy James Stringfield

Student using HRM Sound
Photo courtesy James Stringfield

Case Study 10 (concluded)

Activity 4: Let's hear it for sound!

This activity involved the children in making their own straw oboes, which were numbered to the musical scale. Then, using a "following the bouncing ball" approach, the children used the oboes to blow out simple songs as they watched the waves produced by *HRM Sound*.

After hearing different pitches and intensities of sound in addition to seeing the waves produced on the microcomputer screen, the third-grade students were asked to complete diagrams of five different sounds and then encouraged to reach conclusions about those sounds in relation to their drawings of the sound waves.

The children "discovered" the following: (1) the higher the pitch, the shorter the wavelength; (2) the louder (more intense) the sound, the taller (higher) the sound waves.

In addition, the students concluded that the shorter the column of air being vibrated, the higher the pitch and the shorter the wavelength.

Without the ability to "see" sound via *HRM Sound,* the concept of sound waves would have remained abstract to these third graders. *HRM Sound* showed the students the relationship between sound and sound waves in relation to frequency and amplitude.

The Cost of Microcomputer-Based Laboratories

Commercially available microcomputer-based laboratories range in price from about $50 to $500. *HRM Sound*

Students playing "Hear ye! Hear ye!"
Photo courtesy James Stringfield

is available for $225. Some teachers construct their own MBL systems, but homemade materials can be time-consuming to create and require some knowledge of electronics.

By pooling resources or applying for grants, local schools can buy equipment which they would be otherwise unable to afford. The MBL programs described in this case study were borrowed from the Center for Mathematics and Science Education at the University of Pittsburgh at Johnstown. The center was able to purchase these materials through a Dwight D. Eisenhower grant administered by the Pennsylvania Department of Education.

Conclusions

Microcomputer-based laboratories have been used effectively in K–12 classrooms as a supplement to hands-on science activities. As computers become more powerful, children should have access to even more sophisticated programs.

References

Ideal School Supply Company. *Science Experiments for Elementary Grades.* No. 5403. Illinois: Ideal.

Nelson, L. W., and G. C. Lorbeer. *Science Activities for Elementary Children.* Dubuque, IA: William C. Brown.

Sound: A Microcomputer Based Lab (Apple II series only), Queue, Inc., 338 Commerce Drive, Fairfield, CT 06430; phone 1–800–232–2224.

Talk About It

Topics for discussion based on the case study.

1. What advantages do microcomputer-based laboratories have over simulations?
2. How could *HRM Sound* be adapted for use in high school classrooms?
3. What are the benefits of collecting data in real time?
4. What microcomputer-based labs would you like to see developed? Why?

◼ References

Apple Computer, Inc. *The Impact of Computers on K–12 Education: A Resource for Decision-Makers.* 1990.

Bailey, Robert W. *Human Performance Engineering: Using Human Factors/Ergonomics to Achieve Computer System Usability.* Englewood Cliffs, NJ: Prentice-Hall, 1989.

Bauch, Jerold. Touch 1 For Improved Parent-Teacher Contact. *School Safety,* Spring 1990.

Bigge, Morris L. *Learning Theories for Teachers.* 4th ed. New York: Harper & Row, 1982.

Bruder, Isabelle. Multimedia: How It Changes the Way We Teach and Learn. *Electronic Learning,* vol. 11, no. 1, September 1991, pp. 22–26.

Bruner, Jerome S., et al. *Studies in Cognitive Growth: A Collaboration at the Center for Cognitive Studies.* New York: John Wiley & Sons, 1966.

Capper, Joanne. *Computers and Learning: Do They Work? A Review of Research.* Washington, DC: Center for Research into Practice, 1988.

Goldberg, Mark F. A Portrait of Ted Sizer. *Educational Leadership,* vol. 51, no. 1, September 1993, pp. 53–56.

Hinze, Kenneth E. PC Datagraphics and Mapping. *Social Science Computer Review,* vol. 7, no. 1, Spring 1989, pp. 72–75. See Apple Computer Corporation, 1990.

Jostens. *Jostens Learning Corporation Company Profile.* Press Release, August 1993.

Joyce, Bruce R., James Wolf, and Emily Calhoun. *The Self-Renewing School.* Alexandria, VA: ASCD Publications, 1993.

Kearsley, Greg, Beverly Hunter, and Mary Furlong. *We Teach With Technology: New Visions for Education.* Wilsonville, OR: Franklin, Beedle & Associates, 1992.

Komoski, Ken. Integrated Learning Systems Take Integrated Effort. *School Administrator,* Special Issue, New York: American Association of School Administrators, 1990.

Mageau, Therese. Integrating an ILS: Two Teaching Models that Work. *Electronic Learning,* vol. 11, no. 4, 1992, pp. 16–22.

National Commission on Excellence in Education. *A Nation at Risk.* Cambridge, MA: USA Research, 1984.

OTA. *Power On! New Tools For Teaching and Learning.* U.S. Congress, Office of Technology Assessment-SET-379, Washington DC: Government Printing Office, September 1988. (a)

OTA. *Power On! New Tools For Teaching and Learning.* U.S. Congress, Office of Technology Assessment-SET-379, Washington DC: Government Printing Office, September 1988, pp. 232–36. (b)

Papert, Seymour. *Mindstorms: Children, Computers, and Powerful Ideas.* New York: Basic Books, 1980.

Poole, Bernard John, and Susan Giorgio Bond. *Essential Microsoft Works: Tutorials for Teachers.* Madison, WI: Brown & Benchmark, 1994.

Roblyer, M. D. The Effectiveness of Microcomputers in Education: A Review of the Research from 1980–1987. *T.H.E. Journal,* vol. 16, no. 2, September 1988, pp. 85–89.

Samson, G. E., R. Niemiec, T. Weinstein, and H. J. Walberg. Effects of Computer-Based Instruction on Secondary School Achievement: A Quantitative Synthesis. *AEDS Journal,* vol. 19, no. 4, 1986, pp. 312–21.

Sherry, Mark. The New ILSs: Branching Out. *Technology and Learning,* vol. 13, no. 2, October 1992, pp. 16–22.

Tufte, Edward. *Envisioning Information.* Cheshire, CT: Graphics Press, 1990.

Turkle, Sherry. *The Second Self: Computers and the Human Spirit.* New York: Simon & Schuster, 1984.

Webster's Dictionary. *Random House Webster's College Dictionary.* New York: Random House, 1991.

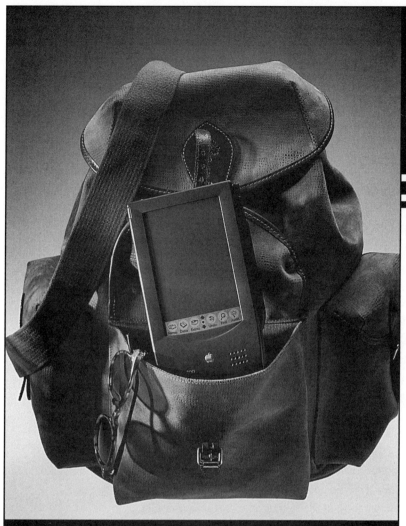

Computers, Communications, and Distance Learning

Laws and Institutions must go hand in hand with the progress of the human mind. As that becomes more developed, more enlightened, as new discoveries are made, new truths disclosed, and manners and opinions change with the change of circumstances, institutions must advance also, and keep pace with the times. We might as well require a man to wear still the coat which fitted him when a boy, as civilized society to remain ever under the regimen of their barbarous ancestors.

Thomas Jefferson (1743–1826)

What would our standard of living be like if we had no knowledge of what was created in Europe—its arts, literature, languages, sciences, religious and philosophic thought, and more? Isn't it equally possible that we are culturally deprived if we do not share in the possibilities of enrichment from the world's people who live elsewhere?

Seymour Fersh (1926–   )

Until recently, electronic communications technology has had only two applications in schools. It has been applied as an administrative tool in the form of the telephone, and it has been used for educational programming through the medium of television. Today, however, computers are making possible new educational uses of communications. As more computers find their way onto teachers' desks, onto students' desks, and into teachers' and students' homes, computer-based communications networks provide opportunities for electronic interaction, opening up pathways to knowledge and social intercourse which are changing the way education is delivered.

This chapter will look at all aspects of computers and communications (C&C) in order to provide a context for the nascent use of this technology in education. Specifically we will cover the following topics.

- Computers and communications
  - Background
  - Technology transfer
  - Explosion in end-user computing
  - The expansion of C&C in schools
  - A vision for the future
- Computer networks
  - The components of computer networks
  - Different kinds of computer networks
  - Applications of computer networks
  - The case for computer networks
  - Implementing computer networks
  - The impact of computer networks in education
  - Recommendations for successful introduction of computer networks in schools
- Home-school communication
  - The importance of the student-parent-teacher Gestalt
  - The *TransParent School* model
- Distance Learning
  - National and international education networks
  - On-line database retrieval services
  - Teaching and learning from remote sites
  - Networked collaborative learning

▪▪ 11.1 Computers and Communications

One of the most important trends in high tech in recent years has been the interlacing of computers with communications (C&C). Many of the major corporations have maneuvered for pole positions in the race to bring to market products that will allow the end-users of computerized systems to easily and safely share data and devices at all levels of activity, whether within the confines of the building in which they work or within the context of the global community.

During the course of the last decade or so, AT&T, the leader in the communications field, has become a serious contender in the computer hardware and software markets. At the same time, IBM, still the leader in the computer field, made inroads onto the telecommunications scene with the acquisition of 16% of MCI and 100% of ROLM. General Motors (GM) acquired Hughes Aircraft Corporation, and formed a powerful business partnership with Electronic Data Services (EDS) before buying the company from H. Ross Perot.

Inevitably, the benefits of C&C have begun to filter down to education. The concepts that led to CIM are being applied in a few forward-looking school districts where computer-integrated education is well on the way to becoming a reality. In these schools, computers and related technologies are integrated into the classroom-based curriculum. C&C systems enable the students, the parents, and the teachers to form an electronic triangle with the interests of the students at its heart. Networked computer systems are linking students with other students, and on-line databases are giving them access to a wide array of knowledge via the computer keyboard at home or at school.

Computers are giving teachers access to a centralized database of biographical, medical, academic, and behavioral student data—the kind of data to which teachers have always been entitled in the interests of students but which, for all practical purposes, has been unavailable to them until now. Finally, computers networked over communications lines are removing the concept of the closed classroom, opening up the students and teachers to the global community of their peers.

But these schools are the exceptions, and it will be some time before they become the rule. It is not unusual for education to lag behind institutions such as business and industry as far as the introduction of technology is concerned. This is partly because the American system of education is so expensive. It glories in "diversity, universal access, and the freedom of choice that comes with local financing and decision-making" (U.S. Congress, Office of Technology Assessment, 1988). Unfortunately, this diversity, universal access, and freedom of choice carry an enormous cost in terms of buildings, equipment, and personnel, which leaves little to cover the expense of rapid integration of technology. In business and industry, the raison d'être is profit; in education, the raison d'être is making do. In business and industry, the weak go to the wall; in education, a measure of strength is the extent to which all, from the most gifted to the most in need, are given an equal opportunity to achieve.

This chapter discusses educational C&C, including an examination of the *TransParent School* model, which is an example of how C&C technology can change the way teaching and learning occur in schools. One of the greatest weaknesses of education, in modern times at least, has been the distancing of the home from the school. There has come about an almost complete dichotomy between what goes on at home and what goes on in school. The result is the loss of an opportunity for "dealing with at-risk students, for reducing the potential for school dropout, for improving achievement and for making [significant] improvements in school/community relations" (Bauch, 1991).

11.1.1 Background

The problem with stand-alone computer systems is their isolation. They not only prevent users from taking advantage of powerful communications facilities such as **electronic mail** (e-mail),[1] but they also cut the user off from on-line data retrieval and data sharing.

Thus, for some time now, the writing has been on the wall for stand-alone systems. In the corporate world, the policy of supplying a stand-alone PC for every desktop has changed because so many of those PCs stand idle, collecting dust and coffee stains. As Jeff Thomson of Hitachi America pointed out in a supplement on Office Automation prepared by the Omni Group (Newsweek, 1986): "It's clear that word processing and spreadsheets on PCs are not office automation. People are reaping positive but limited benefits with that approach. We have now filled all those desks. What we urgently need is clear and simple information sharing among all levels of workers, from entry clerks through senior management."

11.1.2 Technology Transfer

Technology transfer is the process whereby technology finds its way from the workbench of the inventor into everyday use. With regard to computer technology, this transfer is becoming all pervasive as computers become inextricably associated with communications systems. Birnbaum (1985) points out that computer technology has entered the third of four phases of technological evolution. The electronic computer is "manufactured in quantity, has become well known and commonplace, but is used directly by only a rather small portion of the population." This is especially true in schools, since tight budgets continue to severely restrict the spread of computer use in the classroom. The advance to the fourth and final "pervasive" stage, when "computer technology has become integral to daily life," will be effected only when the marriage between computers and communications has become standard at a price that is within the reach of all.

It is evident that we are experiencing a lull before the storm. Heavily funded R&D activity is taking place behind internationally scattered, closed doors. At Bell Labs, prototype fiber optic[2] communications systems have been developed capable of transmitting up to 40 billion bits of data per second. That is equivalent to transmitting about a million pages of text a second (two thousand 500-page books per second!).

Why do we need to transmit data at such incredible speeds? Well, believe it or not, transmitting data from one place to another is actually the bottleneck that slows down the work that computers do. If you have ever tried placing a telephone call on New Year's Eve, you know that it is possible for the telephone system to get overloaded even though the routing of calls is entirely computer-controlled. Yet the goal of companies like AT&T is to establish data highways that will be capable of carrying not only speech communication, but pictures, too.

Videophones, telephones that carry the pictures as well as the voice of the people engaged in the phone call, have been available for some time—decades, in fact. But they

---

[1]E-mail is a system that enables the users to send mail messages back and forth from one computer to another. The mail is temporarily stored in a "mailbox" until the receiver has the opportunity to read it and respond.

[2]Fiber optics uses glass fiber tubes to carry pulses of light (lasers) from point to point. Each pulse of light represents one bit of data.

are still a practical impossibility for the general population because the telephone network is incapable of carrying the amount of data that would be generated by a nationwide, let alone worldwide, videophone system.

A good-quality picture on a computer screen uses about a million **pixels** (dots—or bits of data); that is for a still image. A moving image—such as two people talking to each other on the videophone—requires the picture to be "refreshed" (redrawn and updated) up to 30 times per second. So, if you were chatting with a friend on the videophone, the system would have to transmit about 30 million bits of data per second in one direction and another 30 million bits of data per second in the other. This is fine if you and your friend are the only people using the videophone at the time. But AT&T, British Telecom, and the various other telephone companies worldwide will have to be able to handle millions of simultaneous videophone calls before such a system could become a reality.

So general use of videophones is not possible just yet. But if companies like Bell Labs continue to push the envelope of the technology, it won't be long before schools are setting up videophone links between their students and those in other countries as easily as some schools now set up similarly exciting learning experiences using the voice-based telephone system.

11.1.3 Explosion in End-User Computing

The world is about to experience an explosion of data communications capability that will make the best of current local and wide area networks seem outlandishly sluggish and anachronistic. At the same time, we are witnessing an explosion in end-user computing. Computer use was formerly controlled by information systems (IS) personnel. But today, relatively nontechnical individuals with a modicum of training have taken advantage of the availability of desktop machines to exercise personal control over the processing of "their" data. They want data now, so that today's decisions can be made with today's information. This has led to the rise of state-based educational technology centers, which are responsible for the training and support of computer-using teachers.

Progress toward the goal of bringing all teachers to the point where they are comfortable using computer-based technology in the curriculum is slow. The statewide Information Technology Education for the Commonwealth (ITEC) program in Pennsylvania, for example, had reached no more than 20% of the teachers in the state between 1984 and 1992 (Barnhart, 1992). Many would-be users have been put off by unfriendly human–machine interfaces. They have been frustrated by early attempts to learn the strange sets of sequences and commands which have characterized operating systems such as Apple's DOS 3.3, IBM's PC-DOS (MS-DOS for IBM-compatible computers), and the macro languages of software such as *Lotus 1-2-3*™ or *Dbase*™.

All this is changing with the spread of easy-to-use, graphics-based systems. More and more, the end-user is coming to expect to interact with a computer with a minimum of technical preparation, in much the same way as the modern automobile is relatively simple to drive.

11.1.4 The Expansion of C&C in Schools

Systems that are easier to use will attract an ever-broadening base of computer users in schools. Many teachers who until now have been reticent about making the leap into classroom computing will be more inclined to do so when they see how much easier the systems are to use, and when they see what kind of impact is being made by technology in a growing number of the classrooms around them. It is likely, too, that much of the increased demand for incorporation of the computer into the curriculum will come from parents and students who discover the inequities that may exist in the same school district, or even in the same school, with regard to access to educational computing.

Communications technology is now pervasive, easy to use, and relatively inexpensive compared to just a few years ago. We have reached the point, according to Lewis (1992), where "a growing number of teachers and administrators believe that the full potential of personal computers can be tapped only by connecting them to one another within a school, and by linking each school to others throughout the state, the nation and the world." Hard on the heels of the spread of C&C in government and business, schools are on the threshold of an explosion of networked computing which will further transform education.

11.1.5 A Vision for the Future

"Ah, but a man's reach should exceed his grasp—or what's a heaven for." Robert Browning's words remind us that progress is something we humans seem to strive after instinctively. Progress is most likely to follow if we have a vision on which to focus our endeavors. Shelly Weinstein is director of the National Education Telecommunications Organization (NETO). In July 1992, she was asked to join other leaders in educational telecommunications to address a U.S. Senate subcommittee on the Role of Telecommunications Technologies in Education. Here is Weinstein's vision for schools of the 21st century:

> Our vision is to build an integrated, nationwide telecommunications system, a transparent highway that encompasses land and space, over which teaching and educational resources can be delivered and shared with schools, colleges, universities, and libraries. Our vision is to wire together our classrooms nationwide, and ultimately internationally, through a single dedicated telecommunications system which can be accessed simultaneously through a telephone instrument, a computer, a fax machine, a video camera, and a television set. It would be wonderful if every school could simply pay a single monthly service fee and have unlimited access to a transportation system that carries information in all forms: video, voice, and data from almost anywhere in the nation or world.

This vision is already beginning to take shape. All over the United States are pockets of progress—sometimes the outcome of one individual's efforts, sometimes the outcome of a statewide mandate. It is time to examine more closely the technology involved, and how it can be used in schools.

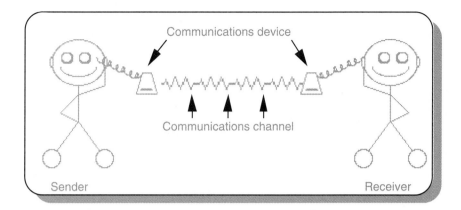

Figure 11.1
Shannon and Weaver model of a communication system

∎ 11.2 Computer Networks

A **computer network** is a group of two or more computers connected electronically for the purpose of sending and receiving data.

11.2.1 The Components of Computer Networks

The following are the basic components of all computer networks.

Computers

The simplest of computers can be used to link users over local and wide area networks. The more powerful the computer, the more sophisticated the communications software it can handle—but hang onto those Commodore 64s, Radio Shack TRS-80s, and Apple IIs. They can serve as excellent dumb terminals to on-line databases, library card catalogs, e-mail systems, BBS, and the like. We will return to this idea shortly.

Communications channels

Shannon and Weaver (1949) formalized the terminology commonly used when describing communications systems. Figure 11.1 illustrates this classic configuration.

As you can see, the communications channel is what connects one communications device with another. Typical media used today for channels include cable-based media (such as copper wire or glass fiber, also called optical fiber) and wireless media such as radio waves (microwave is a type of radio wave). Advances in telecommunications technology are leading to faster and faster transmission speeds (measured in bits per second—bps), making computer networks all the more viable for a multitude of applications both in and out of the classroom, such as those discussed in this chapter.

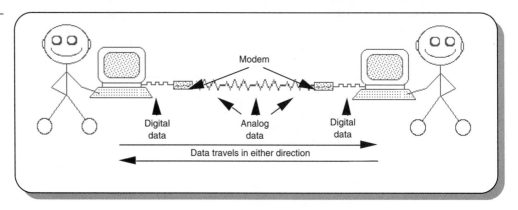

Figure 11.2
A modem converts digital data to analog data and vice versa

Modems and fax/modems

A **modem** is a simple device that is necessary to connect digital computers to wide area networks such as the telephone network which still for the most part transmits data in analog form.[3] The modem converts the digital data transmitted by the computer into the analog data used by the telephone system and back again.[4] Figure 11.2 illustrates this process.

A **fax/modem** is a modem that includes a facsimile (fax) machine, which manages the transmission of digitized[5] copies of images of all kinds. Telecommunications companies such as AT&T are involved in an on-going, multibillion-dollar project to replace traditional, analog electromagnetic media such as variations on copper wire cable by much faster and more reliable digital fiber-optic cable. A time may come when modems will be obsolete—like typewriters.

Telecommunications hardware and software

Telecommunications hardware usually takes the form of circuit boards or electronic components that are plugged into the motherboard inside the computer's system unit. The telecommunications hardware and software together take care of hookups and the other protocols[6] that maintain a trouble-free connection between one computer and another.

11.2.2 Different Kinds of Computer Networks

It is beyond the scope of this book to discuss network topography (Star, Ring, Bus configurations, for example). Readers who would like to learn more about this subject should

---

[3] A digital signal is discrete, made up of separate electromagnetic pulses called bits. An analog signal is continuous, made up of electromagnetic waves.

[4] The word *modem* is a contraction of *mod*ulator-*dem*odulator. The modular component of a modem converts data from digital to analog form; the demodulator converts the data from analog to digital form. Both components are necessary for two-way communication.

[5] The process called digitizing was explained in chapter 6 in the discussion of computer hardware.

[6] Protocols are the rules of the road in communications systems, such as transmission speed and connection conventions (called handshaking).

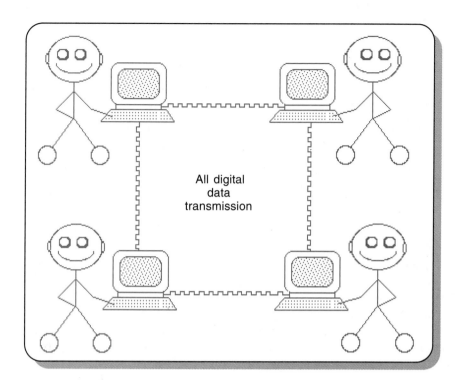

Figure 11.3
Typical LAN
configuration

All digital
data
transmission

consult a general computer-literacy text, or a text devoted specifically to telecommunications. Here, we are concerned only with the broad topic of local and wide area computer networks.

Local Area Networks (LANs)

A **local area network (LAN)** connects computers over short distances (usually not much more than a mile or so). Figure 11.3 illustrates a typical LAN configuration.

A computer network interface device (usually a plug-in circuit board, though more and more computers, including all Apple Macintosh computers, come with this device built in) connects each computer to the communications channel (cable or wireless media) so that data transmission can take place. Today, most LANs include high-speed computers called servers, which also have large secondary memory capacity for storing networked applications software, along with computer network management and security software.

Two or more LANs of the same type (say, in different parts of a school or school district) can be connected using a hardware device called a bridge. A gateway is a similar, though more complex, device used to connect LANs of incompatible types (that is, they use different communications protocols).

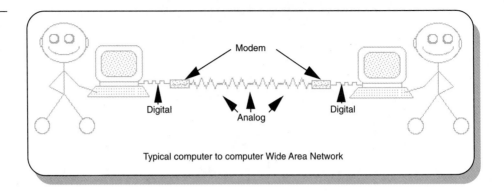

Figure 11.4
Typical wide area network

Typical computer to computer Wide Area Network

Wide Area Networks (WANs and MANs)

A **wide area network (WAN)** establishes communications paths between computers that are scattered over areas that span anywhere from several miles to the area covered by the to-date accessible universe. Figure 11.4 illustrates this concept. A **metropolitan area network (MAN)** is simply a smaller (city-based) example of a WAN.

Schools are exploring the uses of LANs and WANs in the management of the teaching and learning process and, as this chapter shows, innovative communications applications are providing students with exciting collaborative and cross-cultural experiences.

11.2.3 Applications of Computer Networks

Computer networks are commonly used for two kinds of activities: telecommunications and the sharing of hardware and software.

Telecommunications

Telecommunications involves the transmission of data (the spoken or written word, and images and sounds of all kinds) over short and long distances. Examples are

- **Electronic mail (e-mail).** E-mail is, for the most part, used to exchange text (memos, correspondence, and so forth) between two or more individuals using computers. With the proliferation of fiber optic media, communications systems are becoming more powerful and capable of handling larger volumes of data at higher speeds, so that videomail (perhaps it will be called v-mail) is likely to become more common.
- **Bulletin Board Systems (BBS).** A BBS is a central text-based system for sharing information. Users call into the system to share ideas, software, and data with other users.
- **Voice messaging.** Voice messaging is the same as e-mail except that voice rather than simple text is used as the medium of communication. Users do not interact in real time; in other words, they cannot respond immediately as on the telephone. The voice message is stored temporarily in an electronic "mailbox," like e-mail.

- **File exchange.** This is the same concept as e-mail except that formal computer files, rather than informal mail, are transmitted.
- **Local and remote on-line database retrieval.** Here users tap into on-line databases like *CompuServe*™ for data of all kinds.
- **Real time interactive voice, video, and data interchange.** The computer can be used for interactive two-way communication between two or more people all able to communicate at the same time, like a party telephone line. These systems can also use video communication, as well as voice and text. Video conferencing is an example of this type of C&C network.
- **Video conferencing.** Users communicate over live video and voice communications systems from remote locations. This enables people to "meet" electronically, thus saving the time and expense of traveling to a central location.

Hardware device and software sharing

Users can benefit from sharing high-speed, high-quality, centrally maintained peripheral devices such as printers; large-capacity, secondary storage such as disk drives; and high-powered computers (discussed later in the context of dumb terminals). Networks take the hassle out of using such equipment.

Networkable software, accessed from a central host or file server, has several advantages, not least of which is the ability to control the software against viruses and piracy (discussed in chapter 5). Networked software also helps guarantee that users will have access to the same range and version of software. As changes are made to software and upgrades released by software developers, new versions that are centrally controlled can be easily and consistently made available to all.

11.2.4 The Case for Computer Networks

"Computers should be used to tie people together, not to separate them." This is the conclusion of Selfe (1992), warning against the potentially "dehumanizing aspects of technological progress," where computers have been allowed to separate those who have access to computers and those who do not. This is clearly a danger, not just in the English departments described by Selfe, but in schools in general. Selfe goes on to recommend computer networks to "help create communities among groups of students" where they can "share their writing electronically, conference with teachers via electronic mailboxes, and practice argumentation and written dialogue skills on electronic bulletin boards." Practice makes perfect: the more opportunities students have for writing, the better.

Computer networks in schools have more applications than simply improving writing skills. Selfe references Fersko-Weiss (1985) when observing that "networks can expand students' perceptual boundaries, allowing them to tap into rich sources of library data and bibliographic information and become acquainted with the thinking of individuals from other countries or cultures."

Currid (1992) makes a compelling case for networked computing when she reminds us of the kind of anachronistic bureaucracy that still pertains in many professional environments today. She describes the traditional "16-step procedure" for transmitting a paper-based piece of information from one person to another within the same organization (say, from the principal to a teacher). The principal handwrites or dictates the memo and gives it to a secretary, who proofreads it and corrects it before either typing it or getting someone else to do it. Once the memo has been typed, the secretary checks it over again before passing it back to the principal so she can check it over, too. Eventually, it finds its way into the interoffice mail system and gets delivered. Elapsed time: up to several days.

Alternatively, as Currid observes, using networked computing, the same transaction goes like this:

Step 1: [Principal] drafts own document in a word processing program or the E-mail software.

Step 2: [Principal] sends electronic document to [teacher] and files a draft copy.

Step 3: [Teacher] gets message. (Elapsed time: 3 minutes to an hour).

The goal of every school district should be to put a computer on every teacher's desk and to connect that computer to the rest of the world, including not only immediate colleagues and the students' parents/guardians but also teachers in other schools. If every teacher has a personal computer, and if those computers are all linked using networks, there is the potential for change in the way schools, in general, and classrooms, in particular, are run that can be as dramatic as has already been experienced in the business world.

It is already possible for teachers to communicate over federally supported, national and international networks. Shelly Weinstein's vision of the future for education cited earlier is closer to realization than most people are aware. We will examine these and other networks later in this chapter.

11.2.5 Implementing Computer Networks

Before examining applications of networks, let us look at the practical side of implementing networks in schools.

The worst-case scenario: Putting obsolescent technology to work

Many school districts are in the situation of having invested in computer technology that is fast becoming obsolete. During the 1980s and early 1990s, millions of computer systems of all shapes and sizes were purchased for use in schools, especially in the more developed nations of the world. Many of these systems are now considered obsolete either because they are not powerful enough to run much of the software designed for educational applications, or because they are no longer supported by software developers.

E-mail to the rescue

Just about any computer can become a dumb terminal[7] on a network. Whether the computers are Apple IIs, Apple Macintoshes, IBM PCs, or the hundreds of IBM compatible

---

[7]You may recall the two types of network terminals: dumb terminals and smart terminals. A dumb terminal is one that does not have its own processor and therefore cannot perform as a stand-alone computer. A smart terminal is a general purpose computer with its own microprocessor, which can also act as a node on a network.

computers—IBM PS/1s or PS/2s, Commodore 64s, 128s, or Amigas, Radio Shack TRS-80s, and so on—they can be linked together for the purpose of electronic communications as straightforward as e-mail.

This would still, of course, cost money to purchase the various networking software and hardware components and to set up and maintain the network, but it would be money well spent in view of the extended lifespan given to what might otherwise be underutilized, antiquated systems. The amount of money would be a fraction of the cost of setting up every teacher and administrator with completely new computer systems. Needless to say, implementation of this idea would not preclude the necessity to purchase up-to-date systems in the long run, because teachers will eventually want to use their computers for tasks other than e-mail.

But as DeBalko (1992) observes, "E-mail alone, if used properly, can justify the cost of a LAN." In the meantime, there is the possibility of a highly beneficial by-product of putting a networked computer on every teacher's desk—networking could be the Trojan horse that opens the door to more general use of computers by those many, many teachers in our schools who are still resistant to the changes involved in computer-integrated teaching and learning. Simple networks are thus a very practical idea in many school districts that have purchased computers in recent years and are now wondering what to do with obsolescent technology.

Some would argue that it is a waste of computing power to relegate a PC to the functionality of a dumb terminal. But isn't this better than not using the computer at all?

A best-case scenario: Using current technology

Money spent today on computer-based technology will buy considerably more than the same money spent during the early 1980s. This is because the computer industry is one of those rare industries where prices decrease even as the quality increases. For example, the price of secondary storage on hard, magnetic disk drives has fallen from about $100 per megabyte in the mid-1980s to just over $1 per megabyte in the mid-1990s. But not only has the price fallen dramatically; the disk drives are also more reliable, data access is considerably faster, and the drives come preformatted and ready to go with all the necessary disk-management software on board.

This trend toward dramatic increases in value for money is likely to continue into the foreseeable future. Schools investing in technology today can expect to buy systems that will be easily networkable, so it makes sense to take advantage of this facility.

For example, McCarthy (1992) describes the experience of Judy Baker, principal at Hornet's Nest Elementary School in Charlotte, North Carolina. In her school, Baker has installed 150 Macintosh LC workstations connected to eight Macintosh IIsi computers that act as file servers. "In classrooms for grades K–2 there are 5 [networked] Mac LCs; in grades three through six there are six networked LCs. Each classroom has a printer [accessible by each computer on the network]."

Needless to say, the mere installation of systems such as those in Principal Baker's school will not transform the educational process. Teachers still have to be trained and provided with ongoing support—which must include time to integrate the technology into the curriculum.

11.2.6 The Impact of Computer Networks in Education

The implementation of current networking technology opens up the possibility of not only linking students and teachers within a school, but also linking a school to other schools at home and abroad at all levels of the academic spectrum. Mangan (1992) cites just three of many examples of the ways in which schools were proposing to use computer and communications networks in fall 1992 alone.

> Elementary-school students from several schools in Vermont were to work together over the Vermont Educator's Network to write a geography textbook for young children. The students were to conduct research and send the information by network to a central school, which was to assemble the materials and publish the book.
>
> Third graders in Glendora, California, were to communicate with elementary students in Zimbabwe, learning about their school, families, and culture. The link was to be arranged by a faculty member at California State Polytechnic University at Pomona, whose research concentrated on Distance Learning.
>
> Faculty members at Southern Illinois University at Carbondale were working with a local school district on a project designed to improve students' science and computer skills. High-school students served as mentors for elementary-school students in the project. The results were to be shared with other educators on computer bulletin boards.

The benefits of networked computing in schools are compelling. As time goes on, electronic communication will replace much traditionally paper-borne interaction between teachers and administration, between one teacher and other teachers, between teachers and students, between teachers and parents, and so on. But change will be slow, since it is not only a question of buying the equipment, installing it, and maintaining it on an ongoing basis. Teachers and administrators must also change the way they think about education. "There's the rub," for that change inevitably involves both physical and cultural adjustments at the individual and group levels.

11.2.7 Recommendations for Successful Introduction of Computer Networks in Schools

Here are some essential recommendations that will help a school district make the physical and cultural adjustments mentioned above.

Every classroom should be wired for telephone and cable TV communications.

> In the next two sections of this chapter (11.4 Home-School Communications and 11.5 Distance Learning), we will discuss valuable C&C applications that apply in education and become possible when classrooms are wired for telephone and cable television.

All computers should be networked together.

> The people who control the purse strings should understand that it is a wasted opportunity when a computer stands alone, unable to communicate with other computers on a network.

Teachers should be given access to systems that will encourage them to use the computer as a tool.

These would include systems such as the full range of productivity software, centralized on-line databases of student records, calendars detailing upcoming events throughout the year, voice messaging for establishing and maintaining close contact with the students' families, and e-mail systems for sharing messages, memos, and ideas over the network.

Many school districts may hesitate to implement these recommendations because they are strapped for money. But money need not necessarily be a prohibiting factor, since hundreds of millions of dollars every year are made available to support technological innovation in education. Chapter 14 explains how to go about getting a slice of this pie. Of greater concern is the training and support that will be necessary once the teachers' classrooms are on-line to the rest of the world. The next two sections will examine what schools are already achieving along the lines of educational C&C, thanks to the support that they have received on the local, state, and national levels.

11.3 Home–School Communications

11.3.1 Teachers Need Parents

The teacher's best ally in this task of nurturing the student's innate "urge to learn" is, first and foremost, the parents. As Joe Uson, the 1992 Outstanding Early Childhood Teacher from Anchorage, Alaska, observed in his award acceptance speech:[8] "Teachers need parents." *A Nation at Risk* is right in stating that parents do have "an undiminished concern for the well-being of their children," but for the most part they are not culturally encouraged by the education system to intervene in their children's education. For the most part, the schools have paid little more than lip service to the idea of involving parents in schools. On the other hand, very few parents have gone out of their way to insist on being involved. No one is to blame for this state of affairs because no one appears to see anything wrong with it.

According to *The Parent Involvement Report* (1992a), "teachers interact with very few parents on a daily basis." At the elementary level, the "average" teacher has contact with 2.8 parents on a typical day; at the middle/junior high level, the number falls to 2.1; and at the high school level, it falls again to 1.4. These are numbers for the "average" teacher, which means that close to half the teachers have fewer contacts with parents. The statistics are all the more alarming when one considers, as pointed out in the *Report,* that teachers at the higher levels tend to have more students per day, and should therefore have more likelihood of meeting with parents.

The blame must lie with the schools. The parents are on the outside looking in. Culturally—that is, traditionally—they are not supposed to butt in on what goes on in schools, and when they do, they are regarded (respectfully, of course) like students with behavior problems, even when they are only trying to help.

---

[8]Disney American Education Awards, 1992.

Fortunately, some schools are doing something about it—schools such as those that have adopted the *TransParent School* model designed and supported by the Betty Phillips Center for Parenthood Education at Peabody College of Vanderbilt University. There are other schools, too, not affiliated with the *TransParent School* model, where the teachers and the administrators have made that extra effort and taken it upon themselves to bring the parents inside the hallowed halls of academe.

According to data published in *The Voice* (1992), parents on the whole give good grades to their local schools and are deeply interested in what goes on in them, even though this may not always be apparent. Teachers often claim that they seem to meet only the parents of the so-called good children and that these parents visit the school only because they know they will hear good things about their child.

This is a classic example of faulty *post hoc, ergo propter hoc* reasoning, since it accepts as a cause (for parents visiting the school) something that merely occurred earlier in time (the goodness of the child). Instead, teachers should argue the other way round: parents who visit the school show their involvement in their child's education, which contributes significantly to the child's success. Parents should be encouraged to become involved in school life because they are a key component of a successful outcome to the educational process for children.

Unfortunately, the majority of parents have effectively been shut out of the education loop—not intentionally, but by default. The teachers do not think they have adequate time to foster interaction with parents, and the administration cannot be expected to maintain more than cursory contact with hundreds of families. As a result, most schools today are failing to take advantage of a powerful Gestalt, which, were it nurtured, would significantly strengthen the child's all-round educational experience.

11.3.2 The Importance of the Student-Parent-Teacher Gestalt

Wertheimer, the father of **Gestalt** psychology, argued that an organized whole is greater than the sum of its parts (Bigge, 1992). "For example," Wertheimer observed, "a triangle is greater than the sum of the three line segments that form it. This is because of its Gestalt." The triangle is an appropriate analogy for the argument we are trying to make, which is that the triangular relationship formed by the parents, the teacher, and the child is greater than the sum of the three entities taken separately.

You may have good parents, a good teacher, and a good child, but if they do not work together, the strength that could be derived from the Gestalt is lost. This perhaps explains why so many children, academically able or not, simply do not enjoy being at school, no matter how much "fun" they may be having, because they do not consider school to be integrated with the rest of their lives.

It seems reasonable to conclude that the more schools do to weld together the triangular Gestalt formed by the child, the parent(s), and the teacher, the more committed the child will remain through the long process of formal education. And "if time and opportunity to communicate are the barriers [to making the Gestalt a reality], then telecommunications technology can come to the rescue" (Bauch, 1991).

11.3.3 The TransParent School Model

The *TransParent School* model, developed and formalized by Jerold Bauch at the Betty Phillips Center for Parenthood Education at Vanderbilt University, uses telecommunications technology to provide "voice-based information exchange between teachers and parents." The model, described in *The Parent Involvement Report* (1992a) is purposely simple, both technologically and methodologically, to make it as easy as possible to implement.

The components of the model are:

■ **A computer-based voice messaging system is installed at the school site.** Many schools that have implemented the model have raised funds by way of grants from local and nonlocal sources to cover the cost of the hardware and ongoing vendor support as well as the expense involved in running the system on a day-to-day basis.

■ **Each day the teachers prepare a brief script** describing

1. what their students learned during the day;
2. specific homework/home learning assignments;
3. parent education suggestions;
4. any other school information.

■ **The teacher records the message in a voice mailbox.** Ideally, every teacher should have a Touch-Tone telephone in the classroom, but this is not necessary for the system to work since any Touch-Tone phone anywhere in the school can be used. More and more schools, however, are wiring classrooms with phone jacks.

■ **All parents can call and hear the message at any time.**

■ **There are other voice mailboxes on the system,** accessed with different phone numbers, which can contain messages about such items as the daily lunch menu, sports or performance event schedules, and so forth.

Jim Berube (*The Parent Involvement Report,* 1992a), principal at the 600-plus-student Matilija Junior High School, in Ojai, California, reports that the Homework Hotline voice mailbox on his school's system alone "receives about 350 calls on a typical day." The system handled 120,000 calls for teacher messages in the first year and a half of its existence.

11.3.4 Outcomes of the TransParent School Model

The *TransParent School* model has had several interesting outcomes, especially for those families where the parents have taken most advantage of the system.

■ These parents are now more involved with their child's education.

■ They notice that their child completes more homework assignments.

■ They see an improvement in their child's skills.

■ They observe an improvement in their child's grades.

■ They feel better about the school.

One final quote from *The Parent Involvement Report* (1992b) will sum up the parents' reaction to the system:

> The parent response has been overwhelming. Principal Berube said that parents feel that they finally have the necessary tools to support their children. Recently a parent approached him and said, "They should carve your face in Mount Rushmore. You have saved the relationship between me and my son. I now have conversations with him about school, instead of confrontations over homework.

It is beyond the scope of this text to cover the system in more detail. Appendix C (Resources and Recommended Reading) provides information about the Betty Phillips Center for Parenthood Education, along with a brief synopsis of *The Parent Involvement Report*. The center is responsive to all interested parties.

▪▪ 11.4 Distance Learning

Distance learning is the term used to describe learning that takes place over audiovisual networks set up between remote sites. The learning may involve a teacher at one end of the electronic communications lines and students, singly or in groups, at other locations. Alternatively, students from different schools (local, national, or international) may be networked together for purposes of interaction, discussion, joint project work, and so on. In the previous section, we saw some examples of this application of distance learning as described in Mangan (1992). The case study at the end of this chapter further focuses on applications of distance learning as they have been implemented in schools in Waterloo, Iowa.

11.4.1 National and International Education Networks

Think of the world and its immediate, accessible corner of the universe as though it were a human brain: interconnected axons and dendrites link an ever-expanding and potentially infinite collection of neurons. Messages in the form of electromagnetic pulses flash simultaneously and ceaselessly in all directions. Axons and dendrites are equivalent to network systems—computers and transmissions media. The neurons are equivalent to people who are drawn closer and closer together into a global community where every individual depends more and more on everyone else. This is the stuff of science fiction, yet it is becoming a reality today. Computer networks that have been developed over the last 50 years are now capable of interconnection as one vast global and brainlike configuration.

If this is indeed the Information Society, and if our times are aptly described as the Information Age, it is because of the impact that electronic networks are having on the way we live, the way we work, and the way we learn. In the following section, we will discuss briefly a few of these networks. A rewarding exercise would be for you to log on to one of the national or international networks from your college computing center, look around the system, and establish e-mail contact with your friends or whomever you can find. This is recommended as an exercise in the Do Something About It section at the end of the chapter. You will find that the world can quickly become your oyster.

BITNet (Because It's Time Network)   **BITNet** links colleges, universities, and research organizations all over the world. There is no charge for its use, costs being covered by federal government funding. If you can log on to your local college computer system, you can probably log on to BITNet.

Internet   **Internet** is the name given to the electronic mail system that links the various networks that come under the aegis of the federal government and affiliated organizations, including colleges and universities. The Internet is now an "international mesh of interconnected data networks" (Bradner, 1993). In existence for more than a decade, Internet is composed of about two million linked computers worldwide, as of the fall of 1993. According to Bradner (1993), the network is growing at a rate of about 7% per month. BITNet is one of the networks that is linked to Internet. Once again, if you can log on to your college computer system, you can log on to Internet. Internet is now also known as NREN.

NREN (National Research and Education Network)   This network, authorized in 1991 as part of the High Performance Computing Act, will eventually supersede Internet. Its mandate is to "provide access to electronic information resources maintained by libraries, research facilities, publishers and affiliated organizations." Connie Stout, executive director of the Consortium for School Networking, says that the consortium was set up to help ensure that schools K–12 would be well represented when NREN comes on line (Solomon, 1992).

FrEdMail (Free Educational Electronic Mail)   This unique, free service was founded by Al Rogers. **FrEdMail** is a distributed network that connects bulletin boards all over the world. Nodes (bulletin board systems) are located all over the United States. Teachers and students access the local node nearest their school and can use the service to send e-mail both nationally and internationally. International messages are actually delivered during off-peak hours—that is, overnight—to save on expense.

The objective of FrEdMail is to provide students with an environment in which they will be encouraged to write. According to Kurshan (1992), several international collaborative projects have been completed to date, including an international cookbook and a comparison of consumer products and prices.

Other global classroom projects   *AT&T Learning Network* involves students in grades 3 through 12 in interdisciplinary projects and interactive foreign language experience.

Computer Pals across the World engages students in writing, interactive social studies, and foreign language learning projects.

Global Common Classroom operates under the aegis of the National Geographic Kids Network and connects U.S. schools with others in Russia and Eastern Europe.

The TERC[9] Communications' *Global Laboratory* is funded by the National Science Foundation and is designed to enable teachers and students to collaborate internationally on projects related to ecology.

---

[9]Technical Education Research Centers

European systems

The economic unit known as the European Community (EC) has led to a further erosion of barriers between the countries of Europe. This process has been broadened since the tumbling of the Berlin Wall. Students in elementary and secondary schools in these countries now have unprecedented opportunities for on-line access to others all over western and eastern Europe. *Campus 2000* and *TELETEL* are examples of communications networks that are becoming woven into the fabric of K–12 education in Europe.

Campus 2000, as described by Foster (1992), is an inexpensive e-mail and on-line database retrieval system used by almost all the K–12 schools in the UK. Users have access to as many as 150 on-line database retrieval services, including *PROFILE* (a keyword, searchable database that carries back editions of several newspapers, including Reuters), the National Educational Resources Information Service (NERIS), and the Educational Counselling and Credit Transfer Information Service (ECCTIS).

UK students can also interact easily with students in France (via the French TELETEL network) and Germany.

11.4.2 On-Line Database Retrieval Services

America Online, CompuServe, DIALOG, Dow Jones News/Retrieval, Learning Link, and *Prodigy* are just a few of the many national and local examples of on-line database retrieval services. Here we will take a closer look at some of the services offered by DIALOG Information Services, but information about other services and about educational telecommunications in general may be found in many publications including the special issue of *Electronic Learning* on telecommunications prepared by Gwen Solomon (1992), director of New York City's School of the Future.

DIALOG information services

DIALOG Information Services has built over 350 databases with current information on just about any topic under the sun. DIALOG's *CLASSMATE* is one of several classroom instruction programs (CIPs) designed for schools K– college which make the contents of on-line databases available for information retrieval at flat-rate prices. The databases cover the gamut of information services from news to full text sources. There are, for example, over 1,100 full-text publications easily available on-line; extensive coverage from regional, national, and international press; continuously updated news wires for late-breaking stories; and special sources for business, tax, medicine, and technology.

Solomon (1992) has developed an excellent guide to telecommunications for teachers in which she explains the classroom role of a service such as *CLASSMATE:* "The *CLASSMATE* program," Solomon notes, "provides schools easy access to references from over [three] hundred sources including popular magazines, research journals, and specialized data bases. Students can retrieve information in such subjects as agriculture, the sciences, news, environment, medicine, psychology, and education. Teachers can get curriculum materials and guides for directing student activities on-line."

DIALOG Information Services provides special daylong teacher training workshops (*Teach the Teacher*) at a nominal charge and sends out frequent updates on new services available to schools. *DIALOG* is available 24 hours a day, so students can tap into this resource from home if they have their own computer connected locally to their school's network.

It would be interesting to visit a school one hundred years from now to see teaching and learning take place. Although skeptics would say that schools have not changed much over the last 500 years, there is little doubt that the computer as a catalyst for change has already transformed a few schools that have committed to innovative teaching methodologies and learning systems. The communications technologies described in this chapter will further enhance the impact of computers in schools. Will these become the norm? What will be the future in schools? In the Do Something About It section at the end of the chapter, you are invited to discuss this topic with your classmates or colleagues.

11.4.3 Teaching and Learning from Remote Sites

The number of organizations providing on-line programming for education is increasing by leaps and bounds. Joining Shelly Weinstein at the meeting of the U.S. Senate subcommittee on the Role of Telecommunications Technologies in Education (referred to earlier in this chapter) were John Kuglin, 4th-grade teacher at Cold Springs Elementary School in Missoula, Montana, and Kay Abernathy, instructional technology specialist for the Beaumont, Texas, independent school district.

Cable in the classroom

John Kuglin takes full advantage of communications services offered by his local cable company to augment the learning experience of his 4th graders. TCI Cable is one commercial cable company that makes programming drawn from a wide range of cable channels available to schools for use in the classroom. Schools that take advantage of the free service are sent a printed schedule of the times and subject matter of specially prepared commercial-free blocks of programming on the following channels: A&E, C-Span, CNBC, CNN, Court TV, the Discovery Channel, ESPN, the Family Channel, the Learning Channel, Mind Extension University, PBS, and the Weather Channel.

On CNN, for example, a 15-minute summary of the previous day's world news is shown at some off-peak hour (usually early morning). The program is called "CNN Newsroom." John Kuglin is one of many teachers who daily (to be more precise, nightly) make a copy of the 15-minute segment for use in class.

TCI Cable not only prepares the program, the company also has teachers on the payroll who daily prepare a four-page set of materials for lesson plans. These materials are available on-line via the telephone system (Kuglin has a modem on his computer to enable him to connect to the telephone network). Every morning at 8:00 John calls the TCI Cable-maintained, electronic bulletin board system to download a copy of the teaching materials onto the printer attached to the computer in his classroom. The first order of business in his classroom everyday is the showing of the "CNN Newsroom" report accompanied by discussion and related learning activities.

Kay Abernathy was invited by the U.S. Senate subcommittee to describe the Texas Education Network, a distributed computer system that provides local access to a wide range of on-line educational services and material, including the various network services available through the Internet. Nodes for the network have been established in 15 major metropolitan centers and toll-free lines have been set up so that educators outside the local calling area can access the system.

Telephones have also been installed in every classroom in order to "connect our students to the community and the community to our students." The *TransParent School* model thus has competition, though the Betty Phillips Center for Parenthood Education welcomes all the help it can get in achieving the goal of making parents an intrinsic component of the education equation.

The training for the teachers is managed hierarchically and coordinated over the Texas Education Network. The Texas Education Agency has been responsible for the intensive preparation of 40 trainers who represent the school districts throughout the state. These trainers train other trainers at the local level; the local trainers are responsible for training the teachers in the schools, and working with them on an ongoing basis at the grassroots level.

All the schools in Abernathy's school district also take advantage of TCI Cable's cable in the classroom described previously.

11.4.4 Collaborative Learning

Distance learning provides an opportunity for collaboration between teachers and students at elementary and secondary schools and those in higher education. Mangan (1992) cites the experience of the Selma Middle School in Selma, Indiana, "which has been much more involved with nearby Ball State University since the two formed a networking partnership with support from the Ball Brothers Foundation." According to Donald Black, the principal of Selma, "We sit out here in the middle of the Midwest, but we're able to access all over the world. We think this will bring a global classroom to us."

Collaborative learning is not a new concept. Teachers have always encouraged students to work together on learning projects in recognition of the practical and motivational value of peer tutoring and intellectual teamwork. Computer networks are by no means necessary for collaborative work; but they do add an extra dimension to it, enabling collaboration across local, state, national, and international boundaries. A growing number of schools are involving students in intercultural exchange over networks such as those associated with the Internet and the many other on-line networking services.

Foster (1992) describes the National Geographic Kids Network, which was designed, written, and tested at the Technical Education Research Centers (TERC) in Cambridge, Massachusetts, and which enables children to collaborate internationally. He goes on to describe primary schools (in the United Kingdom) that collaborated to write a book with the assistance of an "author-in-residence who picked up [each school's] successive chapters on electronic mail and passed the parcel, duly tied, to the next school."

Foster (1992) describes another program funded by the UK Microelectronics Education Support Unit and IBM, where special needs children were linked around the country. "Chatback encouraged these children to quiz their grandparents, or people of that generation, on what it was like 'in the olden days' and to report to each other by e-mail." The children prepared their reports off-line, which gave them the opportunity to get help when necessary. The children gained self-esteem and confidence from the fact that their audience had no preconceptions about them. "For many, it was a unique experience to be proud of their work."

Groupware

Closely following the proliferation of systems for team-based computing in business and industry, computer hardware and software manufacturers and vendors are now making similar systems available for schools. Called **Groupware,** the systems foster collaboration between students for learning projects of all kinds and in all content areas. Students linked by a network are able to work simultaneously on a piece of writing, for example. Or they might log on to brainstorm on some topic related to material they are studying. The groupware takes care of all the interactive communications back and forth, the capture and storage of material developed in a groupware session, and the screen displays, which are divided to allow each user to see the work contributed by the others in the group while at the same time enter his or her own data.

Technology and Learning (February 1992) outlines a threefold rationale for introducing groupware in schools.

- A growing body of research suggests that collaborative learning is an effective model. There is even evidence that children learn better when collaborating with others than when they learn alone.
- Collaborative work in schools will help to foster interpersonal skills in students. In chapter 14, we will discuss the 1991 report issued by the U.S. Department of Labor Secretary's Commission on Achieving Necessary Skills (SCANS), which spells out the competencies and foundation skills required of workers in tomorrow's labor force. Among them are these interpersonal skills: they must know how to work on teams, teach others, serve customers, lead, negotiate, and work well with people from culturally diverse backgrounds.
- The last rationale is based on the fact that networked computers are becoming the norm in schools, as explained earlier in this chapter. Therefore, groupware can have a viable place in the instructional environment in schools where such networks have been installed.

Looking Back

Naisbitt (1982) describes his high-tech/high-touch formula as the balancing act between the introduction of new technology and "a counterbalancing human response." Naisbitt's intent is to show that the counterbalancing human response (the high touch) is often a reaction against increased implementation of new technology (high tech). But, as discussed in chapter 3, it is as often the case that the heightened human response is an natural complement to new technology. This is especially true of C&C in schools. By putting parents, teachers, and students in touch with each other and with the local and global community, high-tech C&C is extending the reach of education to the high-touch benefit of all.

In this chapter, we have examined the impact of C&C in education, and the conclusion is inescapable that this technology is becoming an integral part of both educational administration and of the learning process itself. It is anticipated (Network World, 1992) that, by 1998, 80% of all personal computers will be networked, as opposed to the 35% networked in 1992–1993. Although this figure pertains to across-the-board PC use, educational environments are undoubtedly due to experience the same change in the configuration of the possibly millions of new systems purchased between now and 1998. And as the new systems are set up alongside the old, a need will arise to integrate the old systems with the networked machines for the purposes of file sharing, communications, integrated learning, and so forth.

As Schmall (1992) points out, institutions that increase the quality of services such as networking "should not lose sight of what [these improved services] cause in terms of user's rising expectations." Once people get a taste for easy and rapid access to others in particular and to on-line services in general, they will quickly reach the point where they will be unable to do without such services. Schools will be obliged to provide network access to all teachers and administrators rather than incur the wrath of those who would otherwise be left out in the cold.

The strains put on computer networks to meet these rising expectations can easily result in performance degradation when the system is pushed to its limits. This is a sufficiently common phenomenon for networks to have sometimes been facetiously named "notworks"! However, if the most common problems associated with networked computer systems arise from overuse, is this not compelling justification for their implementation in schools?

Looking Forward

It is fair to say that teachers today have much going for them. Teacher–pupil ratios are better than ever, education is beginning to be recognized for its central role in preparing children for the Information Society, and the very fabric of education is changing as technologies such as C&C take hold. Computers and related technologies are also transforming the traditional concept of multimedia. Teachers are beginning to have available to them a wide range of audiovisual aids and electronic teaching tools. Given time and training, teachers will learn how to incorporate these new tools into the way they teach, and into the way students learn.

In the next chapter, we will examine the concept of multimedia, along with the equipment that goes to make up a modern, computer-based multimedia classroom. The very entity "multimedia classroom" is, of course, a moving target. New technologies will be introduced which will make what is available today seem anachronistic. But, as will be shown, multimedia has already reached a level of maturity that makes it a powerful application in the classroom. We will conclude part III of this text by examining multimedia in the context of what is being done in some model schools in the United States.

Do Something About It: Exercises and Projects

1. Log on to one of the national or international networks from your college computing center, look around the system, and establish e-mail contact with some of your friends, colleagues, or whomever you can find.

2. How soon, if ever, do you think it will be before it is normal for K–12 students to attend class from home? In your lifetime? Sooner than we think? Will this be beneficial to the student? Under what conditions might it be successful? Are social structures in the United States capable of supporting an educational paradigm that accommodates distance learning of this kind? Would it be more viable with some age groups than with others?

3. Might the time come when a fair proportion of a student's interaction with a teacher will be electronic ("videotronic") in a distance learning mode? What would this imply for the schools for the future?

4. Research the various bulletin boards available for teachers. Be sure to look at the costs of the services as well as the connect costs. Compile a list as a class.

On line with Horton: A telecommunications unit

by Kay Rewerts, Waterloo Community Schools, Waterloo, Iowa

Background

Kingsley Elementary in Waterloo, Iowa, is a building that includes three teachers who are always willing to try something new. These teachers—Linda McCausland, media specialist; Jean Bengfort, second grade; and Linda Blau, fifth grade—wanted to get their students involved with telecommunications and whole language, but wanted their first experience to be in a safe environment.

They decided to try a project within their building using FrEdMail (Free Educational Mail). Having their first project be confined within the building would allow them to support each other as they worked through the process of teaching students about telecommunications while they learned at the same time. They felt this would be a good way to "get their feet wet" with people they knew and trusted.

The pilot project was scheduled to last one month, from Thanksgiving break to winter break. The time frame was established to increase the likelihood that the project would stay on schedule.

The intent of the teachers was that, after trying this unit, they would, if successful, approach teachers in other parts of the state and country for joint telecommunications projects.

Technology Considerations

The access to FrEdMail at Kingsley is through a modem in the media center. The e-mail messages were sent to the main board at night and received back in the building the following morning. The software they used was *ProTerm,* which would allow them to enter the messages on *AppleWorks* and import them for sending.

Objectives

The objectives for their unit were:

1. To use letter writing as a form of communication in a whole language unit.
2. To study characterization.
3. To utilize peer coaches in a cooperative learning format.
4. To introduce electronic mail as a communication mode.

Kay Rewerts, author of the cast study
Photo courtesy Kay Rewerts

Methodology

The focus of the project was a letter-writing campaign to Horton the Elephant (from the book *Horton Hatches the Egg* by Dr. Seuss, Random House, 1940). The letters would be written by second graders, then sent by e-mail to a class of fifth graders who played the role of Horton the Elephant. The fifth graders wrote responses to the second graders' questions and e-mailed the responses to them.

After the second graders heard the story as a part of an animal unit in reading and language arts, they discussed Horton as a character. Then they brainstormed questions to ask Horton before actually writing the letters.

The students dictated their letters to a teacher associate who typed the letters using the word processor in *AppleWorks.* Their questions focused on physical characteristics of the baby as well as on Horton's feelings.

At the same time, the fifth graders were reading the book and discussing characterizations. They brainstormed characteristics of Horton and possible answers to questions the second graders might ask such as: Was the baby a boy or a girl? (a boy) What did Horton name the baby? (Horton, Jr.)

(continued)

Case Study 11 (concluded)

Teacher reviewing the collection of Horton stories
Photo courtesy Kay Rewerts

Collaborative Learning

The fifth graders were concerned that their answers should read as if Horton had actually written every one of the letters, so they all needed to write in character. These students had been using *AppleWorks* for over a year and were comfortable with typing their own letters.

During this time, the media specialist trained peer coaches in order to introduce the students in both rooms to the procedures necessary for successful telecommunications. The coaches were then responsible for helping the other students in their class as they sent and received messages.

In order to practice with the technical part of the unit, the media specialist would send messages to the second graders, telling them to check their mail or saying that Horton was waiting for their letters. In one letter, Horton explained that, with his large feet, there might be errors in his typing. The fifth graders then started writing their own teaser letters to keep the second graders interested while they finished the answers and practiced sending messages through FrEdMail.

When the letters from Horton finally appeared on-line, the media specialist videotaped the second grade class as they watched the large-screen monitor and received a printed copy of their letter and Horton's answer. The video was later shown to the fifth grade class so they could see how enthusiastic the second graders were with their letters from Horton.

One near disaster was averted when a brother heard his sister discussing Horton at home. The quick thinking of the older sister allowed her to explain that she knew so much about Horton because they had met on a field trip several years ago! That was the only snag in the project.

Both classes went on to telecommunicate with other classes in the district and throughout the nation.

Talk About It

Topics for discussion based on the case study.

1. Discuss the logistics of setting up a telecommunications project for the first time in one building where the teachers know each other and, alternatively, in multiple buildings where the teachers have met only through telecommunications. What would be the differences in these situations? What challenges would need to be overcome in each setting?

2. In groups, brainstorm other possible first-time telecommunications projects that would guarantee success for all involved. Share with the group.

3. The Horton project involved fifth graders and second graders working together on writing and communication assignments. What do you think is the value of this collaboration? How might you set up a similar collaboration in your own school?

4. Find other books appropriate for the level at which you teach that would work for a project such as Horton. Describe how you would use the book in a telecommunications project.

References

Barnhart, Barry, David Dunlop, John Kerrigan, Kenneth Mechling, Donna Oliver, Terry Olivier, Thomas Pavelchek. An Update on Pennsylvania's ITEC Project. *T.H.E. Journal,* vol. 19, no. 11, June 1992, pp. 53–58.

Bauch, Jerold. Personal correspondence with the author, July 9, 1991.

Bigge, Maurice. *Learning Theories for Teachers.* 4th ed. New York: Harper & Row, 1982.

Birnbaum, Joel S. Toward the Domestication of Microelectronics. *Communications of the ACM,* vol. 28, no. 11, 1985, pp. 125–135.

Bradner, Scott. The Internet: Why Now? In *Network World,* vol. 10, no. 39, September 27, 1993, p. 20.

Currid, Cheryl. In the "good old days," issuing a memo could take a good week. *InfoWorld,* vol. 14, issue 38, September 21, 1992, p. 81.

DeBalko, Jeff. There is More Than One Perfect E-Mail Package for Every Network. *InfoWorld,* October 26, 1992, p. 59.

Fersko-Weiss, H. Electronic Mail: The Emerging Connection. *Personal Computing,* vol. 9, 1985, pp. 71–79.

Foster, John F. Collaboration: Of Missionaries and "Microids." *T.H.E. Journal,* vol. 19, no. 6, January 1992, pp. 62–65.

Kurshan, Barbara, Tina Dawson. The Global Classroom: Reaching Beyond the Walls of the School Building. *Technology and Learning,* vol. 12, no. 4, January 1992, pp. 48–54.

Lewis, Peter H. Plugging Into the Network. *New York Times,* March 1992.

McCarthy, Robert. Decisions, Decisions: What Computers Should You Buy? *Electronic Learning,* vol. 11, no. 5, February 1992, pp. 18–24.

Mangan, Katherine S. Computer Networks Help Public Schools Forge New Ties with Higher Education. *Chronicle of Higher Education,* September 9, 1992, p. A17.

Naisbitt, John. *Megatrends: Ten New Directions Transforming Our Lives.* New York: Warner Books, 1982.

Network World. *Worth Noting.* Data based on study conducted by Market Intelligence Research Corporation, Mountain View, CA, November 23, 1992.

Newsweek. *Omni Group Supplement on Office Automation.* May 1986.

Parent Involvement Report. What Is the TransParent School Model? *Parent Involvement Report,* vol. 1, no. 1, Winter 1992, p. 1. (a)

Parent Involvement Report. 120,000 Calls at Matilija. *Parent Involvement Report,* vol. 2, no. 1, Fall 1992, pp. 1–2. (b)

Schmall, Eric. Dealing with Users' Rising Expectations. *Network World,* November 23, 1992.

Selfe, Cynthia. The Humanization of Computers: Forget Technology, Remember Literacy. In *Dialogs, Reading and Writing in the Disciplines,* Jeffrey Carroll, ed. New York: Macmillan, 1992.

Shannon, Claude E., Warren Weaver. *A Mathematical Theory of Communication.* Urbana: University of Illinois Press, 1949.

Solomon, Gwen. The Most Complete Guide Ever to Telecommunications. *Electronic Learning,* vol. 11, no. 6, March 1992, pp. 19–211.

Technology and Learning. Groupware Goes to School: New Tools to Promote Group Activity and Learning. *Technology and Learning,* vol. 12, no. 5, February 1992.

U.S. Congress, Office of Technology Assessment. *Power On! New Tools for Teaching and Learning.* OTA-SET-379, Washington, DC: U.S. Government Printing Office, September 1988.

The Voice. Pennsylvanians Continue to Give Teachers and Local Schools Good Grades. *The Voice,* publication of the Pennsylvania State Education Association (PSEA), December 1992, p. 3.

Educational Multimedia

I hear and I forget. I see and I remember. I do and I understand.

Chinese proverb

In time I will utter the truth of my plight.
I will remember the people who helped me.
I cannot do this without help.

*Autistic child
(communicating via computer-based technology)*

The business of education is not to make the young perfect in any one of the sciences, but so to open and dispose their minds as may best make them capable of any, when they shall apply themselves to it.

John Locke (1632–1704)

As far as education is concerned, the term **multimedia** has been used to describe audio-visual teaching aids (AVAs) since some 20 years before computers found their way into classrooms. The modern version of the term differs only insofar as it includes a richer set of AVAs such as scanners/digitizers, videodisc[1] players, and CD-ROM drives that require the use of computers to coordinate their incorporation into teaching and learning activities. Sometimes the computer in question may be a general-purpose desktop computer; other times it may be a special-purpose handheld device such as a remote control for an interactive videodisc system.

In this chapter, we will examine all aspects of the modern concept of multimedia. The chapter will cover:

- The concept of computer-based multimedia
- The physical components of multimedia
  - Data capture devices
  - Data storage technology
  - Data output devices
- Hypermedia systems: Bringing it all together
  - Hypertext
  - The future with hypermedia
- Model schools
  - Room 405 Brookhaven Elementary School, Placentia, California
  - Spring Mills Elementary School, Waterford, Michigan
  - West High School, Columbus, Ohio
  - New American Schools Development Corporation
  - Are model schools a good idea?

■ᴙ 12.1 Introduction

A medium is "an intervening agency, means or instrument, by which something is conveyed or accomplished." (Webster's, 1991). The plural form of medium is *media,* which, in the context of education, includes any of the means used to convey instructional subject matter: chalk and talk, slide projection, video projection (film and tape), visual projection of printed material (as with an epidiascope),[2] sound systems (a record player, radio), and combined sound and video systems (television, video cassette recorders, and computer-based learning systems).

Two centuries ago, the term *media* was first applied to newspapers (Webster's, 1991). By the 1920s, it had come to be used as a singular noun to describe any means of mass communication and advertising. Today, it is usually applied only in this context.

---

[1] Also called laserdisc.

[2] Also known as a visual presenter.

Figure 12.1
Multimedia in the classroom
Photo courtesy IBM Corporation

The term *multimedia* was introduced in the 1960s to describe the combined use of several media, such as films, video, and music. Today, *multimedia* has become closely associated with the computer-controlled, instructional delivery systems that are the subject of this chapter.

12.1.1 The Importance of the Senses in Learning

You will notice that all of the media discussed above target either the eye or the ear of the student. Of the five human senses, vision is recognized as the most powerful data-acquisition device for the brain. Edward Tufte (1990), a professor of statistics and graphic design at Yale University, explains why the most effective presentation methodologies attempt to convey information visually, rather than verbally alone. "Visual displays of information," he says, "encourage a diversity of individual viewer styles and rates of editing, personalizing, reasoning, and understanding. Unlike speech, visual displays are simultaneously a wideband and a perceiver-controllable channel."

The terms *wideband* and *channel* come, of course, from the science of communication. A wideband channel carries more information at higher speeds. A visual display is an example of a wideband channel, carrying more information at higher speeds than simple speech. A visual display is also "perceiver-controllable" in the sense that the person doing the viewing can absorb the data by scanning it at a speed and in a sequence that most naturally fits that person's mental makeup.

Speech, on the other hand, though it is a powerful medium for communication when used by skilled speakers, is not as easy to digest as visual imagery. Plain text in general, and speech in particular, require more effort to follow because less information is conveyed at a slower speed, thus requiring more concentration and extrapolation on the part of the listener. Describing a house verbally will take a lot longer and will be less effective than describing the same house by showing some pictures of it.

Of course, the senses of touch, smell, and taste are powerful learning media, too. The signals that are transmitted to the brain by the touch of a snake's skin will quickly dispel misconceptions of sliminess usually derived from a purely visual experience of these beautiful creatures. This is why good teachers intersperse speech with illustrations and mix verbal presentations with active, hands-on learning methodologies. The younger the audience, of course, the more important are these other sensory vehicles for learning.

12.1.2 Audiovisual Aids

The common term used for the teaching aids that bring media other than speech into the learning equation is *audiovisual aids* (AVAs). The name implies that such aids are only audial or visual, but, in fact, AVAs include tactile, gustatory,[3] and olfactory artifacts. Many chemistry, physics, or biology experiments are good examples of AVA use that are accompanied by interesting other-sensory experiences considered crucial to the success of a lesson. Dramatic reenactment and the use of samples in class have always been part and parcel of a good teacher's box of pedagogical tools for arousing curiosity in young minds.

All teachers recognize the need to make the effort to design their lessons around traditional electronic and nonelectronic AVAs. But few teachers have the luxury of exclusive use of machinery such as VCRs and high-resolution monitors, let alone multimedia units with their computers, CD-ROM drives, videodisc players, scanners, and so forth. Some schools have personnel whose job is to take care of the equipment, coordinate its use, make sure it is where it should be as per the schedule, and return it to the AVA center after it has been used. But such schools are the exception rather than the rule; most teachers have to do this for themselves.

Usually, a great deal of planning and coordination is involved in using electronic AVAs. If special equipment is required, one must plan well ahead, reserve the equipment, and integrate its use into lesson plans. Assuming the equipment is in working order when it is scheduled to be used, it must be set up before class begins, and disassembled and returned at the end of class in case other teachers have scheduled use of the same equipment.

---

[3]Pertaining to taste.

This is all very well if one is teaching three or four classes a day, nicely spaced out with more than ten-minute breaks in between. But most K–12 teachers are lucky if they have one free period each day. It is understandable that there is no great rush to use electronic AVAs in view of the logistical nightmare involved. Instead, most teachers rely on a predominance of verbal subject matter presentation, with sporadic and dubiously effective use of the chalkboard.

This is not to disparage the chalkboard. As a free-form, ad hoc visual aid, it takes some beating and will continue to be a feature of classrooms for some time to come. Mocsny (1987) reminds us just how versatile a teaching tool the chalkboard is. "Walk into any [classroom]," he says, "and observe the chalkboard. Less than half the scribblings can be represented directly by ASCII[4] characters. Instead, one sees a freewheeling set of sketches, graphs, equations, symbols, arrows, etc. The skilled instructor throws it all up there while conducting a [class]."

The traditional chalkboard is, thus, unlikely to be replaced by technology. But it has been *improved* by technology. Electronic chalkboards, commonly used in business environments, accept free-form, hand-drawn text and graphics, and have the added feature that the user (teacher or student) can download a copy of the contents to a printer, rather like a facsimile (fax) machine.

The computer will not supplant traditional AVAs any time soon, but the computer can bring an extra dimension to AVAs in the form of computer-controlled media. A teacher who has access to videodisc technology to coordinate the use of various media—text, images, motion video, speech, sound in general (including music)—in one easily accessible format is going to use that format rather than put up with the fuss of setting up and using a disparate set of AVA equipment. There is still an important premium on careful lesson preparation, of course, but teachers who have had the opportunity to use a multimedia system for themselves have quickly recognized what an empowering tool it is, as much for themselves as teachers as for their students.

As teachers, they appreciate how easy it is to find and incorporate exciting visual and auditory material into their lessons on an interactive basis. Teachers are finding that they can respond audiovisually to the ad hoc reactions and interactions of the students. More to the point, these teachers are finding that their students are able to develop exciting learning materials themselves by way of multimedia project work. As any teacher knows, the best way to learn a skill or concept is to teach it to others. By the same logic, the best way for students to learn is by having the opportunity to prepare materials for presentation to others.

So, teachers are, indeed, voting with their feet. If they are given a realistic opportunity to use multimedia in the classroom, they are doing so. Let us examine why this is the case. We will begin by discussing the concept of multimedia. Then we will proceed to examine the basic components of multimedia systems. After that, we will look at the concept of hypermedia, which combines multimedia with hypertext as a methodology for nonlinear data access and presentation. Finally, we will examine the concept of model schools, which have successfully experimented with technology-rich learning environments, including the use of multimedia.

---

[4]You may recall that ASCII (the American Standard Code for Information Interchange) is a system for representing characters (text and other symbols) in the 1s and 0s of computer language so that they can be stored inside the machine. Appendix A lists the complete set of codes.

Figure 12.2
Students using IBM
Ultimedia equipment
for projects
Photo courtesy IBM
Corporation

12.2 The Concept of Computer-Based Multimedia

As explained in the introduction, teachers have always employed many means to capture children's attention and thus promote learning; as such, multimedia, interpreted broadly, is nothing new. Nor is it reserved to human learning processes. The first time any thinking animal used something other than symbolic utterances, such as sounds to demonstrate an intellectual concept, multimedia was born. When a tyrannosaurus rex, for example, reared on its powerful hind legs and roared thunderously at an aggressor, it was using multimedia: the medium of sound and the medium of mime. The same is true when a bird of paradise displays its plumage while it emits a mating call.

It is human intelligence, demonstrated by a superior ability to conceive and communicate ideas, that raises us above other animal species. To paraphrase Shakespeare, what a piece of work we are!—"how noble in reason! how infinite in faculty!"[5] Yet, with all our intelligence, we rely on very basic tools to express the ideas conceived in the brain. As

---

[5]Hamlet to Guildenstern, William Shakespeare's *Hamlet,* 1602, Act II, Scene II, c. line 300.

Wurman (1989) observed: "There are only three means of description available to us—words, pictures, and numbers. The palette is limited. Generally the best instructions rely on all three, but in any instance one should predominate, while the other two serve and extend. The key to giving good instructions is to choose the appropriate means."

In the classroom, teachers and students alike rely on words, pictures, and numbers to convey ideas. These are the basic tools of intellectual expression. But there are many ways in which words, pictures, and numbers can be conveyed. The concept of multimedia encapsulates these many ways—full motion video, still images, text, and sound—in which words, pictures, and numbers can be delivered for the purpose of conveying meaning. The concept also encapsulates the machinery used to store, edit, project, and transmit the data that are the raw material of ideas.

12.2.1 Multimedia Has Added a New Dimension to the Process of Teaching and Learning

Multimedia has allowed educators philosophically to escape the concept of education as a regimented experience, just as C&C and distance learning, which we studied in the previous chapter, have allowed educators philosophically to escape the concept of the closed classroom. Students who are given access to multimedia learning platforms,[6] whether as individuals or in groups, can take control of their own learning, constructing knowledge at a pace and in a direction that suits their needs and wants.

Amthor (1991) expresses this idea in compelling terms when he writes:

Twice a day, 180 days a year, millions of American young people get on a bus and travel between home and school. Each day, the bus travels the same labyrinthine route through neighborhood after neighborhood. Yet, if you ask students to retrace that route on their own, they might not be able to do it. They were just along for the ride.

The process of learning is more than a passage through new territories. Engagement is crucial. Without true interaction, without a sense of "self propulsion," learning cannot occur. But give students a map—and the power to make decisions and follow their imaginations—and their natural curiosity will have them circling the globe.

For the most part, as pointed out in Bruder (1991), "homegrown approaches in classrooms around the country have become the unofficial testing ground for multimedia—with positive results. Stories abound of ultra-motivated students and rejuvenated teachers working interactively, manipulating and creating projects, [and] producing concrete examples of things they have learned."

12.2.2 Multimedia Authoring Tools

Coordinating the graphics, video, animation, text, speech, and sound in the development of a multimedia presentation is no easy task. For this reason, authoring programs have been developed to assist people in this task. Mann (1992) describes how Marty Colletti developed a three-hour multimedia application to train her company's customer service trainees. The system replaced what previously involved trainees in 20 hours of reading time. A

---

[6]Multimedia as a learning environment includes the thousands of educational software subsumed under the title of CAI (discussed in chapter ten).

multimedia application thus "unites multimedia's pieces" (Mann, 1992), letting the learner cut quickly to the heart of a subject matter. As they say: "An image is worth a thousand words."

Colletti used a multimedia authoring tool called *IconAuthor,* marketed by AimTech Corporation. Authoring tools that are more common in educational circles are *HyperStudio*™, *HyperCard*™, and *QuickTime*™ for the Apple Macintosh; and *Linkway*™ and *Linkway Live!*™ for IBM systems. More powerful (and expensive) tools include Macromedia's *MacroMind Director* and *AuthorWare Professional,* which run on both Apple and IBM platforms. The case study at the end of this chapter describes applications involving *HyperCard* and *QuickTime.* In chapter 13, we will discuss the process of developing multimedia applications, and, in that context, we will take a closer look at these authoring tools.

12.2.3 The Need for Standards

One final observation is in order before we look more closely at the various components of multimedia systems. Typical of most new technology, the marketplace has quickly proliferated with hundreds of multimedia products from many companies without any consideration for compatibility between products. This applies not only to the hardware itself, but, worse still, to the formatting methodologies used for data compression and transmission. One system will use one formula for compressing the data so that it takes up as little space as possible on transmission lines and in secondary storage; another system will use some other formula. The result is that the two systems cannot transfer data between each other without an intermediary system to convert the data back and forth from compressed to normal mode.

According to Jenks (1992), this situation may be close to resolution since the U.S. Department of Defense has developed a new standard for multimedia systems as a whole, including hardware and software. The standard, called 1379D, "defines common technical requirements for interactive video playing and editing systems. Though still incomplete, the standard appears to be emerging as a baseline requirement for systems to play multimedia productions mixing voice, video, graphics and text."

It is now time to examine each of the specialized components of a multimedia system.

12.3 Physical Components of Multimedia Systems

In an earlier chapter, we discussed what one parish in Lake Charles, Louisiana, has decided are minimum requirements for a classroom multimedia system. Figure 12.3 illustrates the equipment configuration that Deirdre Foreman, the social studies supervisor, plans to eventually install in all the social studies classrooms in Calcasieu Parish.

The systems in Foreman's schools, along with the teacher training that has accompanied their introduction, have been funded by an earmarked percentage of local sales taxes. Teachers are not forced to get involved with the scheme, but most have been eager to start incorporating the concept of multimedia into their curricula. To date, roughly half of the 80 social studies teachers in the parish have their own multimedia system, and the other teachers are on a waiting list. Meanwhile, Calcasieu teachers in other disciplines and working with all age groups K–12 are introducing computer-based technology for computer-managed instruction, computer-assisted instruction, distance learning, and multimedia.

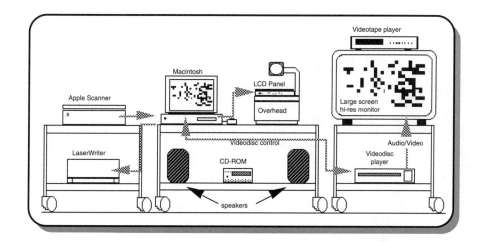

Figure 12.3
Multimedia platform
used in Calcasieu
Parish high school
Illustration courtesy Diedre
Foreman

A multimedia system thus differs from a basic computer system in that it adds to the computer-based learning experience the dimension of computer-controlled integration of images (still photos or artwork); full motion pictures (actual footage or animated graphics), and sound for purposes of teacher/student interaction. A multimedia system thus includes all the components of a basic computer system—the computer itself, a monitor (ideally color), hard and floppy disk drives, a printer (which should be high resolution with color capability), and a mouse. As we saw in chapter 11, the truly computerized classroom will also have a telephone and a modem.

But several other specialized components give the technology its name, *multimedia.* Figure 12.4 illustrates a purpose-built multimedia platform designed by Multimedia Design Corporation. Such a system has the advantage of including all the necessary components, along with wiring and connections, in one convenient, easy-to-move cabinet. Another example of purpose-built multimedia furniture is the lectern designed by Nova Office Furniture, Inc. (see figure 12.5). The ergonomic design tucks both the monitor and the overhead projector, along with its LCD panel, into an adjustable recess below desktop level so that it does not clutter the desk or obstruct the view of students in the class.

In the sections that follow, we will focus on the specialized components of a system such as those illustrated in figures 12.4 and 12.5.

12.3.1 Data Capture Devices

Scanners

Scanners are used to digitize flat (usually paper-based) images or text so that they can be stored and manipulated by a computer. They can be either handheld or flatbed machines.

In chapter 6, we discussed the process of digitizing. You may recall that this process converts data—typically images (pictures, documents, and so on) or sound (speech, music, and so forth)—into the digital 1s and 0s of machine language. The process is electronic and we do not need to concern ourselves with the technicalities of how the images and sounds are digitized. But it is important to understand why the digitization of data is so valuable to us.

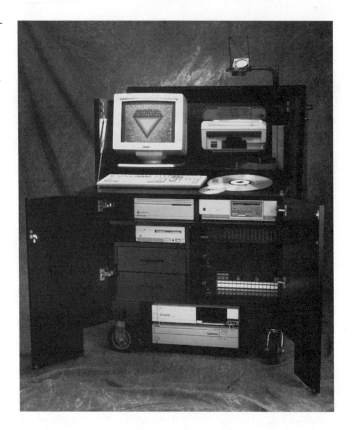

Figure 12.4
An all-in-one
multimedia platform
Photo courtesy Multimedia
Design Corporation

Figure 12.5
Nova's electronic
lectern
Photo courtesy Nova
Office Furniture, Inc.

a

b

Figure 12.6
(*a*) With the help of
one of Hewlett-
Packard Company's
scanners, information
existing in a variety of
forms can be
accessed and used
by customers at any
time. (*b*) Scanners
such as the Complete
PC half-page scanner
can also be
handheld.
(a) Photo courtesy of
Hewlett-Packard
Company; (b) Photo
courtesy BOCA Research

Financial managers like to talk about "leveraging" the value of an investment. They might advise you to make a relatively small investment in this or that stock or venture in the hope of making a high return. In the same way, we use a lever when we want to use a small amount of effort to move a large object. Leveraging, in other words, helps us get the most out of what we possess, whether it be money or strength—or data. The fact is that, once data have been captured in digital form, their value can be leveraged more effectively than if they remained undigitized. This concept warrants further explanation; perhaps a specific example will make it clear.

For example, you organize a class project to put together a monthly newsletter. You tell your students that you want to include their photos alongside the articles they write. The photos the students bring to class will usually be on paper, developed from a negative. The only way such photos can be used in the newsletter is by physically pasting them into the text. If this means they have to be cropped to make them fit, they cannot be un-cropped. If the students working on the newsletter decide to move things around, they would have to un-paste the photos and hope that they would not regret having cropped them in the first place, and so on, and so forth. Photos and other pictures on paper are thus awkward to work with because they are inflexible.

If, on the other hand, you collect your students' photos and scan them into the computer, they become digitized and, as such, they can be duplicated, cropped, restored, moved, enhanced, dubbed, and otherwise manipulated and saved on disk in any of myriad edited versions. The value of the photos has thus been *leveraged* in an infinite variety of ways—without detriment to the originals. The digitized student photos are much more useful because they are in a much more flexible format.

Scanners are either intelligent or dumb

An intelligent scanner is able to scan text, for example, and differentiate one character from another so that the text can be converted directly from the printed page into a word-processor file. The technology used to do this is called **optical character recognition (OCR).** Intelligent scanners are very useful for companies like banks and information service agencies, in general, who need to capture massive amounts of text based on paper transactions like checks and forms.

A dumb scanner simply digitizes a page as if it were a whole image. It makes no attempt to differentiate one part of the page or image from another. As far as a dumb scanner is concerned, a page of text is the same as a student's photo. As one can imagine, the job of a dumb scanner is much less complex than that of an intelligent scanner. For this reason, intelligent scanners generally cost more than dumb scanners. But, for multimedia purposes in schools, dumb scanners serve most needs.

Audio and video digitizers

Like scanners, audio and video digitizers convert analog (continuous) sound and video into the digital 1s and 0s of machine language so that they can be stored and edited in the computer. Once again, flexibility is the major advantage of this process. Sound, for example, can be recorded in digital form, then cleaned up once it has been digitized by removing unwanted "noise." This is one reason why CDs are able to produce such pure sound.

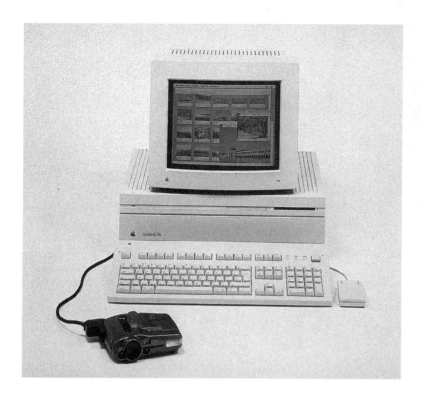

Figure 12.7
Canon's RC-570 still
video camera
Photo courtesy Canon
U.S.A., Inc.

Video cameras and still-image cameras

Video cameras are useful for recording events of interest in many subject areas. After the recording has been made, it can be digitized using the video digitizer, so that it can be stored in the computer. Once in the computer, the video can be edited more easily and commentary added, along with music, and so forth. These are challenging tasks for which students will likely need assistance. A resourceful teacher who has little or no experience in video production can contact local television stations for expert support. Remember, the teacher is the facilitator of learning, not the fount of all knowledge. Once teachers learn to step back and delegate rather than control, students will have more opportunity to exercise resourcefulness and to learn by doing, which is the best kind of learning.

Perhaps a team of students has decided to research some aspect of life in the local community. Perhaps a class has been given the project to record a field trip to some place of historical, ecological, scientific, ethnic, or other interest. A school might have different groups of students every week prepare a half-hour news show. To be effective, the video and other material assembled for such projects must be carefully designed, directed, and scripted, much like any movie. These activities greatly benefit students because they require, and develop, creativity, problem-solving skills, and communication skills.

A still video camera, such as Canon's RC-360™ and RC-570™ systems, which superceded the Xap Shot™ camera, is a useful tool for capturing still images in a form that can be edited in a computer. A still video camera is just like any other camera except that

Figure 12.8
Music in education
Courtesy Yamaha
Corporation of America

it captures the picture in digital form on disk instead of on a roll of film. This picture can then be shown immediately on a television screen, or transferred to a computer for incorporation into word-processed documents. Canon's cameras can store up to 50 pictures at a time. The pictures can be erased and replaced with other shots without the delay and expense of film processing and developing.

Students and teachers might use such a camera for projects that involve the production of printed reports of all kinds. In the Do Something About It section at the end of the chapter, you will have the opportunity to further discuss audio, video, and still video technology.

Electronic music keyboards

Electronic music keyboards are another useful adjunct to a multimedia system, especially if the teacher or one or more of the students in the class has learned to use the keyboard. Modern electronic keyboards can be programmed to provide tempo, beat, harmony, timbre, and other musical features that make even the most inexperienced or untalented of players sound good.

Once again, an audio digitizer can be used to convert the music output to digital form for storage and editing on the computer. Many interesting exercises can revolve around the musical features of multimedia systems. These include music composition and tuition, which is the focus of some excellent CAI software such as *The Miracle Piano Teaching System* by Software Toolworks.

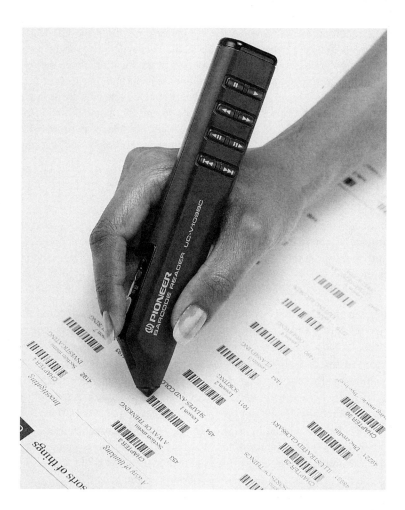

Figure 12.9
Bar codes enable the teacher to quickly access a specific image or video sequence during the lesson
Photo courtesy Optical Data Corporation (photo Carmen Natale)

Bar code readers

Imagine you are giving a lesson on the American Revolution. You have a multimedia system turned on and in position for the class to see. In one hand, you have your lesson plan; in the other, a wireless (remote control) handheld, bar code reader.

At various points in the lesson, you plan to show artwork, video clips, and photos of original documents as AVAs, so you have positioned the appropriate bar code at each of those points in your written lesson plan (or you are using a lesson plan already designed to accompany the videodisc or CD-ROM disc). When the time comes to activate each AVA, you scan the bar code with the pencil-like bar code reader and immediately, without any fuss, the AVA—a still image or video clip—is displayed on the large-screen monitor. The image is high quality, the sound is crisp and clear, the lesson comes alive.

The bar code is exactly the same as those to be found today on every item sold in stores. The black and white stripes stand for 1s and 0s (sounds familiar?). The bar code reader shoots a beam of light at the bar code. Black stripes absorb the light, so there is no reflection; this will be recorded as a 1 (one) in the computer controlling the CD-ROM drive or videodisc player. White stripes reflect the light; this will be recorded as a 0 (zero). The combination of 1s and 0s makes up the address of the location where the artwork, video clip, or photo is stored on the disc you plan to access during your lesson.

Optical Data Corporation's *Lesson Maker*™ software enables teachers to produce their own bar-coded lesson plans from scratch. The bar code and the handheld, wireless bar code reader mean that integration of the technology with the lesson is practically seamless. Even teachers who cringe from technology are immediately impressed with the ease of use of bar code access to audiovisual material.

12.3.2 Using Copyrighted Materials

It will be useful here to consider again the problem of copyright, which we first discussed in the context of software piracy in chapter 5. When scanning published text and images in order to incorporate them into other media such as newsletters or video clips, schools in the United States are covered, in general, by what is known as the doctrine of "fair use." According to Samuelson (1993), four factors are involved in the fair use doctrine:

1. **What is the purpose of using the copyrighted work?** If your use of the material is for the purposes of nonprofit teaching, you may not be infringing copyright as long as you do not abuse factor 3 below.

2. **What is the nature of the copyrighted work?** Copying artistic work of various kinds is usually more legally sensitive than copying instructional material ("factual works"). But teachers are hardly likely to be sued on this account if they act within the constraints of the other three factors of the fair use doctrine.

3. **What is the amount of work copied in relation to the copyrighted work as a whole?** If a teacher copies whole chunks of texts—say, several chapters—and, without permission from the author, hands them out to students, this could well be seen as an infringement of copyright. Software is a case in point. When you copy software, you copy the entire work. Schools that make unlicensed copies of software for use by students are obviously violating the fair use doctrine.

4. **What effect does the use of the copyrighted work have on the potential market for that work?** Artists, composers, photographers, and writers of books or software devote years of effort to their creations. Their work may be their only means of livelihood. If copying undermines that potential, it stands to reason that this would be an infringement of the fair use doctrine.

12.3.3 Data Storage Technology

CD-ROM and interactive videodisc

The only significant difference between interactive videodiscs[7] and CD-ROM discs is size. Interactive videodisc usually uses a 14″ platter to store the data; CD-ROM uses a

---

[7]Note the spelling of *disc*—with a "c." Laserdiscs are spelled with a "c"; electromagnetic disks (floppy disks and hard disks) are spelled with a "k."

Figure 12.10
Videodisc in use in
the classroom
Photo courtesy Optical
Data Corporation

4″ platter. Both use laser technology to make still and full-motion images and text, including multilingual sound tracks, available for integration with other curriculum materials and incorporation into lesson plans. Today, CD-ROM is becoming more and more the norm in school-based computer systems because of its smaller size which makes it easier to handle and build into the computer hardware.

There is a growing number of videodisc/CD-ROM titles available for purchase and use in schools. Optical Data Corporation, founded in 1981, is one of the longest established companies in this field. Their best known product is probably *The Living Textbook*. This is a series of archival, interactive multimedia libraries covering the earth and physical sciences for use at the middle, secondary, and college levels. The full package includes the interactive videodisc volumes that contain the thousands of photographs, diagrams, text frames, narrated movie clips, an Image Directory which is a catalogue of each volume's contents, plus bar coded lesson plans and recommendations for student activities. *Windows on Science* is another of Optical Data's multimedia products.

Schools in Texas were among the first in the United States to be able to select products such as *The Living Textbook* and *Windows on Science* as an alternative to traditional textbooks, thanks to enlightened leadership in the Texas Education Agency.

12.3.4 Data Output Devices

Speakers

If the quality of the audio output that is built into the computer system that controls the multimedia system is unsatisfactory, it is a good idea to add external speakers. This inexpensive enhancement can make an appreciable difference to the quality of the multimedia experience.

Figure 12.11
Overhead display
panel in use with a
class
Photo courtesy InFocus
Systems

Overhead display panels (LCD panels)

Often there will be situations where the computer alone will be used to display material to a large class group. A teacher may want to demonstrate software, or display data sets, or display graphics developed from data sets, or display work such as word processing which is the product of group collaboration. In such situations, the small size of the computer screen makes it impractical when working with more than one or two people at a time.

Overhead display panels such as In Focus Systems' *PC Viewer*® are designed to sit on top of a standard overhead projector for the display of the contents of a computer screen on a large overhead screen.

Overhead display panels are also called **LCD panels** because the technology used to display the data in the panel is *liquid crystal display,* hence the acronym. As color monitors become the norm for classroom computers, the best LCD panel will be one that can

Figure 12.12
Touch-screen
interaction with a
multimedia system
Photo courtesy Jostens
Learning Corporation

project the contents of color as well as monochrome monitors. Products such as *PC Viewer*® include software to help in the development of polished presentations. Screens can be programmed to dissolve smoothly from one to the other, and ideas can be bulleted and presented one by one.

The computer is the ideal vehicle for preparing lesson outlines with their accompanying illustrations. Once the materials are on the computer, they can be displayed directly onto the overhead screen under the teacher's or student's control. Needless to say, student presentations will also benefit significantly from this technology. Teachers tend to shy away from the use of overhead transparencies on an overhead projector for several reasons, not least because they are bulky and awkward to use. If a multimedia system is available in the classroom, the overhead transparency, though still an option, takes a backseat to computer-generated displays.

Touch screen systems

Voice recognition and touch screen systems can motivate students because of the intuitive nature of the interaction. Jostens' *Learning* takes advantage of this facility in its *InterActiveMedia*™ system (figure 12.12).

Large-screen, high-resolution color monitors

The monitor is naturally at the heart of a multimedia system. Indeed, one can say that the quality of the monitor affects the quality of the entire system. No matter how powerful the computer is, or how extensive the collection of laserdiscs, or how super the sound system, if the images displayed on the TV screen are not large enough or crisp enough, the impact will be impaired.

Ideally, the monitor/receiver should be at least 25″ (measured diagonally from, say, the lower left corner to the top right corner of the screen) with a screen resolution of 640 pixels by 480 pixels at the low end, and 1024 pixels by 768 pixels at the high end. You may recall from chapter 7 that pixels are picture elements or dots on the screen. The more pixels your screen can individually paint, the higher the resolution and the greater the precision of the image displayed.

12.4 Hypermedia Systems: Bringing It All Together

Goldfarb (1991) describes **hypermedia** as "the union of two information processing technologies: hypertext and multimedia. Hypertext information is accessed in more than one order. Multimedia information is communicated by more than one means." **Hypertext** information can be accessed only by using a computer, whereas multimedia information can be accessed in many ways, including the use of computer-controlled systems such as videodisc players and CD-ROM drives. Let us examine these concepts more closely.

12.4.1 Hypertext

Hypertext systems are intricate webs of connected electronic data, rather like the neural network that we call the brain. When we think, we often rely on associations to direct us along the path that represents the development of our ideas or train of thought. The more experience and learning we have absorbed in the past, the more associations we will be able to draw on—hence the value of education. A hypertext system is designed in such a way that the user can jump from one data item to the next in a semi-random, *nonlinear,* order. This contrasts with the traditional start-to-finish, *linear* order in which we tend to work our way through a data source such as a book, a video, or a piece of music.

Early hypertext systems were purely text-based. The on-line database was comprised of publications or other textual materials, and the associations or links were bound to words and phrases. The user would select a set of characters from a passage that was being read and instruct the system to find more material related to the selected text. The system would then conduct a rapid search of the entire database and either list the locations where items of related interest could be found for the user to choose from, or inform the user that there was no other text associated with the selection.

12.4.2 Hypermedia

With modern hypertext systems, the user has nonlinear access to a large database of multimedia material—text, still images, full motion video, speech, music, and sound in general. This is the origin of the term *hypermedia.* The database contains what Goldfarb calls "webs" of links, each of which is connected hierarchically or by association with top level links found in the base (or "hub") document(s) in the system.

Many modern, on-line multimedia encyclopedias are, in fact, examples of hypermedia databases. The user selects an item for study and, in the course of the study, may want to delve more deeply into a related topic, which is linked to a video clip, diagram, photo,

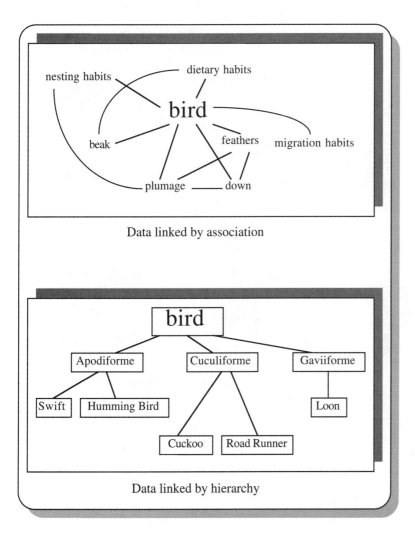

Data linked by association

Data linked by hierarchy

Figure 12.13
Data can be linked
hierarchically or by
association.

and so forth. Following by association, the user might be drawn to tangential information on a voyage of discovery which, like that of Columbus, may not end up at the originally intended location.

Speaking of Columbus, IBM's Ultimedia systems include the videodisc titles *The Illuminated Books and Manuscripts* and *Columbus: Discovery and Beyond.* Both hypermedia textbooks link a rich selection of audiovisual materials on subjects that span the curriculum within the context of the selected area of study.

Columbus: Discovery and Beyond taps the expertise of 60 of the world's leading authorities on Columbus and his times. As might be expected, the knowledge base is comprised of all forms of sources of information—video interviews with the authorities, text from historical documents, dramatic reenactments, and links to both loosely and closely connected text-, graphics-, and video-based background material.

Figure 12.14

IBM's *The Illuminated Books and Manuscripts* links pictures, sound, and text with the click of the mouse button.

Photos courtesy IBM Corporation

a

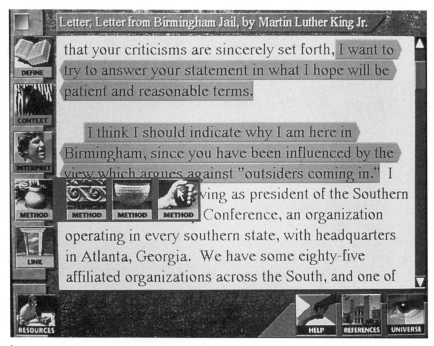

b

Figure 12.15
IBM's *Columbus:
Discovery and
Beyond*
Photo courtesy IBM
Corporation

The system represents a social studies teacher's dream come true. As the creator, Bob Abel (1991), points out: "If you think of the project as a play, Columbus himself would appear only in Act II. Act I would star the Greeks and Romans, and Act III would star those explorers who came after Columbus—up to and including the students of today." Students interact with the system, determining for themselves the pathway that they will take through the knowledge base. They can use the authoring software that accompanies the system to develop projects/presentations of their own, drawing on the audiovisual and textual material to meet their academic needs.

12.4.3 The Power of Hypermedia

If you have seen this technology in use, or, even better, if you have had the opportunity to use it yourself, you will undoubtedly agree that it is a powerful medium for teaching and learning when used appropriately from a pedagogical standpoint. The sense of wonder is a great motivator for learning. "Men love to wonder," said Ralph Waldo Emerson, "and that is the seed of science." When teachers describe some facet of the world, they try to do so in an interesting way; they want to engage the student audience; they want students to remember what they have said; they want students to remember the lesson that is to be learned.

Hypermedia systems meet all these pedagogical goals. Tufte (1990) quotes the photographer Garry Winogrand, who said: "There is nothing as mysterious as a fact clearly described." Pictures and sound can bring to life any verbal description, which is why novelists use simile and metaphor and every artifice to make their characters leap out of the pages of their books. Hypermedia systems, which make the selection and presentation of audiovisual material easier, more flexible, and more extensive than ever before, challenge teachers to employ strategies for teaching and learning which will engage the students' sense of wonder.

We learn a lot with our eyes. As Tufte (1990) observed, the human eye registers 150 million bits of information at a glance. This compares very favorably with a 35mm slide, which contains just 25 million bits of information. In other words, we have an extraordinarily capable visual acuity. Tufte goes on to point out that we are capable of digesting complex sets of data when they are presented visually, provided, of course, that the presentation is well designed. "High information displays," he explains, "are not only an appropriate and proper complement to human capabilities, but also such designs are frequently optimal. If the visual task is contrast, comparison, and choice—as so often it is—then the more relevant information within eyespan the better."

Hypermedia systems are an ideal application of Tufte's ideas since they bring within eyespan a whole world of knowledge entirely at the discretion of the interactive learner. Wilson (1991) describes the value of hypermedia in the educational process when she writes:

> The adults of tomorrow will need to be skilled at accessing, filtering, and managing such multidimensional [multicultural and multisensory] information. And they'll need to be able to reflect on it, question it, and customize it for their needs.
>
> To do this well—to succeed in the information age—interpretive skills such as problem-solving, creative thinking, and a sense of open inquiry are becoming more important than ever. As the complexity of life and work compounds and the boundaries blur between the educational process and life beyond school, abilities such as coping with multiple points of view, working with others, and conflict resolution will become ever more central. As educators, we'll have to treat these skills as key educational goals.

12.5 Model Schools

Let us conclude part III by looking briefly at what happens when teachers are given the time, training, and logistical and technical support to produce "break the mold" schools that incorporate into their curricula the computer-based teaching and learning technologies and methodologies that have been profiled in the last several chapters. The following projects were implemented in the latter half of the 1980s and are representative of the many other schools where a serious commitment has been made to integrating the computer into the curriculum.

12.5.1 Room 405 Brookhaven Elementary School, Placentia, California

As reported by Connie Zweig (1985), Room 405 in Brookhaven Elementary School, Placentia, California, was transformed in 1985 into a prototype classroom, in what the school district superintendent described as "a deliberate decision to create a preferred future." Needless to say, even this affluent school district could not do it without help. The hardware and services were provided free of charge by AT&T. National Information Utilities and Pacific Telesis have provided support. The initial installation was also supported by $50,000 from a district fund set aside for technology acquisitions. A further $500,000 was budgeted for the year following installation in order to purchase additional equipment.

The classroom was refurbished from the ground up, starting with sound-absorbing carpet and cushioned swivel chairs. An AT&T computer sat on every desk. A satellite dish brought in current affairs and educational programming for display on the large-screen television hanging from one corner of the room. Parents were considered an integral part of this classroom of the future. A modem at home gave them access, via their television sets and telephone lines, to data about their children's attendance and homework. They also had two-way communication with the teacher using e-mail, as well as access to an on-line Times–Mirror database and news service to which the school subscribed. The home was, thus, directly involved along with the school in "the responsibility for learning."

The classroom was established as a prototype so that the school district could experiment with a technology-infused classroom and learn from the experience for future implementations of technology in the district's existing and new schools. Margaret Herron, Brookhaven Elementary principal, believes that "if students are engaged with computers, a teacher can be free to give instruction at an individual pace. . . . students will end up with more personal contact rather than less."

12.5.2 Spring Mills Elementary School, Waterford, Michigan

Carol Klenow and Janet Van Dam (Klenow, 1991) describe the Teaching and Learning with Technology (TLT) project funded in 1987 by the Oakland Schools, an intermediate school district serving the 28 local school districts within Oakland County, Michigan. One classroom in each of the third, fourth, and fifth grades at Spring Mills Elementary School was transformed into a "technologically-rich environment" with, at the third-grade level, one computer for every three students, and, at the fourth- and fifth-grade levels, one computer for every two students. Each classroom was also equipped with interactive videodisc players, large-screen video monitors, CD-ROM drives, and telecommunications capability.

Teaching staff members were trained and support was provided by staff from the Oakland Schools, though the latter were present mostly in a facilitative role in order to "observe the changes in teaching and learning that might occur in this new environment while being responsive to teachers' needs."

Particular emphasis was placed on student achievement in writing, though outcomes demonstrated benefits across a broad spectrum of educational experience. Evaluation of the project took the form of "an inferential approach combining classroom observation, interview data and self-report to reveal the characteristics of the teaching-learning process in technology-rich environments."

Statistical analysis of data taken during each of the three years of the project showed an increasingly significant difference in writing achievement between the TLT and non-TLT students. But there was also a "dramatic shift" by the TLT students away from games or drill and practice-type software toward more tool-based use of computers for activities such as word processing, telecommunicating, and artwork.

The project, which is profiled elsewhere in this text, has been successful largely because the project leaders ensured that teachers were well trained and supported throughout the experiment. Even so, teachers did not consider the training sufficient, though they recognized the quality and value of the training they had.

There were several interesting, and sometimes unexpected, outcomes from the project.

- Curriculum change was initiated from the bottom up by what teachers and students were doing in the classroom, instead of being controlled from on high.

- Teachers tended to collaborate more in technology-rich teaching environments. To quote the Executive Summary of the Evaluation Report (Klenow, 1991): "Teachers within the TLT project found it valuable to share ideas, set common goals and assist each other when technical problems arose. This support network now extends to other teachers within the school and district. The TLT project empowered the teachers as change-agents and they are working with other change-agents to achieve common goals."

- The idea was reinforced that "technology will not change a teacher. It will, however, make a good teacher better because it revitalizes both the teacher and the profession."

- The project led to the conclusion that student use of computer technology should emphasize how the technology can be used to promote learning "across a wide variety of tasks and projects," rather than on learning about the technology itself.

- Interdisciplinary teaching and learning, such as writing across the curriculum, was more likely in technology-rich environments.

- Students, empowered by technology, became the center of the learning process and were more likely to assume responsibility for their own learning.

- Technology facilitated "a process and project approach to teaching and learning" because it put into the hands of learners tools for rapid access to, and manipulation of, in-depth knowledge conveyed in a multiplicity of media: text, still images, motion pictures, and sound.

As is happening all over the United States, educational technology in the Oakland Schools' 28 school districts is becoming all-pervasive, and, in the Oakland Schools experience, at least, the model school project has acted as an important springboard for more broadly based action leading to change.

12.5.3 New American Schools Development Corporation

Salpeter (1992) describes the genesis of the New American Schools Development Corporation (NASDC). This corporation was set up in 1991 in response to President Bush's call for help in creating the New American Schools proposed in his America 2000 plan. By 1995, 535 schools, one for each U.S. congressional district, will have been selected to become "break-the-mold" schools designed to further the goals of America 2000. Each school will receive $1 million in seed money to implement the design.

Table 12.1 lists the six goals of America 2000, the attainment of which will further the overall goal of preparing young U.S. citizens for the kind of technological and information-based society envisaged in the 21st century.

Table 12.1	**The Goals of America 2000 (Bruder, 1992)**

1. All children will start school ready to learn.
2. The high school graduation rate will increase to at least 90%.
3. Students will leave grades 4, 8, and 12 having demonstrated competency in English, mathematics, science, history, and geography; every school will prepare students for responsible citizenship.
4. American students will be the first in the world in math and science achievement.
5. Every adult will be literate and possess the knowledge and skills necessary to compete in a global economy and to exercise the rights and responsibilities of citizenship.
6. Every school will be free of drugs and violence and offer a disciplined environment conducive to learning.

The NASDC is responsible for overseeing the competitive planning and design phases of the project. The New American Schools that result from the winning designs must be no more costly to run than "comparable conventional schools."

A useful discussion for preservice or in-service teachers would be to draw up a plan for a New American School in their own neighborhood. In what ways would such schools be different from traditional schools? How would they "break the mold"? What part would technology play in the design? This discussion is offered as one of the exercises in the Do Something About It section at the end of the chapter.

12.5.4 Are Model Schools a Good Idea?

Salpeter (1992) poses three questions about the NASDC plan outlined in the previous section.

1. Will a New American School designed around the six goals of America 2000 be able to "break the mold" of conventional schooling? Are not the goals, especially #3 regarding basic subject competencies, too restrictive?
2. Is it fair to expect a New American School to "operate on a budget comparable to conventional schools"?
3. Will it be possible to model future schools on the New American Schools that will emanate from the gung-ho teams selected to develop those "break the mold" designs?

To some extent, these questions have already been answered in the affirmative by the model schools profiled above. Salpeter, too, is optimistic and, when it comes down to it, we have no choice but to strive after the very reasonable goals of America 2000. With the help of soundly integrated educational technology, students will attain competency in the five core subject areas and have time left over to pursue more personalized interests. There is every likelihood that, in well-managed schools, technology will result in cost savings that will enable the schools to operate within the budget of conventional schools. Poorly managed schools will waste money whether or not they are technology-rich. Finally, we must hope that the schools selected for the project will have presented designs which are replicable in mainstream America.

Technology and Learning (November/December 1992) asked eight educational technology leaders to give their opinions on the value of the NASDC model-schools approach to innovation. As one might expect, there were valid arguments for both sides of the debate. On the plus side, it seems there is a place for model schools, just as there is a place for models in the design of architectural and engineering structures. No matter how expensive the models are to build, they will be cheap at the price if they provide a resource for the development of more generalized systems.

Janet Van Dam, coordinator of computing and technology for the Oakland Schools in Waterford, Michigan, should have the last word on this topic of model schools.

> When we planned our first model in 1986, it was a real risk. Oakland Schools is a regional
> service center and our county has 28 school districts. The idea of spending a lot of money in one
> of them raised many equity questions. But we took the risk and it paid off. In Oakland County,
> we liken our approach to the agricultural extension model. You plant seeds in different settings
> with different growth enhancers, and once you see which conditions work best, you try
> duplicating them in other areas. We used that approach to set up a model technology and writing
> project in an elementary school. It has now been replicated in six other schools. They haven't
> copied exact pieces, but they have incorporated what was learned at the model site—and have
> considerably changed the way they operate as a result. Without heavy intervention in one place
> that would never have happened." (*Technology and Learning,* November/December 1992)

◾ Looking Back

This chapter has argued that multimedia, even though it does not remove the need for careful lesson planning, takes much of the hassle out of using AVAs, especially when the teacher has exclusive use of the multimedia system. Recognizing this, many school systems in the United States are now adopting multimedia programs as textbooks. For the 1992-93 school year, the Utah State Textbook Commission, for example, joined an increasing number of states accepting this practice.

Texas was the first state to do this. As early as 1987, the state amended the law to encourage the adoption of what are referred to as Electronic Instructional Media Systems. The 1991 Progress Report (Texas Education Agency, 1991) noted that "school districts seem to be embracing this alternative to a traditional textbook to a greater degree than expected." As of the writing of the report, the agency "projects that *Windows on Science*[8] will be in use by approximately thirty percent of the elementary teachers in Texas, who will be using this videodisc-based program as the primary delivery system of instruction."

The Texas Education Agency has made an admirable commitment to long-range support for technology use in schools. Fortunately, Texas is by no means unique. Model schools and school districts worldwide are leading the way.

We can learn from them by reading about them, by attending conferences where their representatives present feedback from their experience, and by visiting these schools in order to see for ourselves what can be achieved. American education is a sleeping giant that appears to be on the verge of waking up. Let us hope so, for if the giant sleeps much longer, it may wake up to a world that has passed it by.

◾ Looking Forward

In part III, we discussed the range of applications of computer-based technology in schools. In part IV, we will examine ways in which schools can control their own destinies with regard to teaching in the computerized classroom by creating their own applications, and raising their own funds to support expensive technology projects.

As already discussed, giving computers to students before giving them to teachers is like putting the cart before the horse—it is definitely not the way to foster the best kind of computer use in schools. No matter how sophisticated computer-based learning systems become, children will always need the teacher as director/manager of the learning process. Therefore, the teacher must first be given the opportunity to understand and appreciate the impact that computers can make.

---

[8]*Windows on Science* is a videodisc-based program for elementary science developed by Optical Data Corporation.

Successful applications of computer technology occur in environments where planning and design are supported by leadership at all levels and informed by experience. The best leaders empower their associates. When schools initiate technology projects, those responsible for overseeing the projects should call on all available expertise from the bottom up, as was the case in the Oakland schools in Michigan. Without commitment at all levels, from the teachers on up, attempts at innovation will fail. As Becker observed in *Technology and Learning* (November/December 1992), "people generally forget about a key element to success: 'buy in' on the part of teachers and administrators."

This empowerment of those involved at all levels of an organization is a practice promoted in the concept of quality control circles long advocated by Americans Dr. W. E. Deming and J. M. Juran (Berger, 1986). The idea is that the people with direct hands-on involvement with a project are the ones best placed to monitor and influence the quality of the end product. Deming and Juran's ideas, promulgated during the 1950s, fell on deaf ears in America; however, they found a receptive audience in Japan, a country struggling to recover from the devastation of World War II. Twenty years later, Japan was emerging as a leading industrial power. By the end of the 1980s, America was reeling in the face of relentless Japanese competition. The name of the game was quality brought about by empowerment of the people closest to the production of the end product.

In the case of schools, the end product is the education of students. Teachers are closest to the students, so they are best placed to monitor and influence the quality of the educational process with the students' best interests at heart. Teachers, therefore, must be empowered: given the time, the tools, the training, and the support they need. Without this empowerment, teachers cannot be blamed if the schools fail to meet stated educational goals. When, however, they are empowered by leadership in these real terms, teachers can use the resources provided by technology to become the facilitators of quality education, putting students in control of their own learning and thus empowering them in their turn.

■ Do Something About It: Exercises and Projects

1. Working with a group of your colleagues or classmates, brainstorm to draw up a list of useful applications of audio, video, and still video digitizers for the K–12 school environment.

2. Draw up a plan for a New American School to be established in your neighborhood following the guidelines laid down in the goals of America 2000. In what ways would your school be different from traditional schools? What part would technology play in the design?

3. Investigate the availability of videodiscs in your county either at the public library or in your school district's media services. Draw up a list of the checkout procedures and what types of subjects are available.

4. Instead of a traditional book report or term paper, explain how you would present the material electronically in a multimedia approach.

5. Do a reference search electronically at your university or public library. Then redo the search using a traditional card catalog and note the time difference and difficulties related to the two different approaches.

6. Discuss the differences between XapShot (Canon's RC-360 and 570) still video technology versus 35mm photography. List the advantages and disadvantages of both and describe projects that would be best suited to each.

The magic of multimedia
by Sandi Agle, Franklin Park Magnet School, Fort Myers, Florida

A Commitment to a Hands-On, Multisensory Approach

If the ideal multimedia "heaven" could be envisioned in a K–5 classroom setting, there would be a combination of powerful desktop computers (Apple Macs, IBM PCs/clones, Commodore Amigas) interactively connected to videodisc players, television monitors, camcorders, optical scanners, music synthesizers, Xap-Shot cameras, and so on, all linked together by powerful developmental software such as *HyperCard* or *Linkway* and *Linkway Live!*

This multimedia ideal is what the new Science-Technology-Environment-Math Magnet school in Lee County, Florida, ascribed to when formulating its purchase orders for equipment.

It has long been recognized in elementary education that a hands-on, multisensory approach is the best way to reach the broadest range of students. To this end, Franklin Park Magnet School aspired to create a multimedia "experience" for students in a classroom setting. In so doing, we hoped to create proactive learners by giving students tools that immediately satisfied their creative curiosity and allowed them hands-on manipulation of their technological environment.

In the Classrooms

Each teacher has been provided with an electronic teaching center, or workstation. The computer workstation is comprised of an overhead projector and LCD (liquid crystal display) projection panel, which allows full classroom orientation. Individual stand-alone, student computer stations have also been distributed to each classroom.

In the Computer Labs

One room has been established as a computer lab with 30 computers dedicated to the Jostens Integrated Learning System. Here, upper primary students receive individualized instruction in the Jostens lab weekly.

The lower primary grades have been provided with an IBM lab that features the *Writing to Read, Stories and More* and *Write to Write* learning systems.

Across the Campus

Electronic mail (e-mail) has been provided throughout the school, giving staff and students immediate access to shared information and ongoing communication. The school is currently in the process of routing a *Localtalk* Apple network in the media center to the main e-mail file server, which will allow all personnel and students to access the media center's electronic card-catalog system.

Multimedia Machines: CD-ROM

In addition to the computers, high on the list of hardware purchases for every classroom were CD-ROM drives. Franklin Park Magnet students have found CD-ROMs an invaluable source for research, training, reference, and storage of graphics and clip art.

Use of these read-only drives, which allow access to discs that can contain more than 600 megabytes of information, is rapidly increasing in schools, with prices plummeting to the affordable level. In addition, more and more content vendors such as LucasMedia and National Geographic are producing the software needed in a variety of subject areas.

Our most widely used CD-ROM is Grolier's *Electronic Encyclopedia.* The 21 volumes of the printed text
(continued)

Sandi Agle, author of the case study

Students using Grolier's multimedia encyclopedia
Photo courtesy Sandi Agle

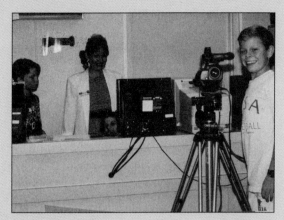

The production team for "FPM News"
Photo courtesy Sandi Agle

take up only 20% of the capacity of a CD-ROM disc. There is a line daily in the media center for the Grolier stations, where students use research and study skills to solve multifaceted research projects in a fraction of the time normally required for such extensive searches.

Interactive Videodisc

Other valuable multimedia tools are level 3, interactive videodisc players. Because of the easy manipulation of the medium, teachers are able to individualize lessons and give special attention to subjects of their own choosing. Recently, I watched our Science Resource teacher use a *HyperCard* application to demonstrate a technique while showing clips of related material from *Windows on Science* from Optical Data Corporation.

Digital Photography

Digitizing still-video images from Canon's Xap-Shot camera and using them in *HyperCard* stacks is a favorite pastime of my after-school team of students who have dubbed themselves "Technology Techs." The days of putting together 35mm slide shows for our end-of-the-year program are over since we purchased six of these marvelous cameras.

As pictures are taken, they are stored on a computer disc that holds up to 50 shots. These shots can then be transferred to videotape or digitized into the computer. Franklin Park Magnet uses the *Computer Eyes*™ hardware/software and video spigot package to enable this transfer.

Mr. Spielberg, I Presume!

What *Computer Eyes* does for still photos, *QuickTime* does for full motion video and animation. *QuickTime* allows the Macintosh user to display, compress, create, edit, and store video clips without other special hardware. I have presented it to students as MTV on a Mac and they love it!

"FPM News" is broadcast each morning live from our school's television studio, which is controlled by a Commodore Amiga enhanced with a Video Toaster by Newtek. This powerful machine enables students to put together professional shows with video fades and wipes or special effects that dazzle and delight. Its equivalent would be over $100,000.00 worth of professional video and editing equipment.

Teams of fifth-grade students rotate each week between the jobs of sound technicians, camcorder personnel, **(continued)** or news anchors. Recently, we implemented a new feature on the program called "Mystery Staff Baby photo," with the help of our trusty Xap-shot cameras and the Video Toaster. The students took still-video shots of faculty baby photos and aired them daily on our news show. Clues were given as to the identity of the faculty member and a prize was awarded at the end of the week to the winner who guessed correctly.

Our after-school Technology Techs are presently working on a Video Toaster project that will superimpose live student images over captured still video to give the illusion that the students are inside the illustrations of books. A voice-over then completes the narration and a super storytelling video or play can be produced for our kindergarteners.

Bringing the World to the Student and the Student to the World

Telecommunication through modems is another alternative learning experience. Our fifth graders have had "computer penpals" in Russia. They shipped out a videotape of Franklin Park Magnet School to their "unseen communicators." The tape was student-produced exclusively on the school grounds with camcorders and Xap-shot images.

In the future, these students will be using similar computer tools, not paper, to disseminate information. By the year 2000, it is predicted that the ability to use computer technology to solve problems and enhance productivity will be a requirement of any job description.

We cannot send students out into the job market with 1950s skills and expect them to survive. We must teach children to be independent learners and researchers, and multimedia use is the answer to opening this world of information to them.

You know, the bell rings at the end of the day at Franklin Park Magnet and my Technology Techs moan and groan as I pull them off projects and send them reluctantly home. And as for me? Well, I come to "work" each day with a smile and the knowledge that I am really teaching students to reach their full potential and preparing them for the exciting times that lie ahead.

Talk About It

Topics for discussion based on the case study.

1. How has the role of librarian evolved to that of media specialist?

2. What would be the advantages and disadvantages of a reference search on a CD-ROM of Grolier's *Encyclopedia* versus the printed textbook set?

3. How could the use of videodisc technology enhance a classroom setting?

4. What advantages would be provided in a school that has access to an e-mail system for faculty?

5. Should e-mail be implemented for student access?

6. If you had access to a modem and could telecommunicate anywhere, how would you use this tool in a classroom?

■ References

Abel, Bob. Columbus: A Multimedia Sweep of History. In *Multimedia: State of the Art, A Special Supplement to Technology & Learning,* sponsored by IBM, 1991, pp. 4–6.

Amthor, Geoffrey R. Interactive Multimedia in Education: Concepts and Technology Trends and Model Applications. In *IBM Multimedia Supplement to the T.H.E. Journal,* September 1991, pp. 2–5.

Berger, Robert W., David L. Shores. *Quality Circles: Selected Readings.* New York: Marcel Dekker, 1986.

Branscum, Deborah. Conspicuous Consumer. *Macworld,* September 1992, pp. 83–88.

Bruder, Isabelle. Multimedia: How It Changes the Way We Teach and Learn. *Electronic Learning,* vol. 11, no. 1, September 1991, pp. 22–26.

Bruder, Isabelle, Herbert Buchsbaum, Maggie Hill, Louise C. Orlando. School Reform: Why You Need Technology to Get There. *Electronic Learning,* vol. 11, no. 8, May/June 1992, pp. 22–28.

Goldfarb, Charles F. HyTime: A Standard For Structured Hypermedia Exchange. *Computer,* August 1991, pp. 81–84.

Jenks, Andrew. A Familiar Refrain: The Search For Standards. *Systems Strategy,* September 24, 1992.

Klenow, Carol, Janet Van Dam, Rebecca Rankin. *Teaching and Learning with Technology: Executive Summary of the Evaluation Report.* Oakland Schools, MI: Division of Information Resources, 1991.

Mann, Mary. Software Unites Multimedia's Pieces. *PC Week,* April 20, 1992, p. 95.

Mocsny, Daniel. Aren't Graphics Necessary? *Byte,* February 1987, p. 186.

Salpeter, Judy. Funding Available for Groups Interested in Designing New American Schools. *Technology and Learning,* vol. 12, no. 4, January 1992, pp. 46–47.

Samuelson, Pamela. Computer Programs and Copyright's Fair Use Doctrine. *Communications of the ACM,* vol. 36, no. 9, September 1993, pp. 19–25.

Technology and Learning. Special Section on Speaking Out. vol. 13, no. 3, November/December 1992, pp. 60–61.

Texas Education Agency. *A Progress Report on the Long-Range Plan for Technology of the State Board of Education.* Austin: Publications Distribution Office, 1991.

Tufte, Edward. *Envisioning Information.* Cheshire, CT: Graphics Press, 1990.

Webster's. *Random House Webster's College Dictionary.* New York: Random House, 1991.

Wilson, Kathleen. New Tools For New Learning Opportunities. *Technology and Learning,* April 1991, pp. 12–13.

Wurman, Richard Saul. *Information Anxiety: What to Do When Information Doesn't Tell You What You Need to Know.* New York: Bantam Books, 1989.

Zweig, Connie. California Elementary School Experiments with Classroom of Future. *Christian Science Monitor,* December 16, 1985.

p a r t

No Problems, Only Solutions

357

13

Creating Computer Applications for Education Environments

The most important method of education always has consisted of that in which the pupils were urged to actual performance.

Thomas Alva Edison (1847–1931)

It's the software that's hard.

Michael Crichton (1942–   )

Trained and experienced teachers should be the best people to create computer applications for use in schools. They have studied education theory and methodology. They have applied what they have learned in the classroom. They understand what will work and what will not. However, most practicing teachers have neither the time nor the inclination to get involved in the development of applications software for computer-based learning. This is understandable enough. Planning, designing, and implementing such applications demands an enormous amount of effort on the part of even technically skilled and motivated teachers.

Fortunately, for the most part, teachers do not need to create their own educational software. One of the fastest growing segments of the computer-related market is comprised of companies such as Claris Computer Corporation, Microsoft Corporation, or Symantec, which develop general productivity and utility software for computer users. Much of their software has application in schools. Then there is a growing number of companies such as Sunburst, Intellimation, MECC, New Media, Scholastic, Brøderbund, Optical Data Corporation, and Cambridge Development Laboratory, to name a few, that specialize in the development of software and systems for the K–12 education market.

But it may be interesting to preservice or in-service teachers to know something of what goes into the planning, design, implementation, and support of software systems. Not only will it help them appreciate the effort involved, but it will also help if and when they either start to develop their own applications using authoring software, or need to advise students engaged in similar endeavors.

In recent years, relatively straightforward development tools called authoring systems have been introduced to simplify the task of constructing learning systems. This chapter will examine two of the better known systems, though it is beyond the scope of this book to teach the reader how to work with them. Readers whose appetite is whetted by this introduction will be advised to acquire from the companies themselves any one of several on-line tutorials and demonstration disks, as well as printed tutorials.

Here is the outline for this chapter.

- Why should teachers learn about software development?
- Characteristics of quality educational software
- How can teachers get involved?
    - Templates and productivity software
    - Authoring systems

■ 13.1   Introduction: Programming Is Hard

Teachers in K–12 schools are not expected to develop computer software from the ground up. After all, this is a tough proposition for a professional software engineer. Indeed, it is accepted in the software development industry that no program is free of errors, or, to put it another way: "Bug-free software is an oxymoron" (Meyer, 1992). Gleick (1992), while noting the importance of the software industry to the American economy, almost in the same breath reminds us that "bugs are its special curse."

The fact is that programmers are human. They develop systems that are recognized as being the most complex that have ever been built (Olson, 1985). Even what appear to be simple programs such as word processors or spreadsheets may today have close to a million instructions. The software designed by AT&T to control its latest electronic switching system has over 25 million lines of code (each line of code represents an instruction). There are 2,500 programmers developing and maintaining the code. Software development is, quite simply, a mammoth undertaking.

A few teachers develop their own educational software from scratch. One such teacher is Donna Mason, a computer education teacher and lab coordinator at the Alice Deal Junior High School in Washington, D.C. When she started teaching at Deal in 1983, there were no computers. When the school did acquire computers, there was no software to run on them, so she developed her own. The system she wrote, *MicroWorks,* was later published. In 1988, Donna was named a Christa McAuliffe Fellow, and in 1991, she was chosen by *Electronic Learning* magazine as one of "10 Who Made a Difference" (Electronic Learning, 1991).

But Donna Mason is the exception that proves the rule: teachers for the most part are not programmers. As Nancy Roberts, director of the graduate program in computers in education at Lesley College in Cambridge, Massachusetts, observed: "Learning a computer language isn't really very important for most people" (Colt, 1984). Of course, some teachers who specialize in mathematics or computer studies are not only qualified, but they usually have a natural ability to put together the step-by-step instructions that tell a computer what to do.

A small percentage of students will also be enthusiastic about programming, and might even create useful software applications. As Muller (1986) pointed out: "It is obvious that youngsters are far more at home with computer technology than are the adults attempting to teach them computer literacy." In some cases, those young people of 1986 are, of course, the young teachers of today, either preservice or in-service. Because of their special affinity with technology and their training and motivation as teachers, they are the ones most likely to lead the process of restructuring education over the next 40 to 50 years.

Many schools have computer clubs in which students get the opportunity to develop programming skills along with other computer-related expertise. A relatively small number of elementary schools teach students the Logo programming language because of its interactive, graphics-based environment which makes programming fun for young children, and, at the same time, helps them develop math and problem-solving skills. Middle and high school students often have the option of pursuing formal programming studies in languages such as BASIC, Pascal, or even Ada. [1]

◆ 13.2 Why Should Teachers Learn About Software Development?

Our concern in this chapter is with the majority of teachers. We need to examine to what extent all teachers can be expected to get involved with the development of software and other higher-level learning systems such as multimedia applications.

---

[1]Named after Lady Ada, Countess of Lovelace, whom we first met in chapter 2 (The History of Computers in Schools).

13.2.1 Historical Background

Software development occurs at several levels. Traditionally, programmers talk about low-level programming, which uses programming languages (machine language and assembly language), which are close to or at the internal machine level of the computer. Low-level programming involves the most detailed and extensive sets of instructions to tell the computer what to do. Such programming is of no concern to the vast majority of teachers.

At a higher level, programming involves the use of languages such as BASIC, Pascal, or Logo. These are examples of what are known as high-level languages (HLLs). They still require some understanding of how the computer works, and they also involve large numbers of instructions to get the computer to do anything particularly worthwhile. Probably fewer than 1% of teachers have ever developed a software application that has more than a few hundred instructions. But many teachers over the last decade, in their efforts to learn about computers, have toyed with programming at this level as part of computer literacy courses. Perhaps you are one of these teachers.

At a still higher level, there are languages such as SQL (structured query language) or QBE (query by example), which are specially designed to simplify access to data in large database management systems (DBMS). These languages are known as very high level languages (VHLLs). Since large DBMS are predominantly used by corporations and central educational administrations, it is unlikely that teachers would need to be familiar with them.

Finally, there are programming languages (more appropriately called applications development tools), such as the authoring systems that we will profile at the end of this chapter, which require next to no understanding of how the technology goes about its work, thus releasing the programmer to concentrate on the application, educational or otherwise, for which the programming is taking place.

13.2.2 Why Should Teachers Know About Programming?

Because of this variety of approaches to programming, different teachers will have different reasons for wanting to know how to go about developing software applications. Here is a cross-section of those reasons. It will be interesting for you, the reader, to see where you fit in this spectrum of rationales.

- Programming a computer helps one understand how the computer works, which leads to a greater sense of control when using the computer for more general and prepackaged applications.
- Knowing how to program a computer helps one appreciate the work that goes into the systems that are used by teachers and students in educational settings.
- If one knows how to use software development platforms such as authoring systems, one can develop applications that are tailored to one's specific local needs.
- Students like to develop their own programs/presentations using multimedia tools. If one understands how these tools work, one can be a better resource for students in their endeavors.
- Teachers who understand what constitutes a well-developed program will be better at selecting applications that will be effective educational instruments.

- Teachers who have survived what they consider to be the trauma of trying to figure out the correct logical sequence of instructions that constitutes a computer program will be sympathetic toward students when they have difficulties with the same process—or any learning process, for that matter.

13.3 Characteristics of Quality Educational Software

Quality educational software puts the nontechnical user's needs first.

Usability engineering is the application of human factors—also called **ergonomics**—to system design. The most time-consuming aspects of software development often have to do with how well the product will fit the "event world" for which it is created (Debons, 1988). The "event world" of K–12 schools is populated by end-users who do not expect to have to learn how a machine works in order to put it to work.

Key to lay acceptance of computer technology are ergonomic considerations that dictate that the designer of a system understand, and cater for, the cognitive and physical constraints that the human user brings to machines. What Tufte (1990) says about the graphical visualization of information applies equally well to software in general and to educational software in particular. "Clutter and confusion," he says, "are failures of design." The best software applies principles of ergonomics to all aspects of design so that the end product—the program—is as easy as possible to use.

Bailey (1989) notes that "a good computer-based system does not require extensive assistance from people." It should be designed in such a way that it marries into the paradigm of normal, everyday practice: business, educational, or otherwise. This emphasis on usability is a relatively recent phenomenon. Systems in the past that had an unreasonable learning curve associated with their use were successful because there was little alternative for people who wanted to use the computer to increase productivity and control. Today, however, it is understood that the benefits of advances in technology should be made available to all, not just the privileged few who were able to master the intricacies of traditional systems.

Moreover, as Stahl (1986) explained in his article enunciating the principle of "least astonishment" in interface design, "system performance is directly dependent on user performance." When users are comfortable working with a system, they will be more productive. Some orientation is, of course, inevitable, and time must be allocated for this in the introduction of a new system. But as Arthur Young & Co. discovered when they selected Apple's Macintosh for their accountants, the adoption of a system that weds functionality to ease of use can bring a convincing bottom-line benefit to the organization in terms of reduced end-user support costs and increased end-user productivity (Garfinkel, 1987).

Fortunately, the last few years have seen the industrywide adoption of standards for the software interface which have greatly simplified interaction between the machine and the people using the machine. These standard interfaces, which we discussed earlier in chapter 7, are known as graphical user interfaces (GUIs). They require the use of the mouse to point and click on icons (pictures that represent processes and files) and menus on the screen. All the information needed to know about how to use an application is there on the screen. Once one application has been learned, the learning curve to master other applications is considerably less steep because the interface is familiar across applications.

As far as teachers are concerned, they want to be able to focus on the pedagogical aspects of an educational package, not the technological ones. Teachers do not want to have to learn technical material in order to use software, nor do they want to have to teach that technical material to their students. One way to help technically shy teachers get involved with technology is to introduce them first to systems that are both easy to use and at the same time manifestly useful for some teaching or learning activity

Quality educational software is crafted with care and is therefore relatively bug-free.

It is almost impossible to guarantee that the software one acquires will be reliable, because it usually takes hours, days, weeks, even months of use before bugs show up. In fact, a corollary of Murphy's law says that bugs show up when least expected and at the worst possible time—for example, you have a ten-page paper in memory that you have not thought to save yet, and the system freezes up. You may never know if it was the applications software you were using that caused the problem, or some utility program running in the background.

It pays to know the reputation of the company that has developed software, and the only way to keep track of this is to read software reviews that appear in educational journals and check with colleagues in your own or other schools who have used the software.

If you ever develop your own software, or if you are working with students who are developing projects around multimedia systems, for example, the most important recommendation is to pay attention to detail. This attention to detail is the hallmark of the best professionals in all walks of life. Here, for example, are the reflections of a television commentator on Curtis Strange as he prepares to make yet another birdie: "He never, ever, pulls the trigger until he feels like he's ready. He ingests all the information that he needs to complete the task and then lets it happen. . . . And there it is, a 2 for Curtis Strange."

As Stephanie Winner, an Apple computer engineer, put it: "Good engineers are always striving to find the best, most innovative solution. Mediocre engineers just find a solution" (Hafner, 1993).

Quality educational software makes the computer appear almost human in responsiveness and anticipation of user needs.

New **artificial intelligence (AI)** and Fourth Generation languages such as authoring software, and better yet natural language itself, greatly simplify human interaction with the machine. *ClarisWorks,* for example, is designed in such a way that it immediately knows whether a user is involved in word processing, or database management, or whichever of the productivity functions that come with the package. When the user wants to create a diagram, or import some artwork, the user simply starts working with the graphics tools, and the system handles the switch to that module of the software.

As we will discuss later in this chapter, authoring software, especially well-designed and comprehensive packages such as those profiled in West (1993), make software development relatively intuitive, allowing the developer to focus on the purpose for which the application is intended rather than on the process of development itself.

Quality educational software will eventually move to far more powerful computer systems than even those that are state of the art in classrooms in the 1990s.

The paradox, therefore, is that, in order to optimize the human resource by designing thoroughly ergonomic systems, we must rethink the design of traditional computer architectures so as to improve the performance of the machines. Execution of one instruction at a time is too slow for the kinds of applications envisaged, for example, by researchers in AI.

Software systems that relieve the human user of the tedious and sometimes traumatic task of coping with unduly complex technology must, of their very nature, be themselves extraordinarily complex. Software systems imbued with characteristics of AI make huge demands on hardware. The processing necessary to allow for the simplest of natural interactions stretches the capabilities of most currently available computing machines. Graphical interfaces have been demonstrated to be among the most natural for the human user, but high-resolution graphics interfaces of the kind demonstrated at the annual SIGGRAPH conferences in Dallas are extremely demanding of machine time and space (SIGGRAPH, 1992). Natural language interfaces, too, which allow users to interact with the machine in their own native tongue, apart from presenting enormously intractable linguistic difficulties, are once again very demanding on machine time and space.

There is no doubt that the bottleneck of the so-called Von Neumann serial computers, capable of executing only one instruction at a time, will eventually be relegated to the halls of the Boston Computer Museum. Parallel computers, computers which have several processors and which can, therefore, execute several instructions simultaneously, are already off the drawing board and available at a cost that makes them viable for schools to use.

The very attempt to hide complexity from the user will necessitate the development of machines with enormous power and "a rich function set" (Birnbaum, 1985). With such machines in place, we will see a world open up which will make the advances made to date in computer technology seem puny by comparison. Most important, these machines will allow for the creation of software systems that will help educators realize the full benefits of technology in the classroom without the kind of mental trauma that has given so many teachers pause until now.

■᛫ 13.4 Authoring Programs: How Teachers Can Get Involoved

Chapters 8 through 12 examined in detail what teachers need to know about computer use in the classroom. If teachers become proficient at a level at which they feel comfortable

- working in a computerized environment;
- using computer-based tools to manage their professional activities in and out of the classroom;

- incorporating computer-based learning into their curricula;
- use computer technology to establish close contact with parents, and encouraging their students to use communications technology to establish cross-cultural links with children all over the world;
- incorporating multimedia systems into the learning process;

they will have made great strides toward providing their students with an educational environment in which their individual and infinitely varied talents can grow. If, on top of this, they are able to use, and direct student use of, authoring tools to fashion learning systems that incorporate hypermedia technology, they will have made the transition into the world of education for an information age. This is not as difficult as it sounds. Let us look at some examples of authoring tools.

13.4.1 Authoring Systems

Traditionally, programs are created by programmers. These are usually people with strong technical skills who have undergone extensive training. Authoring systems are programs that help people who are nonprogrammers develop applications for the computer. They are a natural outcome of the recognition that the best people to develop software are those who are experts in the area of activity or expertise for which the software is intended. This, indeed, was Bill Atkinson's vision when he developed *HyperCard*, the first authoring system for microcomputers and the prototype for most of those that have been developed since 1986. As Atkinson put it: *HyperCard* is "programming for 'the rest of us' " (Goodman, 1987).

People who understand business are the best people to write applications for business. Likewise, teachers have considerable expertise and experience related to teaching and learning methodologies. They are, therefore, the best people to be involved in the development of all types of CAI. Indeed, many of the companies that currently develop software for schools were founded by teachers with the technical skills needed to design and develop software. Other companies that specialize in software applications for schools have teachers on their payroll either as full-time personnel or as consultants.

The case study at the end of this chapter describes a *HyperCard* application authored by a high school teacher in Palo Alto, California. The program describes the Standard Model of fundamental particles and their interactions. With feedback from other teachers and with physicists from the Stanford Linear Accelerator Center and the Lawrence Berkeley Laboratory, Andria Erzberger translated a paper-based, fundamental particles chart into an interactive learning tool that has now received international acclaim. The case study will make interesting reading.

Interactive videodisc systems, according to White (1990), are most effective when used in conjunction with a microcomputer and authoring software such as *HyperCard*. As such, they become powerful tools in the hands of capable teachers and students. Of the many examples of authoring systems available today, we will profile two in the sections that follow. First we will profile Claris Computer Corporation's *HyperCard*™ designed for Apple machines. Next we will examine EduQuest's *Linkway Live!*™ designed for IBM and IBM-compatible desktop machines.

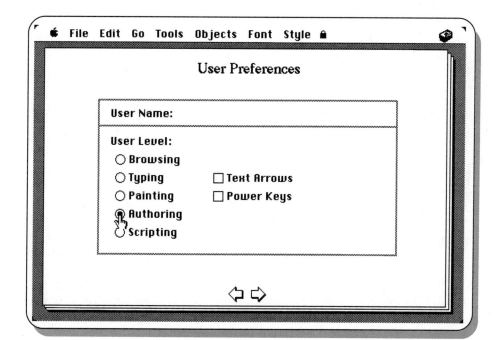

Figure 13.1
Levels of user
interaction in
HyperCard

13.4.2 HyperCard

HyperCard is a software environment that is provided free of charge with every Apple Macintosh computer. In this sense, it is rather like the BASIC programming language, which is built into every Apple II computer. Bill Atkinson has described *HyperCard* as "an authoring tool and an information organizer" (Goodman, 1987). Files in *HyperCard* are called stacks. A stack contains any number of "cards," which contain organized data (or "information," to use Atkinson's term) in the form of text and pictures.

As illustrated in figure 13.1, the system has five levels of user interaction. The least complex levels are the browsing and typing levels. Browsing means that you are looking around a stack to see what is on the cards in the stack. You use the mouse and arrow icons on the screen, or the arrow keys on the keyboard, to navigate around the stack. If you are familiar with any GUI, you will have no difficulty figuring out how to do this. When you are in the browsing mode, you are treating the stack more or less as if it were a database. If there were thousands of cards in the stack, you could have the system search for a specific card if you knew what you were looking for. This would still be in the browsing mode.

If you have selected the typing level as your user preference, you will be able to enter data into the stack, either by updating an existing card in the stack, or by opening up a new card to add to the stack, or by deleting a card from the stack. At the browsing/typing levels, you can also link cards to each other and print out the contents of cards in the stack.

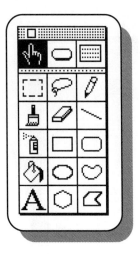

Figure 13.2
The *HyperCard* tools palette

If you want to create cards with graphic designs on them, you can use the painting tools if you select the painting level from the user preferences. At the painting level, you have a selection of tools and options that help you develop artwork.

If you do not feel like creating your own artwork, you can import artwork from other sources such as clip art stacks. Basically, at the painting level, you are in a graphics program such as *MacPaint*. Indeed, *MacPaint* was also created by Bill Atkinson at Apple Computer, Inc.

At the authoring level, you have access to tools to create buttons and fields on the cards in a stack. Fields are places to store data. For example, I might want to set up a stack for the names and addresses of the students in my class. Each card would need one field for the first name, another for the last name, and so on. The buttons are programmable; you can make them *do* things when they are clicked on by someone browsing the stack. For example, you can program a button to send the user to some other prespecified card elsewhere in the stack.

Programming the buttons involves scripting. You are accessing the full power of *HyperCard* when you write scripts. In effect you are assuming control of the *HyperCard* stack you are working in, as well as control of any other stacks stored on the computer system. It is beyond the scope of this text to go into further detail about *HyperCard* scripting. The reader who would like to learn more will find Goodman (1987) a well-written, well-organized source for everything you need to know.

Eventually, it is hoped that this text will have a *HyperCard* supplement. The supplement would consist of a series of tutorials to step one through the fundamentals of the system in much the same way as the Microsoft *Works* tutorials, which are already an optional accompaniment to this text.

HyperTEACH

HyperTEACH is an example of authoring software based on *HyperCard*. The system was developed by Dr. Michael Land at the University of Texas at Wichita Falls. *Hyper-TEACH* acts as a front end to *HyperCard,* simplifying further the teacher's task of

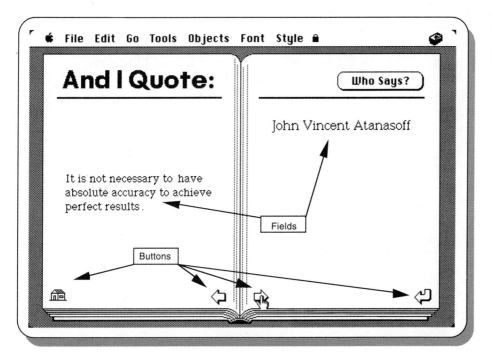

Figure13.3
HyperCard fields and buttons

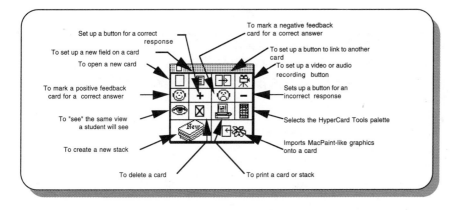

Figure13.4
The *HyperTEACH* tools palette

designing lessons, tutorials, and other computer-assisted instruction that may include computer-controlled multimedia technology. *HyperTEACH* has been put on the Internet network as freeware (public domain), so those who know their way around the Internet can help themselves to a copy of the program and try it out.

13.4.3 Linkway Live!

Linkway Live! is IBM's equivalent of *HyperCard,* insofar as it enables the user to easily create applications that combine text, color, graphics, picture images, and sound. In fact,

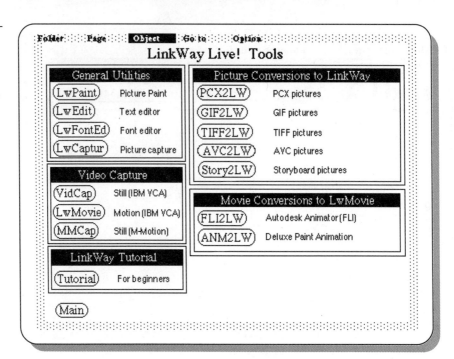

a

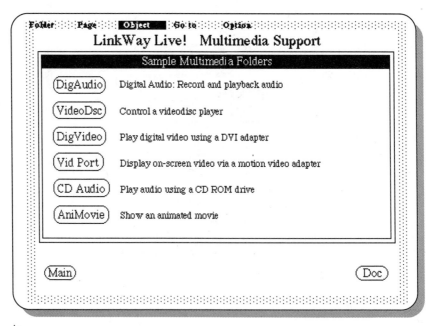

b

it is a hypermedia tool that, like *HyperCard,* links the various types of data in such a way as to allow the user to browse through the "pages" of textual, audial, and visual material following paths selected by clicking on buttons.

Linkway Live!'s pages are equivalent to *HyperCard*'s cards, and *HyperCard*'s stacks are called folders in *Linkway Live!* When teachers or students create applications, they select from menus to set up folders that "contain" the pages of multimedia data. Each page can have text, pictures, and buttons. The text is for reading, the pictures for viewing, the buttons for linking to other pages, and so on. Figure 13.5 illustrates screens from *Linkway Live!* showing a selection of the system's tools and multimedia support.

The buttons are the secret to *Linkway Live!*'s power as a tool for exploration of a selected universe of knowledge. Students need no more than a few hours to learn to use the system. They can then be set free to create multimedia projects of their own. Resourceful teachers will introduce students to the system via IBM's tutorial "comic book" which, as D'Ignazio (1993) explains, means that the teachers "don't even have to know *Linkway Live!* themselves."

Of course, teachers whose students are using the system will probably, almost by osmosis, learn it eventually. The advantage of teachers learning the system along with their students is that they will have a better understanding of the capabilities of *Linkway Live!* and will, therefore, more likely initiate, inspire, direct, assign, and otherwise involve their students in powerful learning experiences as constructors of their own knowledge.

■ Looking Back

It is often difficult for gung-ho computerphiles[2] to appreciate the technological timidity of some of their colleagues. The same problem arises when teachers find it difficult to appreciate the lack of academic motivation on the part of some students. Whatever the reason, it is a fact of life that must be accepted and dealt with through patience, understanding, unwavering support, and encouragement. The panoply of systems being introduced in schools today, exciting as they are to some, can be overwhelming to others. But since the schools exist for the sake of the students, the teachers—whether computerphiles or computerphobes— must come to terms with the technology to some degree in order to provide an adequate educational opportunity for those with whom they are charged.

For many teachers, developing lessons around multimedia systems will not go beyond the simplest application of the technology unless and until comprehensive multimedia curriculum materials are available in an easily adaptable format to meet local approaches and the needs of local populations. Canned multimedia applications will generally not work for all but the minority of cases. For this reason, schools will in the long run need to tap the resources of their own technology-oriented teachers—the computerists—to train and above all work with those teachers who are naturally and understandably reticent about authoring multimedia systems on their own.

In the end, the most avid users of multimedia and other learning systems will be the students who have grown up around technology and consequently are not afraid of it. Given the opportunity, they will use the technology to access and assimilate the knowledge they need to achieve their educational goals.

But children cannot do this without help. Teachers in the information age will need to be able to use technology in support of teaching, but, above all, they will need to know how to establish an environment in which students can safely and successfully control their own learning.

---

[2]A computerphile is a lover of computers. Its opposite is a computerphobe. Which are you?

HyperCard enlivens fundamental particles chart
by Barbara Gasdick, Technical Writer, Mountain View, California

The world of quarks, leptons, and fundamental forces came alive for students when physics teacher Andria Erzberger used *HyperCard* to illustrate the chart of fundamental particles for her students at Palo Alto High School in California. The program quickly gained acceptance, was funded, and eventually published by Science Kit and Boreal Laboratories. Andria Erzberger received a 1991 Presidential Award for Excellence for science teaching.

The software has now been translated into French, German, and Italian and is used in the new Microcosm Museum in Geneva, Switzerland. A Scandinavian country donated a large sum toward the creation of an IBM version so that the software could be used in all their schools.

IBM also unselfishly donated money to support the project in its early days before there was even a way to translate it from *HyperCard* to run on the IBM computers.

An original $2000 budget swelled to over $200,000 with grants from private donors and the Department of Energy. The Contemporary Physics Education Project (CPEP) funded by this money is run by a nonprofit group composed of physicists, high school physics teachers, college physics professors, and accelerator educators.

Description

This *HyperCard* program effectively uses graphics, sound, text, and animation to describe the Standard Model of fundamental particles and their interactions. A colorful wall chart depicting an atom and its subatomic particles, shown in case figure 13.1, served as the foundation for the *HyperCard* program.

In case figure 13.2, the *HyperCard* version of the wall chart, the elements in the chart become "buttons," symbols or icons that open other screens of more detailed information when students select them via a click of the mouse.

For example, clicking on "leptons" would produce the screen in case figure 13.3a. Clicking on "quarks" would lead to the screen in case figure 13.3b, which includes both sound (quark, quark!) and animation for each icon (symbol). Case figure 13.3c shows how

Barbara Gasdick, author of the case study

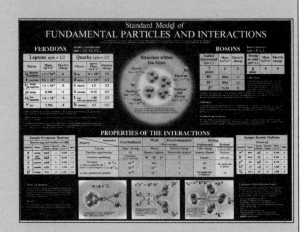

Case Figure 13.1
Fundamental Particles and Interactions chart
Illustration courtesy CPEP

quarks join together to form hadrons (particles like protons and neutrons). When students click on the "Properties of Interactions" in case figure 13.2, the screen in

(continued)

case figure 13.3*d* appears, showing forces resulting from the interactions of the particles. One of Andria's students got involved in the program development by drawing the art shown in this screen.

The icons and names at the bottom of the screen are used to move the student to other parts of the program. For example, the icon in the lower left serves as a "menu" and takes the student back to the full chart screen shown in case figure 13.2. It also highlights the part of the chart that is currently displayed on the screen the student is viewing. Bold names in screens are active buttons, which take students to other screens when they click on them. Some screens have quiz buttons, such as the one shown in case figure 13.3*d*, which display a screen of questions to allow students to check their learning.

How the Program Developed

Andria Erzberger was part of a national, 18-member collaboration of physicists and teachers who initially worked on a fundamental-particles chart project that was to accompany a science textbook. Andria began to learn *HyperCard,* mostly on her own, and used it to duplicate the chart, revising it with feedback from teachers, students, and consulting physicists from Lawrence Berkeley Laboratory and Stanford Linear Accelerator Center. She made additional changes after the project was published and field-tested in *The Physics Journal.* Grants from various governmental agencies and corporations funded her research.

In the process, Andria had to weigh advice from physicists regarding the level of difficulty of explanation. She also learned the importance of knowing about computer hardware limitations and persisted with an earlier version of *HyperCard.* Now *HyperCard* version 2.0 contains many features that expedite the creation of buttons, fields, and cards—the main building blocks of a *HyperCard* program. Andria's advice to *HyperCard* developers is to use the *HyperCard* author help available from Apple Computer and "don't be afraid to just try it!"

The program was eventually published by Science Kit, and today teachers from all 50 states use the software. The program is being translated and distributed in 50 countries. The Smithsonian in Washington, D.C., and various science museums are also using it. Even physicists have requested copies of the program!

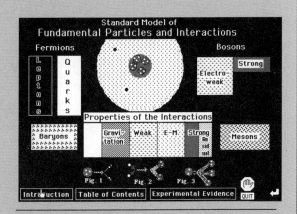

Case Figure 13.2
HyperCard interactive revision of the chart

One Project Leads to Another

In the science area, students use *HyperCard* to create their own projects where they choose an area such as sports, optics, astronomy, and so on, to illustrate a scientific principle. The science teachers are planning to expand the use of computers with an interactive box that measures light and force. The success that Andria and her science colleagues experienced with computers quickly inspired other Palo Alto High School teachers to incorporate the computer as a teaching/learning tool into their curricula. Students now use word processing and graphics to create compositions and newsletters, *HyperCard* to show animated body systems, *Pagemaker* to produce the school newspaper, *Dialog* to tap into databases for research projects, and *AutoCad* to create award-winning engineering and mechanical designs. No doubt, the innovative teachers and eager students at Palo Alto High School will have thought of dozens of other ways to use their computers by the time this book is printed!

HyperCard's Flexibility and Ease of Use

What is great about *HyperCard* programs is that teachers and students can continue to revise and adapt the program to suit their own needs. Teachers at Palo Alto High School found that they can teach students **(continued)**

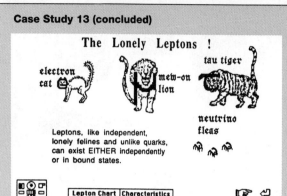

a

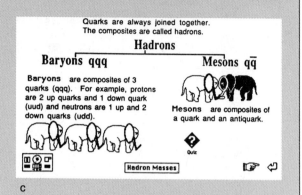

c

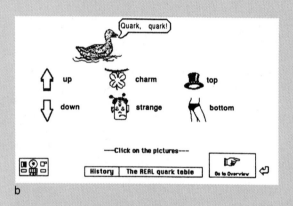

b

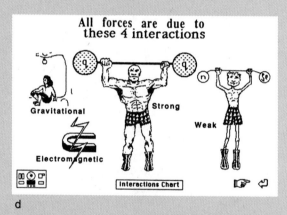

d

Case Figure 13.3
Sample screens from the software

HyperCard—creating cards (screens), buttons, and fields—in one day. Students then direct their own learning. In this way, students are no longer passive passengers in a teacher's vehicle, but active drivers who determine and navigate a meaningful route to learning.

To Order the Program

The Fundamental Particles Chart software costs $19.95 and runs on any Macintosh with *HyperCard*. The colorful particles chart shown in case figure 13.1 comes in various sizes (notebook to wall size), with costs from $7.95 to $12.50. Both software and charts can be ordered from Science Kit and Boreal Laboratories, 777 East Park Drive, Tonawanda, New York, 14150.

Talk About It

Topics for discussion based on the case study.

1. Discuss any collaborative efforts in which you have participated. What facilitated the process? If there were obstacles, how were they overcome?

2. Discuss ways to ensure student participation in educational software development.

3. Brainstorm how you might work with other disciplines to develop a software program for education.

4. Select a lesson or unit in your area and describe how you might automate it.

5. Describe ways in which business and/or industry can assist with educational software development.

■ Looking Forward

Writing one's own software for computer-assisted instruction or multimedia learning is all well and good, and if one can do it, it will save money. But it will not buy the equipment, nor will it generate the funds to release one from teaching so that one can have the time to develop the software!

Money is by no means the only solution to the problem of restructuring schools to meet the needs of an information age, but precious little can be done without it. It is estimated that perhaps billions of dollars are available to fund technology projects in schools, even during this time of economic austerity. The money is offered by foundations and other grant-giving institutions at the federal, state, and local levels. Some schools are making great efforts to win those grants; schools such as the Franklin Park Magnet school, which was the subject of the case study in chapter 12. As a result, their students are benefiting from the best that educational technology has to offer.

It should be of great interest to teachers and administrators alike to learn how to effectively apply for grants. It will also be useful to discuss what steps should be taken to get the most out of a grant that has been won. Chapter 14 will look at all aspects of writing grants.

■ Do Something About It: Exercises and Projects

1. Take a traditional lesson or unit in your area and create a plan for using *HyperCard* or other similar programs such as *Linkway Live!* to teach it. Document what helped and hindered the process.

2. Find two or more colleagues or classmates and create a plan to develop a thematic unit using a software program as a primary tool. Document what helped and hindered the process.

3. Research ways that business and industry have worked together with schools to create educational software.

4. Collaborate with a group of colleagues or classmates interested in educational software development and guide them through program development.

■ References

Bailey, Robert W. *Human Performance Engineering: Using Ergonomics to Achieve Computer System Usability.* 2nd ed. Englewood Cliffs, NJ: Prentice Hall, 1981.

Birnbaum, Joel S. Toward the Domestication of Microelectronics, In *Communications of the ACM,* vol. 28, no. 11, 1985, pp. 1225–35.

Colt, Lois. Learning a Computer Language May Be Easier Than You Think. *Christian Science Monitor,* January 27, 1984, p. B12.

Debons, Anthony, Esther Horne, Scott Cronenweth. *Information Science: An Integrated View.* Boston, MA: G. K. Hall, 1988.

D'Ignazio, Fred. How to Put Multimedia to Work in Your Classroom For $196. *IBM Multimedia In Education,* advertising supplement to *Technology and Learning,* 1993, pp. 8–10.

Electronic Learning. Educators of the Decade: 10 Who Made a Difference. *Electronic Learning,* vol. 11, no. 1, September 1991, pp. 28–29.

Garfinkel, David. An Eye On the Bottom Line. In *Personal Computing,* June 1987.

Gleick, James. Chasing Bugs in the Electronic Village. *New York Times Magazine,* June 14, 1992.

Goodman, Danny. *The Complete HYPERCARD Handbook.* New York: Bantam Books, 1987.

Hafner, Katie. Woman, Computer Nerd—and Proud. *New York Times,* Sunday, August 29, 1993, sect. 3, pp. 4, 6.

Meyer, Steve. Worth Noting. *Network World,* November 23, 1992.

Muller, James H. Learning Must Be More Than Computer Literacy. *NASSP Bulletin,* April 1986.

NBC. Commentator at broadcast golf tournament, summer 1991.

Olson, Steve. The Sage of Software. *Computer World,* 1985.

SIGGRAPH. Annual conferenmce of the Special Interest Group in Graphics. ACM/IEEE, 1992.

Stahl, Bob. Principle of 'Least Astonishment' Can Polish Up Interface Design. *Computer World,* September 15, 1986.

Tufte, Edward. *Envisioning Information.* Cheshire, CT: Graphics Press, 1990.

West, Nick. Multimedia Masters: A Guide to the Pros and Cons of Seven Powerful Authoring Programs. In *MacWorld Special Multimedia Guide,* March 1993, pp. 114–17.

White, Charles E. Interactive Multimedia for Social Studies: A Review of *In the Holy Land* and *The '88 Vote. Social Education,* February 1990, pp. 68–70.

Funding
Technology
Projects

Education pays, unless you are an educator.

Evan Esar

Money enables a man to get along without education, and education enables a man to get along without money.

Marcelene Cox

Technology-rich environments envisaged in the classroom of the future are expensive. As long as school districts have to rely on their own resources, there will be inequities resulting from the disparity of wealth from one district to another. In some countries, such as France, this disparity is largely overcome by the fact that the educational system is nationally standardized. There is a national curriculum and students are ensured equal educational opportunity because all schools are provided with the same facilities.

In the United States, for the most part, this equality of educational opportunity does not exist. A few forward-looking, equity-conscious states such as Texas are attempting to implement a so-called "Robin Hood" allocation of school taxes. Wealthier districts shares the money raised for schools in such a way as to make sure that the poorer districts get enough to make it possible for them to fund equally competitive educational programs.

Unfortunately, this equality is not mandated nationwide. Indeed, in most states it is not mandated statewide. The gap between the quality of schooling for the haves and the have-nots will continue to widen unless disadvantaged school districts fight for the allocations that will enable them to provide the same level of technological infrastructure enjoyed by the wealthier districts. To this end, numerous sources of funding can be tapped through the effective writing of grants.

This chapter begins by briefly reexamining the goals of education in an information age. This will underscore the importance of finding the money to pay for the cost of ensuring that children have the opportunity to achieve those goals. This time, the goals are looked at from the perspective of what the working world requires of schools. The chapter lists many sources of funding, outlines the key components of a strategy for successful grant applications, and discusses how to get the most out of external sources of funding once they have been won. Finally, the chapter discusses the important subject of grant-supported project evaluation.

Here is the organization of the chapter:

- The goals of education for an information age
  - The five competencies of effective workers
  - The foundation skills required of effective workers
- Sources of funding and support
- Writing grant proposals
  - Strategies for successful applications
- Making the most of grants: the seven pillars of success
  - Active support must come from the top
  - A nondictatorial approach is always best
  - Every school should have a core of teacher-computerists
  - Teachers must come first
  - The parents and students must be involved in the evolutionary process involved
  - An ongoing technology training program must be in place
  - Teachers must be given time and freedom to restructure their curriculum around the technology
- Evaluating the technology program

▪▪ 14.1 Introduction

Money is only part of the answer to the challenge of incorporating computers into the curriculum, but it is an important part. As Cheryl Williams put it in Branscum (1992): "Schools need funds and it's not a one-shot deal. . . . you've got to buy the equipment, you've got to buy the software, you've got to buy the maintenance, you've got to buy the training, you've got to buy the updating, and you've got to phase it in."

Money is, thus, necessary to meet the needs of the people on the front lines in the struggle to update and restructure education. These are the teachers and administrators at the local level. Today, it is more necessary than ever for schools to find alternative sources of funding because of the difficult economic times that we are experiencing, and are likely to continue to experience, during this last decade of the twentieth century.

Section 14.3 discusses sources of funding, and they are many. Aggressive school districts, many in underprivileged neighborhoods, are already dipping into this well of financial opportunity. It should be remembered, however, that there is one small problem with grants. Once they have been won, the work has just begun. Applying for a grant implies a commitment to the effort and innovation that the grant will fund. As the old saying goes, "Fortune favors the brave."

14.1.2 Everything Points to an Increase in the Cost of Education

Bork (1987), after presenting the case for technology-stimulated change in our education systems, estimated that an effort to coordinate full curriculum development on an international scale would cost about $10 billion over a period of six to eight years. This might appear to be a prohibitive expense. But, as Bork points out, it represents just one-third of the cost of putting one person on the moon and "is about one or two days of the [pre-end of Cold War] military budget each year."

Here are some of the items that must be factored into the costs of the kind of education essential for the citizens of tomorrow's world.

- Teacher–pupil ratios are steadily improving (from 1:26 in 1960–61 to 1:17 in 1991–92).[1] This means that schools will need more, rather than fewer, teachers as time goes on, assuming a steady or increasing birthrate.

- As pointed out in chapter 3 and as will be discussed more fully in the next section, the changes in society, in general and in the workplace in particular, mean that, more than ever before, children must be given the opportunity for a lifelong education that will enable them to be fully contributing members of the Information Society.

- Everyone must get a fair slice of the education pie. The money needed for education must be shared equitably among all segments of the population, including children from all walks of life, of both sexes, and from all racial and ethnic backgrounds (Stone, 1990). To quote from *A Nation at Risk,* "We do not believe that a public commitment to excellence and educational reform must be made at the expense of a strong commitment to the equitable treatment of our diverse population" (National Commission on Excellence in Education, 1984).

---

[1] According to the U.S. Deparment of Education (1992).

- More money than ever will be needed to provide effective leadership in schools. Teachers especially must be given the time, ongoing training, and logistical and technical support that is necessary for them to get the job done. It would also help if teachers were adequately remunerated for their skills and dedication, as recommended in *A Nation at Risk.* After all, it is the children's lives that are at stake. (In section 14.5, we will further discuss this topic by presenting the Seven Pillars of Success that should form the foundation for effective use of computer-based technology for teaching and learning.)
- Educational technology is attended by a whole gamut of expenses ranging from the cost of the machinery itself, to the infrastructure necessary to support the machinery, to the training and support of those who will use the machinery.

The rationale for winning grants is to help the school maintain a high standard of excellence with regard to the educational product offered to the students and their parents. Before we consider the nuts and bolts of grants, grant proposals, and grant implementation, it will be useful to focus on the expectations that the world of work has of schools in an information society.

▪▪ 14.2 The Goals of Education for an Information Age

The society that will compete most effectively in the 21st century will be the society that realizes the goal of providing high-quality, lifelong education for *all* its citizens. This is an expensive proposition, but the return on the investment to achieve this goal will fully justify the expense. On the other hand, the price that will be paid by a society that fails to commit to this goal will be devastating. This is the message that lies at the heart of *A Nation at Risk:*

> We issue this call to all who care about America and its future: to parents and students; to teachers, administrators, and school board members; to colleges and industry; to union members and military leaders; to governors and State legislators; to the President; to members of Congress and other public officials; to members of learned and scientific societies; to the print and electronic media; to concerned citizens everywhere. America is at risk.

Education is a key that opens many doors.

- Education prepares one to function successfully in a working world where manual skills are less and less in demand as compared to intellectual skills such as communication skills and problem-solving skills.
- Education gives one skills in using the tools to access and assimilate information.
- Education enables one to make satisfying use of leisure time by bringing one to the point where one can educate oneself, broadening interests, acquiring new skills, and pursuing lifelong learning.

Ironically, whereas in 1950 three of four high school graduates went on to pursue a college education, by 1990 that ratio had fallen to two of four, a drop of 25%!

14.2.1 The Five Competencies of Effective Workers

The obligation of schools to prepare students to function successfully in an information age is underlined in a report issued by the U.S. Department of Labor Secretary's Commission on Achieving Necessary Skills (SCANS). The report (SCANS, 1991) identifies "five competencies which, in conjunction with a three-part foundation of skills and personal qualities, lie at the heart of job performance today." The competencies and foundation skills are seen as "essential preparation [for the working world] for all students." They are also essential preparation for further education and for life in general in the Information Age.

The five competencies required of effective workers are defined in the SCANS report as follows (emphasis has been added):

- Effective workers productively use *Resources*—they know how to allocate time, money, materials, space, and staff.
- Effective workers productively use *Interpersonal skills*—they know how to work on teams, teach others, serve customers, lead, negotiate, and work well with people from culturally diverse backgrounds.
- Effective workers productively use *Information*—they know how to acquire and evaluate data, organize and maintain files, interpret and communicate data, and *use computers to process information.*
- Effective workers productively use *Systems*—they understand social, organizational and *technological* systems, they know how to monitor and correct performance, and design or improve systems.
- Effective workers productively use *Technology*—they know how to *select equipment and tools, apply technology to specific tasks, and maintain and troubleshoot technologies.*

14.2.2 The Foundation Skills Required of Effective Workers

The foundation skills that are identified in the SCANS report as prerequisites to competence are:

- Competence requires *Basic skills*—including reading, writing, arithmetic and mathematics, speaking, and listening skills.
- Competence requires *Thinking skills*—including the ability to think creatively, make decisions, solve problems, mentally visualize situations and solutions to problems, a knowledge of how to learn, and the ability to reason.
- Competence requires *Personal qualities*—including individual responsibility, self-esteem, sociability, self-management, and integrity.

The SCANS report (1991) reminds us of the primacy of education to American democracy:

For over 200 years Americans have worked to make education part of their national vision, indispensable to democracy and to individual freedom. For at least the last 40 years, we have worked to join the power of education to the ideal of equity—for minority Americans, for the disabled, and for immigrants. With that work still incomplete, we are called to still another revolution—*to create an entire people trained to think and equipped with the know-how to make their knowledge productive.* [emphasis added]

This new revolution is no less exciting or challenging than those we have already completed. Nor is its outcome more certain. All that is certain is that we must begin.

We *have* begun to overhaul the way we do education. Technology is transforming those schools that have accepted the challenge of change—schools such as Spring Mills Elementary School funded by the Oakland Schools' *Teaching and Learning with Technology Project* (Oakland Schools, 1991; Van Dam, 1991) and the 100 ACOT[2] schools that have been supported by Apple Computer, Inc. You may recall that model schools such as these were discussed in chapter 12 with a view to showing the effective impact of a comprehensive commitment to computer-based technology on teaching and learning.

Change is inevitable. Fifty years from now, learning environments will look very different from most of those we see today. Teachers, too, will have different goals, different responsibilities. They will be more concerned with education and less concerned with classroom and school management. Computer-based learning is essentially constructive and interactive. It is less dependent on a specific location such as a classroom in a school. Children will still come together, but in smaller units, and in less rigidly regimented schools. There will be a great diversity of types of schools unified only by the requirement of preparing students to measure up to standards established by regional and/or national educational goals. With the technology in place and the teachers trained and committed to its use, we will be able to "pay attention to the needs of each student by individualizing the learning experience" (Bork, 1987). No doubt, Herbert J. Klausmeier's dream of individually guided education (Nussel, 1976) will become not the exception, but the rule.

14.3 Sources of Funding and Support

There are two kinds of sources of funds and equipment to support technology projects: steady sources and ad hoc sources. Steady sources of support are represented by institutions such as the U.S. Department of Education, the Computer Learning Foundation, and corporations such as Apple, IBM, and Tandy, which make a certain amount of grant money and/or equipment available every year. Ad hoc support is available on an irregular basis from foundations, local businesses, and other local fund-raising efforts.

Technology and Learning magazine (1992) published a special edition in January 1992 devoted to the issue of where to find funding for technology projects. Many steady and ad hoc sources are recommended. Here, for example, are some of the suggested sources of funding listed by Wilson (1992) in the special edition:

- District general funds

    More and more school districts set aside money to be allocated specifically for educational technology.

---

[2]ACOT—Apple Classrooms of Tomorrow.

- Funds for special educational categories

    Budgets for Chapter 1, learning disabled, and other special needs students often allow for support of technology-related projects.

- State-run educational improvement programs

    Most states today make some provision for budgetary support of technology-based programs for schools. In Pennsylvania, for example, the Information Technology Education for the Commonwealth (ITEC) Act, passed in 1984 and described in Dunlop (1986), was intended "to (1) provide teacher training in computer information technology, (2) help design computer-oriented elementary and secondary curricula, (3) assist teachers and school administrators in the evaluation of educational computer software, (4) administer and fund individual schools' proposals to acquire and upgrade computer equipment and implement computer-oriented instruction, (5) assist in the coordination of the purchase of microcomputer hardware and software for Pennsylvania schools and (6) loan equipment and computer software to non-public schools."

- Parent–teacher organizations

    All over the world, schools rely on such organizations/associations for fund-raising. Computing technology is an ideal focus for their efforts since it has such a direct impact in the classroom.

- Grants

    There are innumerable sources for grants of all kinds, whether governmental at the local, state, or federal levels, or private under the aegis of foundations or corporations. Many of these sources of funding are listed in appendix C. Included in this appendix are details of the various education grant information services provided by organizations such as Capitol Publications, Inc.

- General obligation bonds

    Some school districts win electoral support for school bond initiatives to support improvement of capital facilities, including technology-related equipment. At least one school district has asked the electorate to agree to a one mil increase in local taxation to fund the infusion of the latest multimedia technology (Foreman, 1991).

- Lottery money

    Those states that conduct lotteries can be lobbied to allocate some proportion of the supplemental revenue raised for educational technology.

- Partnerships with colleges or local adult-education programs

    This idea has been successfully implemented at the Minute Man Technical High School in Lexington, Massachusetts (November 1990). By 1990, the program was offering courses for parents and other local citizens with revenues allocated to improving technology-based education at the high school.

- Vendor contributions

    Stanton (1992) provides details of generous programs sponsored by Apple Computer, Inc., IBM Corporation, Matsushita Electric Corporation of America, Microsoft Corporation, NEC Corporation, Tandem Computers, Tandy Corporation, and Toshiba America Information Systems, Inc.. The combined dollar value of the grants and product donations made by these companies alone comes to well over $200 million a year.

- Foundation grants

  NEC (NEC Foundation of America), Toshiba (Toshiba America Foundation), and Toyota Motor Sales USA, Inc. (Toyota USA Foundation) are examples of the many large and small companies that have set up foundations for the purpose of aiding educational institutions with grants and donations (Stanton, 1992).

- Parent workshops and after-school student instruction

  This source of funding is similar to the partnerships with colleges and local Adult Education programs already mentioned. Basically, the school sets itself up in the *business* of education, offering workshops for a fee to parents, students, and local citizens. The teachers are paid for their services as instructors, so it is an opportunity for them to augment their income. Like any business, the program has to be well organized and efficiently run. The potential for net profits can be substantial.

- Lease/purchase agreements

  This arrangement has the advantage of reduced initial financial outlay, thus spreading out the financial burden involved in the purchase of the hardware, software, and support for technology-based programs.

- Local business donations

  As far as computer-based technology is concerned, the major contribution of local business is expertise and training. Many schools are now looking to develop close liaisons with local businesses for purposes of educational support. Of course, financial donations are also available. Outdated computer hardware and software, which a business may be replacing with state-of-the-art systems, can often be put to good use in a school, especially when there is a teacher or staff member who has the motivation and the knowledge to incorporate it into the curriculum. However, such outdated equipment can often be more trouble than it is worth, and may be best utilized as part of an exchange for more up-to-date systems.

As an exercise in the Do Something About It section at the end of the chapter, you will have the opportunity to discuss these ideas in the context of your own experience, either as a practicing teacher or as a student from a school district with which you are familiar.

14.4 Preparing Grant Proposals

14.4.1 Steps in the Preparation of a Grant Proposal

A useful paradigm for developing a grant proposal is the classic problem-solving model advocated by Polya (1945), which we already applied to the problem of designing computing environments in chapter 8. A grant proposal is designed to help solve the problem of coming up with financial support for projects. Polya's four steps in the problem-solving process applied to the development of grant proposals are:

Step One: Understand the problem

This is equivalent to researching the educational environment for which the grant is proposed. Starting with the current state of affairs, identify the way learning currently takes place: methodologies, equipment used, student profiles, and so forth. This will unearth opportunities for improvement that can benefit from technology. These would be stated as *objectives.* The process of understanding the problem will also identify *constraints:* unavoidable limitations on the scope of the project (budget, physical plant, learning abilities, etc.). Very important at this early stage: *involve the teachers and students who will benefit from the grant.* And continue to involve them throughout the process, thus helping them to commit to the project if and when it is funded.

Step Two: Devise a plan

At this stage, you have a reasonably good understanding of the problem the grant proposal is designed to address. Devising a plan involves drawing up in detail the series of steps that will lead to the achievement of the objectives spelled out in Step One, as well as a specification of all necessary equipment and support. It is important at this planning stage to draw up more than one plan. There is never only one solution to any problem. Eventually, of course, you will need to select the one best strategy for presentation in the grant application proposal.

Step Three: Carry out the plan

Prepare the proposal. This should be relatively straightforward if you have conscientiously completed the first two steps. In fact, you will already have written much of the proposal.

Step Four: Look back

Review the proposal carefully before signing off on it and sending it out. Especially important is to have others review it, including people who had nothing to do with the preparation of the proposal. The more objective the appraisal the better. Be open to other people's ideas and perspectives. Only a fool thinks he or she has all the answers.

Following these steps will greatly improve your chances of success. The next section outlines some other strategies that are important in winning grants.

14.4.2 Strategies for Successful Applications

Each school district *and each school* should appoint a grantsperson for grant coordination.

It is important to make an individual staff or faculty member at the school level responsible for coordinating grant applications, and give that individual time to make a difference.

This is the single most important recommendation for success in raising grant money. If you want anything done, make someone responsible for getting it done. In general, it is a waste of time making announcements and putting up signs encouraging people to do this or that, especially if there is any effort involved. Appoint a staff or faculty member to be responsible for coordinating grant applications. Included in that responsibility will be the mandate to make teachers aware of the grants that are available, to encourage them to get involved, and to work with them to develop proposals. This individual might also be responsible for working with teachers in the implementation and evaluation phases.

Teachers should always know that they will have active support if they apply for grants. The more teachers are involved, the better. Schools that rely on one or two heroes to make things happen are not usually as effective as schools where the administration is able to create a spirit of teamwork among the faculty and staff.

Schools should consider the cost involved in freeing up a teacher or staff member to coordinate grant acquisition as *seed money* for the many profitable projects that will result from the investment.

14.4.3 The Qualities of a Grantsperson

- A grantsperson must have excellent organizational skills. He or she not only needs to be able to coordinate the grant application process, but must also be good at delegating work not simply in order to increase the number of proposals submitted, but also to encourage others to commit to the process. If teachers are committed to a project, they will be more likely to be enthusiastic when it is implemented in their school.
- A grantsperson must be reliable when it comes to meeting deadlines. A sure way to lose a grant is to submit the proposal even one day late. The first process carried out by people reviewing grant applications is the development of a short list of candidates. Only those proposals on the short list receive close scrutiny. Proposals that arrive late are the first to be eliminated; they are not even looked at.
- A grantsperson must be a good writer. Much of a grant proposal's success depends on the quality of the presentation. The proposal is designed to sell the project. A funding source will be more likely to look favorably on a request that is couched in credible terms. Not only must the writing be mechanically sound, but it must also get to the point, capture the reader's attention, and convey the strong impression that the funded organization will maximize the potential afforded by the grant should it be forthcoming. If a proposal is poorly presented, no matter what its other merits, it will probably be eliminated from the short list.
- A grantsperson must be good at working with people. So much work is involved in preparing proposals that it makes sense to get others involved in the process, especially those who are likely to benefit most from the resulting grant. People who are good at working with others generally have strong communication skills, lots of patience, and a genuinely friendly personality.

It may seem that anyone with this set of qualities would be difficult to find. As it happens, because these same qualities are required of good teachers, there should be plenty of potential candidates for resident grantsperson in every school.

Allow for the hidden costs of grants.

Grants take expensive time and effort: to prepare the grant proposal, to implement the grant once won, and to evaluate the impact of the grant.

Grants often require a direct or indirect matching investment. Some grants are offered on the condition of matching funds. This is because matching funds imply a commitment on the part of the institution that receives the grant, thus giving the grantor some assurance that the money, equipment, or services will not be wasted. An indirect matching investment might be the lifetime cost of support personnel, power supplies, peripheral (support) equipment, office supplies, and so forth.

Grants carry the cost of resistance to change. Introducing even one computer into a classroom demands change, unless, of course, the computer is not used. That there are so many unused computers in classrooms confirms that change is always difficult. Schools that acquire and implement grants must factor in the effort involved dealing with this very human resistance to change. This is why it is important to involve in the grant proposal process those who will be affected if the grant is won.

Whenever possible, use the computer to write the grant proposal.

The computer comes in handy even when a special grant form must be used. The form itself can sometimes be reproduced on the computer. Most grant proposals have sections that involve freeform text, which means that they can be quickly filled out by cutting and pasting from preused electronic forms. The school's grants coordinator should keep a database of grant applications and make it available for reference. This kind of support can take much of the drudgery out of the task of applying for grants.

Usually, grant proposals must be accompanied by the curriculum vitae of those responsible for implementing the grant. These should be kept on a computer so that they can be easily updated whenever necessary. It is surprising how many people fail to apply for grants because of the paperwork involved. Use the computer to simplify this task.

If at first you don't succeed, try, try again.[3]

Do not be disappointed if you do not win every grant you apply for. Bear in mind that there may be hundreds of others who are applying for the same grants. You are selling yourself and your ideas to the grant awards committees. Unless you are applying for grants that are of interest to a very limited number of people, you should expect to win no more than, perhaps, one in five of those for which you apply. The excellence of a proposal is, therefore, no guarantee of success.

This factor alone discourages many from applying for grants. This is why grant applications should be coordinated. The more people a school or school district can involve in preparing grant proposals, the easier it will be to generate a critical mass of applications, thus upping the likelihood of success. The coordinator should not

---

[3]William E. Hickson, *Try, Try, Again*

simply encourage people to apply for grants. He or she should actively assist in the development of proposals. Most teachers will not apply for grants on their own. Many teachers will get involved if they feel they are part of a team.

A grants coordinator should try to identify the current "hot" area for grant/foundation funding.

The grantor's request for proposal (RFP) will usually indicate a general target, such as "N number of dollars for educational technology." The RFP form will ask you to provide responses to a set of questions that will allow you to map out in detail what use you propose to make of the money or equipment. One year it may be multimedia, another year it may be networks. This "hot" area will differ from grant to grant, as well as from year to year. What this means in practical terms is that experience will help you cut down on the hit-and-miss nature of grant applications. The more grants you apply for, the more you are likely to win, assuming, of course, that you learn from each experience.

If your grant proposal is turned down, find out why.

Often an institution funding grants will tell you why your proposal was turned down, even if you do not ask. Sometimes, indeed, an institution will send a copy of the winning proposal as a model for future applications. When this is not the case, you should write for a formal statement so that you can learn from the experience.

14.5 Making the Most of Grants: The Seven Pillars of Success

You have won the grant. Now, what is your best strategy for achieving maximum yield from the monies and/or equipment that have been allocated to your project? Ideally, you have already thought about this—hence the planning that went into writing the grant proposal in the first place. Indeed, you won the grant as much because you had good ideas as because you had a practical, clearly delineated plan of implementation of those ideas.

What are some of the prerequisites to successful implementation of a technology program? See table 14.1 for a preliminary list of ideas as a basis for discussion. At the end of the chapter, one of the Do Something About It exercises recommends that you get together with some of your colleagues or classmates to brainstorm for more *practical* (capable of innovation) ideas to add to the list.

Let us examine each of these pillars of success one by one.

14.5.1 Active Support Must Come from the Top

A technology program is much more likely to succeed when school superintendents and principals commit to it in word and deed. As already noted, a well-developed grant proposal will include written commitments of support from those who hold the local reins of power. This support would take the form of practical allocations in terms of all necessary release time and training for those teachers and administrators who are responsible for implementing a grant.

Lumley (1992) quotes teachers as saying: "If we don't receive active leadership and support from our principal and superintendent, technology just doesn't happen!" Lumley

Table 14.1	Pillars of Successful Technology Implementation

- Active support must come from the top.
- A nondictatorial approach is always best.
- Every school should have a core of computerists.
- Teachers must come first.
- The parents and students must be involved in the evolutionary process.
- An ongoing technology training program must be in place.
- Teachers must be given time and freedom to restructure their curriculum around the technology.

then goes on to itemize the characteristics of leadership required of effective superintendents and principals: these leaders must be planners, visionaries, supporters, facilitators, and decision makers.

14.5.2 A Nondictatorial Approach Is Always Best

The best leadership establishes an environment in which expected outcomes occur spontaneously. Technology should never be forced on teachers; its use should never come as a mandate from above. Teachers, unfortunately, are no different from other professionals when it comes to sabotaging systems that they do not like and do not want. Teachers must be given the opportunity to prepare for the kind of change that computer technology brings. This is a major challenge, and one that has been sadly neglected in too many school districts during the first decade and a half of computer use in schools. Considering how carelessly computer systems have been introduced, it is hardly surprising that some teachers have resisted accommodating them in their curricula.

The best leadership, therefore, enables teachers to become the best they can be through consultation, collaboration, communication, support, respect, and encouragement. The same, of course, is true of teaching. *The best teachers establish an environment in which expected outcomes occur spontaneously.* The best leadership must also work to supply and maintain an appropriate environment that will function as fertile ground for educationally sound outcomes. Teachers are only one variable in a complex educational equation. Just as students need teachers to help them establish a "prepared environment" for learning, teachers need an administration that is committed to helping them help the students. As the principal at a school founded by Maggie Cromer expresses it so well: "Schools are institutions where people of good will work together for the children."

14.5.3 Every School Should Have a Core of Teacher–Computerists

A teacher-computerist is a person who is committed to using computer-based educational technology and who has been given the opportunity to gain a sufficiently high level of expertise to be qualified to act as an adviser and troubleshooter in matters to do with computer-based educational technology. In every school, there should be one or more teacher–computerists, the number depending on the size of the school and, of course, on the school's commitment to educational computing.

Computerists should be given adequate release time

- to work with other teachers, as individuals or in groups, introducing them to new systems, arranging product demonstrations, and helping them with any technical or pedagogical problems that may arise;
- to work with administration, planning near and long range computing strategies and mediating on behalf of teachers to help ensure that their needs are addressed;
- to work with vendors (suppliers of hardware and software), organizing product demonstrations, making sure that products are delivered as ordered and that warranties are negotiated and fulfilled.

Teachers are the ideal people to work with other teachers because they understand their needs. Teachers who are also computerists will be further suited to help their colleagues learn about computers because they are trained as teachers, and have experience working with computing novices. They are, therefore, less likely to frighten off other teachers who may be timid about using the technology.

14.5.4 Teachers Must Come First

Too many schools put computers in the hands of the students and then magically expect the teachers to take advantage of the situation in their teaching. As Elmer-Dewitt (1991) observed, teachers should be the first to receive hardware and software systems and should be the first to be trained to use them. Teachers are the leaders in the classroom. How can they take advantage of the first of these keys to successful integration of technology into their curricula (*Active support must come from the top*) unless they have sufficient knowledge and skill to feel that they are in control?

It can be done. In the fall of the 1989/90 school year, the Shoreline Public Schools gave each of their approximately 600 teachers an Apple Macintosh or an Apple IIGS as a personal productivity machine (Schlumpf, 1991). The school district began this "Apple for the Teacher" program because it believed in "giving teachers direct access to their own computer [as] the most logical step towards facilitating professional development and maintaining the excellence of [their] staff." Teachers were to feel free to take the computers home if they so wished, and to that end carrying cases were provided as well. Productivity software was supplied for each machine. Three phases of training were initiated to address the needs of different levels of expertise among the teachers. Schlumpf (1991) outlines some of the early benefits derived from the program.

14.5.5 Parents and Students Must Be Involved in the Evolutionary Process

There should be continuity between home and school. This applies to all aspects of education. Parents should feel that their child's classroom is *their* classroom. Although it will often be too much to expect that parents will have a computer for their child in the home, they should at least be provided with feedback on the existence and effectiveness of a technology program. Schools—administration and faculty—should appreciate the value of getting parents directly or indirectly involved in the classroom and commit to it.

Most parents are passive in this regard, especially after the first year or two of a child's formal education. But the best schools appreciate the power of parental involvement and actively foster close relationships between parents and the school for students of all ages—even at the college level. Most schools have PTAs, many have parent–teacher days/evenings, some structure routine home visits by teachers, and, in at least a few schools, the principal accompanies teachers when they visit the homes of their students.

Computer technology is already being used to promote contact and communication between the school and the home. Some school districts, often in collaboration with companies such as Apple, IBM, or AT&T, have provided every child with *two* computers— one for use at school and the other for use at home (Zweig, 1985). As was discussed in an earlier chapter (chapter 11), parents and teachers can maintain close contact on a daily basis via computer/telephone system hookups (Bauch, 1991). There are schools that not only put a computer on every teacher's desk, but also install a phone and a modem alongside that computer which allows parents and students to interact with teachers over electronic mail systems. Information has been defined as "a reduction in uncertainty" (Shannon & Weaver, 1949). Effective communication enabled by computer-based technology can help remove much of the uncertainty that surrounds many parents' perceptions of the education of their children.

14.5.6 An Ongoing Program in Technology Training Must Be in Place

Ongoing training is important for two reasons. First, computer technology is notorious for the pace of change that has accompanied its development and, second, anxiety generally accompanies this change. The technology is advancing so rapidly that faculty skills quickly become obsolete as new hardware and/or software systems are introduced. Commitment to a technology-based teaching and learning program will wane unless teachers are routinely helped with the process of learning new skills.

Anxiety is a human factor that can have both good and bad effects. The best kind of anxiety, such as that experienced by a teacher working with new material or with a new class—or with new technology, for that matter—improves preparation, raises concentration levels, and gives the spark of life to the new experience. This good anxiety is welcomed by good teachers because they know it is productive for all concerned. But anxiety can also be counterproductive, causing retreat from progress into the secure shell of the humdrum. This bad anxiety is often triggered by the careless introduction of innovative methodologies. Bracey (1988) cites the research of Honeyman and Warren of Lehigh and Kansas State universities, respectively, which showed that teachers needed on average a minimum of 30 contact hours with computers before they felt they had overcome initial anxiety about using them.

Bracey (1988) went on to note the findings of Wedman and Heller at the University of Northern Iowa that teachers need first to overcome their anxiety around computers without regard for how the technology might be applied in teaching and learning. An added level of anxiety can easily accompany using the technology in an actual classroom full of students who quite possibly might know more about computers than the teacher does.

Bracey (1988) concluded that technological innovation takes time and that training programs should take into account the negative potential for anxiety induced by unreasonable expectations. Capper (1988) corroborates this conclusion and emphasizes that even experienced teachers who are new to computer technology should be given ample opportunity to feel at ease using the equipment before requiring them to prepare specifically for the incorporation of the computer into their curriculum.

14.5.7 Teachers Must Be Given Time and Freedom to Restructure Their Curriculum around the Technology

This is another recommendation made by Elmer-Dewitt (1991). Typically, teachers K–12 have far too little time to prepare and follow up on classes. It is all very well to say that they have those long summers off when they could be planning new lessons, learning new methodologies, and incorporating them into their curricula. Many teachers already do this. But long-range (what is also called remote) preparation can accomplish only so much. Immediate preparation, designing classes to meet the needs of today's students *today,* must be done in the context of the live situation once the semester is under way. Preparation that involves computer technology puts greater demands on the teacher in terms of time than more traditional methodologies.

In summary, leadership could do worse than apply the secrets of success outlined above for establishing a *prepared environment* in which methodologies involving computer-based teaching and learning will flourish. Provide active support for a project; take a nondictatorial approach; make sure that every school has a core of computerists; put the teacher's needs first; get the parents and students involved; ensure that an ongoing technology-training program is in place; and last, but not least, give the teachers time and freedom to restructure their curriculum around the technology.

14.6 Evaluating the Technology Program

14.6.1 The Purpose of Evaluation

Ongoing evaluation is the key to any system's success. Sometimes we hear programs being lauded on the basis of their existence alone. "Last year, a sum in the amount of $125,000 was spent on the purchase and installation of additional student computing facilities. We feel that this will allow us to continue to offer our children an educational experience that will prepare them for the technological age." Sounds impressive? This is what some school districts pass off as demonstrating their commitment to providing the best possible educational experience for their students. Often there is no mention of computing facilities for the teachers, no mention of allocation of time to teachers so they can learn to use the new technology, no mention of *how* "additional student computing facilities" will make any difference at all, and, above all, no mention of the criteria that will be used to judge the effectiveness of the system being funded. As Branscum (1992) observed, "for far too many, computers are . . . used in tragically misguided ways."

Of course, making money available is important. Computer-based education is a lot more expensive than "chalk and talk." But, if the money invested is to yield an acceptable return, there must be accountability in terms of results clearly demonstrating improvements along criteria laid down by the managers of the educational process. Accountability is possible only if there exists a clear set of criteria based on a school district's educational goals. Routine evaluation is the process that puts accountability under the magnifying glass by examining a system's success against established expectations.

Think of evaluation of a learning system, whether designed around computer technology or not, in the same way as you would think of service on your car or checkups on your health. The idea is to improve the performance, and ultimately extend the life, of the system under examination.

14.6.2 When Should a Program Be Evaluated?

Evaluation that is done with care and sensitivity and that is approached from a positive perspective serves to maintain the healthiest possible status for a system. Therefore, the best time to evaluate a program is when it appears to be working perfectly, in the same way as the best time to service a car is when it is running well, and the best time to check out the human body is when it is in a robust, healthy state. Evaluation of a learning system should also be routine, with the objective of checking to ensure that initially stated goals continue to be met in order to identify opportunities that will lead to those goals being improved upon.

It is usually the case that new and often unexpected negative or positive outcomes for a system are identified during the process of evaluation. Negative outcomes that are identified early can be circumvented and avoided. Positive outcomes can be seized as opportunities for extending the potential of the system. For example, the *Teaching and Learning with Technology* project (Klenow, 1991), which was described in chapter 12, had several unexpected outcomes, among which were:

- Teachers discovered that "they no longer want to teach without technology," and that "they can be omnipresent without being controlling."
- Teachers and students discovered that "they have a greater tolerance for ambiguity and that both parties have ownership in the teaching/learning process."
- "The project forced [the teachers to engage in] conscious discussion of their roles as teachers causing them to take stock of themselves and their work."

There is so much richness in experience that surprises like this are the norm, rather than the exception. The beauty of discovering unexpected outcomes is that, once discovered, they can be controlled: enhanced if they are positive, corrected if they are negative. This is why evaluation should be conducted when the system is in a healthy state, not when it is already on its last legs.

14.6.3 The Components of the Evaluation Process

Draw up evaluation instruments based on the initially stated objectives for the project.

The first step in evaluating a technology program is to identify and delineate the objectives of the program. These objectives should be sufficiently specific as to be *measurable*. In the case of a technology program funded by a grant, they will already have been delineated, for the most part, in the grant proposal. These measurable objectives would then become part of the evaluation instruments, which are comprised of those series of check points and questions regarding predetermined aspects of the project. Questionnaires, pre and post tests, and portfolios of student work are examples of useful evaluation instruments. These evaluation instruments would be used during the regularly scheduled process of data collection about the project.

Reviewing the objectives spelled out in the proposal has the following benefits:

- The objectives will reassume importance before implementation of the grant. Implementors will approach the process of implementation more focused on the outcomes from their efforts. If you know where you are going you are much more likely to arrive at the correct destination.

- With the passage of time, it may well be that stated objectives need to be adjusted or augmented to reflect change in circumstances that have occurred since the grant proposal was originally drafted. New objectives may have become apparent. To the extent that they do not compromise the essential purpose of the grant, these additional objectives should be considered for inclusion alongside the original objectives to help guide implementation and evaluation.

- Some objectives will not be as important as others. Reviewing objectives will enable the implementing team to prioritize them, thus reducing the danger that important goals become sidetracked by an unwarranted preoccupation with ones of lesser importance. For example, one objective of introducing new computer-based technology might be to *foster computer literacy* (familiarity with, and appreciation of the value of, computer technology) among the students involved in its use. Another objective might be to *improve students' writing skills* as measured against norms established by some specific, standardized assessment instrument.

Both are laudable objectives. The first, however, should not take priority over the second—*and should not be touted as a significant outcome from the project*—because, to a large extent, computer literacy will take care of itself in the world of today's child, where computers are, for the most part, taken for granted. On the other hand, the second objective, improving students' writing skills, will always represent a crying need in schools. Computer-based systems for developing writing skills have been shown to augment other methodologies in pursuit of this objective and, therefore, fostering improved writing skills using computer-based systems is a goal worthy of diligent application. As Piller (1992) observed, emphasis on computer literacy can too easily become a cop-out when justifying computer use in schools. It covers up an all too common reality: money spent on computer technology has been wasted on poorly focused, poorly supported, poorly implemented systems.

Use the evaluation instruments to conduct the evaluation.

Each time data are collected, it should give a snapshot of the state of the environment. As Kinnaman (1992) explains, when it comes down to it, evaluation involves "stopping at both predetermined and random points on your journey to look around and answer the questions: *'Do the surroundings look the way we expected them to look at this point?* and *How happy are we with our progress?'"*

Kinnaman (1992) recommends that we look at more than student achievement on tests when conducting an evaluation. Pre and post tests, for example, are a useful barometer, but not a completely reliable one. Tests can be unconsciously biased or inappropriate. Other useful, though more time-consuming, measures involve

- "performance assessment [which] focuses on what the student can *do*" (projects, portfolios of work accomplished);
- questionnaires and interviews to sound out "student attitudes . . . motivation, effort, or enthusiasm";
- and similar instruments to sound out "teacher attitudes and behaviors . . . teacher motivation . . . ways in which teachers interact with each other [or] with students."

Evaluation is an opportunity for improving the quality of a funded project. It should begin the moment the decision is made to prepare the grant proposal and should continue at regular intervals throughout the life of the project. The goal is the pursuit of excellence, which can be sustained only if we accept that it is by no means guaranteed. Educational technology-based projects that are evaluated in this way are far more likely to succeed. They are also more likely to provide a wealth of experience that will lead on to improvements in other areas of educational endeavor. As the English philosopher Aldous Huxley remarked: "Experience is not what happens to a man. It is what a man does with what happens to him."

■ Looking Back

In recent years, education systems all over the world have come under scrutiny and been found wanting. In some countries, the systems are criticized as being too elitist, excluding too many of their youth from access to higher levels of education. In other countries, the systems are criticized for the declining quality of the graduates, at least as compared with 20 or 30 years ago. The United States, "a nation at risk," has also been found wanting. Education is at a crossroads. There is a sense that major change must occur if our schools are to meet the needs of future generations of children. But that change is expensive. In better economic times, schools could expect an adequate level of federal, state, and local support. But, by all accounts, national and global economic constraints are going to hamper educational progress through the remainder of this century, unless we take matters into our own hands.

The Computer Learning Foundation is a nonprofit educational foundation serving the United States and Canada. Its primary focus is on developing computer competence among youth. It is officially endorsed by 54 U.S. and Canadian departments of education and 25 national nonprofit organizations. Funding for the foundation comes from U.S. and Canadian corporations, local businesses, and individuals. It is representative of many governmental and private philanthropic organizations in that it is dedicated to helping the deserving needy pull themselves up by their own bootstraps.

Technology education at David Prouty High School
by Brian Scarbeau, Lake-Sumter Community College, Leesburg, Florida

Background

David Prouty High School is a comprehensive, regional high school with students coming from the Massachusetts towns of Spencer and East Brookfield. Approximately 530 students annually attend the high school, which is located in central Massachusetts 15 miles from Worcester and 60 miles from Boston.

Before 1987, the high school had 10 IBM-compatible computers with monochrome displays, and senior business students were taught basic word processing and spreadsheet applications. Also at that time, a science teacher taught the BASIC programming language on Commodore computers.

In 1987, a decision was made to update the computer equipment at the high school with a local area network. Twenty-five IBM model 30 PS/2 computers with color monitors and an IBM model 60 PS/2 computer were leased for five years. At the same time the school successfully applied for a Carl Perkins grant to purchase the Novell networking software along with the *Word Perfect* and *WordStar* word processing software and the Aldus *PageMaker* desktop publishing software.

Two new courses were offered to all students at the high school: College Word Processing and Personal Computer Applications. The College Word Processing course was a half-year course geared to college-bound students. *WordStar* word processing was taught. The Personal Computer Applications course was a full-year course for business students in which applications using the *Word Perfect* word processor, the *Lotus 1-2-3* spreadsheet, and the *dBase III* database were taught.

The following year, a second Carl Perkins grant was won, enabling the high school to purchase new state-of-the-art equipment. A Hewlett-Packard laser printer was purchased along with a color printer, scanner, and desktop-publishing monitors. Desktop publishing was introduced in the Personal Computer Applications course. Students were taught Aldus *PageMaker* and used the scanner to scan images of various kinds for inclusion in the documents produced using the *PageMaker* software.

IBM *Storyboard,* a multimedia software program, was also purchased with the Carl Perkins grant money and students were introduced to this new technology in the Personal Computer Applications course.

Brian Scarbeau, author of the case study
Photo courtesy Brian Scarbeau

During the next two years, 1989 and 1990, more multimedia equipment was purchased with the Carl Perkins grant: a speech adapter card, a music card, a Pioneer laserdisc player, and the *Business Disc* laserdisc program, along with a new multimedia software program called *Linkway!* Rounding out the purchases were a modem, a laptop computer, and a 350-megabyte hard disk for our network server.

Technology Triggers Change

Thanks to the Carl Perkins grant, our program was able to expand and grow. New objectives were defined and integrated into the course offerings each year in order to introduce this technology to our students. Each year, the program was evaluated and changed to maximize the goals that were established.

The Personal Computer Applications course was offered to all high school students, not just to business students, allowing more students to be exposed to the new technology. In addition, the course, which started out as a full-year course, was offered as two half-year courses to add flexibility to the school's schedule.

(continued)

In the Personal Computer Applications I course, students learn word processing (*Word Perfect*), spreadsheet (*Lotus 1-2-3*), and database (*dBase III+*) applications. The Personal Computer Applications II course covers desktop publishing (*PageMaker*), telecommunications (including electronic mail), and presentation graphics. The students worked on a *Linkway!*-based, multimedia project, which gave them the opportunity to learn to use the scanner and the digitizer. They also used *Linkway!* to create speech and music for the project.

The goals for these two courses were to give students the opportunity to learn new technology and to provide them with job skills. The students who took these courses were prepared for their future in the working world.

The multimedia training component of the course was very exciting for the students. After learning how to use the multimedia software, each student spent four weeks working on his or her assigned project. The guidelines for the project were simple to follow. Each student had to design at least a 20-screen interactive presentation on a subject of his or her choice using IBM *Linkway!* An evaluation screen was created to allow the reviewer of the project to answer appropriate questions about what had been learned while reviewing each screen. In addition, music and speech had to be incorporated somewhere in the project.

Students selected an interesting range of topics for their projects. Among them were a tour of Florida, an overview of the Gulf War, a presentation about witches, and a biography of Michael Jordan, to name a few. Each student was encouraged to be creative and the screens were well designed. The speech and music that were integrated into the presentations were interesting and well thought out in keeping with the themes of the projects.

After the deadline for delivery of their projects had passed, students had the opportunity to view each other's work. Naturally, some students produced better work than others; some took the time to be very creative and others made a bare minimum of effort. We considered it important that the students learn from the understanding that they had a predetermined amount of time to complete this project. A small number of students spent too much time on one aspect of their project, thus failing to complete all the requirements. All in all it was a great experience for everyone involved.

Business Simulation

The Business Simulation class, another new course, also uses the laserdisc player and the *Business Disc* laserdisc program already mentioned. This computerized program uses the interactive laserdisc to instruct students in how to run a business from scratch. Each student is then required to select a specific business to run for the purposes of the simulation that follows. Certain everyday business situations arise and the students must make decisions based on what they believe would be the most practical and profitable thing to do for their business. A monthly report is generated by the system and the students must then make a decision as to what financial adjustments have to be made.

In addition to using the *Business Disc* laserdisc program, each student used a laserdisc program that was developed by Brian G. Scarbeau, the Business department head and teacher of the Business Simulation course. This program is called *The Joy of Stocks* and is interfaced with the IBM *Linkway!* software. *The Joy of Stocks* instructs students on how a business is started. The software then decides to sell stocks to increase capital. In this way, students learn how stocks are bought and sold on the New York Stock Exchange. *The Joy of Stocks* allows students to actually see the activity of the trading of stocks using the Forbes laserdisc of stock quotations. The program is very educational, enabling the students to quickly learn how the stock market works.

Students learned a great deal from this experience and especially liked the incorporation of the new technology into the curriculum. Not all students made money at the end of the business simulation, which led to much discussion as to why they had failed to be profitable.

Other Curriculum Applications

Technology is used in many other courses at David Prouty High School. There is an Ed Center where students use the eight IBM-compatible computers for remedial work. Also, the Tech Ed department uses CAD/CAM software for training. In addition, the English department encourages students to use the word processing software for their projects. An image database was created by Craig Jyringi, a science teacher, for his biology class.

(continued)

Case Study 14 (concluded)

The school won an Alliance for Education grant to enable students to do multimedia research. The Comptons multimedia *Encyclopedia* CD-ROM disc was purchased. The on-line encyclopedia facilitated multisensory research of topics with quick access to text, pictures, and sound (music and speech) related to the subject being researched.

David Prouty High School has come a long way with technology education and will continue its mission of offering the best preparation possible for its student population.

Talk About It

Topics for discussion based on the case study.

1. How can simulation training be used effectively in the classroom?

2. How can science students benefit by doing desktop publishing?

3. How can more teachers get involved in multimedia?

4. Why should all schools consider networking their computers?

5. Should multimedia training be mandatory training for all students?

That is what grants and donations are designed to do. Ideally, they are not given away arbitrarily. It is as if the sponsors are saying: "We have substantial amounts of money and equipment to help you. Show us that you understand the educational needs of children in a modern society, show us that you are likely to make the most of any help we give you, and we will provide you with the wherewithal to pursue excellence."

Sometimes we have to grasp opportunities for change and make things happen.

■ Looking Forward

In the last chapter, we will reflect on the theory and practice of computer-based teaching and learning. Computers have value in schools only to the extent that they reinforce the centrality of the individual student in the educational process while providing opportunities for that individual student to work collaboratively with peers at home and abroad. The cultural change for teachers will be as dramatic as that for students. The most successful teachers will take every opportunity to acquire the skills and concepts that are necessary to provide an appropriate and effective learning environment for their students.

What shape that learning environment will take is still largely a matter of conjecture. Cheaply available, notebook-size computers may eventually replace paper-based grade books and rosters. A computer weighing a couple of pounds, with the power and functionality of an end-of-20th-century supercomputer, and costing no more than a few dollars, will find its way into every teacher's attaché case. We will be able to download into it a lifetime of relevant data regarding our students. We will be able to link them to networks which will put us in touch not only with the entire world of information available at the end of telecommunication lines, but also with our students, wherever they may be. Perhaps much of education will eventually take place from the home—a teleschooling equivalent of telecommuting. Just as many workers now log on to their companies from home-based offices, so tomorrow's children may power up the information center in their room at home to log in to classes that do not require their physical presence at a central learning location.

Student teachers in this last decade of the 20th century will see extraordinary change during the course of their careers. *The key to their survival will be their ability to adapt.* An understanding of reality is the foundation for purposeful adaptation, and an understanding of reality is borne of experience and conscientious study of the wisdom of those who have gone before. Chapter 15 tries to capture past and current wisdom and apply it to the realities of education for an information age.

■ Do Something About It: Exercises and Projects

1. What are some of the prerequisites to successful implementation of a technology program? Get together with some of your colleagues or classmates to discuss this topic. Brainstorm for more *practical* ideas to add to those outlined in this chapter. Select three of the best ideas that you come up with and discuss how each idea might best be implemented. What would be your strategy to turn ideas into innovations?

2. Lumley (1992) itemizes the characteristics of leadership required of effective superintendents and principals: these leaders have to be planners, visionaries, supporters, facilitators, and decision-makers. Discuss each of these leadership characteristics. What responsibilities pertain to each? Are some characteristics more important than others? Are there other leadership characteristics that you think should be included in the list?

3. Review the Wilson (1992) list of suggestions for funding sources (section 14.3) in the context of your own experience either as a practicing teacher or as a student in a school district with which you are familiar.

4. Join with a team of classmates or colleagues to plan and prepare a grant proposal either in response to an actual grant opportunity or for some project that has potential for attracting sponsorship.

■ References

Bauch, Jerold. *Correspondence with author.* July 9, 1991.

Bork, Alfred. The Potential for Interactive Technology. *Byte,* February 1987, pp. 201–6.

Bracey, Gerald W. Still Anxiety Among Educators Over Computers. *Electronic Learning,* March 1988.

Branscum, Deborah. Educators Need Support to Make Computing Meaningful. *MacWorld,* Special Section on Personal Computers in Education, September 1992.

Capper, Joanne. Computers and Learning: Do They Work? A Review of Research. Document prepared for the Office of Technology Assessment, Congress of the United States, for the assessment *Power On: New Tools for Teaching and Learning,* January 21, 1988.

Dunlop, David L. Regional Computer Resource Centers: Opportunities for Excellence. In *Yearbook of the Pennsylvania Council of Teachers of Math,* 1986, pp. 86–97.

Elmer-Dewitt, Philip. The Revolution That Fizzled. *Time,* May 20, 1991, pp. 48–49.

Foreman, Deidre R., Paula Franks. Contemporary Issues in Social Studies Utilizing the Latest Technology. In *Proceedings of the National Educational Computing Conference,* and presented at the conference, June 18, 1991, p. 31.

Kinnaman, Daniel E. How to Evaluate Your Technology Program. In *Technology and Learning,* vol. 12, no. 7, April 1992.

Klenow, Carol, Janet Van Dam, Rebecca Rankin. *Teaching and Learning with Technology: Executive Summary of the Evaluation Report.* Oakland Schools, MI: Division of Information Resources, 1991.

Lumley, Dan, Gerald Bailey. On the Technological Battlefield. *Electronic Learning,* vol. 11, no. 8, May–June 1992.

National Commission on Excellence in Education. *A Nation at Risk.* Cambridge, MA: USA Research, 1984.

Nussel, Edward J., Joan D. Inglis, William Wiersma. *The Teacher and Individually Guided Education.* Reading, MA: Addison-Wesley, 1976.

Oakland Schools. *Teaching and Learning With Technology: Executive Summary of the Evaluation Report.* Oakland Schools, MI: Division of Information Resources, 1991.

Piller, Charles. Separate Realities. *MacWorld,* Special Section on Personal Computers in Education, September 1992.

Polya, G. Gyorgy. *How to Solve It: A New Aspect of Mathematical Method.* Princeton, NJ: Princeton University Press, 1945.

SCANS. *What Work Requires of Schools: A SCANS Report for America 2000.* Washington, DC: Secretary's Commission on Achieving Necessary Skills, U.S. Department of Labor, June 1991.

Shannon, Claude E., W. Weaver. *The Mathematical Theory of Communication.* Urbana: University of Illinois Press, 1949.

Stanton, Susan. The Big Picture: Corporate and Foundation Sources of Nationwide Giving. *Technology and Learning,* vol. 12, no. 4, January 1992, pp. 38–47.

Stone, Antonia. How to Make All Children Techno-Able. *School Administrator,* Special Report on Computer Technology, 1990.

T&L Editorial. Model Schools: Inspiration or a Waste of Money? In Speaking Out section in *Technology and Learning,* vol. 13, no. 3, November/December 1992.

Van Dam, Janet, Carol Klenow. Teaching and Learning With Technology. Report to the *National Educational Computing Conference,* June 1991.

Wilson, Tom. Where to Find Funding for Your Technology Project. *Technology and Learning,* vol. 12, no. 4, January 1992, pp. 36–38.

Zweig, Connie. California Elementary School Experiments with Classroom of Future. *Christian Science Monitor,* December 16, 1985.

Reflections on Education for an Information Age

What avail is it to win prescribed amounts of information about geography and history, to win ability to read and write, if in the process the individual loses his own soul . . . if he loses his desire to apply what he has learned and, above all, loses the ability to extract meaning from his future experiences as they occur.

John Dewey (1859–1952)

A teacher is a person with a touch of immortality, and he should be most envied among men. His profession should be the most sought after, the most carefully prepared for, the most universally recognized.

Samuel Gould (1910–   )

The mind, stretched by a new idea, never goes back to its original dimension.

Oliver Wendell Holmes (1809–1894)

This chapter has four objectives:

- To correlate the practice of computer-based teaching and learning with the significant learning theories enunciated over the past 2,400 years since the time of Plato and Aristotle.
- To argue the importance of individualized education in an information age.
- To make recommendations regarding appropriate use of computers in the classroom.
- To review the needs of teachers during this time of transition in education.

As we will see, the major theories and methodologies have timeless merit and are still applied in classrooms today. After all, as Confucius said: "The nature of people is always the same; it is their habits which separate them" (Fersh, 1982). It will be interesting to see what pedagogical habits, if any, need to be changed when computers are factored into the learning equation.

How might traditional theories of learning be best applied? What are some of the mistakes made by teachers when using computer technology? What help is available for teachers who are new to using computers in the classroom? What is the future for schools if the integration of technology-based education continues apace?

These are some of the questions addressed in this chapter, which will cover the following topics:

- Computers, learning theory, and cognitive development
- Individualized education and the concept of information
  - Data versus information
  - The transfer of data to information is a unique individual experience
  - Computers and the individual's construction of information
- Using computers in the classroom
  - When the computer should be used
  - When the computer should not be used
- Taking care of the teachers
  - Teachers must have time
  - Teachers must have ongoing training
  - Teachers must have technical and logistical support

■ 15.1 Introduction

Chapter 1 presented some of the conclusions drawn from the research into effective computer-based teaching and learning. Many of those conclusions, though tentative, are compelling. For example, Samson et al. (1986) reported in their quantitative synthesis of 43 research studies that "the achievement of the average student exposed to computer-based instruction increased to the 63rd percentile, compared to performance at the 50th percentile for the average student receiving traditional instruction."

Clearly, results such as these are most likely to occur in an environment where computers have been thoughtfully integrated into the learning process. As pointed out in the previous chapter, there is more to computer-based learning than simply tossing a few machines into a classroom and leaving the teachers and students to get on with it.

Success incorporating the computer into the curriculum has been uneven, to say the least. Over the last dozen or so years, schools have spent billions of dollars on computers, presumably with the hope that this would improve the quality of education. Such has been the case in many schools, as evidenced by the kind of research summarized in chapter 1. But several reports (Benderson, 1983; Borrell, 1992; Branscum, 1992; Bulkeley, 1988; Elmer-Dewitt, 1991; McGee, 1982; Perelman, 1990; Piller, 1992) have confirmed the waste that has occurred as a result of the failure to provide adequate and ongoing training and support for the people—teachers and administrators alike—who were supposed to spearhead the use of computers in the K–12 curriculum.

Tentatively, however, these exceptions appear to prove the rule that computer-integrated education works best when it is well-planned, well-integrated, closely monitored as to its effectiveness like any other methodology, and given a fair chance. A fair chance can be guaranteed only if computer-based teaching and learning are constructed on the seven pillars of success that were defined in the previous chapter (see table 14.1).

15.2 Computers, Learning Theory, and Cognitive Development

15.2.1 Computers and Learning

The computer is a general-purpose machine. Indeed, as Alan Turing (1937) demonstrated, it is in theory a "Universal Machine." With the application of human intelligence, the computer is becoming a useful tool for a diverse set of teaching-related tasks, from monitoring attendance to simulating scientific experiments and social conditions to enabling handicapped children to join the mainstream of education on equal terms, to name but a few.

Educators have been quick to imagine ways in which the computer can be programmed to foster the learning process. This was true as early as the 1960s, when computers were mighty, multimillion dollar behemoths owned only by governments and major corporations. A few enterprising teachers were linking up with these corporations and shepherding students across town to give them the opportunity to develop problem-solving skills by writing programs.

As described in chapter 2, from day one, computers have been important research tools, especially for scientists and engineers. By the late 1960s, the latter were joined by researchers in all fields of learning when **database management systems (DBMS)** enabled the easy storage and retrieval of huge amounts of text-based data (Date, 1986). Today, the descendants of these DBMS are the engines driving multimedia and distance learning computer systems.

So, computer use in schools is not new. The question is: Is its use founded on sound pedagogical principles? Before we answer that question, it will be useful to review the various ideas about learning and cognitive development that guide teachers when they formulate methodologies for helping students in their acquisition of knowledge. After all, decisions about how and when to use computers to improve the quality of a child's education must be predicated on the knowledge and experience of the teachers responsible for preparing and maintaining the environment in which that education takes place.

15.2.2 Learning Theory

We will begin our examination of the correlation between pedagogical theory and the practice of computer-based teaching and learning by presenting a brief overview of learning theory and cognitive development. These two areas of study are fundamental to the teaching profession and, as such, are very relevant to the application of computers in the classroom.

How children learn has been the topic of much debate and is naturally an important subject of study for teachers. A reasonable outcome from this study should be that there is no single, best approach to enabling learning that can be applied in all situations with all students (Bigge, 1982). For this reason, student teachers who are well prepared for the classroom are expected to study, experience, and apply (at least in a laboratory setting such as in-course simulations, or during student teaching) a range of learning theories from the time-honored mental discipline (nonexperimental, philosophical) theories advocated by Augustine, Plato, Rousseau, Herbart, and others, to the cognitive (experimental, scientific) theories of Wertheimer, Kohler, Koffka, Lewin, and their followers (Bigge, 1982).

15.2.3 Cognitive Development

A significant body of research helps us to assess our students' academic standing in relation to cognitive developmental expectations based on variables related to their age and intellectual maturity.

Piaget (1954, 1971) observed that all children follow a progression toward intellectual maturity, from the initial sensorimotor stage (birth to 18 months/2 years) to the symbolic or preconcrete operational stage (18 months to 7/8 years) to the concrete operations stage (7 years to 12 years) and, finally, to the stage where the child becomes capable of formal operations (12 to 15 years).

Bruner (1966), acknowledging the work of Piaget, further refines the observation of the stages of human cognitive growth, noting the progression in the ways children "represent their experience of the world": from the enactive mode (where actions are the avenue to understanding) to the ikonic mode (where images are used to represent experience) and, finally, to the symbolic mode (where language in its many forms enables cognitive encapsulation of reality).

Chapter 7 elaborated on this theme in the discussion of the design of modern computer operating systems. Studies in education are designed to help teachers become familiar with a corpus of studies such as this in order to inform their adoption and selection of methodologies in support of the learning process. Well-designed, computer-based learning systems will apply the principles of sound learning theory appropriate to the cognitive development of the learner. The teacher's role is to determine that the learner is suitably served on both counts.

15.2.4 Constructivism

In recent years, there has been growing support for a constructivist theory of learning, which Tobias (1991) describes as "an end product of the cognitive psychologists' emphasis on students' internal representation of external phenomena, and the pivotal role assigned to the cognitive processing of those phenomena." **Constructivism** sees the learner as willingly active in the pursuit of understanding of experience. Driven by curiosity about a world that, in real terms, expands with this experience, the learner seeks answers to questions as they arise: What is this? Where is this? What will happen if I do this? Who is this? and so on.

Finding answers to this constant stream of curiosity-driven questions involves the learner in equally constant, though not necessarily productive (i.e., effective or correct), construction of mental and physical solutions. As Perkins (1991) observes: "Central to the vision of constructivism is the notion of the organism as 'active'—not just responding to stimuli, as in the behaviorist rubric, but engaging, grappling, and seeking to make sense of things."

In this, Perkins (1991) echoes the philosophy of Jean Piaget (1971), who explains what he believes to be the source of scientific knowledge as stemming "neither from sensation nor from perception alone but from the entire action." Piaget goes on to note that "the characteristic of intelligence is not to contemplate but to 'transform' and its mechanism is essentially operatory. . . . We only know an object by acting on it and transforming it."

Good teachers, constructivist or otherwise, given an environment in which they can allow free rein to a child's thirst for understanding, will try to focus the child's quest by providing what they consider to be appropriate stimuli and feedback. The teacher's goal in this collaborative endeavor is not so much to instruct as to educate—*educere*, lead forward—in the belief that the child should not be left to flounder in the discovery of knowledge. It is the rare child, after all, who can discover unaided the kind of intellectual skills required to contribute effectively in today's information-intensive world.

Unfortunately, most teachers are not given "an environment in which they can allow free rein to a child's thirst for understanding." Classes are typically too large to accommodate significant individualized instruction. For this reason, constructivism and the many other powerful theories of learning such as those advocated by Dewey, Montessori, Piaget, Bruner, and others have not found general acceptance in public, or even most private, systems of education.

However, teacher–pupil ratios are falling, and technology is becoming sufficiently sophisticated to take on many of the stimulus and feedback functions of guided, individual student learning. This evolutionary process shows promise of eventually leading to a learning environment in which teachers will manage, guide, motivate, and coordinate, and in which students will actively, individually or in small groups, discover knowledge in the context of the Montessorian "prepared environment" of the technology-rich classrooms of tomorrow.

This is already happening in a sprinkling of schools worldwide, including some of those profiled in this book.

15.3.1 It's Not How Smart the Child Is, but How the Child Is Smart

The extent to which individuals reach their potential as human beings is partially dependent on cultural expectations. The history of education tells the unfortunate story of the many systems that operated under the assumption that certain groups of individuals were less academically able than others. This attitude was able to persist because the education systems themselves were founded on arbitrary definitions of what constitutes academic ability.

To some extent this is understandable, even though it is inexcusable. As explained in the previous section, education has a pragmatic emphasis—where success is measured by how profitable the graduate becomes in adult life. But a more appropriate and equitable definition of academic ability begins with the assumption that every individual is academically able, regardless of whether that ability will yield a profitable return. The school's responsibility is to determine in what respects this is true for each and every student. As one teacher put it: "The question is not how smart the child is, but how the child is smart."

The school as lifelong information system succeeds or fails to the extent that it helps individual students achieve their potential as human beings. "You cannot teach a man anything," observed Galileo; "you can only help him to find it within himself." We may look to numbers as a measure of performance because we do not have a more convenient way of judging success. So, we rate schools and individuals based on numerical criteria. In the end, however, true success can be measured only in terms of the individual's self-fulfillment.

Education must, therefore, continue to broaden its definition of what constitutes a successful student, for no two graduates will be equally or identically shaped by what goes on in schools.

Each individual has a unique, valuable contribution to make. Education's task, with the help of all concerned—students, parents, teachers, administrators, and the local community—is to nurture the unique excellence in each and every one of us. Traditional methodologies developed to cope with large-group instruction tend to overlook individual needs. As the rest of this section explains, information acquisition is a unique experience that is more likely to take place in individual or small-group learning experiences. The underlying argument of this book has been that individualized education is more likely to be fostered where teachers are given the opportunity to design and maintain learning environments that include well-managed and integrated, computer-based teaching and learning.

It will be useful to continue this discussion by drawing an important distinction in the cognitive domain between *data* and *information.*

15.3.2 Data versus Information

Teachers more than most other professionals should understand and appreciate the difference between data and information. Data[1] are the raw material of information. Data are

---

[1] *Data* is the plural form of the word. *Datum* is the singular form. Strictly speaking, one should say "a datum *is*" and "data *are*." However, in everyday usage data is used as a singular or plural noun. Thus, it is correct to say either "Data *is*" *or* "Data *are*." According to Webster's *Random House Dictionary* (1991 edition), the word *datum* is rarely used.

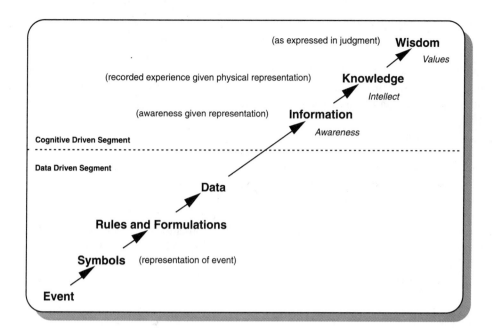

Figure 15.1
The Knowledge
Spectrum
Illustration courtesy
Anthony Debons et al.
(1988)

organized symbols (numbers, letters, pictures) that are representative of events. Data have no meaning in and of themselves. Meaning implies understanding, which implies cognitive activity of some kind. Once meaning is applied to data—once mind acknowledges and assimilates data—they become information.

Shannon and Weaver (1949) define information as data that "reduce uncertainty"—data that extend the realm of understanding lead the mind to new awareness of the world, is accompanied, perhaps, by an element of surprise (the "aha" response). So, we are not informed when we are told something we already know. We are informed when the data that are the subject of the communication extend and renew our receiving mind. When we are informed, our minds and, in some real sense, our lives are changed.

Debons et al. (1988) are careful as information scientists to delineate a continuum they call the Knowledge Spectrum (figure 15.1). The continuum starts with an occurrence called an Event, which constitutes "some condition or change in the state of the world." The Event is captured in our minds using Symbols—essentially meaningless representations requiring Rules and Formulations to give them significance. Once the symbolic representation of the event has been organized using the rules and formulations, Data are produced. Strictly speaking, the mind has not yet been engaged. We are in the Data Driven Segment of the continuum.

Once data are acknowledged by the senses, the mind becomes involved. If the data "reduce uncertainty," information results from the experience. The mind is literally changed physically by the growth in knowledge that information in this Debonian sense brings. As Oliver Wendell Holmes observed: "The mind, stretched by a new idea, never goes back to its original dimension."

The information is added to the mind's store of knowledge when the intellect brings understanding to bear on the information, enabling the mind to use the knowledge "to analyze situations and to put things into their proper perspective" (Debons, 1988). Problem solving does not happen in a vacuum; it arises from a knowledge base sustained by an informed mind. The final stage in the Knowledge Spectrum is wisdom, which brings a set of values to bear on judgments that call on the store of knowledge accumulated through experience.

If it is true that knowledge is power and that those with access to knowledge can compete most effectively for a fair share of the available "wealth" generated in a society, and if it is also true that education is the primary formative experience that puts the keys of knowledge acquisition into a child's hands, then it follows that education is in every sense *the* key to survival in today's information society.

Every teacher is an educator with a mandate to *educate*—to lead out, to lead from, to challenge, to cause to advance. A prerequisite for the formation of an educated individual is the establishment of an environment in which that mind will be encouraged and stimulated to experience a multifaceted world at a level that is consonant with each individual's stage of cognitive development.

15.3.3 The Transfer of Data to Information Is a Unique Individual Experience

Debons (1988) describes the process whereby data is acquired, transmitted, processed, and utilized on the way to becoming of value in decision making. This Debonian model of an information system includes another key component—transfer—which is the end product of an information system. This is when data, because they are new[2], impact the human mind, reducing uncertainty and forever changing the individual's knowledge base.

For the teacher, this has many powerful implications, not least of which are the following:

A student is not informed by the mere attempt by the teacher to convey data. Remind yourself of how many times you have sat through a class, or read page after page of a book, and neither averted to, nor understood, a single thing!

A student is not informed when the data are already known. Remind yourself of how many times you have sat through a class, or read page after page of a book, and learned nothing you didn't know before!

Indeed, a common criticism of poorly designed computer-based learning is that it expects students to mindlessly review material that is already thoroughly learned. On the other hand, well-designed computer-based learning will recognize and remember individual student characteristics and capabilities, and will challenge the user to move to higher levels of learning by addressing that individual's unique learning needs.

The transformation (transfer) of data into information is thus a unique, individual experience even when shared with others. Unfortunately, this is difficult to achieve without the individualizing capability of a well-used tool such as the computer, because of the circumstances where most teachers are expected to work with too many students at once.

---

[2]Data can be "new" even when old. I can know what a particular piece of music sounds like, but, at some later time, I may relive the newness at a deeper level of familiar experience.

The typical teacher–pupil ratio, though much better than 50 years ago, is still unsatisfactorily disproportionate, even when the ratio is closer to the 1:10 which pertains in most private schools. Tailoring course content to individual needs is a major challenge for even the best teachers. Computer-based learning, which helps a teacher individualize instruction, should be given a closer look.

15.4 When Should the Computer Be Used in the Classroom?

The human mind is extraordinarily complex. Tufte (1990) captures this complexity when he describes the information-processing skills of the human intellect:

> We thrive in information-thick worlds because of our marvellous and everyday capacities to select, edit, single out, structure, highlight, group, pair, merge, harmonize, synthesize, focus, organize, condense, reduce, boil down, choose, categorize, catalog, classify, refine, abstract, scan, look into, idealize, isolate, discriminate, distinguish, screen, sort, pick over, group, pigeonhole, integrate, blend, average, filter, lump, skip, smooth, chunk, inspect, approximate, cluster, aggregate, outline, summarize, itemize, review, dip into, flip through, browse, glance into, leaf through, skim, list, glean, synopsize, winnow wheat from chaff, and separate the sheep from the goats.

It is unreasonable to expect children to grow intellectually in some straightened environment where variety of learning experience is reduced to the bare minimum. This is something that a good teacher intuitively understands. But the good teacher also intuitively understands that effective learning requires discipline, concentration, periods of peace and quiet, and a sense of order.

Unfortunately, it is often easier for a computer to be used as a pacifier than as a tool for solid learning. Many applications of computers in schools have the primary objective of occupying the children for a period of time, regardless of learning outcomes. In light of this, it will be useful to examine when and how the computer should and should not be used for teaching and learning.

Although it is never indispensable, the computer is an appropriate tool to use for teaching and learning in many pedagogical situations. Here we will review a sample selection of such situations. In the Do Something About It section at the end of the chapter, you are invited to discuss this topic more extensively.

15.4.1 Computer-Based Learning Enables the Teacher to Tailor the Learning Situation to Suit Individual Student Needs

Turkle (1984) recognizes the value of the computer, "the second self," for those many learning situations when the child's personality, age, and style of learning call for an individualized approach. This puts the onus on the teacher to diagnose each individual child's information needs and style of learning, and then prescribe appropriate learning opportunities.

Although not impossible, this is difficult to do in a traditional classroom where the large class size, coupled with a limited set of learning materials, makes customized instruction an elusive dream. In the computerized classroom, however, access to a wide variety of educational software enables the teacher and student together to select effective computer-based learning situations, especially if the teacher has the training, experience, and motivation to know each child well. There is no substitute for this. As Jean Jacques Rousseau observed in the preface to his 1762 novel *Emile*: "The first thing is to study your pupils more, for it is very certain that you do not know them." It is true that children will apply themselves diligently when their mind is engaged, but it is not true that, unassisted, they will always select activities that will further their education. They need the teacher's help.

15.4.2 Computer-Based Learning Suits Children's Desire to Control Their Own Learning

Piaget (1926) observed that, at least up to the age of about seven, children are essentially egocentric in their thinking, and, therefore, also in their use of language. As Piaget states: "The functions of language are complex, and it is futile to attempt to reduce them all to one—that of communicating thought. . . . For the most part [children up to the age of about seven] are only talking to themselves." A corollary of this, with pertinence to the importance of well-programmed computer-based learning, is the idea that, as Piaget puts it, "The audience is there simply *as a stimulus*" (emphasis added).

The methodologies applied in the schools of Dr. Maria Montessori (Standing, 1962) are also based on a philosophy of education which recognizes the children's preference for control over their own learning. One has only to consider some of the various "discoveries"[3] that she made about the learning modes of the children with whom she worked.

As you consider each of the Montessori discoveries that follow, consider how each might be borne out and amplified in the "prepared environment" of appropriate computer-based learning. Some of the discoveries may come as a surprise if you are not an experienced teacher. If they run counter to your own experience, either as a student or as a teacher in training, suspend disbelief and keep an open mind as you read along. Rest assured that these discoveries are *rediscovered* every day, not just in classrooms modeled after Montessori's ideas, but in classrooms, in general, all over the world. The goal of education is to make these discoveries habitual.

- **Children have "amazing mental concentration" when their interest in anything is spontaneous.** Hence, the importance of the "prepared environment" designed to naturally capture a child's interest and stimulate the desire to learn. This interest and desire to learn will be fostered in the classroom in which the children have access to a range of computer-based learning systems alongside other more traditional learning experiences.
- **Children "love repetition of material even when it is already known."** This is so to the extent that Montessori describes it as a "profound psychological need" during the early years of a child's education. The computer can be a useful vehicle for such

---

[3]"Discoveries" is in quotation marks because, of course, Dr. Montessori was by no means the first to recognize these realities of children in relation to learning. Nor was she the last. They did, however, take her by surprise; thus, for her, they were discoveries, as they may be for you, too. Everyday, teachers make these same discoveries while working with individual children or with groups. They rejoice when they do because it means that the children have become responsible for their own learning, thus taking the awesome burden for that off the teachers' shoulders.

repetitive activity because, unlike teachers, the machine never gets tired. One has only to watch children using their Nintendo™ games or—heaven forbid!—whiling away hours in video arcades to know how easily and exhaustively children are motivated by engaging computer-based activities. When these activities have the added value of being educationally constructive, it seems sensible to take advantage of the computer's motivational capabilities.

■ **Children love freedom of choice when it comes to activities.** This is why Montessori went to such pains to understand and define the appropriate "prepared environment" for the children, depending on their developmental stage. The classroom was set up with carefully constructed learning aids (called didactic materials) of all kinds. The children should be left free to decide what they want to work at or, for that matter, to do nothing at all. Of course, Montessori recognized that one is free only when one has options, otherwise, one has no choice; hence, the considerable variety of stimulating learning materials that she prescribed for her classrooms.

It is beyond the scope of this book to detail all the didactic materials used in the Montessori classroom. The reader is referred to any of the many excellent texts on learning theory for a more extensive description of the Montessori Method. Standing (1962) would be a good place to start. The didactic materials can be purchased from school suppliers or teachers can, of course, construct them themselves. With the computer in mind, didactic materials in the form of the growing selection of learning software would become part of the "prepared environment" in which the child would freely choose from the set of available activities.

■ **Children prefer work to play.** The distinction between work and play is artificial. Culture, to a large extent, determines what we will perceive as either one or the other. For example, Winston Churchill liked to build brick walls to relax. If we create and maintain a learning environment where the children can enjoy what they are doing—which includes the option to do nothing—they will be more likely to busy themselves with useful activities. As one teacher observed: "Kids who have fun will work harder." Even Plato, that advocate of mental discipline as the basis for learning (Bigge, 1982), commented that "early education [should] be a sort of amusement; [for] you will then be better able to find out the natural bent."

Naturally, when work is perceived as play, it will be preferred over activities that are perceived as less enjoyable. Teachers who have had the opportunity to work with small groups of, let us say, ten or fewer students know how much easier it is to maintain a pleasant, flexible, and child-oriented learning environment. One of the problems in most classrooms, however, is that the teacher–pupil ratio is still so high[4] that it is next to impossible to provide an environment where the children can be allowed to "do what they want." So, teachers perpetuate the methodology they themselves endured through their years of schooling, a methodology that depended largely on the principle of regimentation.

---

[4]Approximately 1:17, according to the U.S. Department of Education (1992).

The computerized classroom can go a long way to overcoming the problem of numbers. Classes can be more easily broken up into small groups, or individuals can be left to work on their own. The teacher becomes the facilitator of learning rather than the source of it.

- **Children love silence.** Noise is not usually an accompaniment of mental industry. Children will be the first to appreciate the opportunity to work undisturbed. This is why teachers place so much emphasis on discipline in class; not to stifle intellectual activity, but to maintain an environment in which it can flourish. Classrooms such as those discussed in earlier chapters, in which the children have access to computer-based learning systems, still need adult supervision in order to guarantee that they will have the freedom to learn.

- **Children "explode into writing" once they have learned the letters of the alphabet and the sounds they represent.** They do not need to be taught to write. The *Writing to Read* program, developed by Dr. John Henry Martin and sponsored by IBM, would seem to contradict this approach, but in fact, as the next discovery bears out, there is no contradiction. First, the Montessori children simply learn the letters and the sounds they represent; this leads naturally to the discovery of their ability to construct written words, and only several months later do they learn to read those written words.

- **Children are spontaneously self-disciplined**—and extremely obedient—in a Montessori environment. The reason is simple: the children are engaged in activities of their own choice which absorb their attention to the extent of obviating much of the need for externally applied discipline. Standing (1992) calls it a "cosmic discipline." He quotes Montessori herself as saying: "The quiet in the class when the children were at work was complete and moving. No one had enforced it; and what is more, no one could have obtained it by external means." Teachers who have had experience working with children in well-planned, well-designed, computer-based learning environments can corroborate this "discovery" for themselves.

Software that has been carefully crafted and selected by trained and experienced educationists for the purpose of stimulating learning in children will, in the hands of those children—at their own pace and in their own time—achieve the same effect as a teacher for many learning situations. There are, moreover, significant advantages to the computer-based learning stimulus:

- The child can have 100% of the computer's attention.

- The computer frees up the teacher for important interaction with other children.

- The computer-based learning system gives the child complete control over the pace of learning. This echoes the aspiration of the philosopher George Bernard Shaw, who said: "What we want is to see the child in pursuit of knowledge, not knowledge in pursuit of the child."

- In the long run, computer-based learning will realize significant economies as the cost of teachers continues to rise while the cost of computing falls.

15.4.3 The Computer Is an Invaluable Tool for Classroom Management

We already discussed this aspect of computing in chapter 9. There we noted the value of the computer as a tool to assist in developing useful templates for letters, forms, ditto masters, and so forth. We also saw that the computer is a major time saver when it comes to specifying curricula, preparing syllabi, planning lessons, and preparing learning materials of all kinds. Test preparation and evaluation can also be assisted by the computer. More and more text books come with test-generation software, which takes much of the drudgery out of preparing tests.

The computer is also useful as a visual aid in its own right. Soft-copy materials can be prepared on the computer and then projected directly onto a large screen via an LCD panel and an overhead projector. Student assessment and guidance are supported by the ability to electronically access a database of student information, which more and more schools are maintaining. Finally, communication with parents is facilitated by on-line systems such as those described in chapter 11, which help with attendance management, dissemination of notices of all kinds, including what homework the children have been set, and various other pedagogical eventualities that are best handled by interaction with parents (Bauch, 1990).

15.4.4 The Computer is the Best Writing Implement Yet Invented

The research profiled in chapter 1 overwhelmingly concluded that the word processor and the tools associated with it had a significant effect on the quality of student writing. This is bound to spill over into other areas of the curriculum since writing is fundamental to the acquisition, reinforcement, and assimilation of knowledge in all fields.

At a conference on "Writing Across the Curriculum" offered at Pennsylvania State University in 1987, the keynote address, given by Dr. James R. Squire, was titled "Writing to Learn." The message was simple: the act of writing, of organizing ideas with a view to communicating to others, does more than simply demonstrate what knowledge we have. It reinforces, transforms, and activates that knowledge. Writing is a powerful, often painstaking process, the execution of which is, perhaps, the most educational cognitive activity in which we, and our students, can be engaged. It is a process appropriate to all subjects across the curriculum.

Word processing to learn

If it is true that writing contributes significantly to the confirmation and assimilation of knowledge, and if it is true that the computer is the most versatile writing implement yet invented, then it follows that efforts should be expended at all levels of education to make the facility of computerized word processing available to all students.

The beauty of this goal is that it is based on the simple, but powerful, concept of "writing to learn." Those who control the purse strings of education should feel compelled to support the purchase of all necessary equipment and supplies that will encourage children to write. Computers that have already been purchased, and that perhaps lie idle because people do not know what to do with them, should be dusted off, plugged in, and put to work.

As Mageau (1992) reflected in an editorial in *Electronic Learning:* "For the rest of the world for whom writing is a painful and difficult process (actually, writing is painful even for those of us who like to write), being given a revision tool like a word processor is like being given the key to your jail cell." Mageau goes on to point out that the word processor does not magically turn a poor writer into a good one. Only people can do that. The word processor removes one barrier to the process—the physical difficulty of revision. "What ultimately helps non-writers to write—and rewrite," says Mageau, "is a good teacher who enables students to see that their voice, their ideas, and their ways of thinking are worth exploring and sharing with others."

15.5 When the Computer *Should Not* Be Used in the Classroom

15.5.1 Computers Should Not Be Used for Purely Passive Learning

Computer learning should invite interaction. This interaction can take many forms, among which might be:

- responding to questions;
- finding answers to questions;
- completing verbal tasks;
- reacting to, and interacting with, simulations;
- browsing databases containing textual, visual, and audial material;
- accessing data for inclusion in other research products.

15.5.2 A Computer Does Not Take the Craft Out of Writing

At several points in this text, including the previous section, we have considered the beneficial effects of word processing on writing. There is a danger, however, of putting too much emphasis on the appearance of students' work, rather than on the content. Hill (1992) quotes Hilary Cowan, instructional technology program director for Kanawha County Schools in West Virginia: "It's important that the *process* in process writing isn't skipped. I think it's too easy on a word processor to go from step one to the final finished product with little thought in between."

A carpenter must still understand the nature of wood, and have the knowledge and skills to produce good work, even though he or she will make use of powerful tools to expedite the work.

15.5.3 Spelling Checkers Do Not Have All the Answers

Spelling checkers are very useful for picking up misspelled or mistyped words. However, they are no good for misused homonyms (too, to, two). Nor can they account for ignorance (as when a student thinks the cliché is not "take for granted," but "take for granite!)."

The dictionary that accompanies a spelling checker cannot contain every word under the sun. Students have to be told that if a word is flagged as not appearing in the dictionary, this does not mean the word has been misspelled. It simply may not be in the dictionary. Many spelling checkers will offer suggestions of alternative words for those it cannot find in the on-line dictionary. This can be hazardous to some students' academic health! Sometimes a student will substitute an incorrect word just because it has been suggested by the spelling checker. For example, a student who was writing a story about Samson and Delilah wrote instead about *Salmon* and Delilah. Proper names are usually omitted from on-line dictionaries, and, sure enough, the first alternative suggestion made by the spelling checker for the unknown Samson was *Salmon!*

15.5.4 Computers Cannot Replace the Teacher's Skill and Experience

As already emphasized throughout this text, computers do not replace teachers. They are tools that teachers use to directly or indirectly work more effectively with children: directly, by selecting programs that will address individual and group learning needs based on experience; indirectly, by taking on new roles in the classroom as computer-based learning takes over some of the traditional teaching tasks. CAI can add significantly to the quality of the learning experience, and a skilled teacher will capitalize on the help that technology provides by investing his or her own efforts in a higher level of individual or group-specific attention.

15.5.5 Computers Should Not Be Allowed to Take Away from the Teacher's Responsibility for Careful Class Preparation

The fact that teaching tasks such as preparation (of audiovisual aids, tests, worksheets, and so forth) is simplified should not take away from the teacher's responsibility to plan with the same care, whether or not the computer is used.

For example, computerized test banks make test generation a snap, but teachers still need to consider the design of the tests they prepare. Tests that include only short essay responses may handicap those students who are not good at explaining what they know in the sometimes frantic time constraints of an in-class test. If the objective of short essay tests is to determine whether the student can write, then it is a different matter, though it is debatable whether a timed test is an appropriate method to assess writing ability.

Another problem with test generators is the quality of the questions that are provided in the database. Are the questions unambiguous? Do the questions adequately test the material that is the subject matter? Have the questions been chosen and/or phrased in such a way as to not favor one group or another on the basis of race, gender, or ethnic background? If the answer set is generated by the software, are the answers to the questions correct? This is especially relevant for questions with a single correct answer such as matching, multiple choice, fill in the blanks, or true/false.

When the questions are supplied with the software that accompanies a text, a teacher must verify the accuracy and appropriateness of every question included in a test. When the questions have been created by the teacher, they should still be checked every time they are used. There is no guarantee that each time a topic is covered the same emphasis is given to different components of the topic, so questions may well need to be revised from semester to semester, even from class to class.

The computer makes it easier to update tests. Thus, customizing tests for different learning situations should be the rule rather than the exception. In the same way, computer-based tools should make it easier for teachers to keep their teaching materials current. These tools, therefore, should be seen as providing an opportunity for *seeking* excellence, rather than as an opportunity to short-circuit it.

15.5.6 The Computer Can Be an Excellent Child Minder, but That is Not How It Should Be Used

This is often a question of perception. Assuming that the software available for use in schools is selected on the basis of its educational value, it is possible to argue that, any time the students spend using it, they are in a learning mode. In case it may not be an appropriate learning mode, the teacher must plan for productive student use of the technology. In other words, pacifying students should not be the purpose of computer technology in the classroom.

Learning theory is the foundation for teaching. It goes without saying that the incorporation of the computer into the curriculum should in no sense take away from the teacher's commitment to creating and managing an environment in which learning is of paramount importance. Fancy software that carries the "educational" label may not be effective in achieving its stated "educational" goals—even if the children love using it. Even when a computer-based system has proved effective elsewhere, with other children in other learning environments, it does not abrogate the teacher's responsibility to monitor the impact of that same system on a particular class of students with a view to assessing learning outcomes.

By the same token, a teacher who incorporates a computer-based learning system into the curriculum has the responsibility to validate that system in the context of the learning theory that is the intellectual foundation of the teaching profession. Software evaluation, which we considered in chapter 10, is thus an important skill. The process of evaluation presupposes familiarity with the various theories that have arisen from the study of learning.

15.5.7 Computers Should Not Be Used Purely as Electronic Page Turners

This is a common complaint of teachers unenthusiastic about computer-based learning. The complaint usually stems either from ignorance or from previous unfortunate experience with poorly designed CAI. Certainly, this complaint is justified if the computer is used for no other purpose than to work linearly, page by page, through some passive study of textual material. But this is rarely the case with CAI, especially that which involves multidimensional access to varied types of data—text, images, video, sound—as in multimedia systems; nor is it the case when the study involves the accessing of text in a nonlinear fashion, as in textual database research, where the student moves from one text to another following an associational path linked by key words.

Can you think of other ways in which computers should *not* be used in education? In the Do Something About It section at the end of the chapter, you are invited to consider further inappropriate uses of computers for teaching and learning.

■ 15.6 Taking Care of the Teachers

It is important to recognize that, realistically, it is difficult for teachers to embrace this technology with any success unless they have time, ongoing training, and logistical and technical support. Let us briefly reflect on these prerequisites of successful integration of technology in the classroom.

15.6.1 Teachers Must Have Time

One of the long-standing anomalies of education systems worldwide has been that teachers in elementary and secondary schools spend much more time in class than teachers in non-research-oriented institutions of further education, where the professors' primary responsibility is to teach. Teachers in schools K–12 typically spend well over twice as many contact hours in class than their collegiate counterparts.

Why the discrepancy? Is it because K–12 teachers need less time to prepare their lessons? Is there less need for K–12 teachers to keep abreast of current knowledge in their field of academic interest? Do K–12 teachers expend less energy in the classroom? Of course not. But the anomaly persists. Perhaps it is one of those historical anomalies maintained out of inertia; no one appears to question it because it has always been that way.

The problem, of course, does not lie with the colleges and universities. The proportion of their professional time spent in the classroom (about one fourth) quite closely correlates with the 80–20 rule. Eighty percent of the effort expended teaching a lesson goes into remote and immediate preparation,[5] evaluation, and follow-up, all crucial ingredients of quality teaching. Only 20% of the effort is expended during the lesson itself. Put another way, for every hour that a teacher teaches, he or she probably needs to commit three or four hours of pre- or post-class time for purposes of preparation, evaluation, and follow-up. If we agree that this 80–20 rule applies, we must conclude that the teaching load of professors at non-research-oriented colleges of further education is about right.

The problem, therefore, is in the schools K–12. Elementary and secondary school teachers need, but do not get, adequate time for immediate preparation for class. They need, but do not get, adequate time for student assessment, performance evaluation, and follow-up. They need, but do not get, adequate time to establish and maintain fertile communication with the children's homes. And we have not begun to address the need for adequate time to update teaching methods in line with the latest developments in educational technology.

The status quo in schools K–12 dictates an average teaching load of 35 to 40 hours a week and a teacher–pupil ratio of approximately 1:17 (U.S. Department of Education,

---

[5]Remote preparation is the preparation a teacher makes when attending professional conferences, taking classes, reading current literature, and keeping up with changes in the knowledge base of a field and with changes in the constituent components of the curriculum. Immediate preparation occurs during the days and hours immediately before a class is offered.

1992). Both statistics work against the efforts of teachers to be effective, which in the long run means that students get a raw deal (Borrell, 1992). One bright picture is that teacher–pupil ratios have been steadily declining from the 1:26 that pertained in 1960–61 (U.S. Department of Education, 1992).

A Nation at Risk merits careful reading, identifying as it does various problems with the American K–12 educational system and making specific recommendations to ameliorate those problems. The report recognizes "the dedication, against all odds, that keeps teachers serving in schools and colleges, even as the rewards diminish."

However, nowhere in the report was it suggested as part of a solution to these problems that teacher–pupil ratios should be reduced (say, to 1:10) or that K–12 teachers should be allocated fewer contact hours (say, 25 to 30 hours a week)[6] so that they can give adequate time to class preparation and follow-up and to establishing and maintaining close contact with the children's home environment, not to mention such ongoing educational technology concerns as are discussed in the next section.

A Nation at Risk did note that "not enough of the academically able students are being attracted to teaching," and that "the professional working life of teachers is on the whole unacceptable." The report also recommended, among other things, that teachers should have "an 11-month contract" so as to "ensure time for curriculum and professional development . . . and a more adequate level of teacher compensation." But, as far as teachers are concerned, extending the contract and raising the compensation does nothing to fundamentally change the way the schools are organized. In fact, the burden on teachers might actually be increased if the report's recommendations for a longer school day (7 hours) and a longer school year (200 to 220 days) were implemented, unless, at the same time, schools reduced teacher–pupil ratios and teaching loads.

Unfortunately, many teachers become disillusioned after a few years in a system that works against their best efforts to serve the students. According to Perelman (1990): "One teacher I interviewed could have spoken for thousands when she said: "Why should I do anything different next year from what I did last year? Who cares?"

Are the ideas for reducing teacher–pupil ratios and contact hours feasible? Would the quality of education in our elementary and secondary schools improve if reforms such as these were implemented? Can computer technology come to the rescue by enabling a radical restructuring of the whole process of childhood education? Might the time come, as mentioned in chapter 3 and discussed in chapter 11, when a fair proportion of a student's interaction with a teacher will be electronic ("videotronic") in a distance learning mode? These are interesting questions for discussion, and they are offered as such in the Do Something About It section at the end of the chapter.

15.6.2 Teachers Must Have Ongoing Training

The need for ongoing training in educational technology is not met by a one-day workshop once a semester. Ongoing training means at least a weekly structured session of, say, two to three hours during release time from what would otherwise be teaching

---

[6]We'll go along with the unstated assumption that college professors need more time than K-12 teachers for their professional development.

responsibilities. This structured time would be spent working through on-line or video tutorials, or working one-on-one with the school's technology support staff. This would give teachers at least an even chance of making the transition to teaching with technology without compromising the quality of their day-to-day work with students.

The alternative is for things to remain the way they are, with some 80% of teachers doing no more than paying lip service to the call to update their teaching methods. This includes teachers who began the transition process by attending courses and workshops in the past, but whose enthusiasm waned once they realized how much ongoing effort was involved.

The components of training sessions should include:

- evaluating new software;
- giving or receiving training in newly acquired hardware or software;
- discussing with colleagues methodologies for incorporating new software into the curriculum;
- attending or giving districtwide workshops;
- attending or giving model lessons.

In the Do Something About It section at the end of the chapter, you are invited to further discuss the activities listed above and brainstorm in order to come up with other useful, structured, ongoing training activities designed to keep teachers current with computer-based learning systems.

15.6.3 Teachers Must Have Logistical and Technical Support

Logistical support begets the need for technical support. Once schools commit to computer-based education, there is a logistical price to pay in terms of hardware, software, service contracts, and computer supplies. Piller (1992) and others have reported on the waste that follows when there is inadequate logistical and technical support for educational computing systems. Teachers should not expect to have to support and maintain computer systems. They already have too little time to learn how to use the computer and how to incorporate it into the curriculum.

Consider, for example, the challenge involved learning to use the Apple II and accompanying software and incorporating it into lesson plans. Then consider the further challenge when the Apple IIs were upgraded to Apple IIGS systems, with the new interface, different hardware configuration, and, of course, new software. In recent years, the Apple II has been phased out and replaced by the Apple Macintosh—another new interface, different hardware, new software, which presented another challenge. And, today, it is all multimedia, with laserdiscs, CD-ROMs, authoring systems, and on and on.

Much the same situation has pertained in the IBM world, where teachers have had to learn the relative intricacies of *MS-DOS* and now *Windows*. At least in the IBM world, there has been a measure of stability insofar as the *MS-DOS*-based software has reigned supreme since 1981. But teachers have still been confronted with an incredible array of new tools for teaching and learning which, in practice, they have had to largely ignore.

Now, for a small minority of teachers this challenge is their meat and drink. They love the technology and relish the opportunity to learn and use new systems as they are introduced. Administrators should understand that these teachers are not typical. They are the ones who should be recruited as full-time support personnel, otherwise known as teacher–computerists, whom we discussed in the previous chapter in the context of the seven pillars of successful implementation of educational technology.

The majority of teachers love to teach. They have worked hard to develop skills and methodologies that have proved successful. They recognize the value of computers in the classroom. The majority of teachers welcome the opportunity to integrate the computer into the curriculum and have the instincts and experience to put the technology to its best use. But, unfortunately, the majority of teachers do not yet have a technology-rich classroom, even if they wanted one. Nor do the majority of teachers get the time and funding to support their regular attendance at training seminars and conferences.

This situation must be remedied before schools can ever hope to adequately address the educational needs of students in an information age.

■ Looking Back

There is not likely to be a revolution in education. Instead, there will be a steady evolution that will involve integration of the new along with the tried and true. In this chapter, we have reviewed traditional learning theories and methodologies in order to show that computer-based learning will be most effective if founded on principles and practices that have proved themselves over centuries of experience teaching children.

We have looked at ways in which the computer should and should not be used in the classroom. In all human achievement, quality is characterized by careful preparation, conscientious implementation, and continuous evaluation, revision, and reaffirmation of goals. The same must apply to the incorporation of computers into the curriculum.

We also reflected on the goals for education as set by the future workplace, in order to show how these goals can be effectively reached by schools that take advantage of technology in preparing students to take their place in the working world. Technology can help teachers to individualize education in a way that has been elusive in the past. When classes are large, it is difficult for even the teacher with the best intentions to attend adequately to individual student needs. But carefully integrated computer-based learning environments can both enable the teacher to provide individualized learning experiences and free up the teacher to work one-on-one with students.

■ Looking Forward

We have come to the end of our journey in this book, which is where your journey in the computerized classroom of the Information Society begins. The fundamental content of this book has focused on practical matters relating to computer use in teaching and learning. Although many important philosophical and pedagogical issues relate to the management of computer-based learning, many skills must first be learned—and then practiced so that they are not lost. As the famous French tennis player, Jean Borotra, said about his sport: "Never give it up, my friend. You must play a little every day."

You, too, must keep your computing skills well honed by attending workshops, conferences, and seminars. The technology is charging ahead and is difficult to keep up with. If you are, or hope to be, in a school district where computer-based learning is supported by the community, take advantage of the opportunity to add to your skills and apply them in the classroom. Resolve to provide for your students the best-possible learning environment. This will be the launching pad for the kind of child-centered education described and aspired after by the great American educationist John Dewey nearly a century ago.[7]

His should be the last word in this book. He was born before the American Civil War and lived to see the beginnings of the computer revolution. His perspective on education described here was first published in 1900, but it has a

---

[7]John Dewey, (October 20, 1859, to June 1, 1952). His book, *The Child and the Curriculum and the School and the Life of the Child,* was first published in 1900. The edition from which this quotation has been taken was published by Phoenix Books, University of Chicago Press, 1956.

relevance now more than ever since the "media necessary to further the growth of the child" are being extended beyond most teachers' wildest dreams.

The occupations and relationships of the home environment are not specially selected for the growth of the child; the main object is something else, and what the child can get out of them is incidental. Hence the need of a school. In this school the life of the child becomes the all-controlling aim. All the media necessary to further the growth of the child center there. Learning? certainly, but living primarily, and learning through and in relation to this living. When we take the life of the child [that has been] centered and organized in this way, we do not find that he is first of all a listening being; quite the contrary.

The statement so frequently made that education means "drawing out" is excellent, if we mean simply to contrast it with the process of pouring in. But, after all, it is difficult to connect the idea of drawing out with the ordinary doings of the child of three, four, seven, or eight years of age. He is already running over, spilling over, with activities of all kinds. He is not a purely latent being whom the adult has to approach with great caution and skill in order gradually to draw out some hidden germ of activity. The child is already intensely active, and the question of education is the question of taking hold of his activities, of giving them direction. Through direction, through organized use, they tend toward valuable results, instead of scattering or being left to merely impulsive expression.

If we keep this before us, the difficulty I find uppermost in the minds of many people regarding what is termed the new education is not so much solved as dissolved; it disappears. A question often asked is: If you begin with the child's ideas, impulses, and interests, all so crude, so random and scattering, so little refined or spiritualized, how is he going to get the necessary discipline, culture, and information? If there were no way open to us except to excite and indulge these impulses of the child, the question might well be asked. We should either have to ignore and repress the activities or else to humor them. *But if we have organization of equipment and materials, there is another path open to us.* We can direct the child's activities, giving them exercise along certain lines, and can thus lead up to the goal which logically stands at the end of the paths followed. [emphasis added]

▪ Do Something About It: Exercises and Projects

1. Earlier in this chapter, you were presented with a selection of situations in which computer-based methodologies were appropriate for teaching and learning. Brainstorm with some of your colleagues or classmates in order to come up with as broad a spectrum as possible of other such situations. Rank them according to feasibility and effectiveness and write up the outcome of this discussion.

2. The chapter presents some inappropriate uses of computers in teaching and learning. Brainstorm with some of your colleagues or classmates in order to consider other learning situations in which computers would be unsuitable.

3. Brainstorm to come up with more good reasons why computer technology is not as prevalent in the classroom as one might expect, considering the hype that has accompanied computers over the last 40 years.

4. Are the ideas for reducing teacher–pupil ratios and contact hours discussed in this chapter feasible? Would the quality of education in our elementary and secondary schools improve if reforms such as these were implemented? Can computer technology come to the rescue by enabling a radical restructuring of the whole process of childhood education?

Computer Cadre: A brief history
by Kay Rewerts, Waterloo Community Schools, Waterloo, Iowa

The Waterloo Community Schools in Waterloo, Iowa, have had a computer education plan since 1984. The plan calls for two major strands of emphasis. The first is to teach students about computers and the second is to teach with the computer. The first strand emphasizes the computer as a curriculum topic and the second deals with the computer and the accompanying software as tools that can be utilized in all curriculum areas.

The Computer Cadre was first established during the 1988–89 school year under state staff-development funding. The outcomes for that first year were:

1. A hierarchical list of computer skills needed by teachers was compiled.
2. The list of skills was used in an interview with each teacher to assess the current status of staff computer skill.
3. Data regarding the current status of staff computer skill were compiled by building.
4. A set of materials was developed to be used in in-service/workshops. The focus was on beginning-level skills and awareness of software.
5. A plan for coordinating district, building, and individual goals to bring all teachers to a minimal level of competency was developed. Entry-level workshops were required for all staff who were not able to demonstrate competency. All other workshops were offered as paid workshops through state staff-development funds.
6. A listing of available software in each building, identified by grade level, was compiled.

During the second year of the Cadre, 1989–90, the out-comes were:

1. A schedule of in-service/workshops presented by Cadre members was kept who included data on buildings and teachers who participated as well as evaluations from workshop attendees.

   A total of 370 teachers participated (that was 59% of the teaching staff). The number of hours per workshop varied; however, the total number of

Kay Rewerts, author of the case study

hours taught was 4,295.75. There were 390 hours of the minimum-level workshop offered as required district in-service. People from each of the 21 buildings attended workshops. The workshop evaluations overwhelmingly indicated that the teachers benefited from the workshops and wanted to have more in-service on using computers. A total of $75,595 was paid for workshops. That was in addition to the $30,000 paid to Cadre members for their time.

A packet of in-service/workshop materials available for use by anyone in the district in presenting in-service/workshops was developed. We used the *MECC Computing Tools: AppleWorks* as a guide to develop workshop materials. These are flexible materials that change as we see that revisions and updates need to be made. The major emphasis this year was on *AppleWorks*. Workshops were held on word processing, database, spreadsheet, using the tools together, and advanced uses.

The 1990–91 school year was the third year of the Computer Cadre. The Cadre consisted of 30 representative teachers (14 elementary, 5 intermediate, 5 high school, the media facilitator, and 5 at-large members). These teachers **(continued)** served as mentors for teachers in the district. They provided assistance to other cooperating teachers who were not Cadre members. Their responsibilities included:

1. Modeling effective teaching strategies with the computer.
2. Identifying and providing appropriate computer-related workshops.
3. Serving as building liaison with the district.
4. Participating in professional development.
5. Reviewing and making recommendations regarding computer software and software infusion into the curriculum.
6. Developing a technology plan for the district.

Workshops were again offered to all Waterloo staff members. The minimum-level workshops were paid through district in-service funds for teachers new to the district or for teachers who were unable to take this workshop the previous year.

Computer Cadre members used their Cadre hours to develop computer workshops, prepare and set up for workshop sessions, and to participate in Cadre activities. In addition, a bank of hours was available for teachers to attend and/or present workshops. This was approximately 6 hours per teacher.

The Computer Cadre objectives for the third year were:

1. Continue to develop and revise appropriate workshops based on collected data. Workshops on Microsoft *Works* were developed for the Macintosh and revisions were made on the *AppleWorks* materials.
2. Prepare and present workshops based on building and district needs and individual teacher plans to increase all teachers' levels of competency. A total of 2,949 hours of workshops were held with 532 teachers participating (80% of the staff). The cost for the workshops this year was $77,438. The cost for workshops was teachers' per diem pay for the hours they attended workshops.

Computer Cadre members
Photo Courtesy of Kay Rewerts

3. Develop a five-year technology plan to guide the district's use of technology. This actually became a six-year plan with input from over 10% of the total district employees participating through group interviews.
4. Develop strategies for obtaining districtwide computer hardware and software, such as grant writing, free or inexpensive software, and so on.
5. Expand the computer knowledge and expertise of Computer Cadre members.
6. Continue to infuse computer skills into the curriculum.

The outcomes for the fourth year of the Cadre (1991–92) were:

1. Model appropriate strategies using technology. We tried to focus on using computers in many situations—one-computer classrooms, lab settings, using LCD projection devices, using telecommunications and videodiscs in the classroom.
2. Continue to provide workshops as needed for staff. With the purchase of videodisc players for all buildings, the focus for workshops changed to include *HyperStudio* and *HyperCard*.

(continued)

Case Study 15 (concluded)

3. Continue to be building liaisons for technology.
4. Provide professional development activities for Cadre members.
5. Recommend software purchases for meeting learner outcomes in all curriculum areas.
6. Develop more fully year one of the six-year budget for technology.

Of the many staff development activities provided by our district over the last four years, the Computer Cadre has been the most successful. In fact, it is the only staff development recommended for continuation each year by both the teachers' education association and the administrators' association. The level of technology knowledge within the district has grown tremendously through the years because of the Computer Cadre.

Talk About It

Topics for discussion based on the case study.

1. Apple Computer, Inc. has a model called "Teachers Teaching Teachers" used for in-service materials, which is very similar to the Computer Cadre model. Discuss the advantages and disadvantages of teachers training each other as compared to bringing in an "expert" to share knowledge with a group of teachers.

2. If you work in a small district with only one building, how might you replicate the success of the Computer Cadre model?

3. What areas that are not mentioned in the case study would be appropriate for the Computer Cadre to explore? What topics would you suggest for in-service for the upcoming year?

4. Suggest possible topics for the 10 computer meetings during the year. How might you generate a list of topics?

5. List the possible objectives for another year of Computer Cadre or first-year objectives for a small building just beginning with technology.

■ References

Bauch, Jerold P. Touch 1 for Improved Parent-Teacher Contact. *School Safety,* Spring 1990, pp. 25–27.

Benderson, Albert. Micros: Critics and Critiques. *Focus,* ETS, 1983, pp. 17–19.

Bigge, Maurice. *Learning Theories for Teachers.* 4th ed. New York: Harper & Row, 1982.

Borrell, Jerry. America's Shame: How We've Abandoned Our Children's Future. *Macworld,* September 1992, pp. 25–30.

Branscum, Deborah. Conspicuous Consumer. *Macworld,* September 1992, pp. 83–88.

Bruner, Jerome. *Studies in Cognitive Growth.* New York: John Wiley & Sons, 1966.

Bulkeley, William M. Computers Failing As Teaching Aids. *The Wall Street Journal,* 1988.

Date, C. J. *An Introduction to Database Systems.* 4th ed. Reading, MA: Addison-Wesley, 1986.

Debons, Anthony, Esther Horne, Scott Cronenweth. *Information Science: An Integrated View.* Boston, MA: G. K. Hall, 1988.

Elmer-Dewitt, Philip. The Revolution That Fizzled. *Time,* May 20, 1991, p. 48–49.

Fersh, Seymour. Becoming Self-Educating and Culture-Creating by Being Educated Trans-Culturally. *Reflections,* Winter 1982.

Mageau, Therese. Why Write? Why Rewrite? Editorial in *Electronic Learning,* November/December 1992, p. 4.

McGee, Julie, Daniel Peck. Must Every Student Become Computer Literate? *NEA Today,* October 1982, p. 23.

Perelman, Lewis J. Luddite Schools Wage a Wasteful War. *Wall Street Journal,* September 10, 1990.

Piaget, Jean. *The Language and Thought of the Child.* New York: Harcourt, Brace, 1926.

Piaget, Jean. *The Construction of Reality in the Child.* New York: Basic Books, 1954.

Piaget, Jean. *Psychology and Epistemology.* New York: Grossman, 1971.

Piller, Charles. Separate Realities. *Macworld,* September 1992, pp. 218–30.

Samson, G. E., R. Niemiec, T. Weinstein, H. J. Walberg. Effects of Computer-Based Instruction on Secondary School Achievement: A Quantitative Synthesis. *AEDS Journal,* vol. 19, no. 4, 1986, pp. 312–21.

Shannon, Claude E., Warren Weaver. *A Mathematical Theory of Communication.* Urbana: University of Illinois Press, 1949.

Standing, E. M. *Maria Montessori: Her Life and Work.* Fresno, CA: New American Library of World Literature, 1962.

Tufte, Edward. *Envisioning Information.* Cheshire, CT: Graphics Press, 1990.

Turkle, Sherry. *The Second Self: Computers and the Human Spirit.* New York: Simon & Schuster, 1984.

Turing, Alan Mathison, On Computable Numbers, with an Application to the Entscheidungsproblem. *Proceedings of the London Mathematical Society,* vol. no. 2, 42, 1937.

U.S. Department of Education. *Digest of Education Statistics.* Washington, DC: National Center for Education Statistics, 1992.

ASCII Codes

ASCII is an acronym for the American Standard Code for Information Interchange. ASCII-8, a variation of the original 7-bit code, has become the international standard code for representing text for purposes of transmission over communications media and for processing in personal computer systems. The following table contains the ASCII codes for the most commonly used characters in text communication. You will notice that essential punctuation is included, in case you feel moved to use the code for covert correspondence!

Keyboard character	ASCII-8 code	Keyboard character	ASCII-8 code
0	00110000	T	01010100
1	00110001	U	01010101
2	00110010	V	01010110
3	00110011	W	01010111
4	00110100	X	01011000
5	00110101	Y	01011001
6	00110110	Z	01011010
7	00110111		
8	00111000	a	01100001
9	00111001	b	01100010
		c	01100011
.	00101110	d	01100100
,	00101100	e	01100101
?	00111111	f	01100110
!	00100001	g	01100111
		h	01101000
A	01000001	i	01101001
B	01000010	j	01101010
C	01000011	k	01101011
D	01000100	l	01101100
E	01000101	m	01101101
F	01000110	n	01101110
G	01000111	o	01101111
H	01001000	p	01110000
I	01001001	q	01110001
J	01001010	r	01110010
K	01001011	s	01110011
L	01001100	t	01110100
M	01001101	u	01110101
N	01001110	v	01110110
O	01001111	w	01110111
P	01010000	x	01111000
Q	01010001	y	01111001
R	01010010	z	01111010
S	01010011		

APPENDIX B

Resources and Recommended Reading

Resources

Organizations that support teacher efforts to incorporate the computer into the curriculum:

Organization	Description
Computer Learning Foundation P.O. Box 60007 Palo Alto, CA 94306–0007	The Computer Learning Foundation is a nonprofit educational foundation serving the United States and Canada. The organization's overall goal is to increase the number of people receiving the benefits of technology. Its primary focus is on developing computer competence among young people. To this end, the foundation provides programs and materials that parents and educators need to assist children.
The Betty Phillips Center for Parenthood Education (BPCPE) Vanderbilt University's Peabody College Box 81 Peabody College Nashville, TN 37203 (615) 322–8080	The BPCPE's purpose is to expand and improve parenthood education in the schools through teacher in-service and program development. The activities of the BPCPE are concentrated on increasing parent involvement.

Recommended Reading

You may qualify for a free subscription to many of these publications.

Apple Computer Resources in Special Education and Rehabilitation. $19.95
SRA
P.O. Box 543
Blacklick, OH 43004
(800)843–8855

Comprehensive collection of product descriptions of available hardware and software designed for people with special needs.

Classroom Computer Learning. $3.00
2169 Fransisco Boulevard, East, Suite A4
San Rafael, CA 94901

One of several excellent reviews of what is happening in the field of K–12 educational computing.

Computers and Students With Disabilities. Free of charge
Project EASI
EDUCOM
P.O. Box 364
777 Alexander Road
Princeton, NJ 08540
(609) 520–3340

EASI (Equal Access to Software for Instruction) is an EDUCOM project. Publication is an overview of how people with disabilities use computers in postsecondary education. Many ideas are, of course, applicable in schools K–12.

Computing Research News. Subscription: $20
Subscription Department
Computing Research Association (CRA)
1875 Connecticut Avenue, NW
Suite 718
Washington, DC 20009

Targeted at researchers into computing, for whom it is free of charge. Broad-based data sheet on the subject of the latest developments in the field of applied computer science.

The Computing Teacher. Annual subscription: $47. (8 editions per year)
International Society for Technology in Education
1787 Agate St.
Eugene, OR 97403–9921

Published by ISTE, provides feature articles on language arts, Logo, science, mathematics, telecommunications, equity, and international connections.

Connections: A Guide to Computer Resources for Children and Adults with Disabilities. Free of charge
Apple Computer
Wordwide Disability Solutions
20525 Mariani Avenue
Cupertino, CA 95014

Introduction to key resources and vendors in the adaptive technology field.

The CPSR Newsletter. Basic subscription: $40
Computer Professionals for Social Responsibility
P.O. Box 717
Palo Alto, CA 94302–0717

CPSR stands for Computer Professionals for Social Responsibility. As its name implies, the organization acts as a watchdog on the watch out for social abuses loosely or not so loosely related to computer technology (including most of the issues raised in chapters 4 and 5 of this text).

Electronic Learning. Free of charge to eligible subscribers.
Scholastic, Inc.
730 Broadway
New York, NY 10003

One of several excellent reviews of what is happening in the field of K–12 educational computing. If you use computers and advise on their purchase and use you'll be entitled to a free subscription.

GOLEM: Newsletter of Technology and Education. Subscription: $30
Edizioni Dedalo srl
Casella postale 362
70100 Bari
Italy

There are four English language issues per year of this Italian newsletter which focuses on multimedia development and applications.

InCider/A+. Subscription: $40
80 Elm Street
Peterborough, NH 03458

Must reading, monthly publication for the Apple II user.

Independence Day: Designing Computer Solutions for Individuals with Disability.
$17.95
SRA
P.O. Box 543
Blacklick, OH 43004
(800)843–8855

Explains how to personalize personal computer solutions for disabled youth and adults. Packed with product descriptions and guides to additional information resources.

Inside Microsoft *Works*. Subscription: $39 (12 issues)
The Cobb Group, Inc.
9420 Bunsen Parkway, Suite 300
Louisville, KY 40220

Tips and techniques for Microsoft *Works*™ on the Macintosh.

ISTE Update. Subscription $12 (8 editions per year)
International Society for Technology in Education
1787 Agate Street
Eugene, OR 97403–9921

Subtitled "People, Events, and News in Educational Technology." Articles on current issues including *Future Directions, Washington Watchdog, What's New,* and *Conference Calendar* sections.

Journal of Research on Computing in Education. Subscription $55 for quarterly editions
International Society for Technology in Education
1787 Agate Street
Eugene, OR 97403–9921

Original research and detailed system and project evaluations related to the state of the art and future horizons of educational computing.

Lindsey, Jimmy D. *Computers and Exceptional Individuals.*
Columbus, OH: Merrill, 1987.

Practical discussion of computer technology for handicapped and gifted/talented individuals. Includes references at the end of every chapter, and a useful listing of proven successful applications for use with exceptional individuals.

MacUser. Subscription: $27 (12 issues)
MacUser Subscriber Services
P.O. Box 56986
Boulder, CO 80322–6986

Packed with useful articles and reviews of the latest hardware and software for Apple Macintosh computers.

MacWorld. $3.95
Subscriber Services
P.O. Box 54529
Boulder, CO 80322–4529

Packed with useful articles and reviews of the latest hardware and software for Apple Macintosh computers.

Query. Subscription Free to college administrators; $12, all others
Syllabus Press
P.O. Drawer Q
Sunnyvale, CA 94087

An information source on administrative computing for Macintosh.

Syllabus: For the Macintosh. Subscription: $24
Syllabus Office
P.O. Box 2716
Sunnyvale, CA 94087–0716

Covers technology use in higher education.

Technological Horizons in Education (T.H.E.) Journal. Free to qualified teachers
T.H.E. Journal
150 El Camino Real, Suite 112
Tustin, CA 92680–3670

One of several excellent reviews of what is happening in the field of K–12 educational computing. If you use computers and advise on their purchase and use, you will be entitled to a free subscription.

Technology and Learning. $3 per each of 8 editions per year
Peter Li, Inc.
2451 East River Road
Dayton, OH 45439

One of several excellent reviews of what is happening in the field of K–12 educational computing.

Toward Independence. Free of charge
Apple Computer
Wordwide Disability Solutions
20525 Mariani Avenue
Cupertino, CA 95014

Describes Macintosh computer's built-in features designed specifically to provide access to individuals with disabilities. It also includes a listing of third-party hardware and software products of particular importance to disabled students.

Sources of Funding and Other Resources

The following sources and resources were recommended in editions of *Technology and Learning.*

The Catalog of Federal Domestic Assistance, published annually. $38.
Government Printing Office
Washington, DC 20402
(202) 783–3238

Complete list (occasionally updated during the year at no extra charge) of all federal grants allocated by Congress

Computer Learning Foundation
P.O. Box 60007
Palo Alto, CA 94306

Sponsors *National Computer Learning Month* every year in October. Awards of hardware and software go to winning students and schools.

The Directory of Computer and High Technology Grants, 1991. $44.50.
Research Grant Guides
Loxahatchee, FL 33470
(407) 795–6129

Briefly describes 640 foundations and other sources of more than 4,000 high-tech-related grants.

Guide to U.S. Department of Education Programs, published annually. $4
Government Printing Office
Washington, DC 20402
(202) 783–3238

Contains brief listing of all grants and other programs available from the U.S. Department of Education.

The National Association of Partners in Education (NAPE).
Awards
NAPE
209 Madison Street, Suite 401
Alexandria, VA 22314
(703) 836–4880

This organization recognizes volunteers, teachers, schools, and businesses for contributions to education.

National Guide to Funding for Elementary and Secondary Education, 1991. $125
The Foundation Center
New York, NY 10003–3076
(800) 424–9836

Profiles more than 1,400 foundations and corporate direct giving programs for K–12 education.

Not-So-Common Funding Sources: Computer Technology.
Sloane Reports, Inc.
P.O. Box 561689
Miami, FL 33256

Directory of foundations and corporations funding K–12 educational technology projects (national and state editions available).

State Government Grant Programs.

Several states make available directories of current programs. Check with your local library to find out what is available in your state.

Writing for Grants. $15
National Foundation for the Improvement of Education
P.O. Box 509
West Haven, CT 06516

23-minute videotape with directions and tips for writing grant proposals.

The following sources are published by Capitol Publications, Inc.

The Catalog of Federal Education Grants, published monthly. $190/year.
Capitol Publications, Inc.
P.O. Box 1453
Alexandria, VA 22313–9882
(800) 327–7203

Time-saving reference guide to more than 150 education-related grant programs available from the U.S. Department of Education, National Science Foundation, and more.

Education Grants Alert, published weekly. $299/year.
Capitol Publications, Inc.
P.O. Box 1453
Alexandria, VA 22313–9882
(800) 327–7203

Timely, accurate information on funding opportunities for K–12 programs from federal agencies and corporate and foundation sources.

Foundation and Corporate Grants Alert, published monthly. $227/year.
Capitol Publications, Inc.
P.O. Box 1453
Alexandria, VA 22313–9882
(800) 327–7203

The most complete guide to foundation and corporate grant making for nonprofit organizations. Includes how-to information on winning grants.

A

ABC   Atanasoff-Berry computer; the first electronic digital computer, built in 1939 by John Vincent Atanasoff and Clifford Berry at Iowa State University.

AI   Artificial intelligence; computer-based systems programmed to simulate human intellectual activity.

Apple Computer, Inc.   The company, based in Cupertino, CA, which has spearheaded the introduction and use of computers in schools.

Applications software   Programs that enable the user to use the computer for specific tasks such as word processing or keeping grades.

ASCII   American Standard Code for Information Interchange; a set of codes used to represent characters and other symbols in the computer for purposes of digital data manipulation and transmission.

Authoring software   Tools for coordinating the graphics, video, animation, text, speech, and sound in the development of a multimedia presentation or lesson.

B

Backup   One of the most important, and most neglected, computing activities—making a second, or third, copy of the data produced using a computer.

Bar code   Bar codes are strips of black and white lines which can be read by a scanner and interpreted as data. In the classroom, bar codes are used with optical disc technology to provide rapid access to audiovisual materials stored on the discs.

BASIC   Beginners All-Purpose Symbolic Instruction Code; one of the first computer languages for microcomputers.

BBS   Bulletin board system; a central text-based computer networking system for sharing information.

Big Brother   George Orwell's 1984 fictional concept of an all-seeing force that invades our privacy.

BITNet   Because It's Time Network; a wide area network originally set up to facilitate interaction between researchers at academic institutions. Now part of the Internet. *See* Computer network, Internet.

Booting a system   Bringing a system (hardware or software) up from scratch so it can be used by a user.

Byte   A unit of memory capable of storing the equivalent of one character as a letter of the alphabet.

C

C&C   Computers and communications; the integration of computing and communications technologies.

Caduceus   A computer-based medical-expert system designed to simulate the functionality of a medical general practitioner.

CAI   Computer-assisted instruction; computer-based systems designed to help students learn subject matter of all kinds.

CD-ROM Compact disc-read only memory; laser-based technology for the storage of data. *See* Secondary storage.

CIM Computer-integrated manufacturing; computer-based systems designed to coordinate the various facets of the manufacturing process.

Clip art Artwork that has been prepared, captured on magnetic disk (or compact disc), and made available to computer users to incorporate (cut, copy, and paste) into documents that they produce.

CMI Computer-managed instruction; computer-based systems designed to help teachers manage their professional responsibilities in and out of the classroom.

Collaborative learning Learning environment where students work together in the pursuit of knowledge and educational experience; networks are being used in schools to promote collaborative learning on a local, regional, national, and international level.

CompuServe *See* On-line database retrieval service.

Computerphile A person who has a positive attitude toward computers.

Computerphobe A person who has a negative attitude toward computers.

Computer network Several computers linked together electronically for the transmission and sharing of data of all kinds.

Computer virus Software that infects a computer system by surreptitiously attaching itself to other software and spreading from computer to computer via networks or exchanged disks.

Constructivism The philosophy of education based on the premise that children learn best when they are actively engaged in, and in control of, their own education.

CPU Central processing unit of a computer; controls all the processing carried out by the computer and has the logic circuits that enable the machine to handle math and decision making based on inputs.

Cracking Criminal hacking; using computers to gain unauthorized access to other computer systems and to perpetrate illegal, often damaging, activity in them. See Hacking.

CRT Cathode ray tube. *See* Monitor.

CTS Carpal tunnel syndrome; a debilitatingly painful wrist injury caused by repetitive motion such as extensive use of a computer keyboard or a mouse.

D

Database The productivity tool that manages the collection, storage, access, and organization of data.

DBMS Database management system; software that assists the user in accessing and managing the data in a database.

Desktop The metaphor employed by the Macintosh GUI to simplify the user's interaction with the computer.

DIALOG *See* On-line database retrieval service.

Digitization The capturing of text, still images, full motion film, and sound in the form of 1s and 0s so that it can be processed by a digital computer.

Distance learning Learning that takes place over audiovisual networks set up between remote sites.

Doublethink The use of "conscious deception" while projecting the illusion of "complete honesty."

Drill and practice A paradigm for learning which involves reinforcement of knowledge by frequent repetition.

E

ELFs Extremely low frequency electromagnetic emissions—especially from computer monitors and other peripheral computing equipment.

E-mail Electronic mail; person-to-person, computer-to-computer communication over local and wide area networks. *See* Computer network.

ENIAC The first fully operational electronic digital computer built by Presper Eckert and John Mauchly in 1946 at the Moore School of Engineering at the University of Pennsylvania.

Ergonomics Also called human factors engineering; the study of the interface between people and machines with a view to increasing the ease of usability of those machines.

F

Facilitated communication Methodology that allows nonverbal individuals to communicate by pointing to letters on a keyboard.

Fax/modem A machine that includes the capabilities of a modem, a scanner, and a printer and is used to transmit copies of printed materials over the telephone system. *See* Modem, Printer, Scanner.

File exchange   The transfer and conversion of files from one computer system to another.

Firmware   Software that has been etched (hardwired—usually permanently) onto a computer chip.

Floppy disk drive   The machine used to give the computer access to the data stored on floppy disks. *See* Magnetic disk.

FrEDMail   Free EDucational electronic Mail. A global network tied to the Internet, FrEDMail is set up to encourage curriculum-based learning projects that benefit from a global perspective. *See* Internet.

G

Gestalt   Term used to describe the philosophy that a "whole" system is more than the sum of the parts.

Gigabyte (GB)   1,073,741,824 (a little over a billion) bytes of data.

GIGO   Garbage in, garbage out; the principle whereby a system will produce unreliable output if it is given incorrect inputs or processing controls.

Groupware   Software designed to encourage collaborative learning between students. *See* Collaborative learning.

GUI   Graphical user interface; the computer screen that presents the functionality of the computer to the user via icons (pictures), pull-down menus, and point-and-click interaction (usually with a mouse).

H

Hacking   The computing activity of people for whom extending the computer's capabilities is a consuming interest.

Hard copy   *See* Printer.

Hard disk drive   A high-speed, high-density alternative to the floppy disk drive; so-called because the platter on which the data is stored is rigid.

Hardware   The machinery of computing—the parts one can see and touch.

HyperCard   An authoring tool and information organizer developed by Bill Atkinson for Apple Computer, Inc. *See* Authoring software.

Human factors engineering   *See* Ergonomics.

Hypermedia   The union of two information-processing technologies: hypertext and multimedia. *See* Hypertext, Multimedia.

Hypertext   Database systems, traditionally text only, but now more commonly multimedia, which are intricate webs of connected multimedia electronic data. *See* Computer network, Multimedia.

I

Icon   *See* GUI, Graphical user interface.

Input   Data that comes into the computer from some kind of input device such as a disk drive, the keyboard, or a microphone.

Information center   Location in a classroom where computer equipment is available for use.

ILS   Integrated learning system; a comprehensive, networked instructional system made up of software that is linked to other teaching materials used in a school (textbooks, laserdiscs, etc.), and that incorporates assessment and progress reporting tools.

Integrated software   A single software application that includes several productivity functions—typically a word processor, database, spreadsheet, graphics, and communications.

Interactive processing   Computer process involving interaction with a person or persons during processing. Such interaction may be via a keyboard, microphone, or other interactive input device.

Interactive videodisc   *See* Laserdisc.

Internet   E-Mail system that links the various networks managed by the U.S. federal government. *See* NREN.

ISTE   International Society for Technology in Education.

ITV   Instructional television.

J

JIT   Just In Time systems; computer-based systems that enable the maintenance of a minimum amount of stock in inventory by monitoring the various factors that determine product supply.

K

Kilobyte (KB)   1,024 (just over a thousand) bytes of data.

L

LAN   Local area network. *See* Computer network.

Laserdisc   14″ platter that uses lasers to store and read data.

Launching software *See* Booting a system.

LCD panel Liquid crystal display device; projects the contents of a computer screen via an overhead projector.

Licensed software Software that has been legally acquired.

Linkway Live! An authoring tool and information organizer developed by IBM Corporation. *See* Authoring software.

Loading files Bringing a copy of a file (document or software application) from secondary memory, such as a disk, into primary memory so that it can be used by a computer user.

Logo A graphics-oriented programming language developed by Seymour Papert, professor at the Massachusetts Institute of Technology; the language was designed to help young children develop problem-solving skills.

M

Magnetic disk (diskette) Magnetic medium for the secondary storage of data. *See* Secondary storage.

MAN Metropolitan area network. *See* Computer network.

MBL Microcomputer-based laboratory; science lab in which the computer is used as a tool in the generation and capture of experimental data.

Megabyte (MB) 1,048,576 (a little over a million) bytes of data.

Menu *See* GUI, Graphical user interface.

Menu bar The set of menu items displayed at the top of the screen in most software applications.

Menu-driven Software systems that are menu-driven use layers of menus to help the user navigate through the various functions which the software has been designed to handle.

Microprocessor A computer chip on which are etched the components of a computer's central processing unit. *See* CPU.

Microsecond A millionth of a second.

Modem A communications hardware device that enables the exchange of data between computers over standard telephone lines.

Monitor Otherwise known as a CRT, the screen used to display the data that has been processed by a computer.

Mouse The palm-sized device that is rolled around on the desktop to facilitate interaction with the computer. *See* Graphical user interface.

Multimedia In the context of education, multimedia describes the combined use of several media, such as films, still images, text, speech, and sound in general, for instructional purposes.

Multitasking A feature of an operating system which enables the user to handle more than one task at a time.

N

Nanosecond One billionth of a second.

NCIC National Crime Information Center.

Nonvolatile *See* Secondary storage.

NREN National Research and Education Network; an electronic "super-highway" established to coordinate access to electronic information resources maintained in libraries, research facilities, publishers, and affiliated organizations.

O

OCR Optical character recognition. Computerized scanning technology that can interpret characters on the printed page; typically used for reading bank checks, addresses on envelopes, and so forth.

OMR Optical mark recognition; typically used in schools for gathering survey data or test answers using marks made on paper which are scanned by a computer-based system in the process of analyzing the data.

On-line database retrieval service Provides subscribers (paying or nonpaying) with access to electronic databases containing data on a wide range of subjects such as finance, weather, travel, law, and so forth.

Operating system A set of programs which enhances the performance of a computer and manages the tasks demanded of it by a user.

Optical disc *See* Laserdisc.

Output Data that are produced and transmitted by a computer after they have been processed. The data can be transmitted to a wide array of output devices.

P

Pixel PICture ELement; one dot on a computer's screen.

Portfolio A collection of materials developed by, and demonstrative of, the academic progress made by a student over a period of time.

Primary storage The storage area available on the chips inside the system unit of the computer; it is also called random access memory (RAM). The data in primary storage are volatile, which means that they are lost when the power supply to the computer fails.

Printer Any one of a wide range of devices for producing a hard-copy version of a document, usually on paper.

Productivity software *See* Integrated software.

Public-domain software Software available free of charge.

R

RAM Random access memory. *See* Primary storage.

Real time processing Computer processing that relies on almost instantaneous input of data from external (real world) sources to control subsequent processing. Many microcomputer-based laboratories are examples of real time processing. *See* MBL.

ROM Read only memory. *See* Primary storage.

RSI Repetitive stress injury. *See* CTS.

S

Sans serif Refers to fonts that have no flourishes (extra pen marks); sans serif fonts are plainer, less elaborate, than serif fonts.

Scanner A machine that scans data so they can be captured and manipulated in a computer. *See* Digitization.

Secondary storage Data storage areas outside the computer, such as on disks or tape. It is non-volatile, which means that the data on disks and tape does not need a constant supply of electricity to sustain it.

Serif *See* Sans serif.

Shareware Software the user can "try before you buy." Purchase is based on the honor system: if you like it, buy it and use it—and share it with your friends.

Simulation A learning system that re-creates an artificial environment in which a student can learn concepts and tasks related to the subject of the simulation (for example, running a small business, dissecting a plant, traveling across a continent).

Soft copy *See* Monitor.

Software The programs that enable users to use the computer for a multitude of productivity and other purposes.

Software piracy The illegal copying of software, thus infringing on the software license agreement.

Software protection The use of various methods to protect software against unauthorized (unlicensed) use.

SPA Software Publishers Association; the principal trade group of the PC software industry which, among other roles, acts as a watchdog on software piracy.

Spelling checker Typically available with word processors, along with a dictionary to help the user correct textual errors that result from inaccurate typing or spelling.

Spreadsheet The component of productivity software especially designed for working with numeric data.

Sub-micron technology Technology that enables scientists to visually magnify a subject of study anywhere from a thousand to a million times.

Surge protector strip A set of plug-in sockets which has been wired to protect machines connected to the strip against sudden and unanticipated surges of electrical power.

System unit The heart of a personal computer system, containing the chips that control the computer's operations.

T

Telecommunications The transmission of data—voice, video, speech—over communications media such as telephone lines or wireless channels.

Template A document in outline form, such as a form letter or stationery document, which is easily adapted for specific uses.

Tutorial A learning system that effectively introduces a student to new material.

U

Universal Machine Name given to the theoretical digital computer described by Alan Turing in 1937 (also called the Turing Machine).

UPS Uninterruptible power supply; used to keep the computer up and running in the event of a power failure.

Utility Operating system program that provides the user with a tool that helps in the management of computerized operations (for example, checking a disk, backing up data).

V

VDT   Video display terminal. *See* Monitor.

Videoconference   Remote conference in which the participants use video cameras and televisions at local and remote sites to "come together" for visual and verbal interaction.

Videodisc   *See* Laserdisc.

Virtual reality   Computer systems that simulate reality using computer-controlled 3D video imaging.

VisiCalc   The first electronic spreadsheet designed, in 1978, by Daniel Bricklin and Robert Franston at Harvard's Graduate School of Business.

Voice messaging   A voice-based, e-mail system. *See* E-mail.

Volatile   *See* Primary storage.

W

WAN   Wide area network. *See* Computer network.

Window   An enclosed area on the screen which is an independent object for data-processing purposes. Several windows can be open at the same time, enabling the user to easily switch from one task to another.

Word processor   The component of productivity software used primarily for working with written communication such as text.

WORM   Write once, read many times. *See* CD-ROM.

Wrist rest   A device to support the wrist with the purpose of reducing the damage caused by repetitive motion at a keyboard or mouse. *See* CTS.

WYSIWYG   What you see is what you get; refers to on-screen displays that are close to identical to the same displays sent to the printer.

Credits

Chapter Openers

Chapter opener 1: Courtesy of International Business Machines Corporation.
Chapter opener 2 and Chapter opener 3: Courtesy of Apple Computer, Inc.
Chapter opener 4: © John Coletti.
Chapter opener 6: Courtesy Intel Corporation.
Chapter opener 7: Courtesy of International Business Machines Corporation.
Chapter opener 8: Courtesy of Nova Office Furniture, Inc.
Chapter opener 9: Courtesy International Business Machines Corporation.
Chapter opener 10: Apple Computer, Inc.
Chapter opener 11: Apple Computer, Inc., Frank Pryor Photographer.
Chapter opener 12: © 1993 Optical Data Corp. Photographed by Carmen Natale.
Chapter opener 13 and Chapter opener 14: Courtesy of International Business Machines.
Chapter opener 15: Apple Computer, Inc.

Part Openers

Part opener 1: © Skjold/The Image Works.
Part opener 2 and Part opener 3: Courtesy of International Business Machines Corporation.
Part opener 4: © 1993 Optical Data Corp. Photographed by Carmen Natale.

Name Index

A

Abel, Bob, 345, 355
Abernathy, Kay, 315–16
Ada, Lady, Countess of Lovelace, 41, 361
Adams, Henry, 252
Adams, James Truslow, 111
Adler, Jerry, 206, 227
Aesop, 224
Agle, Sandi, 352–53
Aiken, Howard, 41
Al-Ghamdi, Yousif, 26, 37
Allen, Lyn, 15
Amthor, Geoffrey R., 329, 355
Ankrum, Dennis R., 211, 227
Appel, Lola Rhea, 36
Aristotle, 157, 169, 402
Arrigoni, Bill, 104
Atanasoff, John Vincent, 41–43, 48, 69, 71, 140, 222
Atkinson, Bill, 366–67
Augustine, 404
Ayoubi, Zalpha R., 23, 26–27, 37

B

Babbage, Charles, 41, 222
Bacon, Francis, 77, 93
Bailey, Gerald, 14, 36, 399
Bailey, Robert W., 281, 294, 363, 375
Baker, Judy, 307
Ball, Stanley, 26, 37
Barnhart, Barry, 299, 321
Bauch, Jerold, 202, 227, 251–53, 269, 294, 310, 321, 391, 399, 413, 424
Becker, Henry Jay, 26, 36, 105, 115, 280, 351
Belair, Robert, 102
Benderson, Albert, 403, 424

Bengfort, Jean, 284
Beniger, James R., 63, 75, 83
Berger, Robert W., 351, 355
Berheide, Catherine White, 104
Berry, Clifford, 41–43
Berube, Jim, 311–12
Bigge, Morris L., 270, 294, 310, 321, 404, 411, 424
Bigley, Anne C., 21–22, 37
Birnbaum, Joel S., 298, 321, 365, 375
Black, Donald, 316
Blau, Linda, 284
Blissmer, Robert H., 40, 60, 87
Bond, Susan Giorgio, 4, 6, 45, 166, 210, 212–14, 244–45, 260
Boole, George, 41
Bork, Alfred, 379, 382, 399
Borotra, Jean, 420
Borrell, Jerry, 31, 36, 403, 418, 424
Bracey, Gerald W., 391–92, 399
Bradner, Scott, 313, 321
Branscomb, H. Eric, 87
Branscum, Deborah, 204, 227, 379, 392, 399, 403, 424
Bricklin, Dan, 45, 266
Browning, Robert, 300
Bruder, Isabelle, 32, 82–83, 291, 294, 329, 355
Bruner, Jerome S., 187, 191, 272, 294, 404–5, 424
Buchsbaum, Herbert, 83, 310
Budin, Howard, 30, 37
Bulkeley, William M., 31–32, 36, 231, 253, 403, 424
Burke, Edmund, 91
Burnett, Jamie H., 21–22, 37
Burnham, David, 95, 97–98, 115
Burnham, Robert A., 87

Bush, President, 348
Butler-Nalin, Kay, 22, 37
Byrne, John A., 87

C

Calhoun, Emily, 294
Capper, Joanne, 16, 36, 276, 294, 392, 399
Castine, W. H., 38
Cheever, Maureen Susan, 22, 37
Childs, Terri, 121, 134
Choi, Byung-Soon, 27, 37, 105, 115
Churchill, Winston, 411
Churchland, Patricia S., 58–59, 77
Cimino, Al, 66, 74
Cirello, Vincent J., 21–23, 37
Cohen, Mollie, 28, 37
Colletti, Marty, 19, 30, 329
Colt, Lois, 361, 375
Columbus, Christopher, 274, 343, 345
Confucius, 402
Cornish, Carolyn, 6, 190
Cowan, Hilary, 414
Cox, Marcelene, 377
Crichton, Michael, 359
Cromer, Maggie, 389
Cronenweth, Scott, 375, 424
Cuban, L., 32, 36
Currid, Cheryl, 305–6, 321
Curtiss, Damian H., 23–24, 37

D

Daiute, Collette, 21–25, 37
Dalton, David W., 21–22, 24, 37
Date, C. J., 403, 424
Davis, William S., 173, 191
Dawson, Tina, 321
DeBalko, Jeff, 307, 321

Lengel, James G., 30, 38
Leonard, Elizabeth Ann, 200
Leveson, Nancy, 76
Levitt, Theodore, 33, 36, 79, 87
Lewin, Kurt, 404
Lewis, Peter H., 119, 127, 134, 300, 321
Li, Zhongmin, 227
Lin, Herb, 31
Lincoln, Abraham, 229
Lindsey, Wanda, 113
Linn, Marcia, 27, 38
Linskie, Rosella, 202, 227
Lisker, Peter, 78, 87
Locke, John, 323
Lorbeer, G.C., 293
Lumley, Dan, 388, 399

M

Macdonald, A. M., 75, 87
Machiavelli, Nicolo, 2
Machmias, Rafi, 38
Madron, P., 102
Mageau, Therese, 280, 294, 372, 380,
    414, 424
Mahosky, Nancy, 112–13
Mangan, Katherine S., 308, 312, 316, 321
Mann, Mary, 329–30, 355
Manuth, Tessa, 200
Martin, John Henry, 17, 49, 370, 412
Marty, James F., 26, 38
Mason, Donna, 361
Massialas, Byron G., 28, 31, 38
Matson, Lisa M. Dallape, 44, 84
Mauchly, John, 41, 43
McAuliffe, Christa, 361
McCarthy, Robert, 27, 36, 307, 321
McCausland, Linda, 284
McGee, Julie, 403, 424
McLuhan, Marshall, 45 73, 77, 87, 203
Mechling, Kenneth, 321
Melmed, Arthur, S., 74, 81, 87
Merrill, David M., 197, 227
Metcalfe, Bob, 186, 191
Meyer, Steve, 360, 375
Miller, George A., 64, 87
Miller-Souviney, Barbara, 38
Mocsny, Daniel, 327, 355
Mollenhoff, Clark R., 43, 48–49
Montessori, Maria, 17, 27, 48, 197–98, 227,
    405, 410–12
Mowshowitz, Abbe, 76, 87, 100, 115
Moyers, Bill, 73, 87
Muldrow, Elizabeth, 21–22, 24, 38
Muller, James H., 361, 375

Munsch, Robert, 279
Murphy, R. T., 17, 36
Myers, Jack, 66
Myers, M., 262–63

N

Naisbitt, John, 74, 75, 87, 318, 321
Napier, John, 41
Nelson, L. W., 293
Neumann, Peter G., 98, 115, 130, 134
Newton, Sir Isaac, 39
Nickerson, R. S., 197, 227
Nicklin, Julie L., 231, 253
Niemiec, R., 294, 425
Nietzsche, Friedrich Wilhelm, 117
Noble, Barbara Presley, 104, 115
Norton, Clark, 97, 115, 175, 191
Nussel, Edward J., 382, 399

O

O'Brien, G., 22, 27, 38
O'Connor, Rory J., 204, 212, 227
Ogilvy, James, 72, 78
Okey, James, 37
Oliver, Donna, 321
Olivier, Terry, 321
Olson, Richard, 18, 36
Olson, Steve, 26, 361, 375
Olver, R. R., 174
Orlando, Louise C., 83, 310
Orwell, George, 93–94, 100, 115
Oughtred, William, 41

P

Papagiannis, George, 38
Papert, Seymour, 41, 187, 276, 294
Pascal, Blaise, 41
Pavelchek, Thomas, 321
Pearson, Howard, 21, 23, 38
Peck, Daniel, 424
Penzias, Arno, 77, 87
Perelman, Lewis J., 32, 36, 403, 418, 424
Perkins, F., 405
Perot, H. Ross, 297
Peters, Thomas J., 33, 36, 79, 87
Phenix, Philip H., 61
Piaget, Jean, 15, 36, 43, 182, 187, 191, 276,
    404–5, 410, 424–25
Piele, P., 37
Piller, Charles, 102–3, 115, 394, 399, 403,
    419, 425
Pizzini, Edward, 38

Plato, 402, 404, 411
Pollock, Jodi, 120, 135
Polya, G. Gyorgy, 219, 227, 384–85, 399
Pool, Gary, 63
Poole, Bernard J., 4, 10, 32, 184, 191, 232,
    253, 261, 294
Pope, Alexander, 1
Popp, David, 254, 256
Postman, Neil, 90, 115
Potochar, Charlene, 232, 239
Povich, Rick, 205, 241
Powell, Douglas, 69, 87
Powers, Bruce R., 78, 87
Pressley, M., 26
Publilius Syrus, 240

Q

Quinlan, Tom, 125, 135
Quinn, Jane Bryant, 98, 115

R

Rankin, Rebecca, 36, 355
Rash, Polly, 27, 38
Rewerts, Kay, 171–72, 181, 284, 319–20,
    422–23
Rider, Ron, 186
Roberts, Nancy, 361
Roblyer, M. D., 16, 19–21, 25, 37–38, 105,
    115, 270, 294
Rockman, Saul, 16, 38
Rogers, Al, 313
Rosegrant, 21–22, 38
Rosen, Saul, 41
Rosenthal, Ilene, 127
Rothfeder, Jeffrey, 94, 96, 101, 115
Rousseau, Jean-Jacques, 404, 410
Ruis, Nancy, 99, 115
Rust, Kathy, 22, 38
Ryan, Denise, 56–59, 197

S

Salpeter, Judy, 348–49, 355
Samson, G. E., 26, 271, 294, 402, 425
Samuelson, Pamela, 338, 355
Sanders, Jo Shuchat, 104–6, 108, 110,
    112–13, 115
Scarbeau, Brian, 396
Schlumpf, G., 390
Schmall, Eric, 318, 321

C

CAD/CAM, 397
Caduceus, 61
CAI. *See* Computer Assisted Instruction
Calcasieu Parish high schools, Calcasieu, LA, 330–31
California State Polytechnic University at Pomona, CA, 308
Camcorder. *See* Peripheral devices
Campbell's Soups, 66, 74
Carnegie Mellon University, Pittsburgh, PA, 255
Carpal Tunnel Syndrome (CTS), 196, 205–7, 440
Cassette tape drive. *See* Peripheral devices
Catalog of Federal Domestic Assistance, 435
Catalog of Federal Education Grants, The, 437
CD-ROM. *See* Peripheral devices
Census Counting Machine, 41
Center for Mathematics and Science Education, University of Pittsburgh at Johnstown, PA, 293
Central Intelligence Agency (CIA), 95
Change
    challenge of, 31–32
    need for, 2
Chartjunk, 101
Church-Turing thesis, 64
Claris Computer Corporation
    AppleWorks, 56–57, 184, 261, 319–20, 422–23
    ClarisWorks, 184, 243, 261–62, 264–65, 366
    MacDraw II, Pro, 266
    MacPaint, 368
Classroom Instruction Programs (CIP), 314
CMI. *See* Computer Managed Instruction
CNBC, 315
CNN *Newsroom,* 315
Code of ethics, 90–91. *See also* Software code of ethics
Cognitive development. *See* Learning theories
Cold Springs Elementary School, Missoula, MT, 315
Collaborative learning, 5, 17, 23–24, 186, 222, 316–17, 440
Command and Control, 70
Committee on the Preservation and Use of Economic Data, 95
Commodore Business Machines

Amiga series, 40, 47–48, 175, 237, 307, 352–53
Amiga CD32, 47
C-128, 307
C-64, 47, 301, 307
Pet, 47, 141
Communication skills, importance of good, 2, 261–62
Communications, 3, 5–6, 30, 201, 266, 269, 305–6
Communications channel, 301
Communications software. *See* CAI:productivity software, CMI:productivity software
Compaq Computer Corporation, 48
Compton's *Multimedia Encyclopedia,* 30, 166, 260, 398. *See also* Picture Explorer
CompuServe. *See* Online database retrieval services
Computer Assisted Instruction (CAI)
    drill and practice, 5, 27, 188, 269–71, 440
    Microcomputer-Based Laboratories (MBLs), 26, 186, 188, 288, 442
    productivity software as a platform for, 259–69
    simulations, 5, 26–27, 30, 188, 272, 443
    tutorials, 5, 30, 188, 443
Computer Associates *Cricket Draw,* 266
Computer crime, 119. *See also* Ethical and legal considerations
Computer Curriculum Corporation (CCC)
    CCC Instructional System, 19
Computer Equity Expert Project, 106, 112–14
Computer Eyes, 353
Computer Integrated Manufacturing (CIM), 72, 297
Computer lab, 4, 219–26
Computer Learning Foundation, 382, 429, 435
Computer Managed Instruction (CMI)
    communicating between home and school, 230, 251
    computerizing audio-visual support, 230, 248
    generating and evaluating tests, 230, 243
    managing, assessing and guiding students, 230, 250–51
    planning lessons, 230, 241
    preparing and maintaining curricula and syllabi, 230, 240

preparing learning materials, 230, 242
productivity software as tool for, 232–37
using electronic templates, 230, 238
Computer Mediated Communications (CMC), 254–56
Computer networks
    applications of, 296, 304
    case for, 296, 305
    components of, 296, 301
    definition of, 440
    different kinds of, 296, 302
    impact of, 296, 308
    implementing, 296, 306
    putting obsolescent technology to work, 306
    recommendations for successful introduction of, 296, 308
Computer on a chip, 40–41
Computer operator, 173
Computer Pals Across the World, 313
Computer Revolution, 62–63, 75–78
Computer virus, 118, 130–31, 440. *See also* Vaccine
Computerist, Teacher-computerist, 371
Computerphile, 371, 440
Computerphobe, 371, 440
Computers and Communications (C&C), 4, 30, 70, 73–74, 110, 180, 295–321, 439
Computing inequities. *See* Haves and have-nots
Computing Research News, 430
Computing Teacher, The, 60, 431
Conemaugh Valley Jr-Sr High School, Johnstown, PA, 85
Consortium for International Earth Science Information (CIESIN), 77
Consortium for School Networking, 313
Constitution of the United States, The, 92, 111
Constructivism. *See* Learning theories
Contemporary Physics Education Project (CPEP), 372–74
Control, computers and, 62–63, 66, 68, 75–82
Cooperative learning. *See* Collaborative learning
Copyright, 117–21. *See also* Doctrine of fair use
Copyright Protection Fund, 120
Corel Systems Corporation *CorelDRAW,* 235, 266
Cornell Middle School, PA, 225–26
Cornell University, 130

National Council for Accreditation of Teacher Education (NCATE), 199
National Crime Information Center (NCIC), 95, 442
National Education Association (NEA), 251
National Education Telecommunications Organization (NETO), 300
National Educational Resources Information Service (NERIS), 314
National Faculty, 231
National Geographic, 168, 248, 352
National Geographic *Kids Network,* 313, 316
National Guide to Funding for Elementary and Secondary Education, 436
National Information Utilities, 343
National Organization of Women (NOW), 96
National Parent Teacher Association, 251
National Research and Education Network (NREN), 313, 442
National School of Excellence, 20
National Science Foundation (NSF), 81, 106, 313
National Supercomputing Bill, 255
Native American. *See* American Indian
NBC, 373
NCR, 48
NEC Foundation of America, 384
Network. *See* Computer networks
Network security, 131–32
Network server, 396
Networks and the human brain, 312
Neurophysiology, 64
New American Schools, 348–49
New York City's School of the Future, 314
Nintendo, 411
Nonvolatile memory, 442. *See also* Read Only Memory (ROM), Secondary (external) storage
North American Space Administration. *See* NASA
Northern Telecom, 206
NOVA, 68, 87, 210, 227
Nova Office Furniture, Inc., Electronic Lectern, 332
Novell networking software, 396

O

Oakland Schools' Teaching and Learning with Technology Project (TLT), 347–48, 382, 399

Obsolescent technology, making good use of, 306
Office Automation, 298
Office of Technology Assessment. *See* US Congress, Office of Technology Assessment
Omni Group, 298
Online database retrieval services
America Online, 314
CompuServe, 314
DIALOG, 314
Dow Jones News/Retrieval, 314
Learning Link, 314
Prodigy, 314
Open University, UK, 82
Operating system, 140, 173–74, 442
Optical Character Recognition (OCR), 334, 442
Optical Data Corporation
Lesson Maker, 338
The Living Textbook, 7, 248, 278, 339, 343
Windows on Science, 339, 346, 350
Optical disc, 149, 155, 442
Optical Mark Recognition (OMR), 247–48, 442
OTA. *See* US Congress, Office of Technology Assessment
Output, 442
Outstanding Early Childhood Teacher, 309
Overhead display panel. *See* LCD panel
Overhead projector, 55, 331

P

Pacific Telesis, 347
Palo Alto High School, Palo Alto, CA, 374–75
Parallel computer, 365
Parent, the child and the teacher, 62–63, 67, 90, 110, 237, 251–52, 309–10
Parent Involvement REPORT, The, 311–12, 321
Pascal. *See* High Level Languages (HLL)
Pascaline, 41
Passwords, 125
Patent law, 125
PC Viewer. *See* InFocus Systems
Pennsylvania Department of Education, 84, 86, 293
Pennsylvania Higher Education Assistance Agency (PHEAA), 225
Pennsylvania Science Teacher Education Program (PA STEP), 255
Pennsylvania State Board of Education, 255

Pennsylvania State University, 255, 413
Pentagon, 131
Peripheral devices
bar code reader, 337–38, 439
camcorder, 352
cassette tape drive, 179
CD-ROM, 19, 30, 47, 149, 179, 248, 279, 337–38, 398, 440
digital camera, 352–53
graphics pad, 148
joystick, 148
large screen high resolution color monitor, 341–42
laser printer, 166, 222, 396
mouse, 154, 442
Philco Corporation, 41
Physhare, 255–56
Picture Explorer, 260
Pillars of successful technology implementation, 388–92, 420
Pink. See Taligent
Piracy, software. *See* Ethical and legal considerations
Pixel, 442
Portfolios. *See* Assessment
POWER ON! New Tools for Teaching and Learning. *See* US Congress, Office of Technology Assessment (OTA)
Prepared environment. *See* Montessori
Preparing grant proposals, 384–85
Presentation Manager, 187
Primary (or internal) storage, 443. *See also* Random Access Memory (RAM)
Principles of Computer Equity, 106
Print Shop, New Print Shop. See Brøderbund
Privacy, invasion of, 131
Privacy Act, 98
Privacy invasion. *See* Ethical and legal considerations
Problem-solving, 6, 201. *See also* Arithmetic and problem-solving, research and
Productivity software, 443. *See also* Computer Assisted Instruction (CAI), Computer Managed Instruction (CMI)
PROFILE, 314
Programming. *See* High Level Languages (HLL), Fourth generation languages, Low level programming, Very High Level Languages (VHLL)

Programming languages
  BASIC, 51–52, 225, 240, 318, 355
  Logo, 19, 41, 171, 240, 241, 317
  Pascal, 240, 318
Project Learning 2001, 32
ProTerm, 319
Protocols, 180, 302
Public Broadcasting Service (PBS), 315
Public domain software, 118–19, 122–23,
  131, 369, 443
Pull-down menus, 53
Punched cards, 149

Q

QBE. See Very High Level Languages
  (VHLL)
Quality Educational Data, Inc., 142
Query, Syllabus Press, 433
QuickTime, 330

R

Radio Shack TRS–80, 48, 141, 301, 307
Random Access Memory (RAM) , 149,
  179–80, 443
Read Only Memory (ROM), 149, 170,
  174, 443
Reading, research and, 14, 17–20
Reading programs
  Alphaphonics, 18
  INSTRUCT, 18
  MARC, 18
  MECCA, 18
  TALK, 18
Real time interactive voice, video and data
  interchange, 305
Real time processing, 443
Regional Computer Resource Center
  (RCRC), 54
Remote and immediate class preparation,
  229–55
Remotely Operated Vehicle (ROV), 68
Repetitive Stress Injury (RSI), 205, 443.
  See also Carpal Tunnel
  Syndrome (CTS)
Request For Proposal (RFP), 388
Research findings, sources for, 15
Reuters, 314
Right of public access, 91, 98–99
Right to Financial Privacy Act, 99
Robotics, 68, 72
Role of Telecommunications Technologies
  in Education (US Senate
  subcommittee), 300

ROLM Corporation, 297
Rotary Club, 218

S

Sans serif font, 289, 443. *See also* Serif
  font
Satellite transmission, 72–73, 76
Scanner, hand-held or flatbed, 4, 157, 333,
  352, 443
Scantron Corporation, 247
Scheduling software, 237
Scholastic *SuperPrint,* 266, 279
School Library and Media Services
  (SLMS), Division of, 84–85
Science, research and, 14, 26–27
Science Kit, 372–74
Science Research International (SRI), 186
Secondary (external) storage, 148–52,
  155–64
Secretary's Commission on Achieving
  Necessary Skills (SCANS),
  317, 381–82, 399
Security of computer systems
  access codes, 131
  passwords, 131
  time bomb, 130. *See also* Computer
    virus, Vaccine
  trespass of computer systems, 83,
    118, 131
  vandalism, 83
Selma Middle School, Selma, IN, 316
Separation of church and state, 92
Serial computer, 365
Serif font, 289, 443. *See also* Sans serif
  font
Shareware, 118, 121, 123, 443
Shuttle, 76. *See also* NASA
SIGGRAPH, 365, 375
Simulations. *See* Computer Assisted
  Instruction (CAI)
Site license, 123
Slide Rule, 41
Social impact of computers
  augmenting normal human capabilities,
    69–70
  enriching human experience, 70
  expert systems, 66–67
  extending the boundaries of the
    feasibly finite, 62, 70–71
  extending the capability of the body,
    62, 67–69
  extending the capability of the mind,
    62, 64
  global village, 73–74

help for the handicapped, 68–69
"high tech, high touch," 62, 74–75, 318
implications for education, 73
remote controlled devices, 68
world of work, 62, 71–72
Social studies, research and, 14, 16, 28–31
Soft copy, 144, 443
Software audit, 121, 127
Software code of ethics, 128
Software Copyright Protection Bill, 120
Software development, 188, 359–75
Software evaluation, 200–201, 280–90
  evaluation checklist, 258, 284–89
  evaluation instrument, 281–83
  process of, 258, 290
Software IC, 172
Software license, 123. *See also* Licensed
  software
Software license agreement, 123–24
Software log, 127
Software piracy. *See* Ethical and legal
  considerations
Software protection, 123, 125, 127, 443
Software Publishers Association (SPA),
  31, 117, 119–23, 125–29,
  134–35
Software selection, criteria for. *See*
  Software, evaluation checklist
Software Toolworks
  The Miracle Piano Teaching System, 336
Southern Illinois University at Carbondale,
  IL, 308
Soyuz spacecraft, 76
Space shuttle. *See* Shuttle
Space station, 78
Sperry Rand, 43
Spreadsheet, 443. *See also* Computer
  Assisted Instruction (CAI),
  Computer Managed Instruction
  (CMI)
Spring Mills Elementary School,
  Waterford, MI. *See* Oakland
  Schools' Teaching and
  Learning with Technology
  Project
Sputnik, 76
SQL. *See* Very High Level Languages
  (VHLL)
State Library of Pennsylvania, 84
Students with disabilities. *See* Disabilities,
  students with
Sub-micron technology, 78, 443
Success With Writing, 24
Supercomputer, 54

Surge protector strip, 443
Susquehanna University, 255
System Folder, 175
System unit, 145–48, 443
Systems programmer, 173

T

Taligent *Pink OS*, 54
Tandem Computers, 383
Tandy Corporation, 166, 382–83
Tandy multimedia PC, 166
Tanque Verde School District, Tuscon, AZ, 56, 59
TCI *Cable in the Classroom*, 315–16
Teacher Education Equity Project, 106
Teacher-pupil ratio, 73
Teacher's Pet, 250–51
Teaching and Learning with Technology (TLT). *See* Oakland Schools, Teaching and Learning with Technology (TLT)
Technical Education Research Centers (TERC), 316
Technological Horizons in Education (T.H.E.) Journal, 433
Technological revolution, 75–77
Technology & Learning, 350–51, 355, 382
Technology buddy, 58
Technology transfer, 298–99
Telecommunications, 443. *See also* Communications
Template, 443. *See also* Templates (forms)
Templates (forms), 238–40
Terabyte, 71
TERC Communications
Global Laboratory, 313
Testing. *See* Assessment
Texas Education Agency (TEA), 316, 339
Texas Education Network, 316
Three R's, research and, 13, 16, 65
Tom Snyder Productions
Jack and the Beanstalk, 279
Reading Magic Library, 279
TopView, 187
Toshiba America Foundation, 384
Touch-screen device, 148, 341
Toyota USA Foundation, 384
Trade Secret law, 125
Transac 2000, 41
TransParent School Model, The, 297, 310, 312. *See also* Betty Phillips Center for Parenthood Education (BPCPE)
Trespass. *See* Computer system security

Trinity Area School District, Washington, PA, 282–83
Trojan Horse, network as, 270
Trojan Horse, virus, 130. *See also* Computer virus, Vaccine
TRW, 99–100
Turing Machine, 41. *See also* Universal Machine
Tutorials. *See* Computer Assisted Instruction (CAI)

U

UK Microelectronics Education Support Unit, 317
Ultrasound, 76
Uninterruptible Power Supply (UPS), 443
Universal Machine, 41, 63, 186, 403, 443. *See also* Turing Machine
University of California, San Diego, CA, 31
University of Oregon, Eugene, OR, 120
University of Pittsburgh, Pittsburgh, PA, 66, 255
University of Pittsburgh at Johnstown, Johnstown, PA, 84, 292
University of Stockholm, Sweden, 95
University of Texas at Wichita Falls, Wichita Falls, TX, 368
UNIX, 187
US Bureau of Census, 95, 103
US Bureau of Labor, 79
US Congress, 261
US Congress, Office of Technology Assessment (OTA), 16, 26–27, 30, 36, 141–42, 168, 276, 280–81, 284–89, 294, 297, 321
US Department of Defense, 43, 330
US Department of Education, 10, 18, 20, 382, 418, 425
US Department of Energy, 372
US Department of Justice, 119
US Department of Labor, 317, 381
US Patent Office, 43
Usability engineering, 363
User interface. *See* Graphical User Interface (GUI)
Utah State Textbook Commission, 350
Utilities
alarm clock, 237
calculator, 211
calendar, 237
Find file, 237
print/graphic utilities, 5
Utility, 443

V

Vaccine, 118, 130. *See also* Computer virus
Vermont Educator's Network, 271
Very High Level Languages (VHLLs)
QBE (Query By Example), 362
SQL (Structured Query Language), 362
Video conference, 305, 444
Video Display Terminal (VDT), 444. *See also* Monitor
Video spigot, 353
Video Toaster, 353–54
Videodisc, 338, 352, 444. *See also* Interactive videodisc
Virtual reality, 198, 274, 444
Virus. *See* Computer virus
VisiCalc, 45, 50, 444
Voice, The, 310
Voice mail, 30
Voice messaging, 304, 444
Voice recognition, 70, 75
Voice-based information exchange, 311
Volatile memory, 444. *See also* Random Access Memory (RAM)

W

War on Poverty, 3
Waterloo Community Schools, Waterloo, Iowa, 319, 422
Weather Channel, 315
Weather forecasting, computers and, 72
Westinghouse Foundation, 106
When the computer should be used, 402, 409–14
When the computer should not be used, 402, 414–17
Whole language instruction, 319
Wide Area Network (WAN), 304, 444
Wideband channel, 326
Wireless media, 301
Women Into Information Technology (WIT), 105
Women's Action Alliance, 105
Word Perfect, 243, 397
Word processing to learn, 413
Word processor, 444. *See also* Computer Assisted Instruction (CAI), Computer Managed Instruction (CMI)
WordStar, 396
Workbench, 175, 237. *See also* Commodore Amiga
Workplace Competencies, 3, 72–73

World Book Encyclopedia, 278
Worm, 138, 149, 444. *See also* Computer
    virus, Vaccine
Writing, research and, 14, 20–25
Writing Across the Curriculum, 59, 348, 413
Writing Process Workshop, 24
Writing To Learn, 291, 413
WYSIWYG, 50, 444

X

XapShot (Canon's RC–360 & 570). *See*
    Peripheral devices: Digital
    camera
Xerox Foundation, 106
Xerox Palo Alto Research Center (Xerox
    PARC), 171, 186
X-ray, 76
XWindows, 187

Y

Yale University, 325
Yamaha Corporation of America, 336. *See
    also* Music synthesizer
York Central School, Retsoff, NY, 20